The Process
of Government

The Process of Government

A STUDY OF SOCIAL PRESSURES

ARTHUR F. BENTLEY

With a new introduction by
THELMA Z. LAVINE

Transaction Publishers
New Brunswick (U.S.A.) and London (U.K.)

Second printing 2008
New material this edition copyright © 1995 by Transaction Publishers, New
Brunswick, New Jersey. Originally published in 1908 by The University of
Chicago Press.

This book is printed on acid-free paper that meets the American National
Standard for Permanence of Paper for Printed Library Materials.

Library of Congress Catalog Number: 94-21410
ISBN: 978-1-56000-778-4
Printed in the United States of America

Library of Congress Cataloging-in-Publication Data

Bentley, Arthur Fisher, 1870-1957.
    The process of government: a study of social pressures / Arthur F. Bentley;
with a new introduction by Thelma Z. Lavine.
        p. cm.
    Originally published: Chicago: University of Chicago Press, 1908.
    Includes bibliographical references and index.
    ISBN 1-56000-778-8
    1. Political science. 2. Political psychology. I. Title.
JA66.B4   1994
320—dc20   94-21410
                                                                CIP

TO MY FATHER

THIS BOOK IS AN ATTEMPT TO FASHION A TOOL

CONTENTS

INTRODUCTION TO THE TRANSACTION EDITION

The activities are interlaced. That, however, is a bad manner of expression. For the interlacing itself is the activity. We have one great moving process to study, and of this great moving process it is impossible to state any part except as valued in terms of the other parts.

-Arthur F. Bentley, *The Process of Government*

I can deeply sympathize with anyone who objects to being tossed into such a floating cosmology. . . .The firm land of "matter" or even of "sense" or "self" is pleasanter, if only it stands firm. To anyone whose tasks can be performed on such ground, I have not the slightest thought of bringing disturbance. But for many of us tasks are pressing, in the course of which our firmest spots of conventional departure themselves dissolve in function. When they have so dissolved, and when we are so involved, there is no hope of finding refuge in some chance island of "fact" which may appear. The continents go, and the islands.

-Arthur F. Bentley, *Behavior, Knowledge, Fact*[1]

The scholarly career of Arthur Fisher Bentley encompasses his first major work (*The Process of Government*), which became a classic in the field of political science, and his last major work (*Knowing and the Known*), written in collaboration with John Dewey, which has become a classic text in the history of American pragmatism. These achievements occurred in the course of a life-history that appears to have been marked by hiatuses, discontinuities, withdrawals, and returns.[2]

The world of Bentley's childhood was the small town of the prairie, in Freeport, Illinois, and Grand Island, Nebraska, during the Reconstruction period of the nation. He embarked upon a college education in 1885-86 at York College, close to his home in Grand

Island, leaving after a year for the University of Denver, and dropping out again in a few months. He had experienced one of the many episodes of physical ill health and psychological depression, which were to be lifelong recurrences and interruptions. For three years thereafter, Arthur worked in his father's bank in Grand Island before entering the Johns Hopkins University, from which he graduated in 1892, achieving the distinction of the publication of his undergraduate thesis (1892-93), *The Condition of the Western Farmer as Illustrated by the Economic History of a Nebraska Township*.[3] The collapse of the agrarian land boom, which had been triggered by the Homestead Act's promise of cheap land, and the subsequent disastrous effects upon local Nebraska farmers are examined with a scrupulous methodology based upon data that Arthur gathered with his father. Bentley sees in the resulting situation an interplay of various social forces: the ambitions and naïveté of the farmers with respect to banks and other creditors, land speculators, international grain merchants, market fluctuations, as well as the unpredictable natural conditions of the prairie. With his first venture into the social sciences, there appears what will become the characteristic Bentleyan nonprescriptive, nonreformist view of the social world as a flux of changing forces.[4]

Bentley began graduate work in economics and sociology at Johns Hopkins in 1892-93. He spent the following year in Germany, where he attended the lectures of the economists Adolf Wagner and Gustav Schmoller, as well as those of Georg Simmel and Wilhelm Dilthey. From Dilthey he learned something of the current "revolt against positivism" and the issues involved in the distinctions between the human sciences and the natural sciences. Most important to Bentley were Simmel's seminars in sociology and his teaching on group theory. Returning to Hopkins, Bentley produced a doctoral dissertation, "The Units of Investigation in the Social Sciences," in which he opposed mechanistic or causal explanations (a view he will maintain and share with Dewey) and presented instead a Diltheyan, "idealist" argument for the centrality of "mind" in social scientific analysis (a view that he and Dewey would later reject).

During his lifetime Bentley's only teaching position was a one-year lectureship in sociology at Chicago for 1895-96, a year of job scarcity in the continuing economic depression.[5] After a few days of Bentley's difficult lectures and monumental reading assignments in French and German sociology, students and teacher agreed to abandon the seminar. Bentley appears to have isolated himself while at Chicago from the galaxy of philosophers and social scientists on the faculty, including George Herbert Mead, Thorstein Veblen, Jacques Loeb, James H. Tufts, Addison Moore, James Angell, W. I. Thomas, and Albert Michelson.[6]

From this group was to come the formation of the "Chicago School" of philosophy, under the leadership of Dewey, who had left Michigan for Chicago in 1894-95 (the year before Bentley's arrival as lecturer) to chair the Department of Philosophy, Psychology, and Pedagogy.[7] Under these circumstances, as James Ward observes, Bentley's "natural home would have been at the University of Chicago."[8] Bentley's isolation at Chicago was broken, however, by his crucial encounter with pragmatism and with John Dewey as teacher—he audited (unknown to Dewey) Dewey's seminars in ethics and the theory of logic. Like the German philosophers and social theorists with whom he had just studied, Dewey, too, he found, was enlisted in the revolt against positivism and empiricism, countering these views at that time by a Hegelian idealism, which could provide, unlike positivism, philosophic significance for meaning and value. In the seminar, Dewey rejected Hegel's Absolute, yet he also rejected the primacy of the individual mind and argued against psychological explanation in the social sciences.[9]

These teachings of Deweyan pragmatism and the revolt against positivism were to become components of Bentley's armament. Fifty years later, Dewey and Bentley, no longer strangers, would combine their forces in the revolt against logical positivism and in defense of a pragmatic theory of inquiry. But in the Depression year of 1886, having washed out at Chicago, Bentley could find no academic position. He was finally taken on as a reporter for the *Chicago Times Herald;* by 1903 he had become an editorial writer for the *Times Herald* and the *Record-Herald*. It was as a Chicago newspaper reporter and editor with a "sense of tremendous social activity taking place,"[10] a feeling that "all the politics of the country, so to speak, was drifting across my desk,"[11] that Bentley wrote *The Process of Government* over the years 1896-1908.

The Process of Government, now regarded as a classic in political science, was virtually ignored until the post-World War II period, when American political scientists discovered Bentley to be a forerunner of current interest-group theory and the realism of pressure politics, as well as a scornful opponent of the idealistic pieties of traditional political science, and of its "legalist" and "institutionalist" perceptions of politics. Bentley was hailed on methodological grounds as an early supporter of the "behavioral revolution," which called for the use of natural scientific methods in the social sciences; and on substantive grounds for offering a group theory of politics.[12]

The behavioral revolutionists' view of Bentley is now perceived to have been a misreading. How is this to be understood? There was the bold, hard-hitting, "scientific" tone of the one-line preface to *The Process of Government:* "This book is an attempt to fashion a tool." There were Bentley's behavioral credentials, which appeared to be attested to by his debunking attacks upon "mentalistic" explanations, and upon claims for the causal efficacy of "ideas and ideals," upon the concept of psychological explanation, as well as by his detailed analysis of group theory in relation to interests, values, economics, government, and law. Contributing to the misreading was Bentley's writing in the idiom of behavioral political science (with overtones of the Progressivism that he is in the process of abandoning). Sidney Ratner catches the affect of Bentley's rhetoric, proclaiming that "The raw materials of government . . . cannot be found in the law books; in the proceedings of constitutional conventions; in the addresses and essays on tyranny and democracy; or in the 'character of the people,' in their specific 'feelings' or 'thoughts,' in their 'hearts' or 'minds.'"

> The raw material can be found only in the actually performed legislating-administrating-adjudicating activities of the nation, and the streams and kinds of activity that gather among the people and rush into these spheres.[13]

Unnoticed by the behavioral political scientists was that Part I of *The Process of Government,* which rejects psychological explanation, also rejects the entire category of causal explanation, thus destroying the scientific causal argumentation of the behavioralists themselves, along with common sense explanations of human behavior. Left implicit in Bentley's rejection of causal explanation in *The Process of Government* is his anti-positivism and interpretivism, reflecting the influence of Dilthey, Simmel, and now Dewey. Moreover, under these late Hegelian, Darwinian, and Deweyan influences, Bentley writes as a holistic process theorist in the social sciences: the raw material of these sciences is the group in its meaningful, purposive activity, each group in process, each classifiable by classificatory systems, which are themselves in process. "Mental properties" or specific types of causes are distorting abstractions from the process of group activity. Mental-physical, inner-outer, individual-social, subjective-objective are not discrete elements segmenting the group; they are dissolved into interactional phases of the process of group activity:[14] "We have one great moving process to study, and of this great moving process it is impossible to state any part except as valued in terms of the other parts."[15] With this metaphor Bentley perceives the outlines of his cosmology, in which entities, abstractions, divisions, and separations will be dissolved in their apartness and "interlaced" with other moving parts in ceaseless change.[16]

After the death of his father in 1908 Bentley collapsed into a severe depression which lasted until 1911;[17] that year, following upon the death of his mother, Bentley and his wife moved to Paoli, Indiana. For the rest of his life he would never leave Paoli, except for a few months.[18] He did not resume major writing projects until the 1920's. Prior to the collaboration with Dewey which resulted in *Knowing and the Known* (1949), Bentley produced two important works, *Linguistic Analysis of Mathematics* (1932) and *Behavior, Knowledge, Fact* (1935).[19] These are the works that tie him directly to Dewey.

By the late 1920's Bentley's writing vigorously responded to the revolution in theoretical physics brought about in relativity theory and to the revolution in the foundations of mathematics brought about by the development of non-Euclidean geometries and by the achievement of *Principia Mathematica* in deriving all branches of mathematics from logic. Both developments, as Bentley understands them, carry important implications for scientific inquiry. The success of physics, as evidenced by relativity theory, makes it clear that scientific development requires a clean break with everyday or commonsense beliefs and intuitive understandings of the phenomena of the physical world. Inquiry in the social sciences should be guided by this principle, rather than attempting to show continuity with everyday experience by representing social science as second-order or more precise common sense.

As for the revolution in theoretical mathematics, Bentley's *Linguistic Analysis of Mathematics* opposes the claim of Gottlob Frege and Bertrand Russell that mathematics is reducible to logic, which provides its foundation. Bentley finds a problem with the idea of "foundations" for mathematics which are provided from outside mathematics itself. He presents a counter-foundational view of mathematics as itself an empirical, historical area of inquiry, characterized by changing modes of thought with regard to notions within its subject matter. He argues that with the development of a method of postulation ("the most general form of linguistic control which we may establish" in any area of inquiry),[20] contradictions and controversies within mathematics can be overcome. Thus, the "logical foundations" of mathematics (and, by extension, the inquiry into any subject matter) are constituted by rendering explicit, through postulation, the implicit practices within the field of mathematics, or of the area in question.[21]

Dewey's intellectual delight in finally reading Bentley's *Linguistic Analysis of Mathematics* is understandable: here was a forceful, informative attack on the foundational aspect of mathematics which developed and confirmed the principal argument of *Logic, the Theory of Inquiry*, that the logical "foundations" of inquiry are not external to inquiry but in its practices.[22]

Having quickly established Bentley's supportive anti-foundational stand in the field of mathematics, Dewey does not appear, at least at this early stage in their relationship, to have picked up any clues that would lead him to question how closely allied were their views. He does not appear to have read *The Process of Government* and to have noted its startling picture of the one great moving process of human activity, knowable by an intersection of multiple perspectives that are unable to be prioritized and are themselves in process.[23] Nor had Dewey apparently noted Bentley's argument in *Linguistic Analysis of Mathematics,* based upon his understanding of the revolution in physics, that the development of mathematics, like that of every science, requires breaking the connection between common sense and the notions of the discipline. Nor did Dewey perceive that Bentley viewed science as descriptive only, not experimental, and not instrumental to the ends of culture. These Bentleyan views, from which he never departs, undermine Dewey's biologically based naturalism, his principle of continuity between common sense and science, and his conception of the role of science in society.

In *Behavior, Knowledge, Fact* Bentley presents his philosophy of the behavioral sciences. Bentley's "tellurian-sidereal cosmos" has the "great merit," he claims, of being the only worldview we have that "expands 'inwards' and 'outwards' spatially, and 'backwards' and 'forwards' temporally, to house all branches of knowledge." "Against it," Bentley adds, "no construction built up in terms of some pinpoint 'mind of a moment' has any hope whatever for consideration."[24] The "tellurian-sidereal" cosmos is a scientific construct, and, like each of the sciences, is a part of the cosmic process, "a bit of the cosmos inspecting itself."[25] The circularity of the interpretation of the cosmos, and the cosmic process that it interprets, is characteristic of all modes of knowing that have broken with "Newtonian" traditional epistemology. All sciences are viewed as circular in structure, hence without foundational premises; they are completely postulational and make no references to extra-linguistic reality.[26]

The tellurian-sidereal cosmos is in no sense to be taken as "the hardest of hard Fact" but only Fact as seen from the "local" view of men who have in the course of their history come to "know" it in this way.[27] Moreover, all knowledge, being local, is in the process of change; the future form of the science of physics is unpredictable. This cosmology requires that we pursue our scientific accounts backward across the "few thousand years of social history," and forward to our time, treating all events as phases of one another and all knowledge as local, utilizing cross-sectionally "the ranges of fact, experience, knowledge, and language" toward an expanding spatial and temporal description of cosmic process.

This is what Bentley describes as his "floating cosmology in the course of which our firmest spots dissolve in function. . . . The continents go, and the islands." Against it Bentley sees the "man in the street" arising with objections to the disappearance of things, persons, causes; to surrendering the primacy of his senses and thoughts as the "beginning and end of all knowledge"; to the substitution of "postulates" in place of his "real world"; to the claim that any identifiable object is to be understood as a phase of various scientific inquiries. "His view," Bentley observes, "is that small, prim, assertive, and tenacious view embodied in our practical everyday language."[28]

But the protestations against the floating cosmology are not confined to the man in the street. Bentley has raised major problems with regard to the cognitive status of objects, human individuals, science, and philosophy itself. These problems and their resolution are pivotal in the Dewey-Bentley relationship: the moral dimension of Deweyan pragmatism and the melioristic concern for the "life-career" of the individual human being and of the society find no reflection in Bentley's cosmos. They are pivotal also in current reinterpretations of Dewey and pragmatism, as well as in a wide range of contemporary philosophic and methodological contexts.[30]

Bentley's philosophy of social science in *Behavior, Knowledge, Fact* presents "behavior" as the unit of analysis, defining behavior as "that great type of activity which cannot be held" within the frames of the sciences of physics or biology, "but which requires a directly psychological and social form of research" and its own "behavioral space-time."[31] But how can social behavior be scientifically observed? Not by empiricist sensory responses to stimuli, but by "frames of observability that we possess in fixated or expanding forms."[32] Here Bentley exhibits an affinity with a later Kuhnian rejection of the distinction between observation and theory or with a later Schutzian concept of learned social typifications. His resulting version of "behavior" anticipates in some respects "action" as used by analytic action theory, or "social action" as used in Weberian interpretive sociology. But his analysis of "Social Fact" proceeds by means of a cumbersome, ponderous set of neologisms that are designed to convey process and trans-

action, and to rid the language of behavioral science from involve-
ment with metaphysical, mentalistic, or abstracting elements or with
commonsense notions of the reality of discrete individuals and objects. These neologisms have the function of "'namings' which specify
. . . the range of application for the names we give." Bentley carries
his notions of "namings" and "specifications" to *Knowing and the
Known.*[33]

Following the first exchange of letters between the two men in
1935, there is a lapse of three years; the correspondence resumes in
1938 after the publication of *Logic, the Theory of Inquiry,* reaching a
peak of weekly and daily exchanges as the writing progressed, and
tapering off after 1949 with the publication of *Knowing and the Known.*

Each man was fulfilled in certain respects by the other in the relationship. Dewey found someone more sophisticated than himself in
logic and mathematics, who had already defended a Deweyan position against mathematical foundations, who took Dewey's *Logic* seriously, wishing to defend it against its critics, and who had the
intellectual capacity and vigor to clarify and strengthen its argumentation in the direction of further development. Moreover, this early
admirer-disciple from the Chicago days seemed possessed of a vital,
visionary, driving intellectual force that stimulated and fascinated
Dewey: "I *don't* feel a lot of your positions are divergent from mine. I
think our different modes of approach complement each other. I hadn't
expected at my age (I'm 85 in October) to get a 'refresher course' that
really refreshed. I feel I've got it through this contact with you."[35]

For his part, Bentley found a renowned public figure, an interna-
tionally esteemed philosopher to work with on a specific task utilizing his own logical and mathematical skills to defend and sharpen the
arguments of the *Logic* and undertaking the larger intellectual projects
of battling, with Dewey, against the threat of logical positivism. Moreover, there was for Bentley the intellectual appeal of moving beyond
the issues of political science, mathematics, and psychology that had
previously engaged him to the philosophic frame of pragmatism, which
the relationship to Dewey made possible.

As the two men began their correspondence, they shared the spirit
of the American cultural revolution of the turn of the nineteenth cen-

tury and the early years of the twentieth century; there was for both, as for many American intellectuals at that time, a Hegelian deposit in their thought; both held to a holistic, process philosophy, and were accordingly anti-dualistic, anti-foundationalist, anti-abstractionist, anti-formalist; and in opposition to posivitism and empiricism, they tend to be interpretivist. Dewey and Bentley shared as well a broadly naturalistic, organism-environment frame; a rejection of traditional metaphysics and epistemology; an opposition to a legislative function on the part of mathematics and logic in relation to inquiry; and a behavioral, in opposition to a mentalistic, approach to the social sciences.

From the start there were differences, as noted above, which the amicable respect with which the two men regarded each other could not conceal. In opposition to the moral dimension of the entirety of Dewey's writings, Bentley deliberately precluded as unscientific any moral or political component from his own work; Bentley rejected, as a related issue, Dewey's philosophic consideration of the individual life-career as an abstraction from social transactional process; Bentley's process cosmology threatens dissolution for objects and persons, which Dewey resists with complex and intricate argumentation. Finally, Bentley's conception of science requires discontinuity between ordinary experience and science, whereas for Dewey, intelligent inquiry in the resolution of problematic situations is present throughout human experience. These differences and the conflicting philosophic ideas that they reflect persevere through the nineteen years of the correspondence. In 1950 they were still arguing about the "object."[36] Chapter X, "Common Sense and Science," the only essay signed by Dewey alone in *Knowing and the Known* reaffirms Dewey's well-established reasoning on this issue.

The question of dominance has understandably been raised about this important intellectual collaboration, especially since it is accessible, not only in the completed product but in the making, through a voluminous correspondence. Paul Kress finds it remarkable that

the best-known philosopher of his day carried on an exchange with the obscure orchard owner of Paoli . . . it was remarkable also because the obscure Midwesterner dominates the exchange—identifying problems, proposing and rejecting solutions, tirelessly criticizing, evaluating, and urging. It is the Columbia professor who expresses gratitude and admiration for his friend's insights, and a willingness to entertain challenges to positions held over a lifetime.[37]

Sidney Ratner moves the argument forward by the astute observation that even if it were agreed that Bentley formulates most of the problems, does most of the writing, and that the end product is in Bentley's style, nevertheless it cannot be claimed that Bentley imposes his views on Dewey, since the ideas presented are all to be found in Dewey's work.[38]

In response to Ratner's suggestion it must be said, however, that not all the ideas presented in *Knowing and the Known* are Dewey's, since there are major differences between the two men, as has been noted here. Moreover, Bentley's program is far from being confined to a reflective confirmation of ideas he shares with Dewey. Bentley pursues his own agenda of a process cosmology, and he drives the logic of process, which Dewey shares with him, to its extreme implications, challenging the views that Dewey does not share with him. As *Correspondence* and the finished papers of *Knowing and the Known* disclose, Deweyan pragmatism, as a type of process philosophy, is not immunized against its own dissolving techniques. Vulnerable thus to the force of Bentley's prodding, Dewey falters as the dissolving operations of his own pragmatism are turned against itself. The end result is a *naturalism in extremis,* the dissolution of the structures that Dewey required for his own long-standing agenda, to reconstruct philosophy and to ameliorate the problems of society by bridging the gap between science and morality. Bentley had, however, already warned of this outcome: "[O]ur firmest spots of conventional departure themselves dissolve in function. When they are so dissolved . . . there is no hope of finding refuge in some chance island of 'fact' which may appear."

That pragmatism had been emerging as a potential philosophic framework for Bentley was already evident in his developmental line of thought from *The Process of Government* to *Linguistic Analysis of Mathematics* to *Behavior, Knowledge, Fact,* as his interests focused less on the problems specific to the individual social sciences and mathematics, and increasingly upon the issues addressed by the philosophy of the social sciences. Bentley read Mead, Peirce, and James during the 1930's, and as the relationship with Dewey began to flourish, Bentley appears to have seen himself as a major figure in the further development of pragmatism and as heir to Peirce's philosophic command of all the fields of knowledge.[39] Pragmatism, as Bentley perceived it, was a philosophic movement expressive of the tellurian-sidereal cosmic processes that Darwin had disclosed and Peirce, James, and Dewey had carried forward. In the currents of this great movement, the next evolvement, which neither Peirce nor Dewey had been able to reach, was the development of a theory of linguistic behavior that would be adequate to pragmatism and the circular systems of behavioral science. This next stage in pragmatism Bentley hoped to achieve through the collaboration with Dewey.

In fact the intellectual collaboration, which eventuated as the twelve chapters of *Knowing and the Known,* undertook three distinct but interrelated projects: a critique of formal logicians, in defense of Dewey's *Logic;* a critique of logical positivism, which threatened to usurp the dominance held by pragmatism; as well as the construction of a new language for behavioral inquiry.

The issue with regard to logic: Against the claims of formal logicians, both Bentley and Dewey argue that logic is not an independent foundation for inquiry. For Dewey, logic is continuous with our transactions with nature; it is "the theory of inquiry." For Bentley, logic is a postulational system, neither foundational for inquiry nor developed out of it.

The second project of *Knowing and the Known* was the critique of logical positivism. Anxious attacks upon logical positivism by Dewey and Bentley appeared in the late 1930's and the 1940's in their personal correspondence and in published criticisms in the articles constituting *Knowing and the Known,* as the Vienna Circle, having fled from Nazism, began to publish the views of its members in American journals and to re-establish the unity of science movement.

While the appeal of logical positivism in America seemed to be its bold empiricism and its logical rigor, the pragmatists' case against logical positivism rested on the thorough-going dualism of its empirical and logical components. Dewey and Bentley rejected the foundation in observed atomic facts as the discredited empiricism of subjectivist sense-data; and they rejected the construction of science as a logical system on this foundation as incompatible with the view that the structure of science is not imposed by formal logic, but arises out of scientific practice; they rejected the isolation of observation statements from theoretical statements and also the verifiability test of meaning as further evidence of the strict analytic-synthetic distinction underlying the logical positivists' philosophy of science. However, some points of agreement are conceded: the rejection of metaphysics and the need for the construction of a language appropriate to scientific inquiry.[40]

But the shadow of logical positivism falls on *Knowing and the Known* and its crucial third project of developing a theory of linguistic behavior adequate to pragmatism and the behavioral sciences. Nature is understood as the ultimate field of inquiry; and a transactional approach in inquiry is held to be required at the present developmental stage of science. Here, *Knowing and the Known* presents its best-known contribution to the philosophy of science: the conception of self-action, interaction, and transaction as three successive and progressive scientific modes of viewing the world. Self-action is the classical mode of viewing things as caused by their own essences; interaction is the mode of explanation beginning with mechanistic physics, viewing units that are able to be isolated in causal interconnection with other units; the transactional mode views human behavior "without attribution of . . . action to independent self-actors, or to independently inter-acting elements or relations." At present, epistemology, logic, and the social sciences "are still largely on a self-actional basis" with some movement visible toward an interactional procedure.[41] Physics is the model science, having moved from Newtonian interactional beliefs to the transactional beliefs of Einsteinian relativity theory and to quantum mechanics. Transaction is that "level" of inquiry "where systems of description and naming are employed to deal with aspects and phases of action, without final attribution to "elements" or other presumptively detachable or independent "entities," "essences," "realities," and without isolation of presumptively detachable "relations" from such detachable "elements."[42]

The Bentleyan cosmic vision of systems of local knowledge ranging across time and space, glimpsed in *Knowing and the Known*'s accounts of transaction, recedes as the project of linguistic reform becomes the central issue. The procedure followed, in accordance with science, is postulational and its outcomes are provisional. The "basic postulate" is that "knowings are observable facts in exactly the same sense as are the subject matters that are known."[43] As natural events, knowings and knowns are to be "investigated by methods that have been elsewhere successful in the natural sciences," they are to be "taken together as aspects of one event" observed in a transactional manner.[44]

The immediate inquiry is limited to knowings through namings, and the search is continuous through *Knowing and the Known* for a "firm list of names." Firm names having been scrutinized for vagueness, abstractness, residues of philosophic traditions, self-action, or interaction, and having been studied in a transactional way, are further submitted to specification. Specification succeeds in freeing naming from linguistic barriers by the exclusive "use of widened scientific descriptions."[45]

It may now be seen that the entire conceptual apparatus with which *Knowing and the Known* attempts to construct a theory of language for pragmatism and behavioral science has come from Bentley's *Behavior, Knowledge, Fact*. Postulation, behavior, observation, naming, specification, fact, self-action/interaction/transaction, circularity, the cosmos of knowledge—for all of these, Bentley drew upon his own text. At least in respect to the production of *Knowing and the Known*, Bentley succeeded in his ambition to provide, with the collaboration of Dewey, the next step in the development of pragmatism.

The search for "firm," "leading" names and their specifications led inevitably to the loss of names and relationships which are present in the discourse of Dewey's pragmatism and vulnerable to these structures of transactional analysis. The list of rejected names includes: reality, experience, naturalism, individual, subject-object, problematic situation, concept, meaning, and knowledge. Dewey registers protestations; arguments ensue; Dewey characteristically concedes.[46]

Ironically, the mission of *Knowing and the Known*, to sharpen the language of *Logic*, to provide a theory of language for pragmatism and the behavioral sciences, to combat the foundational beliefs of formal logicians and the looming hegemony of logical positivism, is fulfilled in none of these goals. Instead, *Knowing and the Known* emerges as a rigorous scientific transactional statement, mirroring (despite differences) the logical positivism that it opposes, offering its own formal language, maintaining the exclusive legitimacy of science as a mode of knowledge and as a frame of reference, denying cognitive significance to metaphysics and ethics, and denying connection between science and common sense.

The scientific transactional beliefs of *Knowing and the Known* leaves the philosophic constructions of Dewey hopelessly undermined—the great, unifying Darwinian frame of nature, aesthetically experienced in its precariousness and stability, and the linkages of science and morals, of the individual life career with society, ethics, politics, aesthetics, and science, and the problematic situation, key to the resolution of difficulties. Hopelessly undermined also is the austerely magnificent Bentleyan tellurian-sidereal floating cosmology, spanning millennia in time and space, moving into the future. After the project ended and despite the warmth of the relationship, both appeared to be disappointed in its philosophical outcome and its reception. Dewey wrote again about the transactional relationship of means and consequences ("How, What, and What For in Social Inquiry"). Bentley, perhaps depressed, published a forty-year collection of his papers, including "Kennetic Inquiry," a recapitulation of his intellectual career and his contribution to the transactional approach.[47]

It is, however, pragmatism, not logical positivism that has survived. Pragmatism has become central to current debates concerning foundational beliefs, in which issues of realism, relativism, transcendentalism, idealism, and the "end of philosophy" are involved. And it is plausible that "seen through American eyes, the converging themes of the entire movement of contemporary Western philosophy"—phenomenology, Marxism, hermeneutics, deconstruction—"are decidedly pragmatist in cast."[48] In the course of the development of American pragmatism, the richly complex process philosophies of Dewey and

Bentley played their major roles. The islands go, the continents linger longer.

Thelma Z. Lavine
1994

NOTES

1. Arthur F. Bentley, *The Process of Government: A Study of Social Pressures,* Chicago: University of Chicago Press, 1908, p. 178; *Behavior, Knowledge, Fact,* Bloomington, Ind.: The Principia Press, 1935, p. 183.

2. The Stuhr Museum of the Prairie Pioneer, Grand Island, Nebraska, holds records and correspondence of Charles F. Bentley's bank and of the Bentley family; the Arthur F. Bentley Collection is held by the Manuscripts Department, Lilly Library, Indiana University, Bloomington; additional Bentley materials are held in the John Dewey Papers, Special Collections, Morris Library, Southern Illinois University at Carbondale. For biographical and interpretive materials on Bentley I have drawn upon the essay by Sidney Ratner, "Arthur F. Bentley: Behavioral Scientist," in *Correspondence,* pp. 24-36; Sidney Ratner, "A.F. Bentley's Inquiries into the Behavioral Sciences and the Theory of Scientific Inquiry," *Life, Language, Law: Essays in Honor of Arthur F. Bentley,* ed. Richard W. Taylor, Yellow Springs, Ohio: The Antioch Press, pp. 26-57; chap. 2, "The Intellectual Matrix of Bentley's Social Science," in James F. Ward, *Language, Form, and Inquiry: Arthur F. Bentley's Philosophy of Social Science,* Amherst: The University of Massachusetts Press, 1984, pp. 15-44; chap. 1, "History as Process," in Paul F. Kress, *Social Science and the Idea of Process: The Ambiguous Legacy of Arthur F. Bentley,* Urbana: University of Illinois Press, 1970, pp. 13-42; also upon materials provided by the Stuhr Museum of the Prairie Pioneer and by the Lilly Library, Indiana University. See Ward, Appendix, for a complete bibliography of Bentley's published and unpublished work, including reading notes. These materials are contained in the Arthur F. Bentley Manuscripts Collection, The Lilly Library, Indiana University. The correspondence between Dewey and Bentley has been superbly edited, indexed, and introduced. See Sidney Ratner and Jules Altman, eds., introduction by Sidney Ratner, *John Dewey and Arthur F. Bentley: A Philosophical Correspondence, 1932-1951,* New Brunswick, N.J.: Rutgers University Press, 1964). Succeeding references will be to *Correspondence;* all Dewey Bentley letters are quoted as they appear in the edited *Correspondence.* The present introduction draws upon the author's Introduction to *John Dewey: The Later Works,* vol. 16: 1949-1952: Essays, Postscripts, and *Knowing and the Known,* Carbondale and Edwardsville: Southern Illinois University Press, 1989.

3. *The Johns Hopkins University Studies in Historical and Political Science,* Eleventh Series, nos. 7-8, Baltimore: Johns Hopkins University Press, 1983.

4. See Ward, *Language, Form, and Inquiry,* pp. 25-26; also Richard Hofstadter, *The Age of Reform,* New York: Vintage Books, 1955, pp. 55-58.

5. Aside from a visiting lectureship for 1941-42 in the Columbia Philosophy Department.

6. Bentley apparently made the acquaintance of W. I. Thomas.

7. See Darnell Ricker, *The Chicago Pragmatists,* Minneapolis: University of Minnesota Press, 1969. See Andrew Feffer, *The Chicago Pragmatists and American Progressiv-*

ism, Ithaca: Cornell University Press, 1993, for an account of the social and political activism of the Chicago Department of Philosophy at that time.

8. Ward adds: "Few of Dewey's colleagues and disciples had a first-hand knowledge of currents in European social theory equal to Bentley's. His self-imposed isolation prevented him from contributing these perspectives to the work of the Chicago pragmatists," *Language, Form, and Inquiry*, p. 44.

9. Sidney Ratner has transcribed some of Bentley's notes from the logic seminar: "Dewey urged students to ignore the whole question of subject and object, and to ask instead, 'What is the act of knowing itself?' This for two reasons: first that subject and object are constructions of the primitive acts of knowledge; the second that logical judgment is a form of action, a form of conduct," *Correspondence*, pp. 27-28.

10. Kress, *Social Science and the Idea of Process*, p. 18

11. Arthur Bentley, "Epilogue," in Taylor, *Life, Language, Law*, p. 211.

12. See Ward, *Language, Form, and Inquiry*, pp. 45 ff; Kress, *Social Science and the Idea of Progress*, pp. 22ff. The principal figures in the Bentley revival in political science are David B. Easton, *The Governmental Process: Political Interests and Public Opinion*, New York: Alfred A. Knopf, 1951; Bertram M. Gross, *The Legislative Struggle: A Study in Social Combat*, New York: McGraw-Hill, 1953; Earl Latham, *The Group Basis of Politics: A Study of Basing Point Legislation*, Ithaca: Cornell University Press, 1952.

13. *Correspondence*, Introduction, p. 30, quoting from Bentley's *The Process of Government*.

14. Bentley does not yet use "transactional," which would be appropriate here.

15. Bentley, *The Process of Government*, p. 178. The Romantic and Hegelian doctrine of internal relations is evident.

16. Bentley, like Dewey, resorts to the expressiveness of the revealing metaphor. Whereas the Deweyan metaphors are religious, unifying, and redemptive, the Bentleyan metaphors are cosmic, destructive, yet daringly liberating. See T. Z. Lavine, "Pragmatism and the Constitution in the Culture of Modernism," *Transactions of the Charles S. Peirce Society*, Winter 1984, vol. 20, no. 1, pp. 11-12.

17. See letter from Bentley to Joseph Ratner, 7 September 1948, Arthur F. Bentley Manuscripts Collection 2, Lilly Library, Indiana University. Cited by Ward, *Language, Form, and Inquiry*, p. 240.

18. See Ward, *Language, Form, and Inquiry*, pp. 18-20, for an interesting parallel between Bentley and Max Weber, linking in each case the depression to the death of the father and to the course of subsequent work.

19. See Ward, *Language, Form, and Inquiry*, Appendix.

20. Arthur F. Bentley, *Linguistic Analysis of Mathematics*, Bloomington, Ind.: The Principia Press, 1932, pp. 21-22.

21. See *Logic, the Theory of Inquiry*, New York: Henry Holt and Co., 1938; *Later Works*, v. 12, pp. 23ff., 401 ff.

22. "In personal conversation with [Sidney Ratner] . . . Dewey said that Bentley gave him the final encouragement and push he needed to make the decisive break with formal logic in his *Logic: The Theory of Inquiry*." Sidney Ratner, "A. F. Bentley's Inquiries into the Behavioral Sciences and the Theory of Scientific Inquiry," *Life, Language, Law*, ed. Richard W. Taylor, Yellow Springs, Ohio: Antioch Press, 1957, p. 41.

23. Dewey makes only two, very brief references to *The Process of Government* during the years of the correspondence.

24. Bentley, *Behavior, Knowledge, Fact*, p. 180.

25. Bentley fragment, "Phrasing," 1951-52, Manuscripts 1, Arthur F. Bentley Manuscript Collections, The Lilly Library. Cited by Ward, *Language, Form, and Inquiry*, 232. See also "We observe world-being-known-to-man-in-it; we report the observation; we proceed to inquire into it, circularity or no circularity. This is all there is to it. And the circularity is not merely around the circle in one direction; the course is both ways round at once in full mutual function," John Dewey and Arthur F. Bentley, *Knowing and the Known*, Boston: Beacon Press, 1949, p. 63; *Later Works*, v. 16.

26. "*Circularity*. Its appearance is regarded as a radical defect by non-transactional epistemological inquiries that undertake to organize 'independents' as 'reals.' Normal for inquiry into knowings and knowns in system" ("A Trial Group of Names," *Knowing and the Known*, p. 260-61.)

27. Bentley, *Behavior, Knowledge, Fact*, p. 169. Anthropologist Clifford Geertz, in *Local Knowledge*, New York: Basic Books, 1983, makes a similar point with similar ensuing problems.

28. Bentley, *Behavior, Knowledge, Fact*, p. 172.

29. Dewey's protestation on behalf of the cognitive legitimacy of the notion of the individual "life-career" was noted above. In a subtle interpretation of Bentley as offering a process philosophy of the social sciences, Paul Kress protests that not only "particulars" but also individuals are dissolved in the cosmic flux. By rejecting the individual as analytical unit in political science, Bentley fails to be "appropriate to our sense of what political matters are all about." Kress concludes: "Certainly, *Behavior, Knowledge, Fact* and *Knowing and the Known* may be read as chronicles of a lost mariner, a man who has thrown the compass of reason over the side as so much excess ballast," Paul H. Kress, *Social Science and the Idea of Process: The Ambiguous Legacy of Arthur F. Bentley*, Urbana: University of Illinois Press, 1970, p. 178.

30. See, among others, Karl-Otto Apel, *Toward the Transformation of Philosophy*, London: Routledge and Kegan Paul, 1980; Richard J. Bernstein, *Beyond Objectivism and Relativism*, Philadelphia: University of Pennsylvania Press, 1983; Joseph Margolis, *Pragmatism Without Foundations: Reconciling Realism and Relativism*, Oxford: Basil Blackwell, 1986; John J. McDermott, *Streams of Experience: Reflections on the History and Philosophy of American Culture*, Amherst: University of Massachusetts Press, 1986; Richard Rorty, *Consequences of Pragmatism*, Minneapolis: University of Minnesota Press, 1982; Sandra Rosenthal, *Speculative Pragmatism*, Amherst: University of Massachusetts Press, 1987; R. W. Sleeper, *The Necessity of Pragmatism: John Dewey's Conception of Philosophy*, New Haven: Yale University Press, 1986; John E. Smith, *Purpose and Thought: The Meaning of Pragmatism*, Chicago: University of Chicago Press, 1984; H. S. Thayer, *Meaning and Action: A Critical History of Pragmatism*, Indianapolis: Bobbs-Merrill, 1968.

31. Bentley, *Behavior, Knowledge, Fact*, p. 262.

32. *Ibid.*, p. 204.

33. *Ibid.*, pp. 231, 265; Bentley, *Knowing and the Known*, chaps. 5 and 11.

34. See *Correspondence*.

35. *Ibid.*, 6 June 1944, p. 264. Dewey's capacity to be productively stimulated by persons who project creative vitality was life-long. Among earlier instances is his relationship with the journalist-entrepreneur Franklin Ford.

36. *Ibid.*, 22 January 1950, p. 620.

37. Kress, *Social Science and the Idea of Process*, p. 20.

38. Observation made to the writer by Sidney Ratner, June 1988.

39. See Ward, *Language, Form, and Inquiry*, pp. 201-02, which draws upon Bentley

memoranda of 1939. See also Bentley's article, "The Jamesian Datum," from which this passage is taken, *Journal of Psychology*, vol. 16 (July, 1943), reprinted in Arthur F. Bentley, *Inquiry into Inquiries: Essays in Social Theory*, edited and with an introduction by Sidney Ratner, Boston: Beacon Press, 1954. Bentley shows that James's thought moved on to view the "stream" as behavioral activity, "the flow of the neutral datum in a natural world of organism-environment. This achievement of James was made possible, on the negative side, by the final extermination of the ancestral claimant, 'consciousness'" (p. 248).

40. Bentley concludes a ferocious attack on Rudolph Carnap and other positivists by noting that "with the great objectives of the logical positivists—the expulsion of metaphysics and the development of a linguistic frame for appraisal and organization—I am in the fullest sympathy," "The Positive and the Logical," *Inquiry into Inquiries*, p. 112.

41. Bentley, *Knowing and the Known*, pp. 67-68, 105, 121.

42. *Ibid.*, p. 108. The continuing influence of *Knowing and the Known* is sustained primarily by the concept of transaction. See, for example, as a direct influence in literary theory, Louise Rosenblatt, *Reader, Text, Poem*, Carbondale: Southern Illinois University, 1978; and in psychology, Hadley Cantril, *Selected Essays*, 1988; in cultural anthropology, Clifford Gertz's *Interpretation of Culture* and in hermeneutics, Hans-Georg Gadamer's *Truth and Method* express a transactional viewpoint.

43. *Ibid.*, p. 48.

45. *Ibid.*, pp. 131, 149, 150. "We have chosen the name 'specification' to designate the most complete and accurate description that the sustained inquiry of an age has been able to achieve based on all the inquiries of earlier ages."

46. *Ibid.*, pp. 92-93. In an unpublished review of *Correspondence*, made available to me through the kindness of Sidney Ratner, Herbert Schneider wrote:

> Bentley teased, lured, drove his friend into revising the basic terminology of his thought, using as an incentive the promise that the resulting theory . . . would be stated in hard and fast, clear and distinct language. . . . The genius of Bentley's strategy [was that] whenever Bentley asked him time and time again what he meant when he wrote so-and-so, and how together they could resolve the apparent contradiction, Dewey replied that the contradiction was real and that he should have said thus-and-so.

47. John Dewey, "Means and Consequences—How, What, and What For," Typescript, January 1951, *The Later Works of John Dewey*, vol. 16. "Kennetic Inquiry," published in *Science*, vol. 112, no. 2922, 29 December 1950, pp. 775-83, appears as the final essay in Bentley's *Inquiry into Inquiries*.

48. Joseph Margolis, *Pragmatism Without Foundations*, p. 201.

THE BIBLIOGRAPHY OF ARTHUR F. BENTLEY

BOOKS

The Condition of the Western Farmer as Illustrated by the Economic History of a Nebraska Township. Johns Hopkins University Studies in Historical and Political Science, Eleventh Series, Nos. VII-VIII. Baltimore: Johns Hopkins Press, July-August, 1893, 92 pp.

The Process of Government: A Study of Social Pressures. Chicago: University of Chicago Press, 1908, 501 pp. Second Edition, Bloomington, Indiana: The Principia Press, 1935. Third Edition, The Principia Press, 1949. Fourth Edition, The Principia Press of Illinois, Evanston, Illinois, 1955.

Relativity in Man and Society. New York, G. P. Putnam's Sons, 1926, 363 pp.

Linguistic Analysis of Mathematics. Bloomington, Indiana: The Principia Press, 1932, 315 pp.

Behavior, Knowledge, Fact. Bloomington, Indiana: The Principia Press, 1935, 391 pp.

(with John Dewey) *Knowing and the Known.* Boston: The Beacon Press, 1949, 334 pp.

Inquiry into Inquiries: Essays in Social Theory. Edited and with an Introduction by Sidney Ratuer. Boston: The Beacon Press, 1954, 365 pp.

ARTICLES

"The Units of Investigation in the Social Sciences," *Publications of The American Academy of Political and Social Science,* No. 149, June 18, 1895, pp. 87-113.

"Remarks on Method in the Study of Society," *American Journal of Sociology,* Vol. 32, November 1926, pp. 456-60.

"A Sociological Critique of Behaviorism," *Archiv für systematische Philosophie und Soziologie,* Bd. 31, Heft 3/4, 1928, pp. 334-40.

"L'individuel et le social: les termes et les faits," *Revue Internationale de Sociologie,* Vol. 36, March-June 1929, pp. 243-70.

"New Ways and Old to Talk About Men," *The Sociological Review*

(London), Vol. 26, October 1929, pp. 300-14.

"Sociology and Mathematics I & II," *The Sociological Review,* Vol. 23, July, October 1931, pp. 85-107, 149-72.

"The Linguistic Structure of Mathematical Consistency," *Psyche,* Vol. 12, January 1932, pp. 78-91.

"The Positive and the Logical," *Philosophy of Science,* Vol. 3, October 1936, pp. 472-85.

"Physicists and Fairies," *Philosophy of Science,* Vol. 5, April 1938, pp. 132-65.

"Situational vs. Psychological Theories of Behavior: Sights-seen as Material of Knowledge; Situational Treatment of Behavior; Postulation for Behavioral Inquiry," *Journal of Philosophy,* Vol. 36, March 30, June 8, July 20, 1939, pp. 169-81, 309-23, 405-13.

"Observable Behaviors," *Psychological Review,* Vol. 47, May 1940, pp. 230-53.

"The Behavioral Superfice," *Psychological Review,* Vol. 48, January 1941, pp. 39-59.

"The Human Skin: Philosophy's Last Line of Defense," *Philosophy of Science,* Vol. 8, January 1941, pp. 1-19.

"Decrassifying Dewey," *Philosophy of Science,* Vol. 8, April 1941, pp. 147-56.

"Some Logical Considerations Concerning Professor Lewis' 'Mind'," *Journal of Philosophy,* Vol. 38, November 6, 1941.

"The Factual Space and Time of Behavior," *Journal of Philosophy,* pp. 634-35.

Vol. 38, August 28, 1941, pp. 477-85.

"As Through a Glass Darkly," *Journal of Philosophy,* Vol. 39, July 30, 1942, pp. 432-39.

"The Jamesian Datum," *Journal of Psychology,* Vol. 16, 1943, pp. 35-79.

"Truth, Reality and Behavioral Fact," *Journal of Philosophy,* Vol. 40, April 1943, pp. 169-87.

(with John Dewey) "A Search for Firm Names," *Journal of Philosophy,* Vol. 42, January 4, 1945, pp. 5-6.

"On a Certain Vagueness in Logic: I, II," *Journal of Philosophy,* January 4, 1945, pp. 6-27, 39-51.

(with John Dewey) "A Terminology for Knowings and Knowns," *Journal of Philosophy,* April 26, 1945, pp. 225-47.

(with John Dewey) "Postulations," *Journal of Philosophy,* November 22, 1945, pp. 645-62.

"Logicians' Underlying Postulations," *Philosophy of Science,* Vol. 13, January 1945, pp. 3-19.

(with John Dewey) "Interaction and Transaction," *Journal of Philosophy,* September 12, 1946, pp. 505-17.

(with John Dewey) "Transaction as Known and Named," *Journal of Philosophy,* Vol. 43, September 26, 1946, pp. 533-51.

(with John Dewey) "Specification," *Journal of Philosophy,* Vol. 43, November 21, 1946, pp. 645-63.

(with John Dewey) "Definition," *Journal of Philosophy,* Vol. 44, pp. 281-306.

(with John Dewey) "Concerning a Vocabulary for Inquiry into Knowledge," *Journal of Philosophy,* Vol. 44, July 31, 1947 pp. 421-34.

"The New 'Semiotic'," *Philosophy and Phenomenological Research,* Vol. 8, September 1947, pp. 107-31.

"Signs of Error," *Philosophy and Phenomenological Research,* Vol. 10, September 1949, pp. 99-104.

"Kennetic Inquiry," *Science,* Vol. 112, December 29, 1950, pp. 775-83.

PART I
TO PREPARE THE WAY

CHAPTER I

FEELINGS AND FACULTIES AS CAUSES

The most common way of explaining what goes on in society, including of course the processes of government, is in terms of the feelings and ideas of the men who make up the society. For the last fifty years we have heard a great deal about the environment as a supplementary cause, and in later years much also about the biologically described man. For the purposes of this book the environment will take care of itself, while the vital factors can in due time be assigned their place with little difficulty. As for the old-fashioned feelings and ideas which make the whole of interpretation much of the time and which crop out awkwardly all of the time, they must be given thorough attention before our real work can begin. They are irresponsible and unmeasurable, giving indeed an animistic semblance of explaining society, but actually, to use their own method of speech, blocking explanation as much as the animism of the forest would block the study of nature. It is necessary to come to close quarters with them and to annihilate their false pretenses, before attempting to build up an interpretation out of the underlying facts which they dimly hint at, but never actually define. If in this preliminary task I use many words and seem a long way from the processes of government which are my subject-matter, it is because I feel the need of making sure against misinterpretation later.

My concern is at no time with psychology, but always with the process of social life, and this, while it is always psychic, can at no time be understood or explained with the catchwords and verbal toys of psychology as the starting-point.

The present chapter will deal with interpretations in terms of feelings and faculties; the next chapter will deal similarly with interpretations in terms of ideas and ideals. In each case I shall treat first of the use of the factors in common speech for the every-

3

day purposes of life, attempting impressionistically to reveal their
defects; and then pass to close examination of certain systematic
theories built up out of them.

I may say now as well as later that I have no care for the fine
discriminations which psychological terminology draws between
motives, feelings, desires, emotions, instincts, impulses, or similar
mental states, elements, or qualities. If I separate such factors
from ideas and ideals it is solely for convenience in discussing
two ill-defined types of social theory. It is not, I repeat, psychic
process that I am going to discuss, but social life, which from the
point of view of functional psychology appears as content. The
material is the same, but fine discriminations in psychological terminology used as criteria for classifying the content are not merely
useless but positively harmful.

Section I. In Everyday Speech

We are all of us engaged every day in interpreting our social
life. This person, we say, has deceived us; that one has helped
us. Here we gave way to anger, there we maintained our high
standard of conduct, elsewhere we yielded to a temptation that
forced itself upon us. That man in public life is a charlatan, and
that other is corrupt—therefore they acted in the way they did,
which we disapprove. Here a reform could be accomplished,
if only people would realize it; there you cannot expect anything
better of men; in some other place the physical limitations to this,
that, or the other desired enterprise are showing themselves.

Out of such material our interpretations of politics and government as well as of other phases of social life are worked up.

The one secure point in all these interpretations is that they
answer fairly well for the immediate purposes we have in hand.
If experience shows they do not answer fairly well we revise them;
changing not their character but the proportions of their mixture.

For most of us all of the time, for all of us most of the time,
it is quite sufficient to regard human beings as "persons" who
possess qualities or motives which are phases of their character
and who act in accordance with these qualities or this character,

under certain conditions of life in which they are placed.   Much of
the time we subordinate the conditions or ignore them entirely.
Indeed the greater conditions are never known to us.   A full understanding of the conditions of action is as yet possessed by no one.
When such an understanding is achieved—I do not mean in all
the details in every life, but in principle, in technique—when the
"conditions" are absorbed into the action, sociology will be an
established science, not a struggle to found a science.

We put the main weight then upon the character, or the motives,
of the actors in the social drama.   A man is kind, or violent, or
careless, or "smooth," or stupid, or dishonest, or tricky, or insincere,
or clever, or trustworthy; or, more generally, good or bad, wise
or foolish.   These are his qualities.   They designate "him."   They
are put forth not merely as habits of action, labeled by us, but as
his very personality.   All this in the current life of one man,
judging the others around him.   Out of material of this kind we
have built up many theories of the causes of man's activities in
society.

If we are going to come to an understanding of the process
of government, it will be necessary first of all to reckon with these
theories, and, what is more to the point, with the material of which
they are built up.   We must test them in social life and activity to
discover what we can "do" with them scientifically, how we can
make them work.   We must find out what use they are to us.
Where they are not of use or where they lead us into difficulties
and confusions, we must clear them away.

Let us begin by picking up a few illustrations from everyday
experience.   I am walking along the street and see a man bullying
a boy.   Some big fellow steps out and knocks the street tyrant
down.   A little crowd gathers and cheers the rescuer.   I turn to
my friend and ask:

"What made him do it?   Why do they praise him?"

"He's a big-hearted fellow," he answers.   "It's sympathy for
others.   He's a credit to our civilization."

It is useless to show my friend that he has not answered the
question.   He has used a word or words that describe the man's

act, that indicate a difference between the action of the man in question and the action of some other men. That is all he is interested in specifying. If he generalizes it in terms of civilization, he goes far beyond his depth, but since he is ignorant of the deep water, it is useless, as I have said, to show him the point.

What I wanted to know was why this particular kind of "sympathy," concretely, is manifested in our social life today; why "sympathy" expresses itself in this form of protecting a boy who is merely being hectored or tormented without serious hurt.

The man who got the praise from the crowd is known to me. Half a mile from where he lives there are women and children working their lives out for less than a nourishing living. Nearby an old woman starved to death a few days ago. Child-labor under most evil conditions is common in the city. A friend of his is making his wife's life a burden by day and a horror by night. Yet he does not intervene to save the starving, or to alleviate the condition of the half-fed workers. He does not join the society for the prevention of child-labor. He does not use his influence with his friend to show him the brutality of his ways.

Is it pure "sympathy," pure "love of man," pure "big-hearted-ness" that made the man go to the rescue of the boy? If so our definitions of the words are indeed inept. The "love of man" is a strange thing if it can exist as a lump-sum quality of our hero and yet not influence him to give his aid where aid—anyone will admit—is so much more needed. And indeed in earlier ages this same man with his same physiological structure, as well as we can judge, would have shown the "sympathies," that were in him—and the egoism too—in very different forms. And did his life lie along other lines today, his sympathies would manifest themselves differently.

When my friend said that sympathy had moved the man to his act, he did, then, but restate in other words the very question I had asked. We cannot really put the question—put it, that is, in an intelligent form—without broadening it out so as to make it an inquiry about the existence of the particular form of sympathy in the particular society, manifesting itself with greater or less vigor through the various members of that society. We cannot avoid the difficulty merely by positing sympathy as such, and then limiting it or modifying it in special cases to correspond with external conditions. That is the method of popular speech, but it is arbitrary and artificial; it uses sympathy as the hypothesis for explanatory purposes, and then modifies the hypothesis to meet the needs of every particular case brought up for explanation. It will not serve for our purposes.

Again there is the case of the ill-treatment of animals. Let us choose terms for the illustration so that it will be put more socially, less individually.

Why are horses treated with so much more gentleness now than they have been at various times in the past? Why has bear-baiting come to an end? Why is cock-fighting comparatively rare? Why is the torture of cats and dogs a rare happening instead of an almost daily sight in the streets and alleys of our city? Is it because among English-speaking peoples in the last two hundred years there has been a net increase in some soul quality known as love, sympathy, kindness? My friend would compare Elizabethan England with the manners of today and answer out of hand, "Yes, the proof is there in the facts. Men are growing in sympathy."

And yet I am not answered. For if love of living beings is increasing so markedly, why does so much cruelty to animals continue without the slightest degree of widely spread condemnation? Why do we torture animals in the zoölogical garden cages? Why is the killing of cattle wholesale carried on with the greatest possible regard for expedition and a lesser regard for the feelings of the animals? Why do our hunters shine in the chase of game, enjoying social admiration, not social condemnation? Why, in short, are some particular forms of street and alley torture suppressed and some immensely larger and more common forms of public torture erected into institutions? That pure innate quality of soul, love, sympathy, kindness, or whatever you wish to call it, will have trouble in replying.

Is it some absolute humanity which our city people possess in unique measure which makes the pigeons so safe at a curbstone in the crowded district that not even a newsboy will throw a peanut shell at them with hostile intent? Yes? When those same newsboys are sleeping behind garbage boxes in the alleys?

Keeping still to the love and sympathy qualities, in their function of explaining the events of social life, let us take a still broader illustration from the field of social progress. The extension of child-labor legislation is found in every country in which the factory system of industry has become established. Some regions or states have little of it. Some backward states may be able to show as yet only the unsuccessful struggle to secure it. But all will have it in time, and in whatever measure is necessary—which under similar conditions will be much the same for all.

We see some men and some women abandon their other concerns in life and devote themselves, as it seems, altogether to this one cause from which they can hope for no personal gain in any way proportional to the labor they expend. They appeal for laws in the name of humanity. They deplore the barbarism of the times when they are failing to get their results. They praise the increase of humanity whenever they succeed. When they sit quiet and describe the progress of society they do it in terms of some meliorism which is founded on an improving human nature. My friend says: "Yes, we are growing more humane."

But again I am not satisfied. I know that some of the men who most grievously abuse the children in their factories are most tender-hearted in other relations of life. I know that some of the strongest workers for the reform are harsh and bitter at times and in places. I see the bitter draught come from the honey hive, and the sweet savors come from rancid life.

Nor is that all. I see the workers most eager for the legislation to protect child-labor shrink back in anger from a proposal which means fewer deaths by starvation in our cities. I see them tolerate abuses with indifference which would stir the heart of an Arab tribe of raiders to its depths, which would bring from the Arabs the instant relief our own society denies. I have my doubts about the net growth of human kindness. I want to know why the mixed mass of loves and hates and wants which, we say, make up man have taken this new form of action. And the mere say-so that there is more of love in the mass tells me nothing. Its existence is an inference, and if true its given working seems a strange one to follow from the facts.

Here is an illustration of a different kind. A railway rebate is an act which, considered by itself, is in a class with some simple courtesy we show to a friend and not to a stranger. It is akin to the act of the grocer who gives his best box of berries to a regular customer and his worst to some stranger he never saw before and expects never to see again. In itself it has no more wrong. Yet we denounce the rebate-giver and rebate-taker as wicked men. Rockefeller is made out to be a loathsome villain. But does not the difference here lie clearly in the importance the two different kinds of acts have for society at the given time and place? It is not, we admit in our calmer moments, some psychic quality in Rockefeller that makes him different from the grocer. Nor is it a higher morality in us that makes us condemn him. The social factors are there. The content of our lives takes different forms. We must deal with the facts, but we must be careful how we depend on moral qualities selected to suit our momentary view of the facts for our explanations.

Again we see the people rise against the "iniquities" of the Chicago packers. Those iniquities consist of trade tricks and lack of cleanliness. The packers are denounced as immoral. The people imply that they themselves would never be so evil in their hearts. Everyone knows that during the last strike special houses of ill-fame were provided within the limits of the stockyards for the use of the strike-breakers. Popular morality condemns such conduct in most stringent terms—theoretically. But the people took no action. Was it just their morality that led them to strike at the beef trust when they did, and in the way they did?

In another sphere we find a group of men whom we call "plutocratic." Some of them are frankly engaged in pursuing what we call extremely selfish ends. Among them, however, are others who in the most detached manner imaginable aid them, argue for them, and vote with them—men whose influence could not be secured for money or for any price. But we call them all plutocratic, and we talk of the increase or decrease of the plutocratic spirit, as though it were a quality of the human soul. We condemn them all in a lump for the most part, even though in calmer moments we are willing grudgingly to admit of some few of them that they are "plutocratic yet honest." But surely all of these "plutocrats" are men like the rest of us. They have the same mixed motives, the same varieties of character. There is no soul-mark that stamps them, that governs their action.

If we are going seriously to maintain that the increasing desire for riches, love of wealth, passion for fortune, or what not is the thing that is ruining the country, as pulpit and press and book-man so often do maintain, we shall have to close our eyes very tight to avoid seeing how little, on the side of soul qualities, our explanation fits the facts, and how, rather, it is nothing more than a rough verbalism adequate to indicate what the facts are which we have under discussion, but not adequate to explain them.

Again, we read in our reform newspaper that the "boss" of the city is a corrupt man, that his cohorts are corrupt, and that if they were not corrupt by nature and dishonest through and through our political evils would not be with us. I will not deny that corruption is a good word to describe the facts, nor that facts exist which can be conveniently labeled in this way. But let us us see whether it is wickedness of the heart, evil of the character, that will explain the activities of the machine.

Here is a "boss," a well-known man of great power in one of the largest cities of the country. In the interval of his real work as boss he serves as congressman at Washington, where he is intelligent and fairly useful. At least his record there is marked by no scandal, while his efficiency is enough to place him among the minor leaders. His local machine, however, annexes everything of value it can get its hands on. If there is ever any local bribery, jobbery, or thievery on its side of the political fence which it has not itself directly organized and shared in, that will count as a grave oversight for it.

I heard this boss's most persistent enemy (from the reform side) say of him one day: "If X were only honest, he would be a very useful man in public life." But is X dishonest from moral defect in his own nature? He is self-educated, self-controlled. He neither drinks nor smokes. He cares most affectionately for his family. All his pleasures are taken at his own fireside. One never looks for him at the haunts of the "good fellows." He is engaged in various private business enterprises. Once he failed. Later he paid all his debts. His credit is of the best. His word is as good as a business man's word can be. If he ever operated any kind of confidence game "on the side" as many "reputable" business houses do, the fact has never leaked out. He never deceived a friend. His lieutenants need nothing from him beyond his simple word. They get their share in the spoils and are never deserted.

But "spoils" is, of course, his main line of goods. The looting of the public is his occupation. He plans and campaigns and snatches the booty with no more scruples of conscience than if he were exploiting a gold mine, or dealing wholesale in clothes from the sweatshop, or running a "pure-food" factory—in the days before pure food legislation—or merely living idly on the income from a fine holding of valuable land. If X is dishonest by nature, if his soul is corrupt, he has a queer way of showing it—everywhere except in politics. Take him all in all, I cannot make myself believe that the reason the people groan under the burden of machine politics in his city is because he and some other forceful men like him have wicked hearts.

It is perfectly true that if he did not act in politics as he does, he would be acting differently, but how does that help us? What is there to show that the way he acts is due to his specific moral quality or character? Our problem is to find out why in a city-full of men known to us in terms of all their loving-grasping-vice-virtue complexes of character there develops in the political field a certain form of systematized corruption. If anyone says that a growing evil in the hearts of men causes it, he is as ignorant of the character of the Fathers as he is blind to the full life activities of the men of his own times.

One more illustration, this time drawn from a most mighty manifestation of the social life of America. Through the year 1905 the big mutual life-insurance companies of the country were under fire. Everyone knows now how the officials of those companies had been acting with perfect complaisance in the management of the enormous properties: how favored men's incomes had been swollen, how families had been built up in wealth, how policy-holders' dividends had been withheld and squandered, how legislatures had been bribed, how taxes had been dodged, how books had been falsified, how political campaign funds had been aided. When the facts became known a tremendous public wrath gathered and broke on the heads of the responsible men. It denounced those men as evil and corrupt, as grafters and thieves and swindlers. It compared them with all kinds of detested malefactors in and out of jail. Finally, it thrust them out of their offices and drove at least one to death, and others to sanitariums and to exile. It overpowered the legislature of New York State, suppressed there in a winter evils that had taken years to develop, and drove a most efficient legislative machine into astonished servility, before it was through with its rage. The guilty companies meanwhile, with new officials, made some reforms, and more pretenses of reform, and saved as much of the old system and its perquisites as they could out of the disaster.

What are we to say of the mental and moral qualities of the various actors in these events? Were the presidents who did wrong and paid the penalty men of lesser moral stamina than the presidents of an earlier day when different customs prevailed? Did some mental or moral quality decline and did its decline bring about the evils and losses of which the nation justly complained? Were the men who, in the pulpit, press, and platform, denounced the evil-doers men who themselves possessed a higher morality, a greater quantum of the needed mental quality? Were the new officers who took charge of the companies after the evil-doers had been driven out men of personally higher standards?

Did the reform come, in short, because the decline in virtue had been stopped and because an increase in virtue had come in its place?

For anyone who knows the lives of the actors, who looks straight at their lives in the very moment of action, I think the answer inevitably will be, No. The reforms came. They brought new forms of action, and these new forms we call more moral and more honest. And the old forms will certainly not recur in all their crudity on the moment and perhaps not at all. But as for a change in the character of men which brought these things about, if it is here at all, we know of it only by inference from the facts of the change itself. It is a figure of speech rather than a quality of men useful to explain their deeds.

What was to be seen, in actual human life, was a mass of men making use of their opportunities. The insurance presidents and trustees saw opportunities and used them. Their enemies in the fit time saw opportunities and used them. The "public" by and by awoke to what it had suffered, saw its opportunities for revenge and for future safeguards and used them. All these things happened, all of them had causes, but those causes cannot be found in a waxing and waning and change or transformation of the psychic qualities of the actors.

Who will agree today with Aristotle's explanation of the relations of slaves and freemen? Slaves, he says, are slaves by nature. Freemen are freemen by nature: "From the hour of their birth, some are marked out for subjection, others for rule."[1] "He who participates in reason enough to apprehend, but not to have, reason, is a slave by nature."[2] "It is clear, then, that some men are by nature free, and others slaves, and that for these latter slavery is both expedient and right."[3] "For the slave has no deliberative faculty at all; the woman has, but it is without authority (or, "inconclusive"), and the child has, but it is immature."[4]

Yet what Aristotle was doing in these passages was to trace social relations down to psychic qualities, just as we trace them today,

---

[1] Aristotle, *Politics* (Jowett trans.), I, 5, 2.   [3] *Ibid.*, I, 5, 11.

[2] *Ibid.*, I, 5, 9.   [4] *Ibid.*, I, 13, 7.

so far as the method of the explanation goes, when we use psychic factors to explain social life. The inadequacy of such an explanation becomes strikingly clear to us when we disagree with the concrete use of it.

We have been considering in the main illustrations dealing with the feelings or moral character of men. These phrases of Aristotle's concern not only character but intellectual capacity. Let us turn to this latter phase of such interpretations and examine intellect considered as a power or quality of the individual man; directing attention still to our everyday methods of speech with a view to seeing just how much authority they have.

Here is a man whom the world calls great. Here is another who lives the life of a clod. The one produces a great scientific work, a great painting, a great poem; the other digs the soil under a foreman's orders and never rises above such work. Our ordinary speech forms put it that the one has a great intellect and the other is stupid. We modify this manner of statement by qualifying factors, so that in case of its manifest inadequacy we can take into account variations of "character" or the influences of the "environment," but we do not desert the theory that a difference of brain or mind power is behind the respective achievements·

The theory with its qualifications works fairly well for our practical purposes. We know that dog brains do not produce written poems. We know that idiots are similarly ineffective. We know that in the acquirement of the education of the schools there are great differences between individuals. We know that we can easily explain something that interests us to one man, but only with the greatest difficulty to another. We readily forget that if something different were being explained the relative alertness might be just the reverse. We build up a scale of intellectual capacities, with an Aristotle or a Shakespeare or a Kant or a Goethe or a Darwin or a Lionardo or a Michelangelo at the top, and grade it down to the peasant or day laborer.

But what after all do we have upon which to base our judgments as to the relative ranks of different men, except just their accomplished works? What are we grading except their achievements, as we estimate them? What personal factors have we behind the achievements to explain the achievements by?

I am not insisting that there is no difference in "brain power," if that phrase may be used, between men. I am not saying that such differences can never, in some respects at least, be taken into account; it would be foolish indeed to erect a verbal barricade against the future. I am only saying that as our knowledge now stands, within the range in which we find men in social life, we observe nothing in the facts before us to justify the assertion that any achievement, as socially judged great or small, rests directly on an intellectual capacity correspondingly great or small—nothing, that is, to justify the assertion scientifically, however well the common phrases may suit our practical everyday needs.

Everyone knows how men who today have world-wide fame were neglected by their own generations, and how the favorites of one generation may be forgotten by the next. A Rembrandt closed his life in poverty and neglect. A Mendelssohn has passed from idolization to comparative indifference inside of a century. The great schoolmen have passed into deep obscurity. There are nation-wide and world-wide fads in literature and in all the arts and in science too. We recognize this, but we continue to emit judgments as though our own standpoint were the stable base to which all others must relate themselves as aberrations. We are apt to forget that all of these scales of valuation are relative; that, with but a sufficiently long sweep, there is reason to suspect that even our firmest substratum of scientific knowledge would show the same relativity; and that we have no way of disproving in all this limitless variety of different standards of judgment that possibly the man humblest now would stand out most strikingly in another setting: and that by this very token we must rest our judgment on the achievement itself, not on some alleged genius or ability lying behind the achievement.[1]

[1] Tolstoi's articles on "Shakespeare and the Drama" (*Fortnightly Review*, December, 1906, January, 1907) are illuminating from this point of view; his own outlook on life so clearly determines his entire criticism.

I am perfectly well aware that the point I am trying to make is utterly indifferent so far as the processes of ordinary speech are concerned, but I will show later on how very important it is when the question is the exact interpretation of society, and how weak are the methods of interpretation built up out of these speech forms.

What few attempts have been made to estimate the capacity of the man behind his achievement only serve to show the tenuous nature of the theory. Laboratory studies in experimental psychology do not hitch the man on to the social achievement; at the most they indicate in a limited way different degrees of fitness in different persons for different kinds of achievement, something there is no thought of denying. Measurements of skull capacity throw no light on genius. Raymond Pearl as the result of an elaborate statistical study of nationalities, concludes that "there is no evidence that brain weight is sensibly correlated with intellectual ability."[1] Hansemann, in his study of von Helmholtz' brain, says the same thing as the result of a different line of investigation.[2] Nor do studies of the shape of the skull—the long-headed, the broad-headed—give any aid.[3] The convolutions of the brain do not differ among different peoples. The human convolutions can be matched even in the brains of chimpanzees. If a discriminative investigation is to be made it must be pushed much deeper into the brain processes than any microscope or stain has yet penetrated. It would take statistics of tens of thousands of cases to give results, and even then who could say that the structure showed the cause of the work that was done, rather than being merely the track of the function which was the work itself?[4]

The illustrations I have given thus far in this section have been chosen to show what kinds of explanation we currently make and

[1] *Biometrika*, Vol. IV, p. 83.

[2] *Zeitschrift für Psychologie und Physiologie der Sinnesorgane*, Vol. XX, p. 4.

[3] See, for example, Ripley, *Races of Europe*, p. 40; Reid, *Principles of Heredity*, p. 292; Pearl, *loc. cit.*, p. 83.

[4] Compare also the criticism of Pearson in sec. v of this chapter.

currently find satisfactory for events around us. Their common characteristic is that some psychic quality, of goodness or badness, of love or hate, of intelligence or lack of intelligence, or some mixture of such qualities, is taken to explain what the actors have done. The explanations do not make impossible an attempt to go back of the psychic qualities and ask what caused them. Some event in Tom's career may be pointed out to show why he became kind-hearted, or his quality may be traced to "mental heredity." One insurance company president may be said to have seen another suffer for his sins, and to have learned from him to be a better man himself. But usually it is not felt necessary to go behind the personal quality.

Now the feature of these personal qualities to which attention must specially be given is that they are looked upon as a sort of "thing" acting among other "things" in the social world. They are a sort of "stuff," different, or not different, as one likes, from the material "stuff" of the world, but in either case interacting with the latter in series of events that can be linked together, with each event in the series explaining the other that comes after it. For example, Tom sees the bully maltreating the boy. The bully act is there first. It knocks against Tom's "sympathy." The sympathy makes Tom act in a particular manner. The bullying is stopped by the impact. Brain states, or soul states, forming this "stuff"—it is all one in the practical explanation.

It is like billiard balls on a billiard table. The cue ball is some moral or other feeling, or capacity, and it knocks against another ball, which is some other person or thing or institution, and shunts it off to knock in turn against a third ball, which may be either a feeling or a thing. Thus the social process is supposed to go on.

Is this too crude a statement of such explanations? I readily admit its crudity. But does not the ordinary discussion of the place of education in social life adopt just this theory? Does it not treat so many boys and girls as having so many minds made up of so much feeling- or thought-stuff? Does it not say, Come, let us heap up thought-stuff in such and such ways and it will produce the results we desire later on ?[1]   And is it not by the proof of experience forever and ever wrong ?   Does it ever get results in that way ? I am not denying that education exists and that it has its place and that there are good reasons for its existence, any more than I have denied in the illustrations above that kind-hearted acts occur, that child-labor laws are passed, that bosses exist, that insurance-reform laws have been passed, or that great works of art have been produced.   I am only denying the "stuff" theory or explanation that is used in connection with them.   I am denying that such an explanation explains anything.

The ordinary question concerns the creating of new psychic qualities, the increasing of the amount of some old ones, the suppressing of some other old ones.   The real question—the question we must face—is, why the living, acting men and women change their forms of action, cease to do now what they did formerly, use their "qualities" in some places and not in others, in short live the particular social lives they do live.   Whenever anybody steps forward with any method by which he can show that there actually exists at one time more of one of the psychic qualities, the "stuff," than at any other time, it will be perfectly legitimate to take it into account.   So long as such "stuff" is used in explanation of the forms of our social actions on no better ground than that we assume changes in the "stuff" from the mere fact of the changes in the modes of action, then it is no explanation.   It may answer the purpose of the bystander as he compares Tom with Bill. But it explains nothing at all.   When real explanations begin to appear, the use of the old forms ceases even to deserve toleration as harmless.   It becomes positively harmful as continually creating a false sense of security and comprehension, when no security and no comprehension exist.   It is only in the most superstitious circles that people nowadays say a man is "lucky" by nature, because they observe he has what they call luck; and the doctrine of original sin as explaining men's shortcomings is

[1] For one among a hundred crass illustrations see J. W. Jenks, *Citizenship and the Schools*, pp. vi, 37, 51, 52.

not often seriously discussed.   But both the luck and the original sin are at bottom just as substantial as these soul qualities I am criticizing.

We find that if we are going to use this soul-stuff to explain social activities we must be able to show either qualitative changes in it, or quantitative increases of some forms of it, or our explanation will come to nothing.   What is more, we must show this in some other way than by mere inference from the facts we propose to explain.   If we are going to infer a soul quality from the social fact and then use the quality to explain the fact, we put ourselves on a level with animists in the most savage tribes.   A branch falls. It was the life in it or behind it that threw it down.   Thunder peals.   It is a spirit speaking.   The grain grows.   It is the spirit of the corn pushing it up.   This man is a slave.   It is because such is his nature.   The pigeons are left unharmed.   It is because we are growing more humane.   We pass child-labor laws.   It is because we will not tolerate abuses our fathers tolerated.   That man is a boss at the head of a corrupt machine.   It is because he is dishonest by nature.   This man wrote a great book.   It is because he had a giant intellect.

The stick, the storm, the crop need no spooks to explain them. The child-labor laws, the sparing of animal life, the corrupt politics, and even the great book will not be explained while such spooks interfere.

It may be said, however, that while these feelings and capacities do not manifest themselves so that we can make sure of them in restricted areas and in brief periods, nevertheless a glance across the ages or a comparison of high races with low races will bring an underlying soul-stuff difference to light.   Suppose we examine some of the facts which lie on the surface with reference to this hypothesis, not, of course, in order to make an exhaustive study of them, but merely to bring to light the character of the problem that is involved.

It used commonly to be said that modern men had greater brain power than men of "ancient-history" days.   Aristotle, in his generation, had much the same feeling, for we find him contrasting the times "of old" when "men of eminent virtue were few," with his own period in which "many persons equal in merit arose,"[1] and even using this as the basis of a theory of government. But few students now have any interest in such assertions. The crudity is too apparent. Hear, for instance, Ratzel, who says that it is doubtful whether we are today "in physical or intellectual power, in virtue, in capacity, any farther ahead of our generations of ancestors than the Tubus are of theirs."[2]

Suppose one should try to get light on this question by comparing Italian art of the Renaissance with the Hallstatt culture or with Etruscan art. Could he possibly hope to disentangle from the complex of social achievement anything that would justify him in saying that greater brain power had been shown in one period than in the other? Or suppose he should start proudly with Sir Isaac Newton, or, if he liked, with Darwin, and find himself suddenly under necessity of comparing these men with the men of Chaldea who discovered the eclipse period. Would the very problem he had set himself not reduce itself to an absurdity? Or, again, suppose he should compare the steam locomotive of today with the first seizure of iron from its concealment in the ore. Only a blind confidence that he was dealing with the very basal problem of society, and that he must get an answer to the question in terms of soul capacity, would nerve him to produce one.

If instead of comparing antiquity with modern times one tries to make comparisons between the races of today as to their mental capacity, one must face at once such difficulties as that presented by Japan. Twenty years ago all the world "knew" that Japan was lacking in brain capacity and that the Japanese were of a lower order of humanity. And today? Yet the Japanese people has not been physically or psychically remade in a generation.

But Japan is only an illustration on a great scale of what is manifest in isolated cases in a thousand places. A few months

[1] *Politics* (Jowett trans.), III, 15, 11.
[2] *History of Mankind*, Vol, I, p. 4.

ago a pure-blooded Zulu took first honors in oratory at Columbia University. A pure-blooded Indian, Benite Pablo Juarez, president of Mexico, was a man of admittedly high rank among constructive statesmen. Another pure-blooded Indian, a Mohawk, was distinguished as a physician and as the successful head of a great mutual insurance society in Canada. The Maoris of New Zealand have taken to schooling and civilized life with great ease. There was a famous school of aborigines in Australia that took higher honors for a year's work, once upon a time, than any school of white children. Our own schools in the Philippines have wonder-tales of acquisitiveness to send us. These illustrations do not prove anything positively, but they throw the theory of brain capacity into the most serious difficulties.

Permit a warning again. I am not denying that there may have been in fact a development of nerve and brain structure since human life began, any more than that there was such a development before. Nor am I denying that by a process of selection a greater proportion of the men of today may have a more complex structure than of the men of the Stone Age. I am only insisting that there is nothing in human achievement to *prove* the reality of either of those possibilities, and that, inasmuch as they cannot be independently established, it is a purely arbitrary assumption to place them as causes behind human achievements; and especially is it arbitrary so long as the process of social life and achievement has not been fully studied for itself, apart from any theory of brain power behind it.

So much for the mental capacity in history. And now how is it for the sympathy factors? Here I will put together certain current opinions with facts taken from the works of careful students to show how impossible it is to locate any growth of sympathy in the way the theory demands.

First a bare reference to Kropotkin's *Mutual Aid*, that storehouse of information about institutions and methods of co-operation and assistance, covering not merely ancient village communities and Middle Age guilds, but also animal communities. Kropotkin wrote, it is true, to correct his own misinterpretation of evolutionary theory, and his study led him no farther than to substitute as the underlying motive of society something broader than love or sympathy, namely an "instinct of human solidarity,"[1] a factor of the same kind as the former. His material, however, well serves our purpose here of indicating the ultimate meaninglessness of all such interpretations in terms of instincts; for he shows us sympathetic facts in great masses through the whole range of social life, animal and human. Anyone who will may turn through his pages for their bearing upon this point. Whatever inferences one may draw, certain it is that an inference that sympathy as such has increased quantitatively throughout history will not be among them.

I will cite one or two illustrations from other sources. Americans, because of the wars of the colonists with the Indians, continue to speak of the native tribes of their continent as cruel, bloodthirsty savages. And of course it was the "nature" of the Indians to be such. Here are a few passages to consider, all with the authority of Lewis H. Morgan: "It is a reasonable conclusion . . . . that in all Indian villages and encampments without distinction the hungry were fed through the open hospitality of those who possessed a surplus."[2] "Ordinarily they try to have one year's provisions on hand."[3] "Crimes and offenses were so infrequent under their social system that the Iroquois can scarcely be said to have had a criminal code."[4] Here we have benevolence, foresight, and brotherly love, more than utopian. Evidently one must be careful in the qualities he attributes to the Indian in explanation of his conduct.[5]

There is a good illustration in Letourneau comparing the

---

[1] See the introduction to *Mutual Aid, a Factor of Evolution*, pp. xiii, xiv.

[2] Morgan, *Houses and House Life of American Aborigines*, p. 56.

[3] Samuel Gorman, *Laguna Village Indians;* quoted by Morgan, *House Life*, p. 74.

[4] Morgan, *League of the Iroquois*, edition of 1901, Vol. I, p. 321.

[5] For illustrations of the discipline and self-control of primitive peoples, one may examine Crawley, *The Mystic Rose*, chap. vi.

Indians with the early Germans, which is useful to anyone who is tempted to trace social development back to psychological qualities. At the end of a chapter in which he discusses the political condition of "barbarous Europe," that is, of all European people except Greece and Rome, in the time of Caesar, he mentions some of the most striking social characteristics which these peoples had in common and then compares them with American Indian tribes. In fundamental matters he finds a very close analogy.[1] He compares especially certain Scythian, German, Celtic, and Iberian qualities with the Hurons and the Sioux.   For our purposes we do not need to go behind Letourneau's impression of the resemblance as he states it, his scientific standing being quite sufficient to justify calling him to witness.

Now if the resemblance was there, both in institutions and in character, one would expect, so far as such psychic qualities count as factors, that the lines of evolution would be much the same. The lines of evolution were, however, so strikingly different that one has difficulty in bringing these similar factors into the reckoning at all; and this even though, as Letourneau himself says, Rome played much the rôle in ancient Europe that the Europeans played toward indigenous America.[2] Letourneau is in the habit of interpreting in terms of instincts and similar factors,[3] and so in this case in order to explain the inconsistency which his own remarks draw attention to, he assumes some additional

---

[1] Letourneau, *L'Évolution politique dans les diverses races humaines*, p. 407: "Vue dans son ensemble et en ne tenant compte que des analogies fondamentales, l'Europe préromaine était, pour l'état social et politique, assez comparable à l'Amérique du Nord, alors que Christophe Colomb la découvrit. . . . . Tout cela rappelle fort les mœurs des Sioux et des Hurons. Pour l'état politique, la ressemblance est plus grande encore."

[2] *Ibid.*, p. 408: "Dans l'Europe ancienne, Rome a joué le rôle des Européens dans l'Amérique indigène."

[3] To show how Letourneau himself depends on instincts and psychic characters in his own interpretation, the following is in point: "Old inherited instincts form the basis of the human mind, and the superposition of innate tendencies is exactly comparable with that of the earth in geology. The spirit of progress and liberty is only a thin bed scarce covering the mighty moral strata bequeathed to us by our forefathers."—*Property, Its Origin and Development*, p. 352.

"qualities"[1] in the Germans which would have made them evolve even if left uninfluenced by outsiders. He merely assumes these qualities for his purpose, but does not attempt to elaborate them.[2]

I refer to this here simply to show how such psychic factors as we have in mind are discovered by the persons who use them, how they are put to work to give the appearance of explanation, and how similar supplementary factors *ad libitum* are dragged in to fill out the interpretation. From the given facts one infers the qualities. The qualities are supposed to produce the facts. But conflicts arise. Then one assumes other qualities to fit the varying cases.

It would be easy to take up many of our modern characteristics or institutions which are relied on to prove the existence of an admirable spirit of humanity in our own times, and show the fallacy of the inferences that are made for them. If hospitals are named, they can be offset by ancient "temples of health" and by the spring hygienic festivals of savages—I do not, of course, mean for efficiency as tested by present standards, but for the function they served. If bloodshed is mentioned and we are made out to be milder than our forefathers, there are our huge wars and our factory death-rolls and even our Fourth of July celebrations to take into account as three among many factors that give the lie to our alleged virtue. If education is named, a great array of facts from Egyptian occultism to Polynesian "initiations" should be considered. Our modern forms of prostitution can hardly be called more humane than those of older ages. Do the nations of western civilization utilize their resources as China utilizes its resources, so far as the "virtues" of prudence and foresight go? And when benevolence is mentioned, what can we put forth to

---

[1] *L'Évolution politique*, p. 408: "Néanmoins les populations de l'Europe possédaient déjà des qualités natives, qui les auraient sûrement tirées de la barbarie. Spontanément elles auraient évolué vers une civilisation plus relevée, si Rome leur en avait laissé le temps."

[2] One may get at this same problem on the opposite side by asking why it was that the Aztecs and the Red Indians, being apparently of the same ethnical stock, had such different histories, if psychic qualities determine development.

offset Arab hospitality or the care for the poor in any one of a thousand tribes ?[1]

The truth is that if one should start out on the theory that such psychic factors as these could be discovered and called into play for explanatory purposes, and if one should make a serious attempt to compare races and periods with a view to discovering them, one would need to adopt a very elaborate and careful procedure. It would be necessary to take two peoples and try to fit the one into the exact circumstances of the other, barring only the factor of race character, to see what would develop. It is not enough merely to note that there are in fact differences between peoples, nor is it enough to transplant a lot of adult men bodily from their environment to a strange environment to see what would happen, as, for instance, Bushmen to Wall Street. One would perhaps have to take a selected number of Bushmen babies and an equal number of American babies, give them all the identical home training and outside education, and test the results on a large scale. But while a test with a limited number of individuals may be partially possible, it is manifestly impossible to transport a whole Bushman tribe into the new environment on fair terms with persons born into it. Even less is it possible to isolate the alleged soul qualities of different races in scientific analysis so as to give ground for a fair conclusion. If one could think one race over into the environment of the other he would find that by the time he got it fully enough into the other environment for a fair analysis, it would no longer be the race he started with, but it would actually be that other race, and the very test he was trying to make would have disappeared.

It is easy enough to imagine the bodies of one set of men substituted for the bodies of another set. We can easily see that the habitual social activities of one set would not be reproduced by the other set forthwith. But when we try to give the one set a fair

---

[1] Letourneau says that when a destitute Bedouin tells the chief of his need the chief summons the rich men of the tribe and says: "One of our brethren is in want. If you wish him to die, suffer me to kill him instead of hunger. If not, go: you know your duty." Whereupon the needy man is straightway equipped for a new start toward prosperity.—*Property*, p. 199.

chance to adapt itself to the activities of the other set, we find in
the end that such activities are all we know, and that there is no
underlying "vital factor" left for us to deal with—at least until
that improbable time comes when some tens of thousands of Bushmen, or other "low race," babies are brought up in American or
European homes with the identical love, care, and assimilation
that the born babies of the families receive.

I am perfectly well aware that I have given this whole matter a
superficial treatment.   But the truth is that a superficial treatment
was needed first of all to show wherein the real problem lies.
When I have finished with my examination of the theoretical
systems constructed out of feelings and ideas I shall return in
Part II, in connection with direct examination of the process of
government as it actually goes forward under our eyes, to a consideration of some of the real relations which the biological man
and the conditions under which the social process is carried on
bear to social interpretation.

Section II.   Small

The denial that the psychical qualities of individuals can be
used in explaining social activities will perhaps appear absurd to
some readers, while to others it will appear a quibble. The
former will say that the given fact in human society is the man
who desires and that it will be impossible to build up any interpretation of social phenomena except by taking him with his given
psychical content or capacity, and learning how he "works."
The latter will say that I have been knocking down a straw man,
and that as a matter of fact nobody assumes such soul-stuff as
that to which I have entered objection.

While I cannot hope fully to satisfy the former critics till I
reach the constructive chapters of this book, I shall nevertheless
proceed now to show how such soul-stuff is actually used by
sociologists and other investigators of social phenomena, and what
the difficulties are into which it leads them.   I shall do this through
an examination of the positions of Small, Spencer, and Jhering,
followed by less extended references to some other writers.

Professor Albion W. Small interprets society by the aid of social forces.

> The concept "social forces" has a real content [he says]. It represents reality. There are social forces. They are the desires of persons. They range in energy from the vagrant whim that makes the individual a temporary discomfort to his group, to the inbred feelings that whole races share. It is with these subtle forces that social arrangements and the theories of social arrangements have to deal.[1]

He classifies desires into six kinds which he names desires of (1) health; (2) wealth; (3) sociability; (4) knowledge; (5) beauty, and (6) rightness. Sometimes and for some purposes he calls them interests instead of desires, and sometimes he uses the terms motives or ends.[2] He starts with them as qualities or characteristics of individual persons. Occasionally he uses them as general groups into which many varying desires can be classified. Again he uses them as tests for the classification of social phenomena. But always he comes back to the soul-stuff idea. There is a confusion lurking in all his discussions of these desires, which cannot be cleared away, I think, until he drops the soul-stuff entirely, and takes the facts simply as social phenomena at their simple social value.

I shall criticize sharply his inconsistencies and contradictions, but I do not want to be taken as criticizing his entire method of interpretation. At times, it seems to me, he rises to an entirely adequate use of "interests" as social forces. But, if I am right, it is only in the degree in which he strips off the "personal-qualities" idea and forgets all about the soul-stuff that he succeeds. When the knife is applied to this latter element then the "interests" which are left will prove to be genuine facts, and at the same time forces, of society.[3]

---

[1] Small, *General Sociology*, p. 536.

[2] For a discussion of these terms see *ibid.*, pp. 435, 436, 445, 535.

[3] I shall pay no attention here to the question whether his classification of the interests into these six is well made. My whole criticism will concern solely the validity of the use of any such interests in this manner, without regard to the particular interests that are selected.

The earliest presentation of his theory with which I am acquainted is to be found in the *Introduction to the Study of Society*. In this book we are given man as one of the two elements of society, the other being land, i. e., the physical environment. To learn about man we must go to physiology and psychology. Psychology shows us man as a bundle of wants, or desires. "Social interpretation must begin with an analysis of these desires, and must observe the conditions of their emergence."[1] "History is the record of social action with reference to conceptions of human wants."[2] The first duty of the sociologist is to classify these wants. The preliminary classification offered to us is as follows:

GROUPS OF PERSONAL WANTS

a) Wants immediately connected with the activity of the physical functions.

b) Wants immediately connected with the use of material goods.

c) Wants immediately connected with the activity of social instinct.

d) Wants immediately connected with the activity of intellect.

e) Wants immediately connected with the activity of aesthetic judgment.

f) Wants immediately connected with the activity of conscience.[3]

These are immediately rechristened with the six terms already mentioned, health,[4] wealth, sociability, knowledge, beauty, righteousness (since called rightness).

Now the first thing to note is that the criterion for this classification seems to come from the individual physique or intellect. We find the specific marks to be in one case "physical functions," in another the "using" of goods, in a third an instinct, and in the three others faculties of the soul.

Apparently, then, the standards are of a kind which the man brings into society ready made—in other words, his body and soul-stuff. But if that is the case Professor Small tends immediately to abandon the position, for in his next paragraph he tells us in effect that these wants are experienced by different persons in

---

[1] Small and Vincent, *An Introduction to the Study of Society*, p. 173.

[2] *Ibid.*, p. 174.   [3] *Ibid.*, p. 175.

[4] The health interest includes such various things as sexual desire, hunger, and the "work interest," or impulses to play and to feats of skill. See *General Sociology*, p. 197.

very different and even contradictory ways, and we get the table
worked over in the following somewhat more objective form:

CONCEPTIONS OF PERSONAL SATISFACTIONS

a) Satisfactions of physical functions, from unrestrained animalism to the
perfect body, as an instrument of highest life.

b) Satisfactions of possession, from "material possessions the ultimate
good" to "the trusteeship of wealth."

c) Satisfactions of social instincts from wolfishness to brotherhood.

d) Satisfactions of mental activity; from being in servitude to the physical
to becoming the ultimate end of effort.

e) Satisfactions of aesthetic feeling; from delight in the hideous to deifi-
cation of beauty.

f) Satisfactions of conscience; from fetichism to theosophy.[1]

I do not quote these tables to call attention to the curious
assumptions involved, though all of these assumptions are significant, and Professor Small has never been able to get rid of the
tangles they set for his feet. The old classification of "faculties"
must be valid and it must be capable of co-ordination with "physical functions" and instincts, if the classification is to have any
value at all. For each want in the sense of "thing wanted" there
must be a peculiar desire in a brain. This must be true down
to the finest shades of desire, and at the same time the "wants"
and desires must be capable of classification in identical schemes,
and the most general terms describing desires must in a very
real sense, involving a certain psychical unity, include all the
lesser shadings of desires under them. There must be six definite
great desires, each including an infinite number of definite varieties.

The point I wish particularly to make is that if "wolfishness"
and "brotherhood" are two satisfactions flowing from one kind of
desire; if works of ugliness and works of beauty both satisfy the
same aesthetic feeling, if greed acts and benevolence acts are
similarly linked together; we have ground for the suspicion that
what is here classified is not desires at all, but rather social activities
grouped with a rough empiricism, and attributed for their origin,
in purely gratuitous manner, to desires—as soul-stuff—which are
called into existence to match. And indeed this suspicion is not
weakened by the fact that the three "faculties" are used as criteria

[1] *Introduction to the Study of Society*, p. 176.

in the first table.   There is reason enough to believe that those
faculties themselves have been empirically inferred to exist because
certain groups of social activities have been found which they are
needed to explain on a good old-fashioned soul-stuff basis.

We may say that what Professor Small's theory comes to then
—stating not merely his own contribution but also its social setting—
is that certain rough groups of social activities are first taken; that
it is inferred next that there must be desires or wants corresponding
to each; that these main desires or wants are set up, six in number,
as the springs of social action; that all specific desires as found
from day to day in individual men are brought under these six
classes, no matter how they quarrel when fastened together;
and that finally it is asserted that because the six great desires
have been named, we are given in them a classification of social
activities which is for that reason valid.

It is all a vicious circle which starts with a rough, untested
guess, and comes out in a rough, untested guess, with nothing but
metaphysics in between.   It is no better when it finishes than
when it began, and no appeal to "desires" or other things in the
soul makes it any more plausible.

Professor Small would no doubt say that it is exceedingly unfair
to take this early statement of his theory and judge him by it.   I
have however only taken it to show the confusion at its fountain
head.   Later on he adopted the term "interests," which, I believe
does not appear at all in his first discussion.   With it he has worked
the theory over, but only to fall into deeper and deeper morasses,
except at those times when he disregards it entirely and goes
straight ahead with actual social facts as they present themselves
to his trained eye.

To show Professor Small's difficulties I will first of all quote a
few sentences from various parts of his writings.

Every desire that any man harbors [he says] is a force.[1] . . . .

An interest is a plain demand for something regardless of everything
else.[2] . . . .

[1] *General Sociology*, p. 536.

[2] *Ibid.*, p. 201.   This sentence applies, Professor Small tells us, to interests
"in the most general sense" and also to interests "in the most particular sense."

Interests are the simplest modes of motion which we can trace in the conduct of human beings.[1] . . . .

While biology and psychology have to do with the individual when he is in the making, sociology wants to start with him as the finished product.[2] . . . .

All action that goes on in society is the movement and counter-movement of persons impelled by the particular assortment of these feelings which is located in each.[3] . . . .

Before science that is properly social begins, ... analysis of individual traits must have taken into account all the peculiarities of individual action which betray the individual impulses or springs of individual action which are the units of force with which social science must deal.[4]

All of these quotations make the interests or desires, whichever they happen to be called, individual qualities, and so place them in the category of soul-stuff, with everything that that inevitably implies.

Compare now with the above quotations the following, also brought together from various parts of his writings:

Of course this analysis of human interests is from the standpoint of the observer, not of the actor. Real human beings are not such prigs as to start by saying: "Go to now. I propose to secure health, wealth, sociability, knowledge, beauty, and rightness."[5] . . . .

We have mainly to do with interests in the same sense in which the man of affairs uses the term.[6]

Interests in the sociological sense are not necessarily matters of attention and choice. . . . . They are indicated spheres of activity which persons enter into and occupy in the course of realizing their personality.[7] . . . .

All human experience is thus not merely a fabric of personal desires, but those personal desires operate in a very large measure impersonally.[8]

[1] *Ibid.*, p. 426. Small here is not thinking of a social "mode of motion" but of an individual logically presocial, "mode of motion." Hence, despite the phrasing, he does not take a *descriptive* but a *causal* point of view with reference to the desires. The desires remain for him forces in the metaphysical sense.

[2] *Ibid.*, p. 430.   [3] *Ibid.*, p. 480.

[4] *American Journal of Sociology*, Vol. IV, p. 381.

[5] *General Sociology*, p. 198. (And this, within three pages of the second quotation in the list just given, that from *General Sociology*, p. 201.)

[6] *Ibid.*, p. 436. Illustrations are the railroad interest, the tobacco interest, the sugar interest, the labor interest, the Cuban interest, the army interest, the canal interest.

[7] *Ibid.*, p. 434.   [8] *Ibid.*, p. 539.

Now this second set of sentences just as surely tends to break loose from the soul-stuff conception as the first set adhered to it. Professor Small finds the reconciliation which carries him over the gap in a distinction between objective and subjective interests.[1] But even if he reaches a reconciliation for purposes of personal or logical equilibrium, for sociological purposes he does not want a genuine reconciliation. He wants to make the subjective side of these interests explain the phenomena on the objective side, which are sometimes institutions and sometimes not. In doing it he attempts to work out a calculus of desires. A few typical sentences to this end now follow.

Here is, to start with, an excellent specimen of the billiard-ball method of using interests:

In brief, either the social process in the large or that portion of the process which is comprised within the limits of an individual life is a resultant of reactions between the six interests, primarily in their permutations within the individual, secondarily in their permutations between individuals, and always in their varied reciprocity with the non-sentient environment.[2]

Here is an italicized proposition as to the relation of interests to everything else in society, the institutions, etc.:

At all events the appropriate order of procedure, from a sociological point of approach, is analysis of social situations, in connection with analysis of purposes of the persons involved in the situations, to the end of arriving at generalizations of regularities and uniformities of sequence between types of social situations and types of human volitions.[3]

Here the purposes or volitions (i. e., the desires or interests) are set aside in one series and after an independent study of them they must be used to explain the "situations" in the other series. Again he writes:

In order to have an adequate analysis of any social situation, past or present, it is necessary to have an account of the precise content and proportions of the several wants, both in typical persons of the society and in the group as a whole.[4]

Here is a sentence in which the things to be explained are set

---

[1] *General Sociology*, pp. 431, 445 ff., 537. For the possibilities in the use of subjective and objective see sec. iv of this chapter, on von Jhering.

[2] *Ibid.*, p. 446.   [3] *Ibid.*, p. 649.

[4] *American Journal of Sociology*, Vol. VIII, p. 206.

still more distinctly over against the desires which are to be used to explain them:

The social problem involves the task of discovering the general laws of interrelationship between the individual element in society, represented in terms of desire by the product $a\ b\ c\ d\ e\ f$, and the institutional element, represented collectively by the product $g\ h\ i\ j\ k\ l\ m$.[1]

Here the first set of letters, a–f, represent the health-rightness series, while the last set of letters, g–m, represent De Greef's seven types of social phenomena, economic, genetic, artistic, beliefs, moral, juridical, and political, which are used simply as illustrative of the social facts that need to be explained. It is worth noticing in passing that while normally Small should have as many classes of phenomena as he has desires, each class corresponding to one desire, he finds no difficulty in correlating his six desires with De Greef's seven varieties of phenomena.

One more quotation will show him setting up a classification of social facts to correspond with the six desires. He says:

We might plan our description of human association under the following titles: (1) health associations; (2) wealth associations; (3) sociability associations; (4) knowledge associations; (5) beauty associations; (6) rightness associations.[2]

This, he continues, would be the "most direct way ideally" to classify the phenomena. The process would be "to find out what men as individuals want, not merely in detail, but in the principles implied in details—then to discriminate the associations that cater to these several wants." He does not believe this can be done today, but he is sure it can ultimately be done despite "the tremendous difficulties of the undertaking." It will indeed be tremendously difficult, considering that the facts are to be forced to correspond to a sixfold scheme set up at the beginning of the investigation on a hodge-podge basis, instead of being classified by direct study as they exist.

Professor Small has not stopped with these general statements, but he has attempted to indicate how an "algebra" or "calculus" of desires can be worked out to explain the facts of social life.

[1] *Ibid.*, Vol. IV, p. 382.   [2] *Ibid.*, Vol. VI, p. 493.

This calculus rests on assumed qualitative and quantitative changes in the six kinds of interests, or, better said, on quantitative variations within each of the six interests.   Beginning at the so-called bottom of the social scale,[1] he finds the much-abused "horde" to consist of "simply a mass of practically identical specimens of a species, just like a shoal of fish or a herd of buffaloes."   This is because the health interest is about the only interest that manifests itself in the horde-men.   "So long as the health interest alone is in working force, there is no such fact present as a human individual."[2]   As the sociologist surveys rising grades of society he is supposed by this theory to see other varieties of interests appear and develop themselves, here in one proportion, there in another, and create all the multiform institutions we now have. The theory of increments of desire is explicitly stated in many places, for example thus:

We shall be very far from taking for granted the real individual with whom sociology has to reckon if we picture either desires or wants as fixed in quantity or quality. Human desires are not so many mathematical points. They may rather be represented to our imagination as so many contiguous surfaces stretching out from angles whose areas presently begin to overlap each other, and whose sides extend indefinitely.[3]

Or again:

The problem of changing the facts is the problem of transforming the interests (desires) that make the facts . . . . the social pedagogy and politics and diplomacy . . . . which convert less into more social desires.[4]

Also:

The ends which the groups pursue . . . . vary in two ways, which we may call extension and content.[5]

Now by providing these desires with coefficients and exponents the social calculus is achieved.   We are told for instance as a

---

[1] In discussing the classification of governments and types of society later in this work the reason will appear why the horde is not necessarily a "bottom" form, and how on the contrary it may be a highly perfected form of society as tested by the equilibration of interests.

[2] *General Sociology*, p. 428.   [4] *Ibid.*, p. 442.

[3] *Ibid.*, p. 446.   [5] *Ibid.*, p. 541.

hypothetical case that Athens in the age of Pericles may have included many individuals whose desires may be represented thus:

$$\text{Desire} = a^x + b^{vi} + c^v + d^{xi} + e^{xiv} + f^{vii}.$$

A compound of individual desires might show "as to content" the social end of Athens at the time as follows:

$$\text{Social end} = a^{vii} + b^{iii} + c^{ii} + d^{viii} + e^{xii} + f^{iv}.$$

This is "a qualitative end which is the algebraic sum, so to speak, or better a chemical compound [sic] of the desires cherished by its individual members within the realm of the several great interests."[1]

Now the practical outcome of this theory of Professor Small's is to reduce the whole business of the use of soul-stuff for social interpretation to an absurdity; for the reason that although he has been for a dozen years arguing it in print he has nowhere and at no time, so far as I am aware, taken the slightest step to isolate these desires or prove their existence apart from the social phenomena they are intended to explain. His theory taps popular psychology and the practical terminology of everyday speech for some of the desires. It gets the rest by a cursory inspection of social facts themselves. The popular terms have been created by the identical methods, though in an even cruder use of it. They have proved their utility only for the purposes of distinguishing between Tom and Jack, and never for the purposes of explaining both Tom and Jack in their actual content of social life.

Moreover the utter uselessness of the theory for the sociologist's purposes appears from the fact that Professor Small has never accomplished anything by its aid. He has talked about it, systematized it, bridged over the gaps in it, and tunneled the barriers, but he has not used it. When he wants to study social phenomena directly he takes the active men or groups of men as he finds them without reference to this soul-stuff. He says in words we

---

[1] *Ibid.*, p. 543. Cf. *ibid.*, p. 218, and also the article attempting a mathematical statement of the working of the desires by one of Professor Small's seminar students (Amy Hewes, *American Journal of Sociology*, Vol. V, p. 393). In the latter article the quantities dealt with are stated thus: "The forces that produce motion in social groups are the sum of the wants and desires of human beings."

have already quoted: "We have mainly to do with interests in the same sense in which the man of affairs uses the terms." But this sense, as for example, the "railroad interest," indicates a very complex piece of social structure. It indicates the social fact, but not the individual soul's desire. It cannot actually be built up, piece after piece, out of those soul's desires; or, better said, to avoid being too absolute on the point, it has not been so built up either by Professor Small or by anyone else. They have hitched some of the desires to it, just as one might hitch a demon to a thunderstorm, but they have not pushed the analysis through to satisfy anyone else.

What could Professor Small do, for example, that would be really worth while toward showing the transition from extermination of enemies to the institution of slavery in early times? He could easily, of course, introduce a wealth desire (making the prisoner work) in place of a health desire (self-protection by slaughter). But how artificial such a procedure is! He would then have to assume something as to the reasons for the appearance of this new desire. Of course the observed conditions of the transition would be at his service, and those conditions would be certain relations of groups of primitive men. But how would he gain by translating those conditions into terms of individual desire and then making the desire explain the resulting institution, over what he could accomplish by taking the group conditions just as they stood for his whole explanation? He would be continuing to keep "soul-stuff" at work in his system, and if that is considered a gain, well and good.[1] But for the rest he would simply be making his interpretation vaguer and less exact than he might make it without such desires.

Without further argument, it seems to be sufficiently clear that this theory of social interpretation reduces itself to the identical

[1] I am perfectly well aware that the use of the word "gain" in this connection may be brought up against me as an example of the very kind of interpretation to which I am objecting. The point would be well taken except for one thing, which is the heart of the whole matter. I am nowhere objecting to such speech forms as convenient shorhand devices in their proper places. I am objecting exclusively to the erection of such speech forms into pseudo-scientific systems of interpretation.

proposition, $A = A$, or in other words, to nothing at all except verbiage.

If I had wished to criticize Professor Small's theory of social causation on other than sociological grounds, the task would have been much more quickly accomplished. There are no desires nor interests apart from content. There are no nerves which carry feelings inward without at the same time carrying ideas (the terms are crude, but let that pass); there are none which carry ideas without at the same time carrying feelings. You never can make a feeling all alone explain an act—not even in the simplest case imaginable. And the ideas bring the whole outside world into the reckoning. Then what is the use of building up a complicated calculus of feelings as though it did explain activity in society? To separate the feelings in a little bunch by themselves with the hope of explaining anything by them is much like cutting off one's arms at the shoulders for the sake of using them as weapons against an enemy. One cannot throw them far nor strike hard with them.

The trapdoor that lets the sociologist through into this pit is to be found at the spot where the complicated interest groups, differing in individual adherents as we actually find them in society, intercept one another. Tom, the miser, and Jack, the spendthrift, go into partnership, and therefore the partnership is an outside thing caused by miserliness in one and extravagance in the other, and the metaphysics begins. As a matter of fact, Tom is a member of a lot of interest groups, and so also is Jack. In each of these groups they reflect the social world around them in some of its phases. In their partnerships some of the groups to which each belongs cross and interlace. How this is and what its meaning, will be discussed in detail later in the book.

Section III. Spencer

Herbert Spencer[1] started his philosophic career with a proposition that he considered fundamental as to the relations between

---

[1] In criticizing Spencer's theory of feelings as the forces of society, I hope I shall not be understood as meaning to criticize his work as a whole. I have only

man and man in society: "Every man has freedom to do all that he wills provided he infringes not the equal freedom of any other man."[1] He came out at the end of his life at exactly the same place. This with the wording a little changed is the central thought of the *Principles of Ethics*.

He started life holding that his desires were one thing and that what he desired was another thing. He saw his desires "there" on one side, and the unachieved satisfactions "there" on the other side. He came out at the end of his life at exactly the same place. Each man has certain desires, given or acquired. If you can get the right mixture of desires inserted in these men you will get a perfect society—so, and not otherwise.

He started life believing that "the ultimate man will be one whose private requirements coincide with public ones. He will be that manner of man who spontaneously fulfilling his own nature incidentally performs this function of a social unit; and yet is only enabled so to fulfil his own nature by all others doing the like." He came out at the end of his life in exactly the same place, choosing these words from *Social Statics* for the closing sentences of the third volume of the *Sociology*.

What this means is that Spencer did not learn to know the

---

too much admiration of it in many of its phases, and I recognize that many a sociological reputation has been made with crumbs from his pages. It may seem that when I discard his psychology, his ethics, and his theory of the relation of the individual to the state, I discard everything of importance. On the contrary, the massive work he has achieved with so poor a mechanism marks the way most usefully for further work with a better mechanism.

I wish to make now, just as I have already made in criticizing Small, a somewhat similar avowal with regard to the other writers whose methods of social interpretation I am about to analyze in detail and reject. I can in almost every case say that the men I criticize have been helpful to me vastly out of proportion to the evil in their works which I feel it necessary to point out as a means of safeguarding myself against misunderstanding of the method of interpretation I shall later advocate.

As between Small and Spencer it may be remarked that Spencer is clear and precise as to what he means, where Small is often confused and diffuse. But Small faces much troublesome social material which Spencer simply shuts his eyes to, and his very honesty in facing it adds to the appearance of confusion.

[1] *Social Statics* (Amer. ed., 1865), chap. vi, sec. 1, p. 121.

relation of the individual to society from his life-long study of social facts. He imported his view of this relationship into his philosophy at the start and he built the whole philosophy up around it without even an attempt to test it as such. If the individual's desire and his satisfaction (or, better said, in place of his satisfaction his method of satisfying his desires, this method being the typically social act) are not two separate things capable of reciprocal action on one another, then Spencer's interpretation of social life stands not merely as false, but as a bald, assumption, without any effort to prove it.

I will indicate his views by quotation in detail, show some of the consequences that flow from them in the construction of his system, and finally point out more precisely the weak spots, keeping always, I hope, to social facts as the test.

As simple a statement as any can be found in *The Study of Sociology*. In talking of rational legislation he tells us that such legislation "must recognize as a datum the direct connection of action with feeling." He admits there are some "automatic actions which take place without feelings" and at the other extreme some feelings "so intense that they impede or arrest action." These can be disregarded as insignificant, and so, speaking generally, we can say that "action and feeling vary together in their amounts."[1]

As to the importance of these exceptions I shall have something' more to say later. Here I am interested in noting that Spencer takes his position in opposition to the views of those people who believe that "knowledge is the moving agent in conduct." He is interested in proving that if one increases a person's knowledge it will not influence his conduct, but that if one operates on that person's feelings, it will influence his conduct. He does not say that knowledge can be found that is not based on feelings. But he treats them for all practical purposes as separate. A few pages farther on, he gives some examples of the application of this principle in legislation. For instance, the English people are improvident. That is because for ages they have been disciplined in improvidence. Various factors have built up this trait of

[1] *The Study of Sociology*, p. 358.

character in them. Once built up it is a fixed fact. You can explain their actions by referring to this trait of character. You can explain a trait of character by various other things, but the trait is for all sociological purposes as fixed and definite a thing as, say, a poor law, or a house, or a shotgun, or a tavern. Spencer does not state his position as crudely as this, but the phrasing is not unfair to him.

What it comes to in the case of the English he is describing is this: that those Englishmen select out of all the ways of living open to them certain ways that land them in the poorhouse, when if they were not in their soul of souls "improvident" they would even now select out of their opportunities other ways of living which would keep them comfortable in their old age. And if you could only change those "feelings" of theirs, they would be able to get, even under the same conditions of life and with the same industrial opportunities, ever so much more out of life. He does not either here or anywhere else tell us that any desired alteration of the feelings whatever is possible, the type of society being fixed. He insists, rather, that the change in society and the change in feelings must go along hand in hand. But nevertheless they are separate things, and if the feelings can be pushed forward a little here and there, the actions will change with them in the desired direction. Hence their progress will not be simply the direct outcome of all their ways of acting as such but it will be engineered through specific selected feelings.

Farther along in this same chapter Spencer takes up instances in which feelings as such are selected by the survival of the fit.[1] Also he argues that there are specific thoughts as well as specific feelings which are built up in the individuals and which control their progress.

How absurd [he says] is the supposition that there can be a rational interpretation of men's combined actions without a previous interpretation of those thoughts and feelings by which their individual actions are prompted.[2] . . . . Always the power which initiates a change is feeling separate or aggregated, guided to its ends by intellect. . . . . How then can there be a true account of social action without a true account of those thoughts and sentiments?[3]

[1] *The Study of Sociology*, p. 375.   [2] *Ibid.*, p. 382.   [3] *Ibid.*

Let us trace Spencer's theory of the action of the individual in and upon society through the volumes of his *Synthetic Philosophy*, allowing the statement to be for the most part in his own words. In the *First Principles* we are shown the individual's mind in process of manufacture by the outer world.

The modes of consciousness called pressure, motion, sound, light, heat, are effects produced in us by agencies which, as otherwise expended, crush, or fracture pieces of matter, generate vibrations.[1] . . . . Hence if we regard the changes of relative position, of aggregation, or of chemical state, thus arising, as being transformed manifestations of the agencies from which they arise, so must we regard the sensations which such agencies produce in us as new forms of the forces producing them.[2] . . . . Besides the correlation and equivalence between external physical forces, and the mental forces generated by them in us under the form of sensations, there is a correlation and equivalence between sensations and those physical forces which, in the shape of bodily actions, result from them."[3] . . . .

Next as to thoughts and as to those feelings which arise from "internal stimuli":

The forces called vital, which we have seen to be the correlates of the forces called physical, are the immediate sources of these thoughts and feelings, and are expended in producing them.[4]

These feelings and the ideas that he builds out of them become for Spencer definite "things," just as a sun, a crystal, or a tadpole in the physical world. They are psychical, it is true, and how the physical things turn themselves into psychical things it is "impossible to fathom." But we know that they do, and we have just got to go ahead with them, he holds, on that basis. The following passage, although it is taken somewhat out of order, will show fairly well this concrete view of mental states.

The limit toward which emotional modification perpetually tends, and to which it must approach indefinitely near (though it can absolutely reach it only in infinite time), is a combination of desires that correspond to all the different orders of activity which the circumstances of life call for—desires severally proportionate in strength to the needs for these orders of activity, and severally satisfied by these orders of activity. In what we distinguish as acquired habits, and in the moral differences of races and nations produced by

---

[1] *First Principles*, sec. 71.

[2] *Ibid.*   [3] *Ibid.*   [4] *Ibid.*

habits that are maintained through successive generations, we have countless illustrations of this progressive adaptation, which can cease only with the establishment of a complete equilibrium between constitution and conditions.[1]

In the *Biology* there is nothing that need detain us. One comment may however be made. In his later years Spencer seems to have felt that he had not been entirely fair in his treatment of life. He seems to have felt that perhaps he had not given the animal or vegetable organism sufficient recognition as a peculiarly individualized "center from which a differentiated division of the original force is again diffused." So in the last edition of his *Biology*, revised after his system as it stands had been completed, he interpolated a chapter (Part I, chap. vi, *a*), in which he said that "that which gives substance to our idea of Life is a certain unspecified principle of activity,"[2] and that "life in its essence cannot be conceived in physico-chemical terms."[3] In this he only gave to life a little of that concreteness which from the start he had naïvely given to feeling, but his extra chapter created for a time a great stir among his followers, many of whom were inclined to believe that in this chapter he had withdrawn the problem of the origin of life from the evolutionary mold in which his entire philosophy is cast, and had permitted at this one point the unknowable to break through into the knowable.

Coming now to the *Psychology*, we are to learn how the "multitudinous, diverse forms of feeling have been evolved from a primitive, simple sensibility."[4] Also how ideas are built up out of feelings. "The relational element of mind is the intellectual element."[5] The Spencerian mechanism for this is too well known to need description, and besides it is aside from our purpose.

He tells us that "no kind of feelings, sensational or emotional, can be wholly freed from the intellectual element."[6] But this does not mean for him any unity of the sensational-intellectual process. Feelings are one kind of "thing," and ideas are another

---

[1] *First Principles*, sec. 174.

[2] *Biology*, revised and enlarged edition, 1898, p. 114.

[3] *Ibid.*, p. 120.   [5] *Ibid.*, sec. 209.

[4] *Psychology*, sec. 60.   [6] *Ibid.*

kind of "thing" superimposed on the feelings. "Sensations are primary indecomposable states of consciousness; while perceptions are secondary decomposable states consisting of changes from one primary state to another."[1]

A large part of these feeling "things" are brought by the individual human being bodily—I use the word advisedly—into the world at his birth. "The doctrine that all the desires, all the sentiments, are generated by the experiences of the individual is so glaringly at variance with the facts that I cannot but wonder how anyone should ever have entertained it."[2]

These inborn feelings, modified and developed by the conditions of life, are the things, he holds, which the individual uses to make society. They make his acts, and his acts worked together into a tangle with other people's acts are society.

It is manifest that the ability of men to co-operate in any degree as members of a society presupposes certain intellectual faculties and certain emotions. It is manifest that the efficiency of their co-operation will, other things being equal, be determined by the amounts or proportions in which they possess these required mental powers. It is also manifest that by continuing to co-operate under the conditions furnished by any social state the amounts and proportions of these mental powers may be modified, and some modified form of co-operation may hence result; which again reacting on the nature is itself again reacted upon. Hence in preparation for the study of social evolution there have to be dealt with various questions representing the faculties it brings into play, and representing the modes in which these are developed during continued social life."[3]

Now these "manifests" and "hences" are not manifest at all, except for the first one of them, and that only if understood as indicating a psychical process, not a soul-content. But of that more later. Notice in passing the concrete character of these powers or faculties in the individual, the quantitative increase of them as "things," and the engineering of society by or through them.

It is when Spencer reaches this stage in his psychology that he classifies cognitions on the one side and feelings on the other, each into four groups, with the same group names in each series:

[1] *Ibid.*, sec. 211. [2] *Ibid.*, sec. 216. [3] *Ibid.*, sec. 477.

presentative, presentative-representative, representative, and re-representative.[1] One can recall what all this means sufficiently well by the bare statement that a re-representative feeling would be such a feeling as the "love of property" as distinct from the love of or desire for particular pieces of property. This is for him not at all love of property "in the abstract," but very concretely. It is a feeling thing that he means.

Each one of these faculties or powers or feeling things or whatever they are—excepting, of course, those that have been already evolved when man first is man—has been built up with the progress of civilization. He sets forth that men living in social life and coming up through history gradually add to their facultative equipment such things as foresight, modifiability of belief, abstract conceptions, conceptions of property, of cause, of uniformity, ideas of measure, definiteness of thought, exactness, consciousness of truth, skepticism, and criticism, and finally imagination, first reminiscent and then constructive.[2]

Intellectual evolution as it goes on in the human race along with social evolution, of which it is at once a cause and a consequence, is thus, under all its aspects, a progress in representativeness of thought.[3]

As always, however, this last statement must be taken to mean not merely a process of experience, but the evolutionary creation of a faculty or power which is a thing which encounters, pushes, and interacts with, other world-things.

Only as social progress brings more numerous and more heterogeneous experiences can general ideas be evolved out of special ideas, and the faculty of thinking them acquired.[4]

I call attention here to his remark in this connection that in later stages of social evolution "there is an increasing originality which tells at once on the individual arts, on science, and on literature;" and ask whether anyone can name an invention today that can be compared for boldness and power with early man's invention of fire-using, field-tilling, or animal-domestication, or that can be compared with the many social inventions of the bees,

[1] *Psychology*, sec. 480.
[2] *Ibid.*, Part IX, chap. iii.
[3] *Ibid.*, sec. 493.
[4] *Ibid.*, sec. 493.

which have produced their complex hive-life. These things are comparable generically. It will be a bold man who says that our modern inventive genius often equals them. I wish to refer also to Spencer's illustration in this connection of the mental equipment of modern woman, which he compares in many ways with that of primitive man. This illustration seems to me a most beautiful disproof of his theory. Anyone who chooses to read the passage can see that on inspection and enjoy it, especially if his eye falls also on the troubled reference that is somewhere made to George Eliot and her work.

Making express psychological preparation for his *Sociology*, Spencer next discusses sociality. Sociality is the product of evolution, but it is only possible through a specific mental accompaniment—a feeling content, which it "implies and cultivates;" a feeling which "can begin only through some slight variation," and is "maintained and increased by the survival of the fittest."[1]

This feeling which lies at the foundation of society is sympathy. Sympathy can develop only in proportion as there is power of representation.[2] Three causes of sympathy can be traced in three sets of relations: (1) the relation between the members of a species; (2) between male and female; (3) between parents and offspring. Sympathy accomplishes especially great work in human society because there we find all the three causes just mentioned, "along with the coessential condition, elevated intelligence."[3] "No great social advance has been possible without an increase in this feeling."[4]

Following these propositions Spencer gives a page or two of illustrations[5] of the working of sympathy in society. I challenge anyone to read these and point out from them where Spencer finds any "sympathy" as a feeling thing which is not itself merely his own bald inference from the external facts this sympathy is supposed to explain. Watch him as he describes a primitive custom, which when found nowadays is condemned as cruel and "unsympathetic." Watch him as he infers from it that the primitive

[1] *Ibid.*, sec. 504.   [3] *Ibid.*, sec. 509.   [5] *Ibid.*, secs. 509 ff.
[2] *Ibid.*, sec. 507.   [4] *Ibid.*, sec. 510.

people whose custom it was were weak in sympathy. See him here guilty of as flagrant a "bias" as ever he assailed in his *Study of Sociology.* We may call it, if we please, in parallel to his other forms of bias, the "civilization bias"—it takes the content of feelings as they are found today and sets them up as the standards of feelings for all races and all times.

On the spot he tangles himself badly in his explanations. After showing how weak were the sympathies "among the lower races," he starts to trace the evolution of greater sympathy. This goes beautifully while he is portraying the good deeds of our own times. But when he turns to the other side of the picture, he finds that he has got to account for just the reverse condition of affairs— the cruelty of today—and he has only one way to do it, namely, by denying modern times the faculty of sympathy. Our human institutions of today are due to the sympathy we have. Our inhuman institutions are due to the sympathy we lack. But are not these identical statements, from the given point of view, true also of the most primitive clan, which is bloodthirsty in war, but never lets its humblest member suffer from hunger while a luckier mouth is filled ?   And if so, how can sympathy as such be relied on to explain anything at all ?

He tells us, however, that

the relatively slow development of sympathy during civilization, notwithstanding the high degree of sociality and the favorable domestic relations (i.e., monogamy), has been in a considerable degree due to the slow development of representative power.[1]

It is almost cruel here to refer back to his assertion about the modern increase in originality, quoted a few pages back, but the inconsistency is too vital to be overlooked. Another hindrance he notes is that we are still a "predatory race," which, apparently, we could not exactly cease to be, but at least take a step toward ceasing, any day we wished, merely by taking an injection of Dr. Spencer's choice extract of sympathy.

Now Spencer finds the solution of this unpleasant conflict between theory and fact, in which sympathy as a "thing" must

[1] *Psychology,* sec. 509

explain society, and yet in every phase of society both is and is not at the same time, by striking a compromise between different influences at work on human character, the outcome of which is "a specialization of the sympathies." We are sympathetic here and unsympathetic there, all at the same time, and yet sympathy itself is a thing, a real thing, indeed the most real thing for interpretative purposes.

Fellow feeling has been continually repressed in those directions where social safety has involved the disregard of it; while it has been allowed to grow in those directions where it has either positively conduced to the welfare of the society or has not hindered it.[1]

This is perfectly true—to tolerate the use of such phrasing for the moment—but it is also true that Spencer here clearly abandons sympathy in any way in which it is worth having as an aid to the interpretation of society. He has thrown it aside, but does not know it.

We might follow him as he builds up first of all egoistic sentiments and fits them on to the social facts for which he needs them, according to the lights of his theory; then ego-altruistic feelings, and then altruistic feelings. But what is the use? The defect is the same throughout. They are little puppets made by hand; little spooks miraculously appearing. They are all of them surviving traces of the animism which Spencer himself studied so carefully among primitive men, and so scornfully condemned as violating all reason.

We pass next to the *Sociology*. The character of the units (persons) and the conditions under which they exist (the environment) are the primary factors as primarily divided.[2] With the latter, the external factors, we need not concern ourselves.[3] They,

[1] *Ibid.*, sec. 510.   [2] *Sociology*, sec. 6.

[3] As for these external factors we may note in passing the "superorganic environment," which determines the governmental organization of society, while inorganic and organic environments determine mainly the industrial organization (*Sociology*, sec. 11). This distinction is dogmatic and harmful to later constructive work. The "secondary environment" (sec. 12) also deserves a reference because it is so typical of Spencer's whole method of interpretation to divorce the tool from the hand of the man who uses it—a divorce fatal to any clear interpretation of social activity.

of course, have helped to create the internal factors, the people, and they are "there," outside, all the time pressing against the internal factors and interacting with them.   Of the internal factors, i. e., the individual man, we must take account, in addition to his physique, of his emotional and intellectual traits.[1]   We are also given an opportunity for that most interesting study, "the effect of the whole on the parts, and of the parts on the whole"[2]—a naïve investigation which would do credit to primitive man, which indeed by its very announcement makes primitive man a living reality to us.

As to early man physically the most that Spencer is able to say of him, in contrast with the man of today, is that "some traits of brutality and inferiority exhibited in certain of these ancient varieties, have either disappeared or now occur only as unusual variations."[3]

The chapters[4] which deal with primitive man, emotional and intellectual, indicate how much and how little can be done with these feeling and compound feeling, or idea, factors.   The quotation from the *Psychology* in the first section of the first of these chapters[5] could be accepted in a general way if it were made to refer exclusively to the forms of the psychic process through which the social life is achieved.   But Spencer does not mean it in this way.   Each item that he mentions is a mass of feeling, and it is always masses of feeling he has in mind.   One or two instances of his interpretation will bear fruit for our critical purpose, as fully as if we took up every instance in turn.   Take for instance

---

[1] *Sociology*, sec. 7.   [3] *Ibid.*, sec. 22.

[2] *Ibid.*, sec. 10.   [4] *Ibid.*, Part I, chaps. vi, vii.

[5] Compare also the opening paragraph of sec. 52, which sets up the "truth that the laws of thought are everywhere the same; and that, given the data as known to him, the primitive man's inference is the reasonable inference;" which would be a highly useful principle if he adhered to it and did not make his whole interpretation rest on an evolution of "faculties," including the faculty of reasoning, or getting reasonable conclusions.   Practically he is always insisting that one must get more "reason" or more mental what not in order to move society upward.   Here his words are in flat contradiction to his practice.   This will not be considered a quibble on my part, after I have pointed out the practical difficulties he gets into through the use of his method.

his quotation from Burton's description of the East African.[1] Compare the savage traits set forth with those of the people of our present society. Can they not be easily matched, either separately or in groups? Indeed if the fairer comparison is made, a comparison, namely, between this description and some description, similar in character, of the traits of any civilized people, the decision would be sharper still against Spencer's view. Such soul qualities as he mentions could only be useful for social interpretation if they could be found, identified exactly, and verified independently. But when they are both inexact and knowable to us only from the actions which are supposed to result from them, they are utterly useless, and, as will appear later, highly harmful. Spencer's quotation from Wallace about savage respect for law[2] may be compared with the one just mentioned for further illustration as to the feelings of the primitives.

I cannot resist, however, referring to one other passage in this connection, that, namely, setting forth instances of "credulity"— the Indian choosing his totem, the negro choosing a god for the moment, the Veddah thinking his arrow goes wrong because his deity is not propitiated.

We must regard [he says] the implied convictions as normal accompaniments of a mental state in which the organization of experiences has not gone far enough to evolve the idea of causation.[3]

If these savages do not have the idea of causation, I cannot conceive what causation means. They have not Spencer's idea of causation, it is true, but perhaps, all things considered, their own idea is more useful to them under their own circumstances of life than Spencer's would be, and if so it is to that extent more true. We have our world strung together differently nowadays and the great social change (mind, I do not say result) is manifest; but as for the "faculties," there is at any rate nothing in the facts as given to prove any difference.

Spencer continues with his well-known chapters on primitive ideas which make up the great bulk of his *Data of Sociology*. Perhaps the best test in his whole system is to take these "data" and

---

[1] *Sociology*, sec. 32.   [2] *Ibid.*, sec. 36.   [3] *Ibid.*, sec. 44.

apply them to the rest of his sociology with a view to seeing what can be done with them in interpreting the social phenomena. It is hard to keep any respect for the man when one experiments in this direction. It is so clear that these "data" or "ideas" or what not are forms of social action, just as much as any of the social structures he later describes; that the "ideas" do not have an independent life which creates social activity outside of them, but that rather all social life is stated in terms of "ideas" by the actors, and that all ideas have reference to nothing else except social life, even such ideas as the *First Principles*, even the "synthetic philosophy," even the "unknowable."

I will merely quote one more well-known passage before leaving the *Sociology*.

> While the conduct of the primitive man is in part determined by the feelings with which he regards men around him; it is in part determined by the feelings with which he regards men who have passed away. From these two sets of feelings, result two all-important sets of social factors. While the fear of the living becomes the root of the political control, the fear of the dead becomes the root of the religious control.[1]

If it be possible to find any factors more superficial than these out of which to erect a system of social interpretation, I cannot conceive what they are. This "fear of the living" and this "fear of the dead" alike are crude ways of stating certain very important social facts, certain hard facts of everyday existence. Such crudities of statement form poor stuff for "causes" in sociology. And yet Spencer says:

> Setting out with social units as thus conditioned, as thus constituted physically, emotionally, and intellectually, and as thus possessed of certain early acquired notions and correlative feelings, the science of sociology has to give an account of all the phenomena that result from their combined actions.[2]

Now what of the *Ethics?* I confess I have had few harder problems than to find a way to place Spencer's *Ethics* in the proper relation to his sociology. And the only way I have been able to achieve this necessary task has been by making the whole world of social activity as it presents itself to me distort itself into con-

[1] *Sociology*, sec. 209.   [2] *Ibid.*, sec. 210.

formity with Spencer's separation of his vivid "want" from his far-away "thing wanted"—a separation which he never got over all his life long. Even then much difficulty remains.

In the *Ethics* Spencer seems to distrust fundamentally the adequacy of the feelings as engineers of the social process. Upon the naïve feelings he superimposes a still more naïve control of the feelings. His *Ethics* implies that we can set up a standard for society, and that we can doctor the feelings of the individuals so as to realize this standard in society.

These implications must be stated more fully. They amount to something like this: We, the individuals, made up of feeling things (plus some complex idea things) and living in the midst of a lot of outside things (other people included), can set up a standard of what we all ought to be, either with reference to the world of outside things made over and controlled the way we should ultimately like to have it, pure pleasure existing unalloyed—absolute ethics; or with reference to the world of outside things patched up in the best manner available for our own day—relative ethics. By manipulating the feelings of the individuals—who may be regarded as conceivably all alike for ethical purposes—we can arrive at the relative standard, and work on toward the absolute. This may be done, perhaps, by some social wisdom which plays on the feelings of the individuals and continually forces them all together upward; perhaps, by presenting the truth to the individual in Spencer's *Principles of Ethics*, or in some other fit form, the individual then seeing the desirability of starting out to make himself over on such lines;[1] or perhaps, on the general principle that morals guide society and when you get morals understood properly they will guide it correctly. The alternatives are vague enough and mean little, but they indicate possible points of approach.

The following quotations bear on the technique of the *Ethics:* " Only by gradual remolding of human nature into fitness for the social state can either the private life or the public life of each man be made what it should be."[2]

---

[1] Cf. in *Ethics*, Vol. I, p. 561, the suggestion of "moderation in self-criticism."
[2] *Ethics*, sec. 244.

Speaking of the "capacity for modification which makes possible an approximately complete adjustment of the nature to the life which has to be led,"[1] he tells us we can get a good idea of it from the contrast between people who torment animals and people who cannot be induced even to look on such tortures—an illustration which may do credit to his heart, but which shows a complete forgetfulness of the history of the movement toward humanity in the treatment of animals, and an ignorance of the true meaning of that "specialization of sympathies" which was set forth in earlier quotations.

Happiness, which is itself a kind of feeling, is inevitably "the ultimate moral aim."[2] It is also the thing which ought to control and guide the other feelings. "The essential trait in moral consciousness is the control of some feeling or feelings by some other feeling or feelings."[3] Duty is an unpleasant kind of feeling that "will diminish as fast as moralization increases."[4]

Conduct in its highest form will take as guides innate perceptions of right, duly enlightened and made precise by analytical intelligence; while conscious that these guides are proximately supreme solely because they lead to the ultimately supreme end, happiness, special and general."[5]

So much for Spencer's system of interpreting social life by individual feelings.

Now what of the results that flow from it in the course of his own work? In the first place there are the inconsistencies which have been mentioned from time to time above. If feelings are to be specialized to fit each and every case in which they operate, each bit of specialization is a fresh bit of inconsistency in the theory. If the "amounts and proportions" of the feelings must be made to vary so as to explain each and every social institution and social change, then there is no reason whatever for pausing and calling the feelings the "causes." We may for all practical purposes ignore them.

Another difficulty that the feeling theory leads to is that if the

---

[1] *Ethics*, sec. 244.   [4] *Ibid.*, p. 127.
[2] *Ibid.*, Vol. I, p. 46.   [5] *Ibid.*, pp. 172, 173.
[3] *Ibid.*, p. 113.

individual "as made" is the unit, then it is natural to conclude, by the use of pure reason, re-representatively or otherwise, that all individuals may ultimately be made alike in their feelings so far as these operate on society, or rather on their own social activities. This opens the way for a whole range of individualistic speculation, which has the least possible relationship to inductive science. Indeed this whole proposition that one standard can be set up for all men, and that all men can conceivably be brought up to it (or, alternatively, all men of any given society), however in accord it is with religious codes, is in sharp conflict with the observations of every unbiased pair of human eyes that ever looked out on the world. It conflicts with the experience of the very religions that most earnestly insist on it. It conflicts even more with other phenomena of social activity. Men differentiate themselves in all kinds of groups all the time, each with its own standard. That is the fact. Even the Spencerian individualists themselves are forever asserting the right to disport themselves along the lines of their passing feelings, not the duty of evolving toward the Spencerian ethical ideal. Even the Spencerian ethical ideal, quoted in the opening paragraph of this section, insists on the greatest possible amount of this individually defined liberty. The inconsistency is self-evident. The Spencerian may say that the propositions as I have put them above are just the reverse of what they ought to be properly to represent Spencer's views. Granted, and yet the inconsistency will be as great as ever. In other words, for all his emphasis of the external environment, Spencer, in his specific interpretations, persists in regarding individuals as individuals *per se*, not as individual factors or forms in the particular social institutions in which they actually find themselves, in which they always have found themselves, and in which, so far as any student of facts has a right to say, they always will find themselves.

A third difficulty that flows from Spencer's theory of feelings is that which involves the "natural." It is best exemplified in his views of government and government functions. His followers show the difficulty in their positions. They can get anywhere in the whole range of social speculation by taking a good running start from Spencerian feelings. They can reach socialism or anarchy. They can reach anything they want to reach. The "natural" is not what socially is, but what conforms to the "natural" feelings, as the individual upholder of the "natural" insists they must work out.

All this is not science. It is an eighteenth-century distillation of a seventeenth-century deity, curiously garbing itself in a nineteenth-century "knowable" force. Straight out of these Spencerian feelings come those "innate perceptions of right," which suddenly popped up in one of the passages from the *Ethics* quoted above.

The true Spencerian has plenty of other troubles besides these. But these will do for our needs.

And now two more points. The first will show what Spencer leaves out of his social world. The second will show what poor little service the feelings render him, and how much better that service can be rendered without them.

Turn back to the early quotations from the *Study of Sociology*, in which Spencer put the feelings in quantitative relation to action, but passed over as indifferent the whole range of "automatic" action, as something that could be disregarded without any harm in social interpretation. The unhappy truth for him is that the greater part of our social life is carried on in just this discarded realm. Our feelings, after the Spencerian mode, are seen pushing a little here, pulling a little there, and playing around some features of life. They make a fuss over big things and have free scope with little things, but they do not even in superficial appearance directly secure results with the big things, and in the range of intermediate activities which make up the bulk of social life they hardly appear at all.

We are living in days of great popular agitation over our forms of government. "Feelings" are red hot. They break in some waves over the Supreme Court, and in others over the Senate. They reach in little waves our city councils and city police forces. They pound away in a good many other places. But what are our feelings doing with the great structural features of our American constitution? Just nothing. The constitution—I am not talking of the written document, nor of constitutional conventions, but of the actual working everyday organization of our political society—goes hammering along in its great features undisturbed and uninfluenced, unprodded by specific Spencerian feelings of any kind. Does anybody want the referendum? All right, let him have it. The change would not be much. Or government ownership of railroads? We can make a terrific noise about it, and shake our feelings till our hair stands straight up, but the innovation, if established, would be but a trifle compared with the steady-moving, "automatic" functions of our government, which Spencer deems negligible so far as his theory of feelings goes. If all this process of government were some "external" thing waiting to be pushed by feelings, or now and then pushing feelings in return, that would be one thing. But such is not the case. It is "internal," it is human, as much as anything we know of is internal and human. And the moment it is taken into the reckoning, good-by forever to the Spencerian interpretation.

The case would be stronger still if I took up other and wider phases of our social life, which are touched very little by the emotional play as compared with government. But I will omit that, only to approach such phenomena immediately in a different way.

What service do the feelings render Spencer in his social interpretation? Well, they strive to hold together various forms of activity into groups. They are meant to make all the activities of each individual stick together with the activities of the other individuals in his particular tribe, state, or society. The feelings raised to the higher powers, and finally to the re-representative stage, are supposed to collect together many forms of activity, and make them cohere. They actually give this interpretative help in a feeble way. They keep the Spencerian social world from being a house of cards, but they quickly break in pieces when they are used, and then we have to shut our eyes and open the throttle. We have to "specialize the feelings." It is all over.

Is it the processes of mentality that Spencer places at the foundation of society? Well and good. But then these processes must be filled with a social content. They must be worked up socially all the time. But is it a content of individual mental states? Then they never can be worked up. The unfortunate manipulator shoots off into the infinite at every step.

Just as Spencer flew to "feelings" to get rid of the "knowledge-rules" theory,[1] so we must fly to action—purely positive—to get rid of the abuses of the "feeling" theory.

The interpretation that will hold scientifically will ignore these feelings. It will watch the social situations build themselves up, one unfolding itself out of the other. It will look to the future only through these unfolding situations. It will not put a grain-spook in the wheat-field, nor a brain-spook in the class war or the reform of government or the social movement. It will see every bit of social activity as psychically functioned, and it will see nothing concretely psychical that is independent of society and yet dominating it. It will calmly, "positively," in the Comtean sense, grasp social facts just for what they are, study them for what they are, analyze and synthesize them for what they are, and leave all the mental "spooks" for men and women so hard pressed with the actual doing of things that they need convenient catchwords and symbols to save them the trouble of pushing their thinking back into a region that would inevitably send forth great disturbance for the day's work they have in hand.

Section IV. Von Jhering

It is a pleasure to pass from the confusions of Small and the crudities of Spencer to the patiently powerful work of Rudolph von Jhering.[2] If there is any man who has set out with equal ability, equal equipment, and equal scientific determination to face without flinching every difficulty in this field, I have not

[1] *The Study of Sociology*, pp. 365, 366.

[2] The quotations are from *Der Zweck im Recht*, 3d ed., Vol. I, 1893; Vol. II, 1898; which will be referred to as *Zweck;* and from *Geist des römischen Rechts auf den verschiedenen Stufen seiner Entwicklung*," Theil I, 5th ed., Theile II and III. 4th ed., which will be referred to as *Geist.*

come across his work. *Der Zweck im Recht* must be reckoned with, page for page, by everyone who seeks to understand the process of government and the function of law in social life. And yet with all admiration for the work of this master I cannot but think that the psychological system he has elaborated to function the individual in society has achieved, not a success or even a partial success, but a complete collapse.

With the great majority of his interpretations of laws, moral rules, and institutions, such as are found especially in the second volume of *Der Zweck im Recht* and in *The Evolution of the Aryan*, I feel so substantial a sympathy that I may say my only wish is to go somewhat farther, abandoning the personified society and the race character,[1] which he still retains, and making the interpretation entirely in terms of social groups.

With his psychology, his technique of "Zwecke," objective and subjective, used to connect the individual man with the social processes in which he participates, it is a very different matter. It is solely with this phase of his theory that the present section deals. I must leave it to the second part of this work to show how society can be investigated without such a technique. Here I wish to show his own downfall, and the inherent impossibility of solving the problem he set himself.

Jhering first came to close quarters with the psychological problems of the origin and meaning of law at the close of his *Geist des römischen Rechts*, or rather at the close of that portion of this work which was all he ever wrote. He had been interpreting broadly in terms of national spirit and folk psychology. Now he declared himself for a theory of interest or utility ("Interesse," "Nutzen"), the two words not being well distinguished, but the one being used with a somewhat more subjective, the other with a somewhat more objective, reference.

He set himself in opposition on the one hand to theories which made laws take their origin in any kind of absolute will power, and on the other hand to theories which placed the origin in mere might. It was the usefulness of the law, he said, that counted.

[1] See *infra*, Part II, chap. ix.

Stripped of terminology and disputation, this came to saying that you cannot get law out of simple head work, and you cannot get it out of mere preponderance of force; law must always be good for something to the society which has it, and that quality of being good for something is the very essence of it.[1]

The formal element of law he placed, at this time, in the legal protection by right of action ("Klage," "Rechtsschutz"); the substantial element in "Nutzen," "Vortheil," "Gewinn," "Sicherheit des Genusses." He defined laws as legally protected interests,[2] and said that they served "den Interessen, Bedürfnissen, Zwecken des Verkehrs."[3] The "subject" of law, using the term habitual among the jurists, is the person or organization to whom its benefits pass. The protection of the law exists to assure this benefit reaching the right place.[4]

It is evident that at this time he was not at all clear as to the distinction between the things the individuals wanted and the things that were socially useful. He set forth that he was discussing the "subjective" side of law, and yet most of the terms he uses bear more on the objective utility. He had in mind much such an objective usefulness as the biologist employs in his rough interpretations of organic evolution, but he also insisted on the relativity of laws, on a usefulness "as recognized" by the lawgiver.[5]

---

[1] *Geist*, Vol. III, p. 350: "Kein Recht ist seiner selbst wegen, oder des Willens wegen da, jedes Recht findet seine Zweckbestimmung und seine Rechtfertigung darin, dass es das Dasein oder das Wohlsein fördert, kurz in dem Nutzen in dem oben angegebenen weitesten Sinn. Nicht der Wille oder die Macht bildet die Substanz des Rechts, sondern der Nutzen—die Bedeutung des Willens erschöpft sich lediglich darin dass er die Zweckbestimmung des Rechts für das Subject vermittelt, die der Macht, welche das Recht ihm gewährt, darin, dass er rechtlich daran nicht gehindert wird."

[2] *Geist*, Vol. III, p. 339. "Rechte sind rechtlich geschützte Interessen."

[3] *Geist*, Vol. III, p. 338. Cf. also p. 340: Every law exists "dass es dem Menschen irgend einen Vortheil gewähre, seine Bedürfnisse befriedige, seine Interessen, Zwecke, fördere."

[4] *Geist*, Vol. III, p. 336. "Subject des Rechts ist derjenige dem der Nutzen desselben vom Gesetz zugedacht ist. . . . . Der Schutz des Rechts hat keinen anderen Zweck als die Zuwendung dieses Nutzens an ihn zu sichern."

[5] So, *Geist*, Vol. III, p. 343.

Naturally enough he was not satisfied. He felt the need of working out a theory which would both make full allowance for the relativity of law, and would bring individual interests and social utilities into one effective system. He had something of the progress to make that the economists made in disentangling their idea of value from the idea of utility. He gave most of the rest of his life to the task, and he never completed it. He set up a revised theory, but some of its worst difficulties remained for the chapters, or rather volumes, he did not live to write.

Fortunately or unfortunately, his language contained a word which seemed a guiding star. That word was "Zweck," already used without well-specified meaning in the *Geist*, a word with great tangles of metaphysical implications which lent itself all too readily to the jurists' distinction between subjective and objective law, between law as the social rule and law as the individual's right. I shall use the word "Zweck" directly in this discussion without attempting to find an English word—purpose, aim, end, object, intention, teleology—to substitute for it.

Jhering abandoned, then, "interest" as his chief verbal tool,[1] and substituted for it "Zweck." The motto he placed on the title-page of his great work was "Der Zweck ist der Schöpfer des ganzen Rechts"—"Zweck" is the creator of all law. And to this he added when he pursued his subject from law into morals: "Der Zweck ist der Schöpfer der ganzen sittlichen Ordnung"[2]— "Zweck" is the creator of all moral order. The change from interest to "Zweck" was hardly so great as it appeared to be, for it was a change rather of words than of substance, and indeed a considerable proportion of the old interest remained unassimilated in the later system. But such as it was he utilized it vigorously— it is for us to see with what result.

The word "Zweck," as I have said, lends itself readily to both subjective and objective uses.[3] On the individual side it is for

---

[1] *Zweck*, Vol. I, p. vii.   [2] *Ibid.*, Vol. II, p. 214.

[3] For the distinction between subjective and objective, see *The Struggle for Law*, p. 5; *Entwicklungsgeschichte des römischen Rechts*, pp. 1, 21 ff.; *Zweck*, Vol. I, chap. iii, and pp. 448, 449; Vol. II, pp. 97 ff., 135 ff., and the prefaces to *Zweck*, Vols. I and II.

Jhering the motive or end of action. On the objective side it is the value or meaning or purpose of the laws or institutions or customs it is called on to explain. Now as it, on its subjective side, may be regarded by some analysts of the illusive psychological vocabulary, as rather idea than feeling, and as I have grouped Jhering with the men who interpret society through feelings rather than with those who interpret it through ideas, some explanation of this arrangement may be necessary. Whether necessary or not it will be useful as indicating where Jhering's theory actually stands as to this point.

The writers whom I shall discuss in the next chapter, Morgan, Giddings, and Dicey, use ideas or ideals in interpreting society, but they use them as capable of a highly generalized statement in which they appear detached from the individual souls, in which, of course, they are supposed to exist. Their ideas are broad social facts, to be found by inspection of the general field of social ideas. The procedure is much too superficial for Jhering's purposes. His aim is to link his "Zwecke" together, from the broadest objective forms down to the most intimately individual subjective forms. It would not be true to say that the whole stress of his interpretation falls on the individual, but certainly the stress of this psychological schematism of Zwecke falls on the individual. He has, it is true, personified society for many important purposes, and no one has insisted more strongly than he that the individual exists for and through world processes ("ich bin für die Welt da"); but on the other hand he emphasizes the reverse of this statement and insists that the world exists for the individual ("die Welt ist für mich da").[1] He maintains the existence of this distinction, and aims continually to use the individual for his social interpretations. This is of the very essence of the difficulty in the other writers discussed in this chapter. He does not give the individual any extra-social substantiality, any more than does Spencer; the point is that he uses him very concretely in his social interpretations.[2]

[1] *Zweck*, Vol. I, p. 67.

[2] For example, *ibid.*, p. 512: "So ist es doch schliesslich das Individuum an dem das Recht seine Wirksamkeit aüssert, ihm kommt es zu gute, ihm legt es

This will be apparent from the specific character of the subjective "Zwecke" which he uses in his theory. To mention the important ones we have the two altruistic "Zwecke," duty and love, and the egoistic "Zwecke," compensation or reward, and compulsion or coercion. There are also egoistic motives which do what he regards as a more strictly individualized work than those just named. His specific use of these qualities will be observed as our analysis proceeds.[1]

Let me next give a preliminary sketch of his theory and of the problems it raises. One of the first points upon which he insists is that there is no human action without a "Zweck." Even when we hand a purse to a highwayman at the pistol's point we have our "Zweck" in so doing, namely to exchange our purse for safety, which we value higher. It is only when we are physically con-

Beschränkungen auf." In Vol. I, p. 258, he speaks of "rein individuelles Dasein," and says "Unser Zielpunkt ist der Staat und das Recht, unser Ausgangspunkt das Individuum." In Vol. I, p. 92, he asks the question: "welche Garantien besitzt die Gesellschaft dass Jeder zu seinem Theil den Satz verwirkliche auf dem ihr ganzes Dasein beruht: Du bist für mich da?" and adds: "Darauf soll die folgende Ausführung die Antwort ertheilen." On p. 291 he says that "der letzte Keim des Zwanges als einer socialen Institution . . . . liegt in dem Individuum," and adds that "der Daseinszweck des Individuums ۔ . . . ist der erste, und in ihm liegt daher der Urkeim des Rechts als der rechten Gewalt." For a passage in which he puts the individual at the end instead of at the beginning of the process, and therefore from one point of view contradicts the passages quoted, see Vol. II, p. 102; "Auch ich gelange schliesslich zu dem Resultate, dass das Individuum das Sittliche als Gesetz seiner selber in sich tragen soll, und dass es, indem es sittlich handelt, nur sich selber behauptet, aber ich gelange dazu, ich gehe nicht davon aus."

[1] Many references to such specific use of psychic factors might be given. For example there is his separation of "Zweck" from action (so, in Vol. I, p. 5); his use of the words, "Vorstellung" and "Gedanke" (as in Vol. I, p. 11); such references as those to "der nackte Egoismus" (Vol. I, p. 248,), to the work of the "Rechtsgefühl" (Vol. I, pp. 379 ff.), to the "moralische Macht des Staatsgedankens" (Vol. I, pp. 319 ff.). There is his appeal to *Ehre* and similar factors (Vol. I, pp. 444, 445), the passage in Vol. II, p. 118, referring to "qualitativer Fortschritt," the concluding words of the first volume in which he asks what it is that holds a man back from doing wrong when he can do it without detection, and many of his remarks in connection with his investigation of morals as portrayed by speech forms in the first part of the second volume (Nos. 4–14). The whole contrast between subjective and objective "Zweck" might also be appealed to, as for example it is phrased in the

strained that we do not act with a "Zweck," and then we cannot properly be said to "act" at all; we are the object of someone else's action.[1] This reasoning is summed up in the propositions that acting and acting for a "Zweck" are one and the same;[2] and that willing and willing for a "Zweck" are the same.[3]

Interest ("Interesse") must also be taken into account. Jhering never fully stated its relation to "Zweck," this discussion having been left for a chapter of his work which was never written.[4] He makes it, apparently, the peculiarly personal desire side of the subjective "Zweck." He calls it the relation or reference ("Beziehung") of the "Zweck" to the actor,[5] and elsewhere he defines it as the feeling of the dependence of life upon the surrounding conditions.[6] There must always be some "Interesse" with the "Zweck," and he asserts, similarly to the sentences quoted a

preface to Vol. II, p. x. Also his reasons why "Zwang" remains necessary (Vol. I, pp. 565 ff.), "die mangelhafte Erkenntniss" and "der böse oder schwache Wille;" and perhaps his emphasis of "hervorragende Geister" in *Entwicklungsgeschichte*, p. 23. In *Zweck*, Vol. I, p. 97, he distinctly contrasts "die praktische Bedeutung" of the "Zwecke" for society with "die Art ihrer psychologischer Einwirkung auf das Individuum." I may also refer to the fact that Bouglé who studied Jhering's work at short range felt justified in saying: "Toute tendance pour Jhering part des individus et revient aux individus" (*Les sciences sociales en Allemagne*, p. 125); further that all causes are "cachées dans les âmes (p. 123); that "le desir, c'est le véritable créateur du monde social (p. 133); and that "le vrai moteur du monde social reste le désir" (p. 105).

[1] *Zweck*, Vol. I, p. 16.

[2] *Ibid.*, p. 14: "Handeln und um eines Zweckes willen handeln ist gleichbedeutend."

[3] *Ibid.*, p. 22: "Wollen und um eines Zweckes halber wollen ist gleichbedeutend." Cf. also, Vol. I, p. 5: "Kein Wollen oder was dasselbe, keine Handlung ohne Zweck."

[4] *Ibid.*, pp. 30, 52, 61. I, of course, regard the unwritten chapter as really unwritable.

[5] *Ibid.*, p. 53: "Die Beziehung des Zweckes auf den Handelnden." Cf. also *Geist*, Vol. III, p. 341: "Der Interessenbegriff erfasst die Wertheigenschaft in besonderer Beziehung auf die Zwecke und Verhältnisse des Subjects." Interest is "ein realer Druck," *Zweck*, Vol. I, p. 51.

[6] *Zweck*, Vol. I, p. 30, "Gefühl der Lebensbedingtheit."

moment ago, that there can be no action without "Interesse."[1] Sometimes however "Interesse" appears as "objective."[2]

In analyzing the "Zweck" we find in it first of all the satisfaction the action gives. The satisfaction and the action are held sharply apart as different orders of phenomena, with the satisfaction as the thing that brings about the action. He does not say the thing that "causes" the action, but only because he regards the "Zweck" process as a sort of active causation, as distinguished from the passive causation of the material world.[3] It is the "Zweck" indeed that is the main thing; the action is merely the means to the "Zweck," which means—at this stage of his progress —the satisfaction.[4] This is radically different from asserting that all action is purposive, with purpose strictly as process, because of the very separation which he establishes between the action and the purpose. It is on this separation that his system is built up. It is in this separation that his unsolved, and insoluble, puzzle problems lie.[5]

"Zweck" is, however, soon made very different from satisfaction, and indeed in the most objective forms to which it rises is entirely stripped of its satisfaction aspect. The "Zwecke" of nature come within Jhering's creed, though not within the immediate purview of his work, but the "Zwecke" of society as such play a very important rôle in it. They include the social "condi-

[1] *Ibid.*, p. 52: "Ein Sich-Interessiren" für den Zweck, oder sagen wir kurz: Interesse, ist die unerlässliche Voraussetzung einer jeden Handlung. . . . . Ein Handeln ohne Interesse ist ein eben solches Unding als ein Handeln ohne Zweck."

[2] So *ibid.*, p. 38. It appears as "gesellschaftliches," in Vol. II, p. 285. In Vol. I, p. 257 he talks of the "Kampf der Interessen;" on p. 294 of "gemeinsame Interessen," and on p. 372 of "praktisches Interesse."

[3] *Ibid.*, chap. i.

[4] *Ibid.*, p. 13. "Die Befriedigung welche der Wollende sich von der Handlung verspricht ist der Zweck seines Wollens. Die Handlung selber ist nie Zweck, sondern nur Mittel zum Zweck." Cf. also Vol. I, pp. 28, 29, where "der individuelle Zweck" (of animals) is said to be "pleasure;" p. 22, where the "Entschluss" is separated from the "That," and p. 31, where the "That" is called "äussere."

[5] For the positive discussion of "purposive action"—without the separation —as the material of social study, I can again only refer to Part II of the present work.

tions of existence," and the state, the church, and other forms of social organization. They grade all the way down from these through the connecting link "Zwecke" (compensation, compulsion, duty, love) to the immediately seen purposes of the individual and even to desire in its most individual statement.

For instance, he gives an illustration of the building of a railroad. Many men join, and the state has a share. Each participant has his individual "Interesse;" perhaps no two have the same; and none will have an "Interesse" that covers the whole enterprise. The railroad itself is the "Zweck."[1] But there exists a coincidence of the individual interests with the general "Zweck."[2]

With this great range of meanings for "Zweck" it is not strange that we find him using now one, now another term, as synonymous with it. We have just seen "Interesse" so used. We also find "Motive,"[3] "Triebfeder"[4] (spring of action), "Hebel"[5] (lever), "Mittel"[6] (means), and finally organization forms,[7] and conditions of existence.[8]

By means of the term "Zweck" Jhering gives a definition of life which is significant. Life is the practical application through "Zwecke" of the outer world to our own existence.[9] The life of the race as a whole can be summed up as the substance or the

[1] *Zweck*, Vol. I, p. 43; "Jeder hat sein eigenes Interesse im Auge: keiner den Zweck."

[2] *Ibid.*, p. 37: "Coincidenz ihrer Interessen mit dem allgemeinen Zweck;" also, p. 46; "Coincidenz der beiderseitigen Zwecke und Interessen."

[3] *Ibid.*, p. 28, footnote.

[4] *Ibid.*, pp. 60, 94 ; Vol. II, p. 11, and frequently elsewhere.

[5] *Ibid.*, Vol. I, pp. 60, 95.

[6] *Ibid.*, p. 96.

[7] *Ibid.*, p. 42. Compare also p. 97 where in defining "Verkehr," he uses motives, means, and form as distinct.

[8] *Ibid.*, pp. 435 ff.

[9] *Ibid.*, p. 9: "Leben ist praktische Zweckbeziehung der Aussenwelt auf das eigene Dasein;" also Vol. II, p. 197; "Leben ist Zweckverwendung der Aussenwelt für das eigene Dasein." Cf. also Vol. I, p. 25, "In dem Zweck steckt der Mensch, die Menschheit, die Geschichte," and Vol. II, p. 178, where he talks of the unity of society "durch die Gemeinsamkeit des Zwecks hergestellt."

essence of all human "Zwecke."[1]   It will be noted that this is a definition of life in terms of "Zweck," not of "Zweck" in terms of life, which alone is possible. He proposes to show the inner dependency of the "Zwecke," how the higher are connected with the lower, and how some of them by an inevitable "Zweck" necessity give rise to the others in one great system.[2] The foundation of society lies in the process by which one man's "Zweck" is bound up with the interests of all.[3] These interests must be found converging on the common "Zweck."

In this brief statement of Jhering's theory we have observed "Zwecke" and "Interessen" which are not too sharply distinguished from each other. We have found "Zwecke" (and "Interessen") scattered through all the individuals in the society, where they are, so to speak, on a common level, that is alike in quality or kind. We have found "Zwecke" also running in an ascending series—on different levels, so to speak—becoming ever more and more objective. The problem is to harmonize them in all three lines: to harmonize the "Zwecke" with the "Interessen;" to harmonize the "Zwecke" and "Interessen" of many individuals with one another; to harmonize the objective "Zwecke" with the subjective.

In order to pass a fair judgment upon Jhering's success or failure in effecting these harmonies, it will be necessary to look through his whole system of "Zwecke" in all its typical presentations.

It is through a "Systematik der menschlichen Zwecke" that he works up his theory.[4] All human "Zwecke," he tells us, fall

---

[1] *Ibid.*, Vol. I, p. 57: "Das menschliche Leben in diesem Sinn, d. i., das Leben der Gattung Mensch, nicht des Individuums, heisst der Inbegriff der gesammten menschlichen Zwecke."

[2] *Ibid.*, p. 57: He proposes to show "den inneren Zusammenhang in dem sie unter einander stehen," and further "wie einer an den anderen anknüpft, der höhere an den niedern, and nicht bloss anknüpft sondern wie einer in der Consequenz seiner selbst mit zwingender Nothwendigkeit den anderen aus sich hervortreibt."

[3] *Ibid.*, p. 37; "Die Verknüpfung des eigenen Zwecks mit dem fremden Interesse. Auf dieser Formel beruht unser ganzes menschliches Leben: der Staat, die Gesellschaft, Handel und Verkehr."

[4] *Ibid.*, pp. 58 ff.; pp. 94 ff.

into two great groups, those of the individual, and those of the collectivity (society)—" Gemeinschaft," " Gesammtheit," " Gesellschaft." One must not think that this distinction between the individual and society is the same as that between subjective and objective. It is not. The individual "Zwecke" may be worked up objectively, and the social "Zwecke" we shall find treated largely as individual motives or "Triebfeder." We are supposed to get these "Zwecke" by a study of the actual individual as he exists ("greifen sie aus dem Individuum"). They are not prior to society, but are the actual "Zwecke" of men in society.

The "Zwecke" of the individual are those in which the individual has merely himself in mind, not the society or any other person.[1] These are to be called "egoistische Zwecke." They are directed toward individual or egoistical self-maintenance ("Selbstbehauptung"). There are many kinds of them, but attention may be centered for the purposes of his work, he says, on three kinds: those that have to do with (1) physical; (2) economic; and (3) legal self-maintenance.

The second group, those of the collectivity, may be called "sociale Zwecke." They are likewise borne in the individual man—there is nowhere else for them to exist—but they have to do with his social activity ("sociale Handeln").

A first subclassification (more objective) of this second group is into the unorganized and the organized. Unorganized "Zwecke" may be found in the scientific activity of men—all the scientists pushing along from their own personal "Zwecke" and "Interessen," and building up a great scientific world—or again in a political party, which he conceives of as made up of a lot of separate men with separate "Zwecke," combining in a social whole or "Zweck."[2] The organized "Zwecke" are found in their typical form in the state, which is the crowning work of the organization

[1] *Zweck*, Vol. I, p. 59: "bei denen das Individuum lediglich sich selbst, nicht die Gesellschaft: d. i., irgend eine andere Person oder einen höheren Zweck im Auge hat."

[2] *Ibid.*, p. 42: The political party "beruht lediglich auf dem Dasein und der Stärke des Interesses in den einzelnen Mitgliedern."

of "Zwecke." They also appear in the church, the "Verein," the "Genossenschaft," the "Gesellschaft" and the legal "Person."[1]

A different sub-classification (more subjective) of the "sociale Zwecke" is into the egoistic and the ethical. The egoistic social "Zwecke" here must not be confused with the egoistic individual "Zwecke" above, although they are made out of the same stuff ("der uns bereits bekannte Egoismus"). They are egoism on its social side, or in its social phase, and they appear in two forms, "Lohn" (compensation or reward), and "Zwang" (compulsion or coercion), the "Lohn Zwecke" having their typical manifestation in commerce in a very broad sense of the term ("Verkehr"), and the "Zwang Zwecke" producing for us the state. Of the ethical "Zwecke"—those of the "ethical self-maintenance of the individual"—we likewise find two forms, "Pflicht" (duty) and "Liebe" (love). The theory of these four forms of social "Zwecke," compensation, compulsion, duty, and love, is the "social mechanics."[2]

The remainder of my statement of Jhering's theory will be devoted to showing seriatim, how first the individual "Zwecke," and then the four social "Zwecke," are utilized by him in his social mechanics to build society up out of individuals, and to hold the individuals in their social bonds. But first I will indicate briefly the central line which criticism of the theory must follow.

The four social "Zwecke" are variously called, as stated a few pages back, motives, impulses, means, and levers, in addition to being called "Zwecke." The fact that they belong to an elaborate hierarchy of "Zwecke" does not save them from being used very concretely, as "things" separated from the external "action" and appealed to to produce it. This despised "action" is nevertheless ultimately or immediately the basis for the classification of the "Zwecke," and since it is resorted to not clearly but obscurely, it not only takes the assumed causal (or "Zweck") value out of the

---

[1] These "Zwecke" will appear at times as organization forms of "Zwecke," and some of them from a still different point of view, as "Zwecksubjecte."

[2] *Zweck*, Vol. I, p. 94: "Sociale Mechanik" . . . . "der Inbegriff der Triebfedern und Mächte."

"Zwecke," but throws the whole system askew. A classification of "Zwecke" into organized and unorganized is clearly a classification of institutions. The two ethical "Hebel," duty and love, come from the old ethics, retaining their specific "thingness." The egoistic social "Hebel," compensation and compulsion, are constructed to match duty and love in quality, for the express purpose of being used to explain commerce and the state, as we shall see as we go along. The egoistic individual "Zwecke" are kept separate from the egoistic social "Zwecke" to serve the purpose of an intermediate stage in the series, and make its schematism more plausible. In all this, soul-stuff is being used, and what coherency there is, is verbal, not actual.

　　1. *The individual* (*egoistic*) *"Zweck."*—Taking up now the individual "Zwecke" it will be recalled that the classification was, into (1) physical, (2) economic, and (3) legal self-maintenance. The series of "Zwecke" that he works up out of these is as follows: Person — Property — Law — State　("Person" — "Vermögen" — "Recht" — "Staat").[1] We seek to protect and foster our personal welfare as physical creatures. In the course of such endeavors we annex inanimate and later animate objects to ourselves. These are property. We bring all our properties into a system which guarantees each of us in the possession of his own. Thus we have arrived at legal rights. Behind the law, to keep it in effective working order, we establish the state. Our egoistic "Zwecke" evolve in the three stages and are working away for our welfare all the time. In this condensed statement I do not mean to imply that Jhering's theory is that we consciously create the institutions which correspond to these "Zwecke" out of purely individual egoistic motives, or that he treats such motives ("Zwecke") as furnishing a full explanation of this development. But "Zwecke" of this individual egoistic character are, he holds, continually at work against and upon the social institutions; the evolution presses forward without halting.[2] While the individual is operat-

---

[1] *Zweck*, Vol. I, chap. v.

[2] *Ibid.*, p. 74. "Wie die Person und das Vermögen das Recht, so postulirt das Recht den Staat: die praktische Triebkraft des Zwecks drängt mit Nothwendig-

ing on the world solely from the standpoint of his own interest ("lediglich unter dem Gesichtspunkt seines Interesses"), he both makes the world serviceable ("dienstbar") to his interest, and his interest becomes serviceable to the world.[1]

2. *The social "Zwecke" (egoistic) "Lohn."*—Passing now from the individual "Zwecke," we have next to examine the first of the four social "Zwecke" or "Hebel," which Jhering makes use of. It is "Lohn," compensation or reward. Whereas before he was showing the individual's interest, considered all by itself, in everything social, he is now aiming to show how a lot of different individuals adapt themselves to one another and to the society. The "Lohn Zweck," he believes, gives him the explanation for all the phenomena of what he calls "Verkehr," which may be translated either commerce, in a very broad sense, or intercourse, in a specialized sense. "Verkehr" includes all forms of commerce and all forms of voluntary association.[2]

The commerce and trade phenomena ("Tausch") are the lower form of "Verkehr." Here the different individuals have different "Zwecke," but by getting compensation from one another they harmonize themselves. In his proof Jhering uses much such a range of facts about individual surplus values and utilities as the economist uses in analyzing trade. Barter is the simplest of these forms. Money and credit and the trades and professions build themselves on top of it, and so also all the commercial, financial, and industrial customs and methods. Competition is the social self-regulation of egoism.[3] The trades and professions are the organization of "Lohn."[4] Not only material rewards are listed under "Lohn," but also "ideal," the latter including all the immaterial goods which men gain in their dealings with one another. Ideal compensation again may be divided into external and inter-

---

keit von dem einen zum anderen." P. 76: "Der Zweckbegriff drängt von der Person zum Vermögen, von beiden zum Recht, vom Recht zum Staat—es ist kein Halten in dieser Evolution des Zweckgedankens, bis die höchste Spitze erreicht ist."

[1] *Ibid.*, p. 76.   [2] *Ibid.*, chap. vii.   [3] *Ibid.*, p. 135.

[4] *Ibid.*, p. 150. Cf. p. 117: "Verkehr" "is the completed system of egoism."

nal, the former being illustrated by fame, and the latter by soul satisfactions of one kind and another.[1]

A higher form of "Verkehr," which is likewise the product of the "Lohn Zweck," is voluntary association. His terms are "Societät," "Societätsvertrag," "Association."[2] Here instead of having complementary purposes all the individual participants have the identical purpose. The individuals line up side by side for some common work. As illustrations of the special "Zwecke" found in the "Societät," one may name such things as care for public security, the making of roads, the building of schools, care of the poor, provision for preachers, and the building of churches; all of these, of course, only when the state does not provide them and when voluntary combination is necessary.[3] All co-operative organizations and associations from the lowest to the highest, "even to church and state," are to be arrayed with the "Societät."

Now although the "Societät" is from the point of view of "Lohn," which is the "Zweck" or "Hebel" behind it, a second form of "Verkehr," it is nevertheless an organization form of such general applicability that it is deserving of being called the second fundamental form or type of social existence,[4] the "Tausch" society being of course the first fundamental form. In it we find people exhibiting "Gemeinsinn," which is an ennobled form of egoism ("nur eine veredelte Form des Egoismus").[5] This "Gemeinsinn" is brought in by Jhering for use later in interpreting the transition from egoism to altruism, and we shall meet it again.

[1] *Zweck*, Vol. I, pp. 181 ff.

[2] *Ibid.*, pp. 208 ff. P. 208: "Der Tauschvertrag hat die Verschiedenheit, die Societät die Gleichheit des Zwecks zur Voraussetzung." He thinks (p. 126): "der Gedanke einer gemeinschaftlichen Verkehrsoperation war das Werk eines findigen, denkenden Kopfes."

[3] *Ibid.*, pp. 209, 210.

[4] *Ibid.*, p. 215: "Die Association ist eine Form von der allgemeinsten Anwendbarkeit, sie ist in der That das, wofür ich sie oben ausgegeben: die zweite Grundform des gesellschaftlichen Daseins." At p. 125, however, he calls it a "Grundform des Verkehrs," instead of "des gesellschaftlichen Daseins," and the additional statement is made: "Eine dritte Grundform gibt es nicht, kann es nicht geben."

[5] *Ibid.*, p. 219.

One further point about "Verkehr" must be noted. Jhering says that it is perhaps the only bit of the human world which is the natural product of the free development of the "Zwecke;"[1] and while I am trying to avoid inserting criticisms in the midst of this description of his theory, I cannot forbear pointing out the striking contradictions in such a statement. We shall find in a moment that while the state is mentioned as the highest development of the second fundamental form of "Verkehr," nevertheless his elaborate interpretation throws it outside the operation of "Lohn," and in the field of the operation of the next of the four "Hebel," "Zwang" (compulsion). And with the state goes law. Yet here we have him excluding the state and law from the "free development" of the "Zwecke," in the very face of the fact that law and the state are themselves "Zwecke," that they rest on a "Zweck" ("Zwang"), and that the motto of his book is, "Zweck" is the creator of all law. It is but a sample of the contradictions involved in his terminology.

3. *The social "Zwecke" (egoistic) "Zwang."*—So much for the working of the "Lohn Zweck." We have next to examine the "Zwang Zweck" as it supplements "Lohn" in knitting the individuals together into society, and as it carries the social process to still higher levels. We shall see it take up the "Societät" and build it up into the perfected state. It must be remembered that the "Zwang" which Jhering uses is not a mechanical, but a psychical compulsion, or coercion. He uses "Gewalt," the broader word, to describe all exertions of force, both mechanical and psychical, but "Zwang" where the force is applied by influencing the will.[2]

We must note this peculiarity in the working-out of his system at this point. He tells us that "Zwang" is "lower" and older than "Lohn," but that nevertheless it is the basis of a "higher"

---

[1] *Ibid.*, p. 97. "Diese Organisation ist wie vielleicht kein anderes Stück der menschlichen Welt das natürliche Product der freien Zweckentfaltung."

[2] *Ibid.*, pp. 234 ff. So, p. 234, "Unter Zwang im weitern Sinn verstehen wir die Verwirklichung eines Zweckes mittelst Bewältigung eines fremden Willens, der Begriff des Zwanges setzt activ wie passiv ein Willenssubject, ein lebendes Wesen voraus."

form of social organization.[1]   As a motive he thinks that "Zwang"
is found among animals, but that "Lohn" is unknown to them.
Moreover "Zwang" is the basis of the earliest interactions among
men, while "Lohn" only appears later.   On the other hand the
organization through "Zwang," the state with its law, comes later
and is more complex and more highly evolved than the organization through trade, commerce, and other "Verkehr" forms.   He
conceives of highly evolved commerce, structures, and organizations as possible without the intervention of "Zwang," while he
conceives of the state as appearing in and upon "Verkehr" society
and working up portions of it in a more effective way[2]—a point
of view which is a natural by-product of his dependence upon
"Zwecke," but which must be regarded as exceedingly unfortunate
considering what is now known of the solidarity of horde life, of
mutual aid in early organizations of living beings, and in general
of the community setting in which such institutions as private
property develop.

"Zwang" begins of course in the individual, and without
"Zwang" the individual cannot realize his "Zwecke," but through
"Zwang" his "Zwecke" rise straight up to law and to the state.[3]
Law and the state are the organization of "Zwang," just as "Verkehr" was the organization of "Lohn," but there is also a field
of "unorganized" "Zwang,"[4] a social as opposed to legal "Zwang,"
which we shall meet later when he uses it in connection with his
interpretation of moral phenomena.

In working up his organization through "Zwang" Jhering finds
it necessary to draw a distinction between a system of "Zwecke,"
and a system of the realization of "Zwecke."[5]   He develops

[1] *Zweck*, Vol. I, pp. 96, 97, 238.

[2] *Ibid.*, p. 232: "Längst bevor der Staat sich erhob vom Lager . . . . hatte
der Handel schon ein gut Theil seines Tageswerkes vollbracht."

[3] *Ibid.*, p. 291: "Jeder der Zwecke den es (das Individuum) . . . . als
Lebensbedingung empfindet postulirt den Zwang.   Mit diesem Postulate ist aber
das Recht postulirt als die Organisation des Zwanges."

[4] *Ibid.*, p. 236: "Der staatliche Zwang hat zu seinem Object die Verwirklichung des Rechts, der sociale, die des Sittlichen."

[5] *Ibid.*, p. 74; also p. 311: "Die Organisation schliesst zwei Seiten in sich—
die Herstellung des aüsseren Mechanismus der Gewalt, und die Aufstellung von
Grundsätzen welche den Gebrauch derselben regeln."

the distinction by discriminating between the elements of "Norm" and "Gewalt." "Norm" is the rule or precept element in law and the state. "Gewalt" is the law-enforcement element. It will be noted that while "Zwang" is psychic, nevertheless Jhering finds it desirable to revert to "Gewalt" to describe the organized power of the state. The change of terms does not speak well for the adequacy of his "Zwang" as an agent of interpretation, but it is usefully employed to set forth the "heavy hand" of the state as a social fact. He asserts a steady progression from "Norm" to "Gewalt" and from "Gewalt" to "Norm."[1] "Gewalt" answers in a general way to conditions in a despotic state and "Norm" to conditions in a republic.

I will proceed to describe first his position with regard to the "Gewalt," then with regard to the "Norm" element, and finally his completed statement in terms of "Zwecksubjecte" and "Lebensbedingungen," letting him speak for himself in quotations as far as is practicable.

His formal definition of the state, from the point of view of force, is that the state is society as the possessor of the regulated and disciplined "Zwangsgewalt": from this point of view law is the substance of the principles in accordance with which the state so acts; it is the discipline or applied science of Zwang.[2] The organization of the "Zwang" for the "Zwecke" of society rests on the building-up of the power ("Macht") which applies the "Zwangsgewalt and on the establishment of rules for its application[3] "Gewalt" drives out of itself law as the measure of itself: law as the politics of force.[4] Law without "Gewalt" is an empty name with no reality.[5] The state is the final form of the applica-

[1] *Ibid.*, pp. 248, 249: "Die Norm gelangt zur Gewalt, die Gewalt zur Norm."

[2] *Ibid.*, p. 308: "Der Staat ist die Gesellschaft als Inhaberin der geregelten und disciplinirten Zwangsgewalt. Der Inbegriff der Grundsätze nach denen er in dieser Weise thätig wird: die Disciplin des Zwanges ist das Recht."

[3] *Ibid*, p. 236: "auf der Herstellung der Macht welche die Zwangsgewalt ausübt, und der Aufstellung von Regeln über die Ausübung derselben."

[4] *Ibid.*, p. 249: die Gewalt "treibt das Recht als Maass ihrer selbst aus sich heraus—das Recht als Politik der Gewalt."

[5] *Ibid.*, p. 253: "Das Recht ohne die Gewalt ist ein leerer Name ohne alle Realität."

tion of "Gewalt" for human "Zwecke." It is the social organization of the "Zwangsgewalt."[1] The great "Zweck" of the state is the law "Zweck," the formation and safeguarding of the law. The nurture of the law is the vital function in the life of the state.[2] The state is the single source of law.[3] There is no test of law except its recognition and realization by the power of the state.[4] A legal rule without legal "Zwang" is a self-contradiction.[5]

Looking back from the state to the "Societät," we find the latter called the prototype of the former, for in both of them the method of the regulation of "Gewalt" by "Interesse" is the same.[6] The "Societät" effects the transition between the unregulated form of "Gewalt" in the individual and the regulated form in the state.[7] The one is built on "Lohn," and the other on "Zwang," but both together make a single form of social organization as opposed to that "free development" of the "Zwecke" which we saw in "Verkehr." To appreciate the patchwork of his position we may remember that the "Societät," which was at first a fundamental form of Verkehr," became later, as here, a fundamental form of social existence.

This "Staatsgewalt" would normally be maintained by the majority of all the people of the state. But often we find a minority possessing and exercising it. To understand this we must add

[1] *Zweck*, Vol. I, p. 307: "die endgültige Form der Verwendung der Gewalt für die menschlichen Zwecke, die sociale Organisation der Zwangsgewalt."

[2] *Ibid.*, p. 309: "der Rechtszweck: die Gestaltung und Sicherung des Rechts. . . . . Die Pflege des Rechts ist die vitale Lebensfunction des Staates."

[3] *Ibid.*, p. 320: "die alleinige Quelle des Rechts."

[4] *Ibid.*, p. 321: "Anerkennung und Verwirklichung durch die Staatsgewalt."

[5] *Ibid.*, p. 322: "Ein Rechtssatz ohne Rechtszwang ist ein Widerspruch in sich selbst."

[6] *Ibid.*, p. 295: "Soweit sonst auch der Staat und die Societät auseinander gehen, das Schema in Bezug auf die Regelung der Gewalt durch das Interesse ist bei beiden ganz dasselbe—die Societät enthält den Prototyp des Staates." Compare also p. 305: "Der Verein ist die Organisationsform der Gesellschaft schlechthin," and p. 307, where the series, "Individuum, Verein, Staat," is made the "geschichtliche Stufenleiter der gesellschaftlichen Zwecke."

[7] *Ibid.*, p. 295:. "Sie vermittelt den Uebergang von der ungeregelten Form der Gewalt beim Individuum zur Regelung derselben durch den Staat."

two other factors to mere number. The first is the organization of the minority, enabling it to use its strength more effectively ("die Organisation der Macht in den Händen der Staatsgewalt"). The second is the moral might of the state idea ("die moralische Macht des Staatsgedankens").[1] The "Staatsgewalt" can therefore be described as a differentiated portion of the power of the people ("ein ausgeschiedenes Quantum der Volkskraft"). It is the preponderance of organized might over unorganized might ("Uebergewicht der organisirten Macht über die unorganisirte Macht").[2]

Given now this differentiated state power, resting at times and places in a minority of the people, then the critical point in the whole organization of law and of the state, the kernel problem, is that of the preponderance of the common interests of all of us over the particular interest of the single individual. The common interests are upheld by all of us. The particular interests have only single individuals to uphold them. With equality of strength all of us will come to suppress the individual interests, and this so much the more rapidly as the total number of members in the society increases. Power is brought upon the side of the common interests.[3] I call attention in passing to this statement in terms of interests, and more particularly to the moral might of the state idea mentioned in the preceding paragraph. This "moral might"

[1] *Ibid.*, p. 319: "Ich verstehe darunter alle diejenigen psychologischen Motive . . . . die Einsicht in die Nothwendigkeit der staatlichen Ordnung, den Sinn für Recht und Gesetz, die Angst vor der mit jeder Störung der Ordnung verbundenen Bedrohung der Person und des Eigenthums, die Furcht vor der Strafe."

[2] *Ibid.*, p. 316.

[3] *Ibid.*, p. 294: The "springender Punkt" is "das Uebergewicht der gemeinsamen Interessen Aller über das Partikularinteresse eines Einzelnen; für die gemeinsamen Interessen treten Alle ein; für das Partikularinteresse nur der Einzelne. Die Macht Aller aber ist bei Gleichheit der Kräfte der des Einzelnen überlegen, und sie wird es um so mehr, je grösser die Zahl derselben ist." The "Schema für die gesellschaftliche Organisation der Gewalt" becomes: "Uebergewicht der dem Interesse Aller dienstbaren Gewalt über das bloss dem Einzelnen für sein Interesse zur Verfügung stehende Maass derselben, die Macht ist auf Seiten des Allen gemeinsamen Interesses gebracht."

—a factor akin to the "Rechtsgefühl"[1] soon to be introduced—is assigned a very important function in his system, although only a brief paragraph is given to its treatment. It represents an area of social fact never fully functioned in his theory.

We pass now to the Norm. A Norm is a "Satz praktischer Art": it is an "abstracter Imperativ."[2] Besides the legal norms there are the norms of morals ("Moral") and of socially enforced habit ("Sitte," as distinguished from mere social habit, "Gewohnheit"). In law alone, however, it is the state that realizes ("verwirklicht") the norm, and in law alone does the state establish the norm, although there is some law here and there established by society directly. For "Moral" and "Sitte" it is society that both establishes and enforces it. The distinction is between the organized and unorganized "Zwang."

Among "legal imperatives" Jhering distinguishes three grades,[3] forming a hierarchy, among which only the last two are "legal norms," and only the last one is perfected law. First there is the direct command to an individual to do a particular act ("Individualgebot"). This is concrete, not abstract, and is a norm only in the sense that it contains within it the undifferentiated material of norms. Next comes the norm which is binding on the people to whom it is directed, but not on the "Staatsgewalt" itself which issues it. This is abstract and so a norm, but not full law: it is the "einseitig verbindende Norm," binding in one direction only. Finally comes the norm which is binding not only on the people but on the state authorities as well, the "zweiseitig verbindende Norm," binding in both directions. With this the "Staatsgewalt" has come into subordination to its own laws,[4] and now at last the real "Rechtszustand" has been reached.

Were we to follow his analysis farther here we should find under the "norms binding in one direction" an examination of

---

[1] Of course he insists: "Nicht das Rechtsgefühl hat das Recht erzeugt, sondern das Recht das Rechtsgefühl" (so p. xiv), and the same would of course apply for the "moralische Macht des Staatsgedankens," but that is not sufficient.

[2] *Zweck*, Vol. I, pp. 330, 331.   [3] *Ibid.*, p. 338.

[4] *Ibid.*, p. 358: "Die Unterordnung der Staatsgewalt unter die von ihr selber erlassenen Gesetze."

the order thereby established, of the measure of equality produced, and of the subjective "Recht," or sense of legal rightness and desire to obey the legally right, which is developed in the individuals. Under the "norms binding in both directions," the chief problem raised concerns the reasons which hold the "Staatsgewalt" in subordination to its own laws. The motives for this subordination are placed in self-interest, inasmuch as law is not merely the politics of force, but the intelligent politics of force ("wohlverstandene Politik der Gewalt").[1] The guaranties of the subordination are found in the developed legal consciousness ("Rechtsgefühl") and in the professional cultivation of the law ("Rechtspflege").[2] The independence of the judiciary receives consideration here as a factor, and there is also a discussion of the proper limits of subordination which is entirely apart from our present purpose. Government respects its law, Jhering sums up, because of the actual power which lies behind the law, a people which has recognized in the law the condition of its existence, and which feels an injury to the law as an injury to its own self; a people which, we may rest assured, will in extremity take up arms for its law. Thus in the end, he adds, the safety of the law rests on the energy of the national consciousness of legal right.[3]

Now even with "Norm" and "Zwang" thus analyzed Jhering feels that he has not yet got beyond a "formal" statement of the facts. The content ("Inhalt") of the law must still be studied. To correspond with his definition of law and the state in terms of force we now get a definition in terms of content. Law is the form which the conditions of social existence assume under the guarantee of the state.[4] We have next to discover what these conditions of

---

[1] *Ibid.*, p. 378. Cf. also p. 566: "Die Vereinigung der Einsichtigen und Weitsichtigen gegen die Kurzsichtigen."

[2] *Ibid.*, pp. 379 ff.

[3] *Ibid.*, pp. 381, 382: "Lediglich die reale Kraft die hinter dem Gesetz steht, ein Volk, das in dem Recht die Bedingung seines Daseins erkannt hat, und dessen Verletzung als eine Verletzung seiner selbst empfindet, ein Volk von dem zu gewärtigen ist, dass es äussersten Falls für sein Recht in die Schranken tritt. . . . . So hängt die Sicherheit des Rechts schliesslich nur an der Energie des nationalen Rechtsgefühls."

[4] *Ibid.*, p. 443: "Die Form der durch die Zwangsgewalt des Staates beschafften Sicherung der Lebensbedingungen der Gesellschaft."

social existence ("Lebensbedingungen") are, and how they are apportioned to certain "Zwecksubjecte" as their beneficiaries.

These conditions of social existence embrace all that is the goal of human struggling and striving: they are the presuppositions upon which subjectively life in the wider sense depends—life, that is, as including both existence and weal ("Dasein" and "Wohlsein"); they are the goods and enjoyments through which man feels his life conditioned.[1]   Ideal as well as material blessings are included; and honor, freedom, nationality, love, activity, religion, culture, art, and science are not to be omitted from the list. Some of these "conditions" are non-legal in their method of operation, some mixed legal, and some pure legal.   Such a "condition of existence" as "thou shalt not steal" is pure legal.   Of mixed-legal conditions, he discusses four—the maintenance of life, the propagation of life, labor, and commerce—on the basis of three "Motive," the impulse to self-preservation, the sex impulse, and the economic impulse.[2]

Now, he says, if all legal precepts have the safeguarding of the social conditions of existence as their "Zweck," that is the same as saying that society is their "Zwecksubject."[3]   He takes the word "Subject" from its old legal usage, and gives it a meaning, not with reference to the law of the codes, but with reference to the "Zwecke."   He makes society a "person" or living being ("lebendes Wesen"); he develops a "social teleology" similar to "individual teleology;" and in so doing he personifies society in a way which we shall find to have very important results for the ultimate characterization and criticism of his system.[4]

---

[1] *Zweck*, Vol. I, pp. 444, 445: "Sie umfassen alles was das Ziel des menschlichen Ringens und Strebens bildet. . . . . Die Voraussetzungen an welche subjectiv das Leben in diesem weitern Sinne geknüpft ist nenne ich Lebensbedingungen. . . . . Die Güter und Genüsse durch welche der Mensch sein Leben bedingt fühlt."

[2] *Ibid.*, pp. 542–60.

[3] *Ibid.*, p. 462.   "Wenn alle Rechtssätze die Sicherung der Lebensbedingungen der Gesellschaft zum Zweck haben, so heisst das: die Gesellschaft ist das Zwecksubject derselben."

[4] *Ibid.*, Vol. II, p. 88: "Ein Subject, d. h. ein lebendes Wesen." "Princip des Sittlichen kann nicht etwas Unpersönliches, sondern nur die Person, ein lebendes

But it does not satisfy him to say that society, personified for the purpose, is the subject of all law. He carries his analysis farther than that. He recognizes that for certain of the laws their "Zwecksubject" must be looked for directly in the individuals, for others directly in the state, for still others directly in the church, and finally for others directly in voluntary associations (here "Vereine"). But when all is said and done there are an immense number of laws which cannot be attributed so far as their "Zweck" is concerned to any one of these four "Subjecte." A good illustration of what he means can be found in property;[1] private property has the particular individual for its "Subject;" government property has the state, but the public uses of property as, for instance, of public parks, or of state churches, cannot be located in either one or the other. To meet such cases he brings into account as an additional "Zwecksubject," society in the narrower sense of the term ("Gesellschaft im engeren Sinne") which he distinguishes sharply from society in the broad sense.[2] Society in the narrower sense includes the mass of the people in their common (not separate individual) interests. He defines it as the indefinite many, the mass ("die unbestimmte Vielheit, die Masse").

Adding this to the four other "Zwecksubjecte," we have the following series:

1. "Individuum."
2. "Staat."
3. "Kirche."
4. "Vereine."
5. "Gesellschaft (im engeren Sinne)."

All of these, be it remembered are included in society in the wider sense, the state and society in the narrower sense being so included just as much as the others. In the wider sense society is the whole range of organized and unorganized social interaction. The state appears within it, for example, only as society specially

---

Wesen sein;" Vol. II, pp. 150, 193. In contrast compare Vol. I, p. 87: "Die Gesellschaft ist zu definiren als die thatsächliche Organisation des Lebens für und durch Andere," etc.

[1] *Ibid.*, Vol. I, pp. 446 ff.   [2] *Ibid.*, pp. 464 ff.

organized to use compulsion ("Staat ist die Gesellschaft welche zwingt)."[1]   The five "Subjecte" in the table embrace the whole range of society in the broader sense, and give a complete analysis of the beneficiaries of law and legal institutions.[2]   Society in the narrower sense is the beneficiary of all laws not to be attributed to one of the other four.

Discussing crime from the point of view of the "Zwecksubjecte," Jhering asserts that punishments are established wherever society cannot get along without them; that crime is such legally marked injury to the necessary conditions of social life as cannot be warded off without punishment; and that the scale of punishment is the foot rule of social values.[3]

His exhaustive ("erschöpfende") definition of law, which follows the earlier definitions as to form and content is: Law is the substance of the conditions of social existence in the widest sense of the word social as made secure by external compulsion through the power of the state.[4]

4. *The social "Zwecke" (ethical), "Pflicht" and "Liebe."*— With this we have traversed society in its main outlines as far as

[1] *Zweck*, Vol. I, p. 309.

[2] *Ibid.*, pp. 464, 465: "Auf diese fünf Zwecksubjecte bezieht sich das ganze Recht: sie sind die persönlichen Zweckcentren des gesammten Rechts, um die sich sämmtliche Einrichtungen derselben gruppiren." The "Zwecksubjecte" should be distinguished from the bearers of the power of the state, the organs, namely, to which is intrusted the duty of enforcing the law. Jhering does not regard any law as directed at the people who must obey it. It is directed ("gerichtet") instead, "an die Organe die mit der Handhabung des Zwanges betraut sind" (p. 336). Compare also pp. 337, 338: "Die Rechtsnorm enthält einen abstracten Imperativ an die Organe der Staatsgewalt, und die externe Wirkung, d. i. die Befolgung derselben von Seiten des Volks, soweit dazu Anlass geboten ist, muss von diesem rein formaljuristischen Gesichtspunkt (nicht vom teleologischen) jener primären gegenüber lediglich als secundäre bezeichnet werden."

[3] *Ibid.*, pp. 490–92. We find "Strafe überall da wo die Gesellschaft ohne sie nicht auskommen kann. . . . . Verbrechen ist die von Seiten der Gesetzgebung constatirte nur durch Strafe abzuwehrende Gefährdung der Lebensbedingungen der Gesellschaft. . . . . Der Tarif der Strafe ist der Werthmesser der socialen Güter."

[4] *Ibid.*, p. 511: "Recht ist der Inbegriff der mittelst äusseren Zwanges durch die Staatsgewalt gesicherten Lebensbedingungen der Gesellschaft im weitesten Sinne des Wortes."

Jhering has been able to build it up out of "Lohn" and "Zwang," the two egoistic "Hebel." But he did not hold that these two "Zwecke" gave a complete picture of society. There were still phenomena beyond, which he could only explain by appeal to the two ethical "Hebel," duty and love ("Pflicht" and "Liebe"). Duty and love were necessary motives both to complete the work of "Lohn" and "Zwang" in the very fields of commerce and the state, and to hold men together socially in other fields lying outside of these two.

Moral phenomena are according to Jhering just as completely social as any others. They have their origin and function and "Zweck" in society and are to be studied nowhere else than in society and in no other way than through society. This is as true of them in their subjective aspects, that is as motives, as it is of them in their objective aspects, as social norms. His purpose is now as before to get a system of objective "Zwecke" and a system of subjective "Zwecke" built up, and to connect the two with each other and also with individual interest. On the objective side he sets himself the problems of the origin of the norms and of their "Zweck," and on the subjective side the problem of the motives.

On the subjective side he intended to build altruism up out of egoism, and while the exposition was left for the unfinished portion of his work, many sentences were written showing the line he would have taken. Egoism, which is a work of nature, is transformed, he tells us, by history into its opposite.[1] The altruistic qualities are very real qualities; they exist just as surely as the egoistic qualities, once they have appeared, and they can be reckoned on just as surely. The "Gemeinsinn," which he

---

[1] *Ibid.*, Vol. II, p. 118: "Der Egoismus ist in sein gerades Gegentheil umgeschlagen. Er hat sich selber negirt. Die Aenderung, die hier vor sich gegangen ist qualitativer Art, die Geschichte bildet aus dem Thone, dem Teige den die Natur ihr geliefert hat: dem natürlichen Menschen, dem Thiere ein Wesen höherer Art; welches das gerade Widerspiel des ursprünglichen bildet: den sittlichen Menschen; der Egoist ist das Werk der Natur, der sittliche Mensch das der Geschichte;' p. 119: "Wissen und Wollen des Sittlichen, das sittliche Gefühl und die sittliche Gesinnung sind das Werk der Gesellschaft."

showed as appearing in voluntary organization, the higher form
of "Verkehr," will be recalled as a transition step.   "Gemeinsinn"
was set forth as "ennobled egoism."   From pleasure in a common
good he would have effected a transition to pleasure in others'
good ("die Freude am fremden Glück" he calls it in one passage).
He would have thus worked out that full identification of the subjective with the objective "Zweck" which is for him the essence
of the moral.[1]   Once developed the ethical motives become an
absolute postulate of the existence of society.[2]

Taking the moral phenomena objectively, he has to do with a
field of unorganized compulsion as contrasted with the organized
compulsion of the state.   He distinguishes moral phenomena from
"Sitte" (socially enforced custom) on the one side, and from law
on the other, and he adds "Mode" (fashion) as a further field
capable of investigation by similar methods.   A large part of Vol.
II of the *Zweck im Recht* is devoted to an analysis of the objective
"Zwecke" revealed in two forms of "Sitte," courtesy ("die Höflich-
keit") and propriety ("der Anstand").

The "Zwecksubject" of the moral is society itself personified.[3]
Morality is the egoism of society.[4]   The moral is the socially
useful or necessary.[5]   The existence and welfare of society is the
"Zweck" of all moral norms.[6]

It is significant to note in passing that despite the omnipotence
of the "Zweck" in all moral affairs, there are some forms of "Sitte"
for which Jhering can find no "Zweck,"[7] and which he is com-

[1] *Zweck*, Vol. I, p. 60: "völlige Einheit des subjectiven mit dem objectiven
Zweck."

[2] *Ibid.*, Vol. II, p. 12: "Sie bilden ein absolutes Postulat des Bestehens der
Gesellschaft. . . . . Und sie sind da."

[3] *Ibid.*, p. 156; and p. 104: "Die Gesellschaft bildet das Zwecksubject des
Sittlichen. . . . . Alle sittlichen Normen sind gesellschaftliche Imperative."

[4] *Ibid.*, p. 194.

[5] *Ibid.*, p. 214: "Sittlich ist das gesellschaftlich Nützliche oder Nothwendige."

[6] *Ibid.*, p. 156: "Das Bestehen und die Wohlfahrt der Gesellschaft ist der
Zweck aller sittlichen Normen."

[7] *Ibid.*, pp. 280 ff.   So with debts of honor and standards of excessive liber-
ality; p. 284: "Einen gesellschaftlichen Zweck kann ich bei ihnen nicht ent-
decken."   It is worth noting that he also finds points where "der Zwang versagt,"
as with monarchs and juries, Vol. I, p. 329.

pelled to assign to a realm of the morally indifferent.   All through this part of his discussion there are traces of a predominance of "Zweck" which is nothing more than the appearance of the world from his own personal standpoint in it.

I have devoted a great deal of space to this account of Jhering's system, although it would have been easy to state in a page or two its fundamental propositions.   But if I had taken the latter course I would have only been in a position to answer a theory with a theory: and that would not be worth while.   I want to show right on his own social facts that his theory of "Zwecke" is merely a mess of words.   It is, if I may so state it, merely one great elaborate pun upon the word "Zweck," and as a theory entitled to no more scientific respect than any other pun.

Let us recall his great merits.   He broke away from "pure reason" as a principle of interpretation.   He broke away from the presocial or extra-social individual as a principle of interpretation. With this he saved himself from falling into the worst crudities which attend the extension of physical causation to the social field.   (By physical causation I mean that simplified statement of causation which thus far has been adequate for most interpretations of physical facts.)   He brought moral phenomena into a systematic working relation to legal phenomena, and studied both in connection with economic phenomena.   He strove to make all his interpretations in social terms, explaining in this way the individual's psychic life, both in its egoistic and altruistic phases. His point of approach in this attempt was, I feel safe in saying, far superior to that of Spencer's, for he did not merely project a biological man into an unreal and hazy social world, but studied a (comparatively speaking) very real social man directly.   His special studies of laws, of morals, and of institutions showed a very rich insight into social meanings and values, and were indeed epoch-making.

But—and here is the crucial point for the "Zweck" theory— his individual man, even after he had socially interpreted him, was kept in concrete contrast to society which was personified in

opposition to the individual; and his whole theory of social interpretation was made to rest throughout on just this contrast or
opposition.[1]

The word "Zweck" is made to do duty at the one end for the
individual's pleasure, and at the other end for the social welfare
which society is supposed to seek, for the "Interesse Aller,"[2]
"das Wohl und Gedeihen der Gesellschaft,"[3] "das Bestehen der
Gesellschaft,"[4] "das Bestehen und die Wohlfahrt der Gesellschaft," "das gesellschaftlich Nützliche oder Nothwendige."

Between these extremes it stands for a thousand things, among
them two classes to which we have given special attention; subjectively, the four "Hebel" ("Triebfedern," "Motive," "Mittel"),
"Lohn," "Zwang," "Pflicht," and "Liebe;" objectively, certain
institutions or forms of organization (some of which appear from
certain points of view as "Zwecksubjecte") and the immediate
aims or objects of these institutions or organizations.

I suggested earlier in this section that Jhering's problem as
he stated it required him to harmonize the "Zwecke" with "Interessen," to harmonize the "Zwecke" and "Interessen" of many
individuals with each other, and to harmonize the subjective with
the objective "Zwecke." We have found nothing in our progress
to show any clear distinction, to say nothing of harmony, between
"Zwecke" and "Interessen;" sometimes our author has used one
word, sometimes the other, without precision. We have found,
however, that the "Zwecke" and "Interessen" of the many individuals are brought into harmony by him by a process of subordinating them to the objective "Zwecke," which seems to depend
at times on the very vagueness of meaning of the words "Zwecke"
and "Interessen" for its strength. We must approach the solution of all these questions then through a consideration of the extent
of his success in harmonizing the subjective and the objective
"Zwecke." We must ask for the subjective and for the objective

[1] In Vol. II, p. 157, he says that while the individualist theory has no room
for society the social theory has plenty of room for the individual. Instead of
being a merit this is a defect for his form of social theory, for room for a concrete
individual opposed to society is just what it should not have.

[2] *Zweck*, Vol. I, p. 315.   [3] *Ibid.*, Vol. II, p. 103.   [4] *Ibid.*, Vol. I, p. 250.

"Zwecke" respectively what the phenomena are which the words he uses are intended to indicate, where he finds them, and how he analyzes them; and in short not merely what the words are which he fits together, but what the facts are, with a view to seeing whether through one set of facts the other can be interpreted, or vice versa. We can best do this on the two groups of "Zwecke" mentioned in the preceding paragraph, the four "Hebel" as subjective, and the institutions and institutional activity as objective.

The social world presented itself to Jhering as composed of four great groups of facts. This is not set forth explicitly in his book, but may easily be discovered by reading between the lines. First there were the phenomena of commerce, then the phenomena of voluntary association, then the phenomena of law and the state, and finally moral phenomena.

Commerce is a field in which the individual seems—to the ordinary observer commenting on the fact in ordinary speech forms—to be freely adopting lines of action as he wishes at each and every step of his course: and in which the structure or organization of what is done seems to be the free result of this free choosing. Voluntary organization is a field in which the individual, once arranging with other men a policy or line of action, must, it seems, continue on those lines unless he steps out of the process altogether; and in which, so long as he continues to participate, he shares on one or another basis the resulting satisfactions. Law and the state show us a field in which the individual seems to have lost this freedom and to be under compulsion to play the part he does under penalty of punishment. Moral phenomena are a field in which compulsion likewise appears to exist, but not to be exerted in an organized form on the individual.

I wish I could state these four fields of phenomena less superficially, but I cannot, because at bottom Jhering distinguished them from one another only from the point of view of the individual; that is as groups of facts they presented themselves to him fundamentally on an individual basis.

The phenomena of commerce were the simplest, but even here it was apparent that they had a meaning or value beyond the meanings which the individual participants put into them at the time of action. The illustration of the railroad as "Zweck" in contrast to the "Zwecke" ("Interessen") of the individual share-holders will be recalled. But Jhering held firmly to the position that this meaning or value was a meaning or value for men, although it was a meaning which he could not state in terms of the individuals, nor in terms of any conglomeration of individual meanings. By using a common word, "Zweck," for both the social and the individual meanings, he was able to approach, in his opinion, to a coherent statement of the facts. By establishing a principle of "value received" ("Lohn"), to cover all the essential individual acts of participation in the process, he felt that he effected the transition between the individual "Zwecke" and the higher social "Zweck." And this higher "Zweck," being capable of statement as detached from the individuals, could be called objective as opposed to the subjective "Zwecke."

To pass voluntary association for the moment, how was it with law and the state? Here there was equally that higher purpose or meaning, which was human, but his "Lohn Zweck" as he had defined it would not answer to interpret or bridge over the individual's relation to it. Compulsion was the prominent fact, and so compulsion ("Zwang") had to be made itself a "Zweck" for use as a connecting link.

The phenomena of voluntary association occupied a peculiar middle place between commerce and the state. The individual could withdraw; therefore "Lohn" might be taken to explain his presence. But while he remained in he was identified with his companions and under a certain regulation; therefore, we had the application of a simple form of "Zwang," and voluntary organization was the prototype of the state.

But there were still the moral phenomena in which the proportion of "Lohn" was infinitesimal and the "Zwang" while clearly present was not applied in organized forms. Neither of these motives would do. But half-generalized agencies similar to the other two could nevertheless be found in the moral impulses, "Pflicht" and "Liebe." A transition to these from "Lohn" could be found in the "Gemeinsinn," which appeared under voluntary association, and the schematism was complete.

What now did Jhering really accomplish in this way? Let us look at "Zwang," where we see his schematism actually in the making. How can anyone hope to find in "Zwang" as a motive anything more than a reflection of the social facts of law and the state which it is assumed to explain? Even people who think they know where to find duty and love, or even "Lohn," definitely, specifically, concretely, as psychic qualities, will hesitate to point to any spot where "Zwang" exists as a capacity or quality or possession of the soul. They know plenty of facts of "Zwang," actual compulsion and coercion as exercised by some men on others. Of course. With Jhering himself in early passages "Zwang" was frequently synonymous with "Strafe" (punishment).[1] But "Zwang" as a "Zweck"? It is nowhere to be found. As a thing in and for itself it is a useless and self-contradictory fiction. And even as an individualized reflection of the facts, it is useless and self-contradictory; which appeared in Jhering's own words when alongside of a system of "Zwang" (or "Verwirklichung") he put a system of other "Zwecke," in the very state which is interpreted as the organization of "Zwang."

But that which is true of "Zwang" is also true of "Lohn," of "Pflicht," and of "Liebe," however difficult it may be to make this appear to people much more familiar with these latter words in such a use, and accustomed by long habit to getting a fairly satisfactory amount of meaning out of them for everyday needs. They come from the same source, that is the social activity itself, whatever prestige of antiquity they possess as words. As Jhering uses them, they are, so to speak, half individual psychology and half social institutions. They are not adequately stated from either point of view. They do not really state the social facts; they serve merely as a verbal bridge between two part statements, which, put together in this way, do not suffice to make a whole.

We can see how this is in the case of "Lohn" by recalling Jhering's idea that "Lohn" alone can build up a complicated "Ver-

[1] *Zweck*, Vol. I, pp. 60, 181.

kehr" system, free from all interference by "Zwang" or any other
motive, a system which precedes the state and is always in great
part independent of it.   Now we know perfectly well how artificial any such extra-legal commercial construction is—I have
already made mention of the defect—but here the point is that
his motive "Lohn," as reflection of "Verkehr" facts in this phase
is likewise artificial and abstract, and that Jhering's dependence
on it as a concrete thing seduced him into his unfortunate statements as to the free and independent development of the "Verkehr" system.

To put this criticism in a more generalized form, "Lohn"
could get nowhere at all by itself; neither could "Zwang," nor
"Pflicht," nor "Liebe."   But putting these four together is not
like compounding four forces each of which would get somewhere,
and noting the resultant motion.[1]   It is rather fitting the four
abstractions together again and getting the full picture from which
we started, but getting it without any more advance in interpretation than we had when we started.   Just because in the intermediate stages of the process we have imagined the various motives
as concrete possessions of the individuals of which the society is
made up, we cannot say that we have made an advance in interpretation; we have only advanced in the sense that we have satisfied some of our kindergarten wonderings about the relations
between a fictitious individual and a fictitious society.

I have already mentioned in footnotes or in the text a number
of instances in which Jhering uses "Zwecke" or motives of one
kind or another with exceptional definiteness and concreteness.
I will now call attention to one form of phrasing he uses in which
he erects these concrete "Zwecke" into the motive power, so to
speak, of his whole system.   He tells us that the lower "Zwecke"
inevitably drive the others forth out of themselves ("hervortrei-
ben"), that the "Zwecke" press ("drängen") upward, and that
there is a continuity in "Zweck" evolution.[2]   I will not accuse

---

[1] I mean this merely as a simile which illustrates a practical difference.   I
do not mean to pass judgment on the abstractions involved in all statements of
causation.

[2] *Zweck*, Vol. I, pp. 57, 74, 76, 98, 237.

him of attempting to use this evolution deductively in interpreting society, for his very latest work is freest from any such abuse. But I am dealing here not with his special interpretations, but with his theory of social process, and in this respect the statements just referred to form a culminating point in his theory, at which its worthlessness becomes more apparent. They are of a piece with his attempt to state life in terms of "Zwecke," instead of "Zwecke" in terms of life facts.

I think now it is sufficiently well established on Jhering's own work that his distinction between the subjective and the objective "Zwecke" breaks down, and that instead of reaching an interpretation of society by harmonizing the two he only succeeds in making it clear that he should never have set up the hard and fast distinction at all. His objective "Zwecke" are at bottom nothing more than institutions, social modes of action, poorly stated; had he confined himself to the study of their meanings, values, functions, just as they are, in society, just as it is, made up of human beings, he would have laid the foundations for an adequate interpretation. His subjective "Zwecke" are little chunks of institutions, variously generalized; had he analyzed the psychic process as process he would again have had a safe field of study. But he did neither of these things clearly and cleanly. Instead of studying the "Zweck" process as process, he sought always "Zwecke" as causes, that is, as anterior facts. He coagulated the individual "Zwecke," so to speak, and at the same time stewed down the social institutions till he got them into about the same consistency. Then, both alike being called "Zweck," he felt that he had attained his explanation. And it is clear that with Jhering's "Zweck" theory we discard also his distinction between the "Zweck" process and the causal process, which is merely a further generalization of his point of view, for the "Zweck" is simply a faulty definition of the activity itself.

Why is it that with all his painstaking work Jhering reaches only confusion in the end? Is it because his work has been poor? Most decidedly not. His work seems to me of the keenest, broadest, and most thorough, granted his presuppositions. His trouble

lies deeper than that, and it will befog and bemire everyone who
works upon his lines. He set himself a fictitious and hence
insoluble problem. Now it is easy to answer insoluble problems
with stupid answers. But the more brilliant and more powerful
the effort, the more glaringly confused the result.

Jhering saw before him a world in which given masses of men
were doing given things in given ways. I am quite confident that
he never saw or studied or came into any kind of contact with any
social phenomena that were not of this kind. Close under his
vision were phenomena of law, and especially of Roman law.
But he never learned to posit the simple answerable question:
"How are these masses and groups of men doing these things
in these ways?" which is the only scientific question. He always
asked: "What is there hidden in these men and in other men
which makes them be doing these things which I, or somebody
else, can easily think they ought not to be wanting to do?" He
asked: "Why are these men doing these things and not some other
things?" and not, "How are these processes of men working?"
He asked, "Why does a society of men set up certain laws and then
why do these men obey these laws?" and not: "How do these
socially and legally organized men function along? What are the
various elements of their functioning? And how do these elements fit into one another and condition one another?" He
might as well have asked why is gold gold and not silver, and why
is silver silver and not gold, instead of simply studying all the gold
and silver phenomena under as many conditions as possible, and
trying scientifically to make out their similarities as distinguished
from their differences.

He had an assumed individual to start with. As he progressed
he found himself compelled to assume and personify a society to
set over against this individual. His entire theory consisted in a
desperate struggle to bring his two assumptions into harmonious
relations. And of course the harmony he established was as fictitious as the assumptions upon which he established it.

If instead of setting the concrete individual over against the
concrete society, he had taken the individual point of view and

the social point of view merely as points of view, that is, each as covering the whole range of the social life of men, he would have had both his individual and his society capable of being broken down, that is of being analyzed, without the interpolation of fictitious "Zwecke." His personified society with its five compartments (the "Zwecksubjecte") would have become capable of statement as immediate social fact, without the confusions that are involved in the distinctions between "Norm" and "Zwang," between "Lebensbedingungen" and "Zwecksubjecte." He would have had social force and the forms of force and the purposes of force and the beneficiaries of force, all taken up in one unified statement, which would have come very much closer than his *Zweck im Recht* comes, to an adequate reflection of the method which he himself used practically in his own social interpretations.

SECTION V. OTHER ILLUSTRATIONS

Feelings are used in so many widely different ways that a few more illustrations will be profitable. I will give brief consideration to one or two other general theories of the feelings, then show in a series of instances how specific feelings are practically used by investigators in special fields, and finally discuss certain recent attempts to study feelings and faculties statistically in their guise of specific properties of living beings.

First to consider is Professor Lester F. Ward. He makes his whole system rest on the feelings, and indeed he claims that this part of his work is most highly original. The feelings are the neglected factor, which he has brought to light. We will not, however, examine the process of biologic evolution by which he works them out and gets them ready for action. We will take instead his classification of the feelings, and ask what good it is to him, what he is able to "do" with it, for it can have no value for us in any other way than by being useful. It will appear, I think, that his classification satisfies crudely his desire to hitch the social world on to the vital world, but that it serves no other purpose in his system.

His classification of the feelings (desires, social forces) is as follows:

Physical Forces (function bodily)
    Ontogenetic Forces
        Positive, attractive (seeking pleasure)
        Negative, protective (avoiding pain)
    Phylogenetic Forces
        Direct, sexual
        Indirect, consanguineal
Spiritual Forces (function psychic)
    Sociogenetic Forces
        Moral (seeking the safe and good)
        Aesthetic (seeking the beautiful)
        Intellectual (seeking the useful and true)[1]

Professor Ross regards this classification "for the purposes of philosophy" as "by far the most helpful that has been made,"[2] but he objects to it as based too largely on the functions to which the desires prompt, and says that, "for practical purposes," he prefers a classification "based more immediately upon the nature of the desires." Is it not evident that Professor Ward's classification is in no sense a classification of desires or forces in his meaning of the word, but that it is solely and simply a grouping of activities? Certainly this is true of all but the first pair of "forces," pleasure and pain, and in a way it is true even of them. That is, so far as they indicate activities they are entitled to a place in such a table as is in question, but so far as they are regarded as feelings abstractly, they are not entitled to a separate subdivision in the table, but should rather be treated as cutting across all the others.

But if what Ward really gives us is a grouping of activities, then why posit desires behind them to correspond, and think thereby to have made progress in explanation? Certainly when such desires as he lists cannot be detected independently of their manifestations, when they can merely be posited as behind those manifestations, one has no way to test them or to handle them.

---

[1] *Pure Sociology*, p. 261. Compare also *Dynamic Sociology*, Vol. I, p. 472.

[2] *The Foundations of Sociology*, p. 167.

If one uses them in interpretation the whole use must be hypothetical. Of course if the hypothesis is of the kind which gives us aid in understanding the operations under examination, well and good. But even with the two hundred pages of Professor Ward's *Pure Sociology*, in which he works out a detailed treatment of the three groups of forces, the ontogenetic, the phylogenetic, and the sociogenetic, lying before me, I am compelled to say that in my opinion his hypotheses do nothing of the kind. We have here a sort of evolutionary history of social man, described along three general lines, forming the three chapters referred to, headed with the names of the three groups of "forces." But how the theory of the underlying feeling forces helps this history I utterly fail to see. The history could have been built up just as it is without the theory; and the alleged "forces" represent merely the principle on which the facts are classified by Dr. Ward, nothing more.

Another use of desires that is very common is found among the socialists and other writers who tell us that sex and food desires are the sole motors of life.[1] When a man who does this sort of thing is honest with himself he soon is forced to admit that there are a lot of other desires which cannot be reduced as such into one or other of the pair, and then his proposition becomes one to the effect that these are the two dominant motors and that all others can be disregarded as negligible in serious study of society. But we really have in this nothing more than an assertion that sex and food institutions are the most important institutions of society and so no progress has been made toward interpretation by dragging in the desires.

In Westermarck's *History of Human Marriage* we find some apt illustrations of the misuse of solidified feelings and instincts. I shall here, as before, leave on one side the solid and substantial portions of the book and confine what I have to say to the abuses of interpretation in the use of the feelings and instincts, with a view to showing why those factors are brought in and what they stand for. My belief is, it is hardly necessary to repeat, that they are brought in to satisfy the writer's need of systematizing

---

[1] A recent example is M. A. Lane, *The Level of Social Motion*, pp. 46 ff.

his work with reference to certain metaphysical problems, and that they stand for ignorance.

At the very beginning Westermarck confesses frankly his reliance on psychological factors, and adds: "More especially do I believe that the mere instincts have played a very important part in the origin of social institutions and rules."[1] His most important use of an instinct in interpretation is in connection with the theory of the origin of marriage itself. After showing the utter lack of proof for the existence of promiscuity among early human beings, and establishing satisfactorily that upon the emergence of social man to our vision, marriage existed in the sense of "a more or less durable connection between male and female, lasting beyond the mere act of propagation till after the birth of offspring,"[2] he sets up an "instinct developed through the powerful influence of natural selection,"[3] to explain this "natural form of the sexual relations of man."[4]

Now the student of bird life, who finds birds pairing with almost unbroken habit, uses the term instinct to explain the coming together of two birds, their nest-building, egg-caring, and offspring-feeding habit. He means by it conduct which, so far as he can observe, is not built up in its given form during the life-experience of the individual. We need not quarrel with his use of the word "instinct," because it serves to mark off a set of facts he has observed; but even here he should not be too positive in reliance on it until he has got into intimate touch with the relations of birds to one another, and knows how much to attribute to that factor.

But when we come to human society, even in its most primitive forms, the case is different. It may be perfectly true that natural selection will account for the survival of marrying apes and human beings, and it is of course possible to use "instinct" to describe the marrying fact in its regularity. But the social problem remains for explanation just as much as before. We have various sets of possibilities of living, various sets of conditions of life, and a large

[1] *The History of Human Marriage*, p. 5.

[2] *Ibid.*, p. 19.   [3] *Ibid.*, p. 537.   [4] *Ibid.*, p. 70.

amount of psychic process going on, including influences from family to family, from larger group to family, and from larger group to larger group. We cannot safely go back to an inherited vital habit till these have been taken into account. We want to know what happens and how, and what variations came and how. When we are answered by the reply of "instinct," we are told little more than that the individuals have a tendency to do as they do. We are merely shown the social action and referred to an individual tendency alleged to conform to it; but all the group life that we know to exist is left out of account. I am not saying that Westermarck or anybody else is at present in a position to give a helpful explanation of the approximate universality of the little marriage groups of early man, and I am of course not attacking him because he did not do it, but merely showing that his "instinct," although it defines and states the problem, does not answer it. It is perfectly true that such an instinct treated merely as an organized habit of action occurring in a presocial life and projecting itself into a social life, without any more modification through social experience than, say, the manner of using the jaws in eating undergoes, may be properly emphasized where it can be positively established. But it should be treated very tenderly and carefully, as systematized action and as nothing more; and when one reaches any stage of development in which, if indeed it really existed before, it has been clearly wiped out or transformed, one should then make a prompt ending with the instinct, even in its clear-cut activity sense. Moreover, when one remembers the infinite pains that a naturalist must take with a chick, for example, to make sure whether he is really studying an activity of prenatal derivation, or one acquired through imitation and experience, he may well hesitate long before settling the exact amount of confidence he will place in a pairing activity, as handed down in fixed form from one generation of human beings to the next. Indeed it may well be asked whether such an instinct can properly be regarded as a factor to be emphasized as "building up" a social institution like marriage as we know it, or whether it is not rather a factor which must be broken down, or at least transformed by society, before what we describe as the social evolution can take its start.[1]

Westermarck does not, however, limit himself to instincts that have come to us from ape ancestors. He makes use of instincts that arise in us through natural selection during social life, and here his fault is very much more serious. The most striking case is his explanation of incest and the whole problem of the prohibition of marriage between kindred. These prohibitions, he insists, are not social: men do not "avoid incestuous marriages only because they are taught to do so;"[2] it is not a case of law, customs, education, or any other form of "social" control. The repulsion to marriage between kindred is "instinctive," not in the sense, however, that the instinct recognizes kinship itself and repulses it, but that it repulses the "household," those who live closely together, among whom the kin make the greater proportion.

For such an instinct to develop through natural selection, the questionable supposition must be made that such marriages of kin are physically injurious to the offspring; the more questionable supposition must be made that they are injurious enough to cause the destruction—in competition at least—of groups that make such marriages; a repulsion to the sexually familiar, much stronger than any mere love of variety, must be assumed as a very common occurrence over the earth; the possibility that such a repulsion can get "set" physically—not merely socially—and transmitted from generation to generation must be assumed; and its strength must be made so great that it lasts through life and only under the most extreme cases can be broken down by any conditions of living in which tribes and people may be placed.

[1] In Part II, chaps. ix and xxi, the place material of this kind occupies in group interpretation will be indicated. It may be observed here, however, that whereas there are many pairing animals, the only one that has both pairing and organized social habits at the same time is probably the beaver. See Letourneau, *L'Evolution politique*, pp. 11, 12.

[2] Westermarck, *op. cit.*, pp. 319, 544. Westermarck does not indeed say absolutely that this instinct is of strictly social origin. He thinks (pp. 352, 353) that a similar instinct may possibly have been of presocial origin, but he has no reasons to offer, and he goes on to say, "it must necessarily have risen at a stage when family ties became comparatively strong and children remained with their parents until the age of puberty or even longer."

Given all these assumptions little progress has been made toward explaining why the varying forms of these prohibitions appear, clan maternal or paternal, phratry, recognized kinship in many degrees or few; nor why villages miles apart are sometimes included in the close living together, while huts side by side are not; nor why indeed the hut and village contrast can sometimes be found in the same tribe at the same time.

To explain these variations, which together make up the whole of the phenomena to be explained, social factors must be superimposed on the alleged "instinct." I have no hesitation in asserting that when we have these social factors completely worked out we will have our full explanation of all problems of marriage prohibitions, and the "instinct" will drop away as a useless bit of verbiage. In other words, when we have marriage interpreted as a form or set of forms of the ordering or control of interests in human groups, we will be done with our inquiry. If there is a selection resting on any real injuriousness in the marriage of kin, it will be a "social selection" not a "natural selection," in the sense in which Westermarck uses the phrase.[1]

I might give a long list of feelings which Westermarck appeals to for help in explanation. For example, polygyny "implies a violation of woman's feelings"[2]—and this even in the face of all the exceptions. There is an "instinct" of women to select the

---

[1] While this matter of exogamy is under view, a method of explaining it which seems to me particularly naïve is worth noting. In the *Zeitschrift für Socialwissenschaft*, Vol. V, p. 15 (cf. also *American Journal of Sociology*, Vol. III, p. 756), Professor W. I. Thomas asserts that since desire weakens for familiar things, since familiarity breeds contempt, and since love at first sight is the warmest love, therefore we may argue specifically that men "like" strange women better than well-known women; that they gradually get the habit of getting their wives abroad, and hence that they build up exogamy as a social institution. Of course he does nothing more than to assume a feeling to fit the fact; in other words he spins the answer out of the term he selects to start the reasoning with. Since he makes the marriage institution as a whole rest on the sex instinct, it is fair to point out the contradiction that at once grows out of his argument. Clearly, the moment exogamy was established, the home women, being forbidden, would become infinitely more desirable than the foreign women from whom the wives are taken. If any such instinct or feeling as he assumes could establish exogamy one day it would smash it to pieces the next.

[2] *The History of Human Marriage*, p. 495.

strong men.[1] In Paraguay institutions bend under "woman's stronger passions."[2] Jealousy is a pervading motive in building up institutions.[3] The spring procreation festivals are explained as survivals of the primitive human "rutting" instinct.[4] The "absorbing passion for one"—otherwise the "true monogamous instinct"—is a powerful obstacle to polygyny.[5] "Fraternal benevolence" is responsible for polyandry under some conditions.[6] The laws of Europe against divorce took their origin in an "idealistic religious commandment."[7] "Endogamy is due to a want of sympathy, and has declined before altruism and religious toleration."[8] In all cases he takes a psychic factor to correspond with one set of customs, which happens to be the prevading one, and then says that all customs that do not correspond are due to perversions of that factor, or to its suppression by some other psychic factor.[9]

On the other hand when Westermarck finds a feeling or instinct in current use as an explanation of something or other, and his broader knowledge of facts enables him to annihilate it, he performs the operation with pleasure and precision. Thus there is his study of the relation of clothing to the feeling of shame, in which he reverses the causal order of everyday explanation and proves that "the modesty which shows itself in covering is not an instinct in the same sense in which the aversion to incest, for example, is an instinct;"[10] insisting that "it is not the feeling of shame that has provoked the covering, but the covering that has provoked the feeling of shame."[11] Similarly he objects to "Darwin's inexplicable aesthetic sense" in sexual selection.

---

[1] *The History of Human Marriage*, p. 256.   [5] *Ibid.*, p. 502.

[2] *Ibid.*, p. 158.   [6] *Ibid.*, p. 516.

[3] *Ibid.*, p. 132.   [7] *Ibid.*, p. 536.

[4] *Ibid.*, pp. 28 ff.   [8] *Ibid.*, p. 546.

[9] A similar illustration can be found in Ratzel, *Die Erde und das Leben*, Vol. II, p. 669. He says that if two peoples join together to form a state, then "übernimmt das politisch begabtere die Leitung." But of course the only way he can know which is "politically more gifted" is by the outcome in fact.

[10] Westermarck, *op. cit.*, p. 211.

[11] *Ibid.*, p. 208. It may be added that that very "desire for self-decoration" which Westermarck uses in his clothes theory (pp. 165 ff.) is itself simply a "soul-stuff" reflection of the fact of decoration activity, and is manifestly of no use in explaining the particular forms of decoration adopted.

Every one of his own interpretations in terms of instinct of feeling is, however, open to the same demolition, on further examination, that he has proved for the "shame" feeling. "Shame" was inserted by others to explain clothing in the same way that the instinct against marriage with close companions is inserted by Westermarck. Demolishment is not the special fate of the one or the other under scientific investigation. It is the sure fate of all such elements when used as independently existing "causes" of anything whatever.

It is interesting to note what happens when an investigator of some special problem, who accepts the instincts and feelings unhesitatingly as the causes of action, tries to make a general statement of cause in such terms for a multitude of phenomena all in the same group. An illuminating case in this respect is that of Gurewitsch, who has studied that perennial puzzle problem about the relative priority of needs and division of labor.[1] Which came first, he asks, the needs, or the division of labor by which those needs are supplied? And this indeed expands into the wider problem: Which came first, the needs, or the technical methods of supplying the needs? We must understand, of course, not generalized needs, but specific needs, as a need for milk, for rye bread, for a meat diet, and so forth.

Now Gurewitsch knows perfectly well the pitfalls of this question. In discussing that great problem as to how men came to keep domestic herds, for example, he puts the dilemma of the needs in this way: If early man had plenty of flesh food, then why should he take the trouble to raise flocks? If, on the contrary, he did not have plenty, then what could induce him to spare part of the little that he needed for immediate use, in the hope of getting ultimate advantage? If one is using psychic factors in interpretation, and faces the difficulty squarely, such insoluble problems as this will appear on every hand, and indeed nothing else will appear.

I am not going to follow Gurewitsch's study in details, since

---

[1] "Die Entwicklung der menschlichen Bedürfnisse und die sociale Gliederung der Gesellschaft," *Staats- und socialwissenschaftliche Forschungen*, Vol. XIX, No. 4.

his interest for us here lies not in what he has accomplished, but in what he has failed to accomplish. After having recognized so clearly the contradictions of the psychic factors when used in specific cases, he nevertheless does not have the courage to break away from them entirely, but when he comes to sum up his theory he bases it on a hypothetical "striving for power" ("Streben nach Macht"), seemingly unaware that this motive, or psychic tendency, or whatever it is, is just as much open to confusions as any of the "need" elements he has excluded. He sets up a complicated law[1] to the effect that the "development of human needs (and all social evolution)" depends on "the continuous abolishing and restoration of the social-economic equilibrium," which in turn depends on the "Streben nach Macht," this "Streben," finally, manifesting itself not merely in efforts to perfect both needs and labor arrangements necessary to their satisfaction, but also in creating the social differentiation, which is the basis of the development of human needs.

In other words, instead of letting his work stand for itself, he makes it all work out into what we may call an "in-and-in-breeding" definition, with a hypothetical "Streben nach Macht" as the vital principle: all because he has not yet succeeded in weaning himself from the psychic factor—a factor which after having shown itself ludicrous in every particular use, at last takes refuge in bare tautology, as its sole safeguard against being completely discarded.[2]

Finally, when all is said and done, if one drives out the soul-stuff, here, there, and everywhere in its specialized forms, from use in social interpretation, but still leaves it lying around as socially unassimilated matter, one will most probably sum it all up in some one broad general principle of self-maintenance. This, for instance, is what Gumplowicz does when he sets up the "Selbstbe-hauptungstrieb."[3] If one arrives at a motive so general that it covers all social phenomena, one has at the same moment arrived

[1] Gurewitsch, *op. cit.*, p. 128.

[2] Giddings' "consciousness of kind" is in similar case. And so also Kropotkin's "social instinct" already referred to.

[3] *Die sociologische Staatsidee*, 2d ed., p. 161.

at a motive which is utterly useless and negligible for purposes of social interpretation. To talk of a "Selbstbehauptungstrieb" is merely to indulge in a passing personification of social activity. It is just as adequate to say that social activities exist as to say they exist because they strive to exist. The striving for existence cannot be used anywhere or in any way that will add meaning to the existence, the activity, the process, considered as fact, apart from the "Trieb" behind it. The outcome of any process of simplifying a system of motives into one great dominating motive is the annihilation of the use of motives in interpretation.

One other method of using mental qualities and capacities in scientific work remains, which I must try briefly to characterize and criticize. It is that which Francis Galton started, which Karl Pearson and his associates of *Biometrika* are laboring with, and which is illustrated by such an American work as that of Frederick Adams Woods, on *Mental and Moral Heredity in Royalty*. These investigators treat feelings and intellectual capacities as definite "things,"[1] and try to measure them. They seek to show exactly how they are inherited and what the correlations are between parents and children, between brothers and sisters, and between race and race. Galton's interesting propaganda for eugenics is in part an outgrowth of this work, but I am not concerned here with any attempt to fix the social value of his practical teaching. The assumptions of the theory and its confusions can best be shown in the studies made by Pearson or under his direction, with some additional illustration from Woods. There is some doubt as to the validity of Pearson's mathematics, but that again is none of my business here.

Pearson has comparatively smooth sailing with his study of the correlations[2] of physical characteristics in plants and animals, such

[1] They may deny that they are dealing with "soul-stuff." I am concerned however, not with what they say about their position, but with what it actually, i. e., practically, is.

[2] For the technique of the study of correlations see Pearson's *Grammar of Science*, 2d ed.; Bowley, *Elements of Statistics*; E. L. Thorndike, *An Introduction to the Theory of Mental and Social Measurements*; the article on "Heredity" in *Buck's Reference Handbook of Medical Sciences*, or the files of *Biometrika*.

as the number of beans in a pod, the number of ribs in a leaf, the length of certain bones, or the shape of the skull.   So far so good.

Advancing to more complex material, however, he at once gets into trouble in two ways.

First studying the color of the hair or eyes, he is able to get correlations, not of definite facts, but of vaguely judged facts.

Next, studying fertility in men or in the thoroughbred horse,[1] he conducts his investigations on material which is affected in very important ways by "social" influences, although he has no way to separate the social from the vital in his material or in his calculations.

When he comes to the study of the inheritance of mental qualities or capacities, both of these difficulties are in his way. He is dealing, not with his material direct, but with very doubtful judgments about it[2] and he has no means whatever of isolating his vital qualities, or even of making a rough estimate of the proportions in which they appear in his material.   An analysis of a single one of the investigations made under his direction will be sufficient to show this.   The paper, "On the Inheritance of Mental and Moral Characters in Man,"[3] does not attempt to measure parental correlations, but confines itself to fraternal correlations, that is, to the resemblances of brothers and sisters, and even this it studies not among adults, but among school children.   The statistical material put under examination consists of school-teachers' reports on some thousands of brother-brother, brother-sister, or sister-sister pairs, obtained only with great labor and long delays.   The children were classified as to ability into the quick-intelligent, the intelligent, the slow-intelligent, the slow, the slow-

[1] *Philosophical Transactions*, Royal Society of London, Series A 1899.

[2] I do not mean to contrast his physical measurements with his psychical judgments as though they were distinct ranges of phenomena.   The distinction is practical.   In his skull shapes he has measurements that have scientific value. In his psychical characters he has no such measurements, or, to put it in terms of vocabularies, in the first instance he has a word equipment—the millimeter series —which has practical results; in the other he has no such word equipment— merely vague general phrases with indefinite meanings.

[3] *Biometrika*, Vol. III.

dull, and the very dull. A seventh class, the inaccurate erratic was ignored in the returns. The moral qualities reported on had regard to vivacity, whether noisy or quiet; assertiveness, whether self-assertive or shy; introspection, whether self-conscious or unself-conscious; popularity, whether popular or unpopular; conscientiousness, whether it was keen or dull; and temper, whether quick, good-natured, or sullen. Handwriting, as an indication of character, was also estimated in six degrees, and the head measurements were taken, as well as certain other physical characters.

To these facts Pearson applied his formulas, and worked out the correlation in all cases as around o. 5, which is just about what the correlation for physical characteristics as between brothers and sisters should be. "There can, I think," he concludes, "be small doubt that intelligence or ability follows precisely the same laws of inheritance as general health, and both the same laws as cephalic index, or any other physical character."[1]

Now this result was a surprise to him, for he had "expected a priori to find the home environment largely affecting the resemblance in moral qualities of brothers and sisters."[2] That is, he expected the ratio of correlation to show the effect of heredity plus environment, and so to be unusually large. Since it is not large he at once draws the inference that home environment counts for nothing at all. He writes:

We are forced, I think literally forced, to the general conclusion that the physical and psychical characters in man are inherited within broad lines in the same manner, and with the same intensity. The average home environment, the average parental influence is in itself part of the heritage of the stock and not an extraneous and additional factor emphasizing the resemblance between children from the same home.[3]

But now consider. His material is the judgments of school-teachers upon the children as these are revealed to them in the school work. When ability in school is under consideration, suppose it should happen that two children from one family were alike ill-fed or over-fed; suppose they had alike contracted some vice; suppose their home surroundings had given them

---

[1] *Biometrika*, Vol. III, p. 149.   [2] *Ibid.*, p. 153.   [3] *Ibid.*, p. 156.

interests which make the routine of a British school peculiarly repulsive to them. These things are not improbable; they are rather almost inevitable in many instances. Under such conditions a correlation might be shown, but it would certainly not be a correlation of the kind that Professor Pearson thinks he has shown. And further than this, the "ability" that he deals with is merely ability for the particular kind of school work in question, and not ability in general.

Bad as all this is, we can still allow weight to the teachers' judgments as to ability in far greater degree than we can to their judgments as to the moral qualities; for these judgments as to moral characters are peculiarly personal, each such "moral character" being indeed itself a relation between two or more persons, and not necessarily equivalent to the relation that would arise between the given child and some other person. We are, then, in reality offered statistics not on certain qualities or faculties of the children, but on certain social judgments about the children, which may be called, not so much fallible, as partial reflections of the facts from the view-point of a small corner in the social mass.

Nor is this all. There is a certain amount of known fact about children and homes and schools, such as that some children can learn rapidly of one teacher, when they cannot of another; that children vary in the ease with which they can be controlled by different people; that when moved from one home environment to another, a considerable change may be worked in their actual conduct. This fact of the reality of discipline, however we may interpret it, is given to us in observation, and Professor Pearson's denial of the influence of the home environment does not do away with it. If therefore we should accept his statistical material as containing real facts about children, we should nevertheless be compelled to conclude that his ratio of correlation must be reduced somewhat to allow for this, and that the correlation of psychic characters he shows us would therefore be less than the correlation of physical characters.

However, I cannot allow to Professor Pearson's work even this vague degree of validity. The material he has investigated is strictly social material. It is foolish to talk of "heredity plus environment," since the environment itself is strictly part of the material under investigation. One could as fairly conclude from the results offered us that the whole thing was a showing of environment without heredity, as that it is a showing of heredity without environment, and indeed one could more fairly conclude thus.[1]

And this leads us to knowledge of the source of his inferences. He wrote frankly in the article to which I have referred:

> I cannot free myself from the conception that underlying every psychical state there is a physical state and from that conception follows at once the conclusion that there must be a close association between the succession or the recurrence of certain psychical states, which is what we judge mental and moral characteristics by, and an underlying physical conformation, be it of brain or liver.[2]

And again,

> Personally I do not think it desirable to draw very rigid lines between the physical and psychical, and the present inquiry has much strengthened that opinion.[3]

---

[1] Perhaps I can make his defect clearest by a comparison. Suppose he should wish to establish correlations in bean-poles between their length and height. Suppose he should gather several thousand such poles. Suppose, then, he was unable to measure them, and instead should set them up in a long row, and put two or three hundred agricultural laborers at work making estimates of their length and thickness from a distance of two or three hundred feet, giving each laborer his proportionate share of the poles to report on. Suppose then when he had passed his statistical material through his mathematical machinery, he should announce a positive conclusion concerning the correlations of these characteristics in the poles, and should proceed on the basis of his results to declare, first, that there is no such thing as a factor of variability among the observers, and second that social elements in the production of bean-poles not merely had no effect but actually did not exist. Laughter would be the mildest greeting that his conclusions would receive. It would be clear enough that his material consisted of man-made bean-poles "as judged" by the observers. And his correlations might indicate the "man-making" factor, or might have to do with the judgments rendered, but hardly could be announced for bean-poles, considered as independently existing. And yet I venture the assertion that there would not be a tenth of 1 per cent. as much vagueness or uncertainty in his bean-pole correlations as there actually is in his "mental and moral characters."

[2] *Biometrika*, Vol. III, p. 147.   [3] *Ibid.*, p. 153.

These quotations show clearly enough that his conclusions follow directly from his presuppositions, not from his investigations as such. I, of course, do not take exception to his conception that the physical underlies the psychical. So long as we hold the physical and psychical apart by our present terminology, I freely admit that without such a presupposition no systematic investigation of any social fact is possible. What I am referring to is the "thing" nature which he gives to these psychical "states," to his treatment of them as "soul-stuff," to his idea that they can be adequately described or defined for scientific purposes by the same verbal methods we use to define or describe an ear or a thigh-bone or a skull, to his idea that lumps of mental or moral qualities can be compared as individual possessions, and can be inherited as such. I do not think that he offers us the slightest proof that his presupposition is well founded; and such proof is of course the whole purpose of his elaborate investigations. The "translation of correlation into causation,"[1] so far as the mental factors are concerned, is merely the translation of an untested presupposition into an unproved conclusion.

It is upon such flimsy foundations as these that Pearson causes to rest his piteous wailings over the mental and moral degeneration of the British stock. Remember, the question at issue is not whether there is actually any degeneracy as a social fact in Great Britain, but whether that degeneracy, assuming it to exist, rests on—or, better said, is the same thing as—a physical (i. e., physically mental and moral) deterioration of the population, carried on through natural selection, or in other words through the dying-off of better grades of the men and women, and the multiplication of poorer grades.

In his *Grammar of Science* he puts his fears mildly enough for him. He says that "if we could remove the drag of the mediocre elements in ancestry, were it only for a few generations," we could create a better stock, just as the breeder does. He tells us that the upper middle class "thinks for the nation" because it is a better stock, and he asks:

[1] *Grammar of Science*, p. 397.

There is apparent today a want of youthful ability in literature, art, science, and politics: who can affirm that this dearth—not British only, but French and German—has not been emphasized by the reduction in the birth rate of the abler intellectual classes which has taken place since the sixties?[1]

But in his *National Life from the Standpoint of Science*, after restating his theory that the characters of parents, including "their virtues, their vices, their capabilities, their tempers," are inherited "in definite amounts," with "a certainty as great as that of any scientific prediction whatever;"[2] after asserting that bad stock cannot be changed to good, and that education and nurture will accomplish nothing in modifying the stock; after setting up a law of "stagnation," when offspring come equally from superior and inferior stocks and there is no wastage, he bursts out: "Woe to the nation which has recruited itself from the weaker and not from the stronger stocks!" And he asks: "Have we a reserve of brain power ready to be trained?" and he sadly answers: "I must confess to feeling that an actual dearth is upon us."[3]

And all this because Kaffirs and negroes, as a social fact, have not developed, as a social fact, great complicated social organizations, and because Pearson himself does not recognize either a Darwin or a Thackeray among his contemporaries.

The presupposition about soul-stuff is all there is to this argument. It is so trivial it is hardly worth answering. But I have felt that I could not ignore it here, because it is by far the most painstaking attempt to apply "scientific" methods, as distinct from sociological theorizing, to the material, that has yet been made.[4]

The interesting work of Mr. Woods gets its material from

[1] *Ibid.*, pp. 457, 466, 467.

[2] *National Life from the Standpoint of Science*, pp. 14, 16.

[3] *Ibid.*, pp. 29, 42, 57.

[4] I might also show the futility of Pearson's point of view by analyzing his discussions of progress in terms of individualism, socialism, and humanism (*Grammar of Science*, chap. ix). These "principles" are put forth as "factors of change" connected with the principle of the survival of the fittest; they are made to rest in instincts; they are described as "formulas;" and they are called "motives" of modern life. It is a frightful confusion. But analysis of such theories of interpretation belongs to the next chapter.

sources very different from those which Pearson used, but it is equally faulty in its naïve acceptance of the soul-stuff at the beginning of the investigation. This investigator thinks it "evident that each human being has certain definite mental, moral, and physical characteristics, and that these are due to not more than three causes—heredity, environment, and free will." Taking the royal families of Europe, he proposes to find out whether the statistics reveal mental and moral heredity. He excludes all royal persons not mentioned in Lippincott's *Biographical Dictionary*, as such persons "could not have been very great, at least as regards outward achievements, which is the standard here employed."[1] One would think that as he wrote these words he would recognize that achievement is not a proper standard, because the relation of achievement to character is the very thing under investigation. But no. His prepossession is too strong. Moreover, he explains that the basis of estimate is "the adjectives that are used by historians and biographers."[2] All of which means that the material he is investigating is social achievement as accredited to the individual by ordinary language, and as socially judged. I hardly need to reiterate the argument that whatever correlations he may reveal, it still remains on this basis an open question whether the "what" of the correlation is social influence, or social judgment, or individual character, or capacity, the very question to which he purports to be seeking an answer.

It is not to be denied that the similarities in the ratio of physical heredity with the heredity he establishes are interesting, but that is entirely apart from the fundamental question. Consider how the case appears when he points out the "relatively large number of exceptional geniuses" in royalty, and argues that therefore the "stock" must be superior.[3] Think how the work of a royal personage is flattered; think how many subjects do work which is put forth in the monarch's name; think what opportunities are given every scion of a royal house in line of succession to fit himself for some or all of his life functions, what compulsion is exercised on him to fit himself, and how he is enabled to get a maximum of

---

[1] *Mental and Moral Heredity in Royalty*, p. 12.   [2] *Ibid.*, p. 10.   [3] *Ibid.*, p. 301.

benefit with a minimum of labor. Can one still safely draw an inference to "stock"?

Again, we are told that the "relative absence of great kings during the last century" indicates that regression has begun.[1] But what value can we give to the inference when we remember the difference of industrial, national, and political conditions between the last century and preceding centuries?

Also, we are told that "for nearly a thousand years the commercial and industrial progress made by both Spain and Portugal has been directly traceable to the character of its chief heads of state."[2] But his tabulation of two columns of epithets, one relating to the state and the other to the ruler, proves nothing. The inference may be made from either column to the other with equal propriety.

We may sum up Mr. Woods's work by saying that while his factor of "intellectual" capacity may be reported with some slight degree of objectivity from the individual standpoint, yet there is absolutely nothing presented to show that this "capacity" as such produces the social achievement, while indeed it is most often inferred from the achievement in a way that gives it no claim to individual objectivity at all; on the other hand his "moral" qualities are "things done" socially, and involve the whole social situations in them to such a degree that they are even more clearly worthless for inferences as to the relation between "stock" and social process than the intellectual factors.

I repeat that I am not denying that men are in fact distinguished from one another by epithets relating to their intelligence and moral qualities; nor that different adults act differently in situations which we describe to ourselves as substantially the same; nor that this method of statement is useful in its own time and place. What I am asserting is that the attempt to erect it into a causal interpretation of society on the basis of fixed individual characters which can adequately be described and defined apart from the society they explain, is a hotbed of confusion and irrelevancy; and the proof is in the works of the men I have studied in this chapter.

[1] *Ibid.*, p. 302.   [2] *Ibid.*, p. 198.

CHAPTER II

IDEAS AND IDEALS AS CAUSES

Section I. In Everyday Speech

We pass now from the feeling theories to the idea or ideals theories. As before I do not pretend to be careful about the use of the psychological terms. I am not here engaged in any analysis of intellectual process, nor in any manipulation of any form of soul-stuff. Leaving psychical "process" on the side for the time being, I am engaged simply in showing that the use of specific forms of soul-stuff gives us absolutely no help in interpreting the doings of social men. We shall first of all try to locate the ideas and ideals in everyday talk, moralizing, and exhortation. Then we shall consider some theories based on such interpretative material.

Let the stump speaker appear at the old-fashioned Fourth of July celebration. What does he tell us? Our forefathers who created this nation were led by a great ideal of liberty. It was their highest good. Without it they would never have made this land what it is. Also they sought independence. Had they not suffered and labored many long hard years to breathe the air of freedom, they never would have been "free." Perhaps also equality was one of the great goals they set before themselves. It was something they sighed for, bled for, and were willing to die for. Let us keep the ideals of our forefathers ever in our minds; let us inspire ourselves with the same lofty spirit that led them to their deeds of heroic devotion—and then we will all live happily ever afterward.

After which, speaker and hearers alike go back to the same old round of buying and selling, laboring and advantage-seeking. Did the speech change their methods of dealing with their fellows, privately or publicly? Did it move the country forward toward anything? Did the renewed assent of all its hearers to its principles have any such results? Do the tens of thousands of speeches and applaudings and assentings like it have such results? The stump speaker himself would be the first to laugh at the folly of the question, give him only time enough to recover from his verbal self-hypnotism.

We know as a matter of fact that the liberty our revolutionary forefathers sought stood for exemption from a certain number of burdensome taxes and trade restrictions which were interfering with their prosperity. We know that formal independence from England was only sought by them in the last extreme after much reluctant discussion and as a war measure of doubted value. We know that any striving after equality, as distinct from facts of existent comparative equality of condition, cannot be found among them with the most careful prying; and that as for the tendency of the times, it was rather away from than toward equality.[1]

So much for the talk of the Fourth of July. Let our stump speaker transfer his activities to the party campaign meeting. Listen to him again.

The Republican party has been inspired by glorious ideals; it set the slaves free; it has ever since been striving to set everybody else free; it is the party of patriotism, the party of all the people, the party of the whole country. It has the monopoly of the genuine love of country. Because it keeps these ideals uppermost it alone can be trusted with the nation's government.

Or, in the hall across the way: The Democratic party is the party of the common people. Their welfare is its sole desire. Thomas Jefferson and Andrew Jackson wrote its immutable principles across the national firmament. It has ever since been fighting the tyrant and the oppressor, in the name of liberty and

[1]For the contrast between the revolutionary Bills of Rights and the revolutionary constitutions with their suffrage restrictions and disregard of the "great unrepresented masses," see a neat summary in J. B. MacMaster, *The Acquisition of Political, Social, and Industrial Rights of Man in America*, pp. 45, 46. If further testimony is desired, one may take Bryce's thoroughly practical remarks that "the abstract love of liberty has been a comparatively feeble passion," and further that "rebellions and revolutions are primarily made not for the sake of freedom, but in order to get rid of some evil which touches men in a more tender place than their pride."—*Studies in History and Jurisprudence*, Vol. II, pp. 24, 25.

freedom. The threatened welfare of the states is in its keeping. The rights of the states shall never be surrendered. It has the monopoly of the genuine love of country. Because it keeps these ideals uppermost it alone can be trusted with the nation's government.

Of course the party meeting is a fact, and an important fact. Of course the party oratory is part of the party meeting, which is part of the campaign. So are the torches in the parade. They all count toward bringing out the ballots on election day. As such they must not be overlooked.

But when it comes to taking the proclamations of ideas and ideals, word for word, at the values set forth in the speeches, what is the use of discussion? It is a case for laughter.

To rise to a slightly higher level, there is the party platform. When a great fight is on and the platform takes a definite stand squarely on the issue, and is backed up with equal strength by the presidential candidate in his letter of acceptance, the platform means something. It has meaning with reference to a specific piece of legislation, a specific line of policy, or a specific administrative course to which it commits the party. But when it proclaims or asserts or argues in terms of the party ideals or heirloom phrases, it is neglected and negligible.

Everyone who reads the newspapers intelligently prior to and at convention time, and everyone who examines the works of students of party problems, is well aware how these platforms are put together; how on the basis of good old phrases a string of pledges or indorsements is wrought; how the pull or haul of interested persons or factions brings about the compromises on the planks; how the nearer to action the party appears to be, the more carefully the decisions are made in terms of what the interested groups desire and the less pains are taken to adapt the planks even superficially to the old-time verbal tests; how when all is said and done the only thing that counts is the specific pledge on some issue that everybody is sure to watch, and how it never is safe to be too certain that even this will count in the event of party victory. Everybody knows how the government moves along much the same with one or the other party in power, barring only the specific issues, definitely fought over in the election. No one is so rash as to try to show a real change in national tendencies according as one or the other party takes power; much less in state tendencies; not by the wildest dreams in city tendencies.

To take an illustration of a kind most unfavorable for my contention: Does anyone believe that a states'-rights Bryan in the president's chair could have taken any other course in dealing with the nation-wide beef industry when the time for its control had arrived than was taken by a republican? I do not mean that a different course could not conceivably be taken, nor that different men with different backgrounds of representation would not react differently, nor that under a Bryan the day of the issue would have been exacty the same as under a Roosevelt; nor do I mean that a Bryan out of office would not announce a policy opposed to that of a Roosevelt in office. But given the national scope of the industry and of its customers, given also its foreign trade, given the emergency for its control which was bound to come through its own growth and methods, if not in one year then in another, given presidential representation of the mass of the people on approximately the same level, could a states'-rights president have found a different solution from any other president? The answer is most decidely, No.

Or again, can anyone who has examined the transportation business of the United States carefully enough to note its interstate foundations, expect a Bryan states'-rights plan of government domination to have a shadow of a hope for success? The answer is not in dispute. If "states' rights" presents itself as an ideal, its weakness and secondary position and trivial importance at once become apparent. It must yield almost without a struggle.[1]

And then there is the antipathy to a strong executive, which, in this late stage of its history during which it has been a high and

[1] Considering the amount of attention that will be given in Part II to the process of ideals and to ascertaining what is actually meant when ideals are talked about, I do not need to touch on that phase of the subject here, where I am solely concerned with demolishing stuff ideals or ideal things as far as concerns their use as social causes.

dry, thin, bloodless, demand—that is, very peculiarly an idea or ideal—is very instructive. In face of the requirements of government it has almost ceased to pretend to amount to anything. Only as it is pumped full of life by some vigorous specific objection to a particular policy of the executive does it now have even the appearance of meaning.

Let us next take a look at socialism as an ideal. The socialist position can be stated, without attempting to allow for various deviations, about as follows. Present economic conditions are judged evil and are to be discarded. In contrast with them an ideal of a different arrangement of social life can be set up. To realize the ideal force will probably be required, but the way to get the force is by spreading the ideal. Hence propaganda. Missionaries of socialism, themselves led by the ideal, impart the ideal to others, and when enough people hold it they will realize it. The ideal according to such theories is the main thing. It is the true cause. The truth of this reflection of the socialist position may be punctuated by recalling the Marxian position that force has ruled past and still rules present society, but that future socialistic society will be on a new level, an affair of virtue, not of force.

Can this ideal-thing, socialism, accomplish any such work ?

I can hardly hope to carry conviction at this stage for my assertion, but I will say, nevertheless, that it is probable that if every man, woman, and child in the United States was a confirmed, inveterate, dyed-in-the-wool idealistic socialist, the progress of events for the next few years and for the generations to come would be very little different from what it will be as it is. If the president and all members of Congress and all governors and state legislators and all mayors and aldermen and minor officials were socialists, our national evolution would be much what it will be anyway. This is not to say that socialism as a fact is not approaching, nor is it to say that it is; nor is it to deny that our present socialist propagandas have any value in the social process. But it is to say that whatever is to come, the differentiated theory, the socialistic ideal thing, will not produce it, nor will it even necessarily state it adequately in advance.[1]

I can call to witness European governments that contain strong elements of socialism, and contrast them with those that have almost no such elements. I can refer to socialistic cities in fact which are without socialism in theory, and to cities dominated by theoretical socialism which are yet no more socialistic in fact than neighboring cities that are not so dominated. I can appeal to socialistic New Zealand operated by "individualistic" Englishmen who never heed the socialism ideal. There is Switzerland, too, teeming with socialistic forms of organization, but in great part bomb-proof against the propaganda of socialism.[2] And to come nearer home, anyone who likes may see municipal ownership making great strides while the socialists stand aside and jeer, knowing not the meaning of step by step nor yet the mechanics of step after step.

Individualism is another ideal, mighty indeed, to judge by its broadsides. Yet the most rabid, cock-sure, intemperate, proselytizing, philosophical individualist I ever knew had the misfortune to live in Chicago while that city was waging its fight with the traction companies. At first he debated and made many speeches against municipal ownership. But, by-and-by, being the possessor of no traction securities and having lively sympathies with the "down-trodden" whose salvation, of course, lay in individualism, he became a municipal-ownership advocate. Soon he was strenuous in proving that municipal ownership was true individualism. After a while the country had railroad rates to regulate, and beef

[1] The work of socialistic propaganda as a representative activity will be discussed in due time. See especially Part II, chap. xix.

[2] See, for example, Jesse Macy's interesting account of his personal observations in Vol. II of the *American Journal of Sociology*. He contrasts the development of public ownership with the lack of interest in socialism. As to the general character of the Swiss he says their predilection for democratic habits appears only in the mountain cantons, and that there "their democratic ways and so-called democratic virtues were the only obvious means of subsistence." They are "victims of democratic habits." For New Zealand see Cockburn, *Publications of the American Academy of Political and Social Science*, No. 264, quoted at length by Ward, *Pure Sociology*, p. 562.

to inspect, and insurance companies' managers to tie hand and foot to legal stakes, and insurance policy-holders to take under its wing, and my friend was for all these movements. But he was just as great an individualist still.[1] Anyone who admires a prestidigital ideal like that, because of its might in molding the destinies of the world, may continue to admire, but he is invited to stop reading this volume right here. It is useless to go on.

I might say something also about the noisy old anti-ideal—if the term may be used—the bugaboo, paternalism. Two or three years ago it would have been worth while. Today the progress of events has made the task useless. The rout of paternalism from its seat on the tips of tongues and the points of pens is so thoroughly accomplished that it is almost admitted.

There is another ideal which may be touched in all reverence because it has meant so much to those unfortunates who for half a hundred generations have had so much need of it, yet which has been as impotent as any of these others in evolving social life. I mean the ideal of the City of God, of the Kingdom of Heaven on earth. And it is most useful for our purpose because of the many centuries and the manifold favorable circumstances which have been given it in which to show its power. It would be hard, indeed, for eyes not blinded—or glorified, if one will—by the vision, to trace the power of this ideal on Christendom's growth. All too clearly history points to this, that, or the other factor, or set of factors, as responsible for this, that, or the other softening of the brutalities of life, but the ideal does not appear among them, unless sometimes in the courtesy guise of their spokesman.

Is the City of God nearer to us today with our slums and our wars of million armed men against million than it was two thousand years ago, fifteen hundred years ago, a thousand years ago?

---

[1] Letourneau says (*Property*, p. 242): "Is it not always seen in critical times of public danger that the greatest individualists lay claim to the social solidarity at which they turned up their noses in days of peace and prosperity?" Dicey in his *Law and Public Opinion* (p. 301) notes that individualists are very apt indeed to wander into the wrong camp at times. And Simmel (*International Monthly*, Vol. V, p. 104) remarks that many thoroughgoing individualists in Germany are to be found enrolled in the social-democratic party.

Has there been progress toward the City of God from the days of the guilds in the Middle Ages down into our factory régime? Has the economic ideal of the Gospels implanted itself anywhere, even with the slightest visible results? The voice of Tolstoi, lifted as it is for the ideal, speaks all too plain a No. The best the world has to offer is for Tolstoi lost with the worst in the perspective. Best and worst alike must, for him, be born again.

These ideals, whatever else they may be, are, as independent or even semi-independent factors in explaining the social life and the social progress, just nothing at all. At every point, at every moment, in any form in which they may seem to be working, they need themselves more explanation than the phenomena which they are said to be producing. They are "talk," and at that not even talk that goes to the point, but talk at long range, talk that colors, that lights up, that pleases aesthetically, that stimulates, but that for the purposes of close investigation is negligible except as its exact meaning at any given time and place may be definitely established. They do not help us to understand. Rather they obstruct our vision. What trifling meaning they have will appear only when they are seen from beneath where lie the wheels within the wheels. On the surface, taken at their own valuation, they are but illusion.

It seems probable to me that when I enter on detailed criticism of certain typical works in which ideas and ideals are used as interpretative agents, I shall be answered not so much that I am wrong in my objections, as that I am falsely attributing to these writers a meaning for the words idea and ideal, and a process of using them, which they do not intend: that, in other words, I have merely knocked down a straw man of my own setting up.

To make it clear that ideals are actually used by scientific writers in the stuff sense, I desire to give a series of quotations, picked almost at random. None of the mystic philosophers of history of an older generation are on the list and with but a single exception none such of this generation will be found there.

First, John Stuart Mill: In discussing the logic of the moral sciences Mill announces without sufficient analysis and with no proof that the "predominant and almost paramount" element in social progression is the state of speculative faculties of mankind, "including the nature of the beliefs which by any means they have arrived at, concerning themselves and the world by which they are surrounded."[1]   Social existence is only possible by a disciplining of the powerful propensities of human nature, "which consists in subordinating them to a common system of opinions."   Every great social change "has had for its precurser a great change in the opinions and modes of thinking of society."   The order of human progression in all respects "will mainly depend on the order of progression in the intellectual convictions of mankind, that is, on the law of the successive transformation of human opinions." In his *Representative Government* he says, "One person with a belief is a social power equal to ninety-nine who have only inter-ests."[2]   In the *Political Economy*—I have lost the exact reference —he says: "I regard social schemes as one of the most valuable elements of human improvement."   These views are mild indeed in their emphasis of the thing-nature of ideals as compared with some that follow.

Professor W. W. Willoughby, opening a volume on mixed metaphysics and formal political science, says: "Ideals of right constitute the essentially active principles in our social and politi-cal life."[3]

Professor Henry Carter Adams, excusing to himself his own vivid appreciation of some of the most substantial elements of social structure, says: "Individualism is an historic force—and not a formal argument."   Also, "the industrial controversies of our own times are an endeavor so to reconstruct the code of ethics," etc.[4]

Bluntschli says: "The ideological acceptation of Liberty and Equality has filled France with ruins and drenched it with blood."[5]

[1] *A System of Logic*, Book VI, chap. x, sec. 7.   The three following quotations are from the same section.

[2] *Representative Government*, New York, 1873, p. 23.

[3] *Social Justice*, p. 1.

[4] "American Economic Association," *Economic Studies*, Vol. II, pp. 12, 19, 20.

[5] *Theory of the State*, 2d ed., English translation, p. 6.

Professor Richard T. Ely says: "The history of ideas is the history of man. . . . . From time to time, in the history of mankind, an idea of such tremendous import has found acceptance in the minds and hearts of men that it has been followed by a new era in the progress of the human race."[1]

Professor Patten, despite all his materialistic interpretation, keeps his ideas in the form of good substantial soul-stuff—always things, not function. He is able to talk of the "ideas that created the French Revolution"—ideas which came bodily from England, but which were kept "within proper bounds" in that country by "the particular conditions surrounding their origin."[2] Also he is able to say of Adam Smith's system of thought, taken concretely: "But for him the reaction against the new conditions would have been more severe and England might have missed the opportunities for development that had been opened up."[3] Some of the democratic ideals, for example, which Professor Patten finds on hand capable of use in this material way after he has given them a sort of physical origin are, in an older group, justice, liberty, equality, and fraternity; and in a newer group, tendencies toward the referendum, the initiative, and proportional representation, and the living wage, surplus values, progressive taxation, the single tax, and the right to live, to work, and to enjoy the fruits of the earth.[4]

Durkheim, despite all the objectivity of his method, is able to say: "As soon as a fund of representations gets built up, these become partially autonomous realities which live their own peculiar life."[5]

---

[1] *Studies of the Evolution of Industrial Society*, p. 3.

[2] *Development of English Thought*, p. 21.

[3] *Ibid.*, p. 243.

[4] *The Theory of Social Forces*, pp. 139, 140.

[5] Revue de métaphysique et de morale, 1898, p. 299: "La matière première de toute conscience sociale est étroitement en rapport avec le nombre des éléments sociaux, la manière dont ils sont groupés et distribués, etc., c'est à dire, avec la nature du substrat. Mais une fois qu'un premier fond de représentations s'est ainsi constitué, elles deviennent des réalités partiellement autonomes qui vivent d'une vie propre."

Ratzenhofer, despite his struggle theory, is led along by his positive metaphysics to frequent assertions such as: "The fundamental principles of civilization are the civilizing ideas working through social politics,"[1] and the importance he gives to the "Zeitgeist" and other kinds of "Geister" is very great.

Seligman, who has made special study of the materialistic interpretation of history, sets forth as one of the three factors of importance which will dominate our industrial future, "the existence of the democratic ideal,"[2] which is "the flower and fruit of all its forerunners," and he makes the new industrial order depend on the "emergence of a healthy public opinion." This in his *Economics*. In his essay on the "Economic Interpretation of History," we find him allowing for "conditions" on the one side, and for "ideals" on the other, and insisting on the use of both factors in interpretation. Ideals are for him so solid and substantial that he can say, "all progress consists in the attempt to realize the unattainable—the ideal, the morally perfect."[3]

Mackenzie in his *Introduction to Social Philosophy* pictures society as engaged in the realization of certain ideals, with which he is so well acquainted that he is able to list them and talk dogmatically about them. Two of these ideals, the aristocratic and that of individual liberty, society has been engaged with in the past. Just at present society is trying to realize a socialistic ideal, but if it is wise it will quit all three and go in for the organic ideal which is of course the writer's pet. Presumably, unless society learns all about the organic ideal, sets its jaw, and hurries after it, it will never arrive. Mackenzie has no difficulty in talking as follows: "Two of these ideals have already been adopted and to a large extent embodied in the structure of society. . . . . We are now presented with the alternative of adopting one or the other of the two ideals which remain."[4]

---

[1] *Wesen und Zweck der Politik*, Vol. III, pp. 396, 397.

[2] *Principles of Economics*, p. 600.

[3] *The Economic Interpretation of History*, Part II, chap. iii, especially pp. 126 ff.

[4] *Introduction to Social Philosophy*, pp. 431, 432.

An elaborate sociological study of the whole group of ideals of equality has been made by Bouglé who has used the method of Durkheim with inspiration also from Simmel.[1] Bouglé treats these ideals as a social product, and shows, or aims to show, how they appear only at particular times and under particular conditions. Then by comparing cases, he strives to determine the objective factors that condition them, such as the size, homogeneity, complexity, and organization and density of the societies in which they exist. That part of his study, whatever its value, does not concern us here, but rather the fact that it never seems to have occurred to him to try to get these ideals into thoroughgoing functioning with the society. Instead he keeps them segregated in concrete masses. After he has built them up from sociological factors he grants them a very vigorous power of their own (compare the quotation from Durkheim above) and indeed attributes to them the leadership and guidance of modern society. "Equality, as directing and explaining principle, imposes on our states civil, juridical, political, and economic reforms, so it seems to us." "Equality is the soul of the greatest modern revolutions," he says, but he adds that he does not mean unqualifiedly that the ideal has the capacity of modifying social forms at its own sweet will. That is, the ideal has to be built up; it has to work in its environment: but it is nevertheless a "thing" which can be taken concretely and applied as a cause of alterations in society. It is the same old personification or, if the term can be pardoned, thing-ification, of the psychic factors, despite all the objective method of study.

A most exceptionally entertaining specimen of what can be done with ideals is Ludwig Stein's conviction that "the anarchists in three days, given a chance, could destroy what authority has labored three centuries to construct."[2] Side by side with these may be put an illustration of what the ideal theory can accomplish in the way of making the world topsy-turvy. It is W. H. Mallock's interesting remark that "socialistic theories merely cause a

[1] *Les idées égalitaires.* The quotations are from p. 239.

[2] Schmoller's *Jahrbuch für Gesetzgebung, Verwaltung und Volkswirthschaft im deutschen Reich,* Vol. XXVI.

barren and artificial discontent."[1]   A system of interpretation
which can make discontent, whether barren or not, follow a theory
is ripe for a process *de lunatico inquirendo*.   But Dr. E. J. Dil-
lon, the writer on foreign affairs for the *Contemporary Review*,
does almost equally well when in his excitement he assures his
readers that "the Russian movement is a revolt, not merely against
this political system or that, but against all authority whatever."[2]
And I cannot forbear referring to Benjamin Kidd, whose method
of dragging in the "future" as a factor in social interpretation and
whose principle of projected efficiency reduces the idea of ideals
to a brilliant absurdity.[3]

I will only mention in addition two naïve expressions, swelling
up from the heart, which show right on its native soil the stuff out
of which are made all the ideas and ideals the scientists use.   There
is the famous resolution adopted by a mass meeting of the people
of Berlin in 1893 that, "This stupidity must be done away with
that the fellow who hasn't any money and can't find any work
must go hungry in the presence of accumulated stores of provisions."[4]   We may heartily sympathize with the feelings of the
mass meeting, even while we laugh at its expression.   Here, however, is another case in which we may laugh without being troubled
by our sympathies.   When it was proposed to abolish the "party
circle" from the official ballot in Chicago municipal elections,
the Cook County Republican Central Committee seriously considered resolutions declaring "against any and all measures infring-
ing in such radical manner on the rights and freedom of such an
enormous proportion of population as would be affected by the

---

[1] *Aristocracy and Evolution*, p. 368.

[2] *Contemporary Review*, January, 1906, p. 121.

[3] "The controlling center of our evolutionary process in our social history is,
in short, not in the present at all, but in the future," *Principles of Western Civilization*, p. 6.   On the same page he calls this his "new master principle."   On
p. 53 he says he has to do with "a struggle in which efficiency in the future is the
determining quality."   Cf. also pp. 8, 12, 94.

[4] "Die Unvernunft muss aus der Welt geschafft werden, dass wer kein Geld
hat and keine Arbeit findet, angesichts aufgehäuffter Vorräthe von Genussmitteln
verhungern müsse."

proposed change in our electoral system," and further, "that we regard this attempt . . . . as an unwarranted move in restraint of the expression of the public will, and an insulting reflection on the intelligence of an enlightened constituency and a treacherous blow to popular liberty."[1] Funny as this is, it is all of one piece, so far as its place in the process of social life goes, with the noblest ideals to which man ever gave utterance.

Section II. Morgan

An interestingly naïve case of the use of ideas in social interpretation is to be found in Lewis H. Morgan's *Ancient Society*, a work highly valued because of the progress it marked in our knowledge of the structure of primitive communities. Morgan, unfortunately, was not content to set forth his results just as he secured them, but felt called upon to string them together on a set of "ideas," which, existing in individual brains, and passing through an evolution there, were supposed to explain the social doings of the individual.

Perhaps it is going too far to say that the work is strung together on these "ideas," for they are prominent more in appearance than in reality. The "ideas" were inserted now and then when Morgan felt the need of touching up his tale in accordance with the psychology he commonly applied to his own everyday life. In so far they were little passing satisfactions of the writer. They also were appealed to occasionally when his material for direct interpretation of facts in terms of facts gave out. Here they served as stop gaps. It is just because his book is so substantial in its main matter and because its "ideas" are so superficially attached to it, that I have selected it for examination before taking up elaborate theories that rest on "ideas" as causes. It reveals with exceptional simplicity how little value such "ideas" have for the student of society.

It may be observed even in the Table of Contents that the writer was not satisfied to discuss first the growth of inventions and discoveries, next the growth of government, then the growth of the

[1] Chicago daily papers of December 12, 1906.

family, and finally the growth of property. It seemed necessary to him, in place of this matter-of-fact statement, to head his four parts; "Growth of Intelligence through Inventions and Discoveries," "Growth of the Idea of Government," "Growth of the Idea of the Family," and "Growth of the Idea of Property." Such a use of terms, we are all ready to admit, does not help the work, and would hardly appear in any book treating of the development of institutions published today.

In the Introduction we find him saying:

The idea of property has undergone a (similar) growth and development. Commencing at zero in savagery, the passion for the possession of property, as the representative of accumulated subsistence, has now become dominant over the human mind in civilized races.

This is one of the very few cases in which he uses a feeling to explain anything, but even here his context seems to make it mean much the same thing to him as an idea. At any rate this idea or feeling is to him a characteristic, or quality, or possession of the individual mind, which spreads and "grows" and brings about a system of life with which he finds serious fault. Later on he tells us that "when the intelligence of man rises to the height of the great question of the abstract rights of property," then "a modification of the present order of things may be expected."[1]

Morgan studied human achievements and found growth. He studied institutions and found growth. He looked upon the achievements—inventions and discoveries—primarily as ideas; and he looked upon the institutions in the same way. This led him to write:

The facts indicate the gradual formation and subsequent development of certain ideas, passions, and aspirations. Those which hold the most prominent positions may be generalized as growths of the particular ideas with which they severally stand connected. Apart from inventions and discoveries they are the following: I, Subsistence; II, Government; III, Language; IV, The Family; V, Religion; VI, House Life and Architecture; VII, Property.[2] . . . . The principal institutions of mankind have been developed from a few primary germs of thought.[3]

[1] *Ancient Society*, p. 342.   [2] *Ibid.*, p. 4.

[3] *Ibid.*, p. 17. Cf. p. 302: "The substance of human history is bound up in the growth of ideas which are wrought out by the people and expressed in their institutions, usages, inventions, and discoveries."

As an evolutionist he holds that we have "the same brains" that our ancestors had, but practically he thinks those brains are solidified into very different organisms—they have different "ideas" in them.

Some of the excrescences of modern civilization, such as Mormonism, are seen to be relics of the old savagism not yet eradicated from the human brain. We have the same brain, perpetuated by reproduction, which worked in the skulls of barbarians and savages in by-gone ages; and it has come down to us laden and saturated with the thoughts, aspirations, and passions, with which it was busy through the intermediate periods. It is the same brain grown older and larger with the experience of the ages. These outcrops of barbarism are so many revelations of its ancient proclivities. They are explainable as a species of mental atavism.[1]

The "few germs of thought" which explain our institutions "have been guided by a natural logic which formed an essential attribute of the brain itself."[2] Applied to the gens, we are told that it was "the idea of a gens" that developed, and that "it came into being upon three principal conceptions, namely, the bond of kin, a pure lineage through descent in the female line, and non-intermarriage in the gens."[3] Surely such "conceptions" as these regarded as existing before the gens and as being responsible for its appearance must have stretched our forefathers' reasoning power very materially. Except in degree they are, however, not worse than any other stuff ideas used as causes.

A little later we find him discussing a tribe which "had not advanced far enough in a knowledge of government to develop the idea of a chief executive magistrate."[4] It is no wonder. We have plenty of chief executive magistrates in this world, but all the political scientists put together have not managed to work out a lucid, coherent "idea" of that official even yet. Montesquieu thought he had it, and our forefathers thought they had it when they drafted our American federal Constitution. And every day's

[1] *Ibid.*, p. 61. Cf. also p. 255, where the "few primary germs of thought" are represented as "working upon primary human necessities" to produce vast results.

[2] *Ibid.*, p. 61. Cf. also p. 266, where a similar phrase reappears.

[3] *Ibid.*, p. 69.   [4] *Ibid.*, p. 119.

telegrams in the newspapers may be said to prove conclusively how wrong they all were.

Proceeding, Morgan takes up the development of the locality unit of government as the successor of the clan unit. He discusses the conditions under which it appeared,[1] but in this he regards himself as merely indicating the background. Greek and Roman brain was necessary for it and was its real cause. "Anterior to experience, a township, as the unit of a political system, was abstruse enough to tax the Greeks and Romans to the depths of their capacities before the conception was formed and set in practical operation."[2] Also of the same development he says that "such a change would become possible only through a conviction that the gens could not be made to yield such a form of government as their advanced condition demanded."[3] This last sentence has a meaning which is fairly well defined, if we take it to sum up in loose words the general tendency of the times. Taken as an explanation of what happened, rather than as a cursory description, its meaninglessness is at once apparent.

Morgan also regards the transition from his consanguine to his punaluan family as "produced by the gradual exclusion of own brothers and sisters from the marriage relation, the evils of which could not forever escape human observation,"[4] this being a case of his use of the "idea," not for self-satisfaction but for the covering up of ignorance as to causes. It is clear he cannot prove that such an idea existed, and equally clear that it is nothing more than the application of his own opinion of the meaning of the change to the minds of the actors. The same explanation is repeated thus: "It is a fair inference that the punaluan custom worked its way into general adoption through a discovery of its beneficial influence."[5] This assertion, it may be added, is almost his only argument in proof of the existence of such a family, beyond his sweeping inference from his "Turanian system of consanguinity." Again we find him indicating what might have happened

[1] *Ancient Society*, pp. 268, 311, 338, 339, 360, 361.

[2] *Ibid.*, p. 218.   [4] *Ibid.*, p. 424.

[3] *Ibid.*, p. 322.   [5] *Ibid.*, 503.

in Rome "had the Roman people wished to create a democratic state."[1] Also in connection with the patricians of Rome, he discusses "the two classes of citizens thus deliberately and unnecessarily created by affirmative legislation."[2]

These illustrations have had to do with Morgan's use of the growth of specific ideas in his explanations. A few quotations may be added to show his use of an expanding intellectual faculty or capacity. He speaks of the "feebleness of the power of abstract reasoning"[3] in early society. Talking of confederacies of Indian tribes, he says: "Wherever a confederacy was formed it would of itself evince the superior intelligence of the people,"[4] a peculiarly felicitous phrase, for our purposes, as indicating clearly the kind of material out of which the alleged "superior intelligence" in sociological theory is made. Again: "As the confederacy was the ultimate stage of organization among the American aborigines its existence would be expected in the most intelligent tribes only."[5] Proofs of the existence of such intelligence apart from the very facts the intelligence is summoned to explain, are, of course, not given, for the excellent reason that they cannot be given, any more here than elsewhere. Again: "An assembly of the people (Greece), with the right to adopt or reject public measures, would evince an amount of progress in intelligence and knowledge beyond the Iroquois."[6] These illustrations are sufficient for our purpose.

If I simply wanted to contend that these ideas and capacities were wrong in their particular uses, it would be foolish and wasteful of time to list them in this way. Instead of that, my purpose is, as already indicated, to show how utterly mistaken any such use of similar elements in interpretation is. What do all these explanations add to our comprehension of the evolution Morgan is discussing? I think any impartial reader will answer, Nothing. Some of them clearly are made to order to fit the facts. Others are bare reflections of the facts in generalized, or "psychic," terms. Others again can hardly be characterized as anything

[1] Ibid., p. 336.
[2] Ibid., p. 339.
[3] Ibid., p. 41.
[4] Ibid., p. 123.
[5] Ibid., p. 126.
[6] Ibid., p. 245.

more than circumlocutions, as, for example, when "the idea of property" is used instead of simple "property."

Morgan's real contributions to our knowledge of ancient society are of an entirely different nature. He worked out the main characteristics of the clan as a social organization, and first identified the Greek and Roman gens with the American Indian clan. He analyzed the nature of the transition from tribally organized to territorially organized societies. He called attention to the connection between property and tribal evolution on the one hand, and between property and marriage evolution on the other hand. He made the first great study of systems of consanguinity. He studied social evolution in terms of technical achievements and of the utilization of the physical environment. He gave a prominent place to such factors as the "commingling of diverse stocks, superiority of subsistence, and advantage of position."[1] Such investigations as these have entitled him to front rank among American investigators of society. But what of his "ideas" and other psychic qualities and faculties? They are long since forgotten because they are utterly useless. Only when he could not lay his hands on substantial factors for his interpretations, or when perchance he wished to nail down his conclusions upon the individual man as he conceived him to be, did he have recourse to them.[2]

As with Morgan so is it with every other writer who uses such factors; only, it is rare in good scientific work that the naïvety of the procedure is so manifest.

SECTION III. GIDDINGS

Professor Franklin H. Giddings has done much careful work in the interpretation of society on what he calls the "objective"

[1] *Ancient Society*, p. 39.

[2] It is not improbable that Morgan's reliance on "ideas" and conceptions in times of difficulty helped to seduce him into building up his fictitious consanguine and punaluan families out of systems of consanguinity. If this is true it adds force to the preceding criticism, for it makes very clear indeed the lurking peril of such factors. The errors he fell into here have called upon his head whole volumes of sarcastic criticisms, which have blinded many eyes to the splendid achievements he secured when dealing directly and unwaveringly with facts.

side—that is in terms of physical and vital facts introduced into sociology as such. He holds, however, that in our own noble times the objective process has become subordinated—though of course still underlying everything—and that now society subjectively decides what it wants itself to be and sets forth to accomplish its aim. He does not confine himself to generalities about the social will, but endeavors to locate these predominant factors of present-day social causation in certain ideals which he thinks he detects controlling our social life.

Ideals for Giddings are ideas touched up with emotion—the exact definition is utterly indifferent for our purpose. The great ideals which, in the latest presentation of his theory, he finds dominant—I merely mention them now to indicate what he means —are unity, liberty, and equality. They are stratified on top of one another in that order.

We are not now concerned with his "objective" interpretation of society. Neither are we concerned with his "objective" interpretation of the ideals themselves in terms of the character of the environment and the composition of the population. The thing that does concern us is that these ideals, once formed, are for him exceedingly concrete positive things, which can be precisely designated by the words used to name them—such as the three given above—and which operate directly and by their own force on social action, thereby producing social institutions.

It is our problem now to see whether he actually shows that these ideals have any such claim to independent operation. I shall quote a series of passages from his works, giving them in chronological order to show his development. In all of them the background of the objective process must be assumed. That does not explain away the "thing-ness" of the ideals; it rather serves to emphasize it.

"A community continually endeavors to perfect its type in accordance with the prevailing conception of an ideal good."[1] This position furnishes the basis for Giddings' "first law of social choices," in which he arranges the series of ideal goods that have

[1] *Principles of Sociology*, 1896, pp. 407, 408.

been influential, as (1) those of personal force; (2) utilitarian ideals; (3) integrity, and (4) self-realization.

For the conservation and perfection of social relations and for the realization of ideals, the social mind creates institutions.[1]

The third stage of civic evolution brings with it as a characteristic product an influence that counteracts the dangers which have been described, and offers to the community an assurance of continued stability and progress. That influence is a growing ethical spirit, and the formation of the highest mode of like-mindedness, namely the ethical.[2]

It is the rational-ethical consciousness that maintains social cohesion in a progressive democracy.[3]

Civilization we found to be a product of the passion for homogeneity, and its policies to be expressions of that passion.[4]

The individualities of nations are a product of their ideals rather than of their institutions.[5]

The creation of ideals is one of the highest activities of the human mind.[6]

When the conditions favorable to rational social choice exist the choice itself is determined by the scale of social values.[7]

The social values in his scale are made to correspond to four types of character which Giddings sets up, the forceful, the convivial, the austere, and the rationally conscientious. These types correspond with the four varieties of influential ideals mentioned in connection with the quotation above from the *Principles of Sociology*. It may be noted in passing that the only way Giddings is able to indicate how these types of character may be studied is through analysis of the very social facts they are set up to explain.[8] The significance of this state of affairs is evident.

The most immediate stimuli and the most important of modern social life are products of past responses to yet earlier stimuli. . . . . Of all the stimuli that move men to mighty and glorious co-operation none can be compared

[1] *The Theory of Socialization*, 1897, p. 33.

[2] *Elements of Sociology*, 1898, p. 320.

[3] *Ibid.*, p. 321.

[4] *Ibid.*, p. 347. See also p. 283.

[5] *Democracy and Empire*, 1900, pp. 315, 316.

[6] *Ibid.*, p. 339.

[7] *Inductive Sociology*, 1901, p. 177.

[8] *Ibid.*, p. 84.

with a great ideal. The ideals of liberty, of freedom, and of enlightenment lift men today in gigantic waves of collective effort like resistless tides of the sea.[1]

The Declaration of Independence was an ideal and nothing more. The federal Constitution was a stupendous ideal.[2]

Again, placing ideals at the top of a series of which the lower terms are danger, menace, bribes, and the strong personality, he says: "These new and higher stimuli are ideals and it is these that presently become a factor of chief importance in the higher forms of social causation."[3]

Following an explanation that "social ideals arise in the minds of exceptional individuals," are communicated to others, and spread until they are generally accepted, he says that they "have the power to call forth persistent effort to transform the external order of things into a realization of the ideal."[4]

A number of passages have to do with the possibility of organizing men by great ideals, when nothing else will serve to bind them together, and he even convinces himself that while democracy is normally not possible for a heterogeneous population, it can be made possible "if there is a practically universal belief in the superiority of democratic forms"[5]—which is a most perfect example of begging the question.

It is after this progress has been made that Giddings, abandoning at least for immediate use his earlier series of ideals, sets up the series of three ideals, which he believes have dominated the history of developed society—the three ideals mentioned at the beginning of this section—unity, liberty, and equality.[6] He shows how first it was necessary to bind the society together, and how the people knew this, and how they thereupon decided that unity was their greatest need, and made this their ideal, and with a view to achieving it took various and sundry measures. By-and-by they discovered that they had been too successful by half, that they had got more unity than they needed, and so they set their

[1] *The Theory of Social Causation*, "Publications of the American Economic Association," Series III, Vol. V, No. 2, 1904, p. 149.

[2] *Ibid.*, p. 149. [4] *Ibid.*, p. 164. [6] *Ibid.*, pp. 164–70.

[3] *Ibid.*, p. 163. [5] *Ibid.*, p. 168.

brains at work under high pressure and hit upon liberty as a better
ideal to chase.   All things social thereupon had to be molded on
the pattern of liberty, till liberty got too irritating, in fact, whereupon another mental commotion produced Minerva-like the ideal of
equality, which nowadays everybody who is not hopelessly anti-
quated is pursuing just as hard and fast as he can.   Professor
Giddings does not write so irreverently about his ideals, of course,
but I am positive I am doing him no essential injustice, in stating
the theory in that way.   One or two later quotations remain to be
given.   In presenting a series of eight forms of social organization
he says:

> Society of the eighth type exists where a population collectively responds
> to certain great ideals that, by united efforts, it strives to realize.   Compre-
> hension of mind by mind, confidence, fidelity; and an altruistic spirit of social
> service are the social bonds.   The social type is the Idealistic.[1]

In a discussion of sovereignty, Professor Giddings sets forth
four well-defined modes of sovereignty, four well-defined modes
of government, and four well-defined "groups of theories or tendencies of speculation on the nature and scope of government."
He says:

> I am concerned only to point out certain conditions under which men do
> as a matter of fact make such assumptions as those which the great political
> theorists have made and do in fact institute one or another of the forms of
> government here described in approximate accordance with their theoretical
> assumptions.[2]

From the same article the following sentences also are worth
quoting:

> Next to theories of religious obligation theories of the rightful forms of
> government and of the rightful scope of governmental power have most pro-
> foundly affected human feeling. . . . . To the extent that these theories are
> formulas of feeling rather than of speculation there is a certain presumption
> that they are true products and expressions of some great collective need.[3]

In Hobbes, Locke, and Rousseau, Giddings finds three well-
known theories to go with three of his four modes of sovereignty

---

[1] *American Journal of Sociology*, Vol. X (1904), p. 169.

[2] *Political Science Quarterly*, March, 1906, p. 21.

[3] *Ibid.*, p. 3.

and modes of government, but for the fourth theory he is compelled to drag up from an obscurity, which he himself admits, Thomas Paine's *The Rights of Man*. This he puts at the basis of the American type of government as we had it in our first century of history. Surely this is forcing things a good deal in the hunt for ideal causes. And one may properly ask why is it if the three great ideals, unity, liberty, and equality, are actually dominating history, that four forms of government are discoverable; for surely in government those three great ideals would make themselves most vividly and characteristically felt. But that is incidental.

Now with regard to this whole theoretical position, if Giddings were merely indulging in enthusiastic talk, or in some form of propaganda or appeal to the emotions, one would have no reasonable criticism to bring against him because of his choice of language; that would be his affair. But it is scientific work he is busying himself with.

If he were merely using his ideals to indicate general tendencies of social development one could, again, accept them providing one thought they fairly reflected the tendencies. But it is a theory of social causation which·he is setting forth, and his ideals are definite, concrete factors in society which can be discovered all by themselves, and when discovered can be used to explain social activities and social institutions.

Here it is necessary to hold the man who uses them to strict account. It is necessary to make him establish his causes, either by holding them up to the light by themselves, apart from the things they explain, or, if they are frankly put forth as hypothetical, after the fashion of the once-flourishing chemical atom, by working them through clearly and cleanly in typical cases to which they are applicable.

Now how does Giddings get his ideals? That is the first question we must face. Unless I am completely blind to the truth, he gets them in one of two ways. Either (1) he takes them up as a sort of essence or general characteristic or tendency of the very facts which they are used to explain, or else (2) he gets them from the talk of the people, from their professions of faith, from their own explanations and defense of what they are doing and in general from their system of conversation.

It is not of necessity the case that there will be any identity between results secured in these two different ways. That would be something to prove, not to assume. If the latter way was frankly followed, then it is not of necessity true that the talk and conversation relied on is what it purports to be; we have no way of knowing in advance that it, so to speak, correctly states itself. That again would be something to prove, not to assume. But passing these difficulties for the moment, and confining our attention to the series of ideals, unity, liberty, equality, let us try to see whether, if speech habits are the source from which they are gathered, they are actually to be found there in the way it would be necessary to find them to justify Giddings' use of them.

Unity, to begin with, has rarely, if ever, been a national passion or enthusiasm. Mind, I do not mean that great nationalizing movements are not found. I mean one does not actually find the unity ideal as Giddings himself describes it, where literally "the passion to make all men within the community more alike begins to be consciously felt and to make itself a power," where literally "the passion for homogeneity seizes upon the whole population."[1] Liberty, no doubt, has been such a passion—it has turned the dictionaries loose in floods—at the time of social action to which it is made to correspond. Equality has also been such a passion, but unfortunately it has been a passion linked with that of liberty, at periods when the tendencies were toward liberty facts (assuming the general correctness of Giddings' analysis), instead of toward equality facts. The future according to Giddings must belong to equality, but it would be very difficult indeed to find any impassioned adoration of equality in and for itself, among the peoples who are making the forward march in that direction.

Where then does Giddings stand? So far as he is giving us general tendency of fact under the name of an ideal, he is not frank about it and he is confusing us. So far as he is using the people's adorations as his source of ideals the adorations do not square at

[1] *American Economic Association*, III, Vol. V, No. 2, pp. 165, 166.

all with the system, either at the beginning or at the end, while in the middle there is confusion. Besides that there is no test of them to see if they really are just what they pretend to be.

How can one take this seriously for social causation?

How can one be satisfied with a theory that comes down hard on the federal Constitution as primarily a great national ideal, in the very face of the struggles and quarrels of the constitutional convention for the maintenance of pressing social interests?

How can one have confidence in the ideal as such a cause when he knows that in all established social creed organizations, a formal adherence is all that is demanded, and this the more inevitably the larger and stronger the organization becomes?

I cannot see.

I will very frankly admit that when an investigator starts out with dead external factors in his interpretation, when he is "objective" to the limit on one side of his work, he will inevitably reach a point, if he is honest with himself, when the "objective" will be recognized by him as not sufficing, when he will be compelled to set up something more "human," something "subjective" to carry his interpretation farther forward.[1] But that is primarily a defect of the hard objectivity with which the start has been made; and whether it is a defect or not—I pass that question here—it will be no excuse for setting up arbitrary, artificial, unreal subjective factors at the upper end of the interpretation. Suppose something is needed to offset the objective interpretation: it will have to be something real, something that will stand a test of examination, something that can be frank about its origin, and definite in its operation. Professor Giddings' ideals answer none of these requirements. They must be shown the door forthwith.

His ideals, even if given the benefit of being hypothetical causes, cannot for an instant be compared with the atoms in the older chemistry. Rather they are color flashes on the surface of the materials with which the student of society must deal. They are

---

[1] Cf. *Elements of Sociology*, p. 350: "Society is not a purely mechanical product of physical evolution. To a great extent it is an intended product of psychological evolution."

mere surface forms or appearances, better, if the issue is sharply drawn, to forget than to attempt to manipulate in social interpretation.

The people believe that the king's touch cures disease. Shall we base pathology on the belief in the touch?

Mumbo-Jumbo keeps order in the African village. Shall we found a theory of the state on the small boy's and the woman's fear of the monster?

The rain-maker makes his magic. The rain falls. The people lie prone in admiration of the supernatural power. Have we here the foundation of meteorology?

The ideals must count. There is no doubt about it. They are involved in the social fact. But they must be properly stated at their real value, not at their own allegation as to that value. They must count for just what they are—now this, now that, now the other thing. They must count honestly. The sociological witchcraft must be abandoned.

Section IV. Dicey

For the purpose of testing the value of the theory of ideas in social interpretation, I know of no work more instructive than the recent lectures on the relation between law and public opinion in England by the distinguished Oxford lawyer and publicist, Albert Venn Dicey.[1] Certainly one could not approach the theory on ground more favorable to it. The author is, to start with, an authority of the highest rank on the material which he is discussing, namely the laws of England. Next, he is sincerely convinced that ideas govern history. Finally he has made it deliberately his special study to discover the variety of ideas—here legislative public opinion—which govern the law-making of England, and to trace the process through all its stages.

I shall attempt to show that Dicey himself does not succeed in establishing clearly what these ideas are, that he produces no proof that they have causal working except by citing certain imperfect,

[1] A. V. Dicey, *Lectures on the Relation between Law and Public Opinion in England during the Nineteenth Century*, London, 1905.

inconclusive, and indeed almost irrelevant sequences of events, that his very statements about the ideas are full of inconsistencies even when most courteously examined, and finally that the trouble lies not in Dicey's imperfect investigation, but in his insoluble problem.

I have no quarrel with the three periods of English law-making which Dicey finds in the last century: the first a period of comparative quiescence; the second of law-making which can fairly well be denoted by the term individualistic; the third of law-making which can fairly well be called collectivistic. It would, of course, be absurd for me to criticize in this field without a vastly more detailed knowledge of the material than I possess. I can assume that the laws do group themselves in these three groups, concretely. This is not to admit that the terms used for the last two periods, with all their varied implications, are the best terms, nor that the analysis has been pushed as deep as is desirable, but simply to accept the three groups concretely, while pursuing the inquiry as to whether Dicey has produced idea systems as a matter of fact, to correspond.

I wish to make the further preliminary remark that to anyone who is thinking solely of the substance of Dicey's grouping of the laws, the passages I shall quote for attack will open against me a charge of verbal quibbling. Such a charge will not be justified for two reasons: first, that it is the causal operation of the ideas that I am investigating; and second, that it is this very causal relation that Dicey sets before us as his fundamental thesis.

Dicey holds that in England in the nineteenth century public opinion has been the great force in producing the laws. He does not mean by this merely that the laws have been the laws the "people" or their delegated rulers wanted; but that a systematic theory, a definite type of thought, has been behind the laws and that as it has changed the character of the laws has changed. It is not public opinion in general, but "legislative public opinion" that has thus prevailed. This legislative public opinion is in a way a branch of general public opinion, i. e., the general thought-system of the times, and in a way also it is influenced by "circumstances." It will be impossible fairly to represent the shadings of his theory without copious quotations.

He begins by declaring that English law is "the work of permanent currents of opinion."[1] The absence of legislation as well as legislation itself may depend on such "varying currents of public opinion."[2] It is not always and everywhere that such public opinion governs. It has not been true of England in earlier centuries. It is not true in nearly so great a degree of either France or the United States as of England. The theory is deliberately confined to England in the nineteenth century.[3] In some countries no opinion proper with regard to change of laws may exist. That is where custom rules; habits, not thoughts are dominant. In other countries the opinion which does exist may not be public opinion: it is the opinion of a small number of people or even of a single individual. In still others there may be lack of a legislative organ which adequately responds to the sentiment of the age; the United States congress is, he thinks, defective in this respect.[4]

Then he gives us a little touch of psychological apology in meeting the objection that it is "interest," not opinion, that governs. Opinion, he retorts, quoting Hume, always governs interest. The citizens of England are not "reckless, governed by mere interest;" they are not "recklessly selfish;" they look out for their neighbors and for their state as well as for themselves. When they seem to be pursuing purely selfish ends, "the explanation of this conduct will be found nine times out of ten to be that men come easily to believe that arrangements agreeable to themselves are beneficial to others."[5] Opinion is master over "callous selfishness." It is not "exceptional selfishness" but some "intellectual delusion unconsciously created through the bias of sinister interest" that makes men go wrong. So heroic an adherence does he give to this proposition that he is able to say of the slavery struggle in the United States:

The faith in slavery was a delusion: but a delusion, however largely the result of self-interest, is still an intellectual error, and a different thing from

[1] Dicey, *op. cit.*, Preface, p. vii.   [3] *Ibid.*, pp. 1, 8.   [5] *Ibid.*, p. 14.
[2] *Ibid.*, p. 1.   [4] *Ibid.*, pp. 3, 9.

callous selfishness. It is at any rate an opinion. In the case therefore, of the southerners who resisted the passing of any law for the abolition of slavery, as in all similar instances, we are justified in saying that it is at bottom opinion which controls legislation.[1]

The weakness of this justification of the proposition that opinion governs the world will at once be apparent. Because one has an antipathy to "callous-selfishness" theories, that is no justification for setting up idea theories. Because self-seeking seems inevitably callous and reckless, and so unpleasant, that is no proof of the power of ideas. Dicey's attitude is like that of the self-styled individualist, who, when driven into some practical corner where theory fails to square with fact, cries out in agony: "But what else can I be ? I can't be a socialist," utterly oblivious to the fact that plain common-sense is a good substitute for both. "I can't be so selfish," says Dicey. "I must stand firm for ideas."[2]

Coming to closer quarters with this legislative public opinion, the first definition of it we get is that it is "merely a short way of describing the belief or conviction prevalent in a given society that particular laws are beneficial and therefore ought to be maintained, or that they are harmful and therefore ought to be modified or repealed."[3] This is exceedingly vague. It might be taken to mean opinion on each law for itself without regard to any others. But really it means much more than this. A sentence or two later it becomes "the speculative views held by the mass of the people as to the alteration or improvement of their institutions." Again it becomes the opinion "held by the majority of those citizens who at a given moment have taken an effective part in public life."[4]

It is, as has been said, "law-making or legislative public opinion"[5] which counts, and of this only the moderate forms, not the extreme or radical forms. "Moderate, though it may be inconsistent, individualism" and "moderate, though it may be inconsistent, socialism"[6] alone count. In passing he remarks that this

[1] *Ibid.*, p. 16.

[2] Cf. *ibid.*, p. 35: "The conduct of a whole nation is governed by something better than sordid views of self-interest;" also p. 493, where "public opinion" is contrasted with "the selfishness or recklessness of politicians."

[3] *Ibid.*, p. 3.   [4] *Ibid.*, p. 10.   [5] *Ibid.*, p. 17.   [6] *Ibid.*, p. 18.

public opinion "is recorded either in the statute book or in the volumes of the reports,"[1] a form of statement which will frequently recur, and which puts the knife at the very roots of his whole theory, because if it is ultimately to the statutes that one must turn to prove the opinion, then the opinion is dangerously near to a gratuitous element in the interpretation, which had better be omitted altogether.

Dicey proceeds to ask several questions about this "body of beliefs, convictions, sentiments, accepted principles, or firmly rooted prejudices,"[2] which together make up public opinion, about its existence, origin, continuity, and checks. The whole body, he tells us, may generally be traced to "certain fundamental assumptions."[3] There are "tides of opinion" that swell till some other tides cross them and check them. Their origin is most often "with some single thinker or school of thinkers." In the ordinary course of events a man of originality or genius has a great idea.[4] He preaches it to his friends and disciples. These soon form a school. The school propagates the creed till it is generally accepted or till some person of eminence, such as a powerful statesman, takes it up—and there you are. The laws result.

Dicey does not, however, maintain that mere argument will bring this about nor will intuitive good sense. There must, he says, be "favorable conditions."[5] But notice how he speaks of these conditions, looking out upon them from the standpoint of the dominating ideas. He calls them "external circumstances, one might almost say accidental conditions." He is talking here of the repeal of the corn laws. The "opinion" was Adam Smith's to start with. These mere incidental circumstances gave it a chance to make itself effective, but all the time "harmony with the disbelief in the benefits of state intervention weighed above every other consideration." And a moment later we have him, in talking of slavery, say that the slave-owners' "honest belief" was "the

---

[1] Dicey, *op. cit.*, p. 17.   [3] *Ibid.*, p. 20.

[2] *Ibid.*, p. 19.   [4] *Ibid.*, pp. 21, 22.

[5] *Ibid.*, pp. 23–27; cf. also p. 111: "Men's beliefs are in the main the result of circumstances, rather than of arguments."

result, not of argument, not even of direct self-interest, but of circumstances."

Already, therefore, we have inextricable confusion: first thought harmonies are in the saddle; next external circumstances: there is no peace for the theory.

This public opinion undergoes a slow development, and often it is a generation ahead of legislation. The young theorists of one generation become the elderly law-makers of the next. There may rarely be a sudden alteration in the laws, never in public opinion.[1]

Cross-currents and counter-currents of opinion must be reckoned with, the latter, when surviving ideas of the last generation or coming ideas of the next, have some fighting power; the former, when currents of thought, "in a measure independent," fight against the prevailing ideas. The cross-currents "arise often, if not always, from the peculiar position or prepossessions of particular classes," such as the clergy, the army, or the artisans.[2] He would not listen for an instant to a suggestion that these classes might have had similar "opinion" to other members of the society of their time, but were urging different laws because of their class interests. All must be transferred into "opinion."

We must also take account of his admission that while laws are made by opinion, they in turn help to create opinion, and the following quotation is good for both phases: "Every law or rule of conduct must, whether its author perceives the fact or not, lay down, or rest upon, some general principle, and must, therefore, if it succeeds in attaining its end, commend this principle to public attention or imitation, and thus affect legislative opinion."[3] Also, the influence of law on opinion "is merely one example of the way in which the development of political ideas is influenced by their connection with political facts. Of such facts laws are among the most important; they are therefore the cause, at least, as much as the effect, of legislative opinion."[4] One might turn this last sentence back on him as indicating that he gave up 50 per cent.

[1] *Ibid.*, pp. 27–31.   [3] *Ibid.*, p. 41.
[2] *Ibid.*, pp. 36–40.   [4] *Ibid.*, p. 46.

at least of his theory when he wrote it, but no matter. We can take it for what he means it, as placing laws themselves as merely one more of the external circumstances which influence opinion, the all-powerful.

With so much of preliminary explanation Dicey enters upon his interpretation of the century's law-making. He distinguishes the following periods:

1. The Period of Old Toryism, or Quiescence (1800–30).
2. The Period of Benthamism, or Individualism (1825–70).
3. The Period of Collectivism (1865–1900).

During each of these periods, he says, "a different current or stream of opinion was predominant and in the main governed the development of the law of England."[1]

In the first period pride in the constitution manifested itself, and a reaction against Jacobinism: inertia ruled Parliament, and there was "no theory of legislation."

The second period, that of utilitarian reform, reveals "a definite body of doctrine," directly applied to the reform of the law.

With the third period Dicey has more difficulty, even while trying to outline it roughly. The school of opinion predominant is called socialism, and it "favors intervention of the state even at some sacrifice of individual freedom, for the purpose of conferring benefit upon the mass of the people."[2] Now despite his previous explanation of the manner in which ideas arise and spread, he is forced to admit that he cannot connect this socialism with any one man, nor "even with the name of any definite school."   In England indeed, it "has never been formulated by any thinker endowed with anything like the commanding ability or authority of Bentham." It has been "rather a sentiment than a doctrine," and "rather an economic and a social than a legal creed." "Even now," he repeats, "it is rather a sentiment than a doctrine."[3]

From this follows what Dicey calls a "curious fact," and what is indeed most curious if there is any truth at all in his theory, the fact, namely, that although the inquirer "can explain changes in English law by referring them to the definite and known tenets and

[1] Dicey, *op. cit.*, p. 62.   [2] *Ibid.*, p. 64.   [3] *Ibid.*, p. 66.

ideas of Benthamite liberalism, he can on the other hand prove the existence of collectivist ideas in the main only by showing the socialistic character or tendencies of certain parliamentary enactments."[1]

Think of it. Dicey is going to explain to us the course of legislation by the legislative public opinion behind it, and here the minute he tries to apply his theory he is forced to confess that for one of three periods the only way you can make sure of the opinion is by inferring it from the laws, while for another of the three periods (the first), not "a theory of legislation," but "no theory" has been the prevailing factor.

To my mind this is so significant that it overturns Dicey's whole theory without more ado. Inasmuch as I want to be perfectly fair to Dicey and make the case against him from the whole of his book, not from single passages, I shall carry the analysis through to the end. But first there is one more unhappy admission on the same page with the one I have just criticized, the admission, namely, that in the transition period between individualism and collectivism he finds lines of Benthamite acts "under an almost unconscious [sic] change in legislative opinion," taking "a turn in the direction of socialism." Here he strikes a blow not merely at his three types of opinion, but at his three types of laws themselves.

Now if we examine his separate discussion of the period of quiescence, or period of "no theory of legislation"—which according to his principles should be stated rather as a period of a "theory of no legislation"—we find him giving illustrations of certain kinds of changes the laws underwent in that period, which he attributes in part (1) to reactionism, and in part (2) to "the irresistible requirements of the day," or to the "humanitarianism which from 1800 onward exerted an ever-increasing influence."[2] One would think that "irresistible requirements" made a pretty sound explanation all by themselves if properly analyzed and studied, but Dicey still regards them as incidental and external, operating only in the absence of a "theory of legislation."

[1] *Ibid.*, p. 68.　　　　[2] *Ibid.*, p. 94.

The factory legislation of the times, he tells us, "was suggested not by any general principle but by the needs of the moment."[1] That this same factory legislation holds its place as a forerunner of other laws through the two later periods does not suggest to Dicey either that he should bring the "theory" back to it, or carry its "needs of the moment" forward to later times.

The combination acts were due to (1) a dread of combinations and (2) a tradition of paternal government, which had two sides, the first setting up the duty of the laborer to work for customary wages, and the second demanding a provision by the state of sub- sistence for those out of work.[2] These factors he calls "elements of the public opinion in 1800," but they are not public opinion in that broader sense he uses to explain his great periods. They are much too specific in their nature for that, and the use of the word "paternalism" does not help out. Certain "selfish" group demands of the people are all too clearly apparent in these "ele- ments."

Humanitarianism, as preached at the time, is used to explain the abolition of the whipping-post for women, of the pillory, of spring guns, of state lotteries, and of the slave trade.[3] Humani- tarianism is defined as "that hatred of pain, either physical or moral, which inspires the desire to abolish all patent forms of suffering and oppression." This comes nearer to an "opinion" cause than the other illustrations, but Dicey, except for mentioning the names of some of the preachers of this humanitarianism, does not attempt to show how the preaching actually did the work; he offers nothing to meet the objection that the preaching may have been merely the verbal embodiment of the movement that was doing the work, and he does not consider in the slightest degree the question as to why only a few selected "forms of suffering or oppression" were eliminated and not a lot of others, riotously "patent" then, and just as "patent" still.

Reaching the end of this period, Dicey thinks that "the English people had at last come to perceive the incongruity between rapidly changing social conditions and the practical unchangeableness of

---

[1] Dicey, *op. cit.*, p. 108.   [2] *Ibid.*, p. 100.   [3] *Ibid.*, p. 106.

the law."[1] The implications of this sentence are hard for his system of interpretation, and still more so is his list of transitional factors: (1) the rapid change in social conditions; (2) the increasing unsuitability of unchanging institutions; (3) the fact that lapse of time had obliterated the memories of the French Revolution,[2] and, finally, (4) the existence of the Benthamite school. Here the "legislative public opinion" makes a poor fourth in a list of causes.

While touching on such "external" causes it is worth noting that he in fact explains the reform bill as due to the shifting of the "population, wealth, power, and trade,"[3] toward the north of England. That leaves Benthamism high and dry, but Dicey, addicted to his opiate, the ideas, does not recognize it. He, of course, is compelled directly or indirectly to bring in just such factors for every concrete piece of interpretation he offers that is definite enough to have value or even meaning.

Now we come to the second period, the period of individualism, where Dicey has the easiest ground for the application of his method. We may accept his assertion that "from 1832 onward the supremacy of individualism among the classes then capable of influencing legislation was for many years incontestable and patent."[4] We may accept also his description of the legislation of the time as in fact individualistic. Does he show a causal connection?

The Benthamism that is in question is "the Benthamism of

[1] *Ibid.*, p. 111.

[2] Dicey tells us (p. 123) that in the ordinary course of things the law of England would have been amended before the end of the eighteenth century. Apparently, then, the process of amendment would not have had to wait for Benthamism which is offered to us as the cause of the change. It may perhaps be that the long damming up of law amendment by the indirect influence of the Revolution was the cause of the ultimate violent efflorescence of Benthamist individualism with all its specious claim to wield the thunderbolt and guide the chariot. If so—I make the suggestion without emphasis—many of the idealistic interpretations of society in the middle of last century are due to that ultimate cause, and the very fallacies and superficialities of Dicey's own method of interpretation must be traced back to it. Needless to say, none of these theories, nor Dicey's own, can have any measurable influence as such on the actual course of legislation. They show their detached extravagance all too plainly.

[3] *Ibid.*, p. 116.   [4] *Ibid.*, p. 176.

common-sense." "This liberalism was the utilitarianism, not of the study, but of the House of Commons or of the stock exchange."[1] It "was not in reality the monopoly of Liberals."[2] The men who guided legislation "were all at bottom individualists,"[3] even when some of them were not avowed Benthamists, or would even have repudiated the individualist fellowship. "Utilitarian individualism . . . . was nothing but Benthamism modified by the experience, the prudence, or the timidity of practical politicians."[4]

On the theoretical side, to which Dicey gives a long discussion, he admits that there are a number of problems which could not be answered by the theory so that all its adherents would agree. For instance, there is the problem of contractual freedom, to which they have "never given a perfectly consistent or satisfactory answer."[5] It is a little rough to make an unsolved theoretical problem play the part of effective public opinion in law-making, but let us not laugh at the theory in its worst entanglements. Let us pass this tenderly by.

The reason that Benthamism swept the nation, according to Dicey, was that it provided the reformers with an acceptable programme and with an ideal.[6] Also it "exactly answered to the immediate wants of the day."[7] Yet "the essential strength of utilitarianism lay far less in the transitory circumstances of a particular time than in its correspondence with tendencies of English thought and feeling, which have exhibited a character of permanence."[8] Also, "Benthamism fell in with the habitual conservatism of Englishmen,"[9] and "its strength lay in its being the response to the needs of a particular era and in its harmony with the general tendencies of English thought."[10] One can take his choice. Also, one can allow for a factor which Dicey emphasizes in another place, namely Bentham's long life and influence, which gave his theory authority, on the principle that "iteration and reiteration are a great force."[11]

[1] Dicey, op. cit., p. 169.
[2] Ibid., p. 179.
[3] Ibid., p. 168.
[4] Ibid., p. 124.
[5] Ibid., p. 155.
[6] Ibid., pp. 124, 167.
[7] Ibid., p. 170.
[8] Ibid., p. 173.
[9] Ibid., p. 173.
[10] Ibid., p. 175.
[11] Ibid., pp. 127, 128.

Now for an illustration or two of the way the individualistic public opinion is actually used by Dicey. The four kinds of laws which he thinks Benthamism aimed at were the transference of political power into the hands of a class large and intelligent enough to identify its own interest with the interest of the greatest number, the promotion of humanitarianism, the extension of individual liberty, and the creation of adequate legal machinery for the protection of the equal rights of all the citizens.[1] He tells us that Benthamism saw "that the unreformed Parliament, just because it mainly represented the interests and feelings of land-owners and merchants, would not sanction fundamental improvements in the law of England,"[2] which is all well enough, but then he asks us to believe that this Benthamism, which could not get results directly, was able to get them indirectly, by demanding that this same selfish Parliament first reform itself in order that afterward it could Benthamize everything else against its own wishes. That is hard to swallow, especially when we recall his statement that the reform of Parliament was really due to the shifting of industrial power to the north of England.

Discussing factory legislation, Dicey quotes from Shaftesbury a list of men who opposed it—Peel, Graham, O'Connell, Gladstone, Brougham, Bright, and Cobden[3]—and says that while Shaftesbury was puzzled at their opposition and inclined to call them wicked and selfish, the truth of the matter was that they were all "individualists," and the genuine explanation of their anti-factory-legislation attitude lies in that point alone. One laughs. We know enough of the industrial interests and affiliations of most of the men on this list to feel certain that theory was a minor consideration for them, however much it was in theory's name that they urged and argued. Shaftesbury himself speaks of "mill-owners, capitalists, and doctrinaires," as opposing him, with the doctrinaires in third place, and also says that "in very few instances did any mill-owner appear on the platform with me; in still fewer the ministers of any religious denomination." One can fairly

[1] *Ibid.*, pp. 183, 184.   [3] *Ibid.*, pp. 233–36.
[2] *Ibid.*, p. 166.

well drop the individualistic explanation of the opposition to such legislation.   It weakens Dicey's own work.

We may end this analysis of his interpretation of the period of individualism with two quotations which may be placed side by side:

> The more closely the renovation of English institutions under the influence of Bentham is studied, the more remarkably does it illustrate the influence of public opinion upon law.[1]
>
> This continuance, indeed, of Benthamite legislation is the main proof, as well as from one point of view a chief cause, of the dominance of individualism throughout pretty nearly the whole existence of the reformed Parliament.[2]

The last quotation is a wonder.   It bobs up with a malevolent grin to give the lie to Dicey's whole system of interpreting the law. So vague does Dicey's public opinion become when he brings it to close quarters with the work he assumes it to do, that he really does not know what a stab he has here given himself.

And now for the period of collectivism which we can handle much more expeditiously because we have already quoted Dicey's preliminary admission that he could find the "public opinion" only through study of the laws.   He proposes to give us, "an attempt at analysis of the conditions or causes which have favored the growth of collectivism or, if the matter be looked at from the other side, have undermined the authority of Benthamite liberalism."[3] The conditions to which the change is due are: (1) the Tory philanthropy and the factory movement; (2) the changed attitude of the working-classes; (3) the modification in economic and social beliefs; (4) characteristics of modern commerce; (5) the intro- duction of household suffrage.[4]   Here we have a set of conditions, without even the naming of a school of thought as one element in the series, such as we found before in his conditions surrounding the transition from the first to the second period.   A typical sen-

---

[1] Dicey, *op. cit.*, p. 208.   This sentence is from a two-page summary of the preceding chapter, entered in the table of contents as "Benthamite Reform an Illustration of Influence of Opinion."   In these pages I can find no hint of argument and no summary of argument.   They consist only of bald assertions, and of facts that do not go to the point at all.

[2] *Ibid.*, p. 183.   [3] *Ibid.*, p. 217.   [4] *Ibid.*, pp. 216 ff.

tence in this part of the book is: "The mere decline of faith in self-help—and that such a decline has taken place is certain—is of itself sufficient to account for the growth of legislation tending toward socialism."[1]

He attempts to set forth the principles of collectivism under one heading and the general trend of such legislation under another. As a matter of fact the distinction is merely formal, and all he succeeds in doing is to divide his set of collectivistic laws irregularly into two groups, when he could better discuss them directly and all together. Indeed it is the principles "as actually exhibited in and illustrated by English legislation during the latter part of the nineteenth century"[2] that are the only principles he presents. It would be absurd for him to appeal to Marx at this point, and quite as absurd for him to name the dreamy English socialists and communists of the first half of the last century.

It is needless to take up any of his illustrations of collectivistic legislation. The sole point at issue is his method of abstracting the essence of these laws in the form of a principle and making the principle explain them. What he sets forth about the combination law may be taken as a ready test by anyone who looks farther into his position.

We find him referring to "that latent socialism, not yet embodied in any definite socialistic formulas, which has for the last thirty years and more been telling with ever-increasing force on the development of law in England."[3] We find him insisting that the difference between the two types of legislation, individualistic and collectivistic, is "essential and fundamental," because "it rests upon and gives expression to different, if not absolutely inconsistent, ways of regarding the relation between man and state."[4] We find him cheerfully adding that "modern individualists are themselves generally on some points socialists," and a paragraph later telling us that "the inner logic of events leads to the extension and development of legislation which bears the impress of collectivism."[5] And finally we find him conjecturing in a footnote that

[1] *Ibid.*, p. 257.   [3] *Ibid.*, p. 299.   [5] *Ibid.*, p. 301.

[2] *Ibid.*, p. 258.   [4] *Ibid.*, p. 299.

if the progress toward collectivism is ever checked it will not be
"by the influence of some thinkers," but by "some patent fact,"
such as overheavy taxation.[1]

Here again, one can take one's choice. The sentences are
absolutely inconsistent. And the reason lies in a theory that will
not stand the simplest test, in a vagueness that will permit any
inconsistency without crying for mercy.

In his chapter on the cross-currents of opinion, Dicey gives
opening for easy criticism. His main illustration is ecclesiastical,
and what it all comes to is that the corporate interests of the English
church, garbing themselves in argument and theory, have succeeded in checking a good deal of proposed legislation and muti-
lating a good deal more. The chapter does not bear on speculative
thought or any other kind of "public opinion" after the style of
Dicey at all.

Then comes the chapter on judge-made law. And here we
have "fiction" treated as the development of judicial opinion,
when really what the facts Dicey brings forward mean is that
through the courts, "fiction" and all, the interests of the nation
have been solving their conflicts.

Another chapter brings law-making opinion into relation with
other public opinion—with "the whole body of ideas and beliefs
which prevail at a given time." So theology, politics, jurisprudence, and political economy are examined with relation to legislative opinion, and the lives of thinkers in their evolution are
brought into touch. It is pleasant to read Dicey's comments on
the way in which freedom of discussion and the disintegration of
belief, the apotheosis of instinct and the historical method have
caused the authority of Benthamism to grow weak; but what it
all has to do with English law, after the mass of contradictions
and confusions that our analysis has revealed, it is hard indeed
to imagine.

And now at the end, Dicey concludes by saying that

the relation between law and opinion has been in England, as elsewhere,
extremely complex, that legislative opinion is more often the result of facts

[1] Dicey, *op. cit.*, p. 301, footnote.

than of philosophical speculations; and that no facts play a more important part in the creation of opinion than laws themselves; . . . . that each kind of opinion entertained by men at a given era is governed by that whole body of beliefs, convictions, sentiments, or assumptions, which, for want of a better name, we call the spirit of the age.[1]

So we come out with the "spirit of the age," as pale a spook as ever walked a lawbook's page.

Dicey's fundamental purpose has been to show that a systematic legislative public opinion can be located in society—that is, in the English society of last century—which is the source of its tendencies in law-making. He does not claim that this public opinion makes itself; he admits many factors, incidental and other, that combine to build it up. But once built up, he treats it as a solid substantial existence, which can be used for itself as a cause or interpretative factor. In other words, he does not make the ideas that form his public opinion absolute in the old metaphysical sense, but he makes them a good phenomenal imitation of that old metaphysical absolute.

In applying this theory to his three periods of law-making, he uses "no ideas" instead of "ideas" as the principle of the first period; he finds a systematic theory of legislation (Benthamism) which answers his purpose in the second period; and in the third he frankly admits that the only way he can get his hands on any such theory is by inferring its presence bodily from the facts of legislation he calls upon it to explain.

In short, his own theory fails him in two of his three periods, and if there is any value in it that value must be shown solely in the Benthamist period. But even here we have found him, toward the close of his study, admitting that the legislation itself is the "main proof" of the existence of the public opinion. We have found him utterly at sea as to whether to place the main weight on thought harmonies, or on accidental circumstances in explaining the rise of the opinion. We have found him admitting that the Benthamist opinion itself had never reached a clear logical formulation in some of its most important central points, and we

[1] *Ibid.*, p. 463.

have failed to find in him a scintilla of proof that it really is opinion which dominates the legislation. A few sequences, such as showing that Adam Smith antedates the reform bill, can hardly be regarded seriously as proof of a causal connection.

Which all comes to this, that Dicey has begun with a naïve belief in the validity of opinion, that he has never seriously thought through the difficulties, and that he has been content to allow vagueness and haphazard concessions to creep in to such an extent that they undermine his whole theory without his seeming to know it. Great as is the value of his book as a study of English legal history, as a causal explanation of the process by which the laws have been created it has just no value at all.

This is not to say that there is not much revelation of causes in the book. It has been impossible for Dicey to discuss laws merely as products of opinion. He has brought in the important factors, but not deliberately, with balanced recognition of their true worth, and not with adequate statement. All such things lie outside in the "external" and the "accidental," and there they miss being properly balanced, weighed, and stated. That is the penalty a man must pay for devotion to the "ideas."

Another comment that follows naturally from the above considerations is that the "ideas" as Dicey uses them are really nothing more than a form of sensationalism—we may call it "yellow" science. They are the spectacular feature. Everybody howls individualism and liberalism; everybody swears to live and die by the creed of Bentham; everybody uses all the brains he has to defend the actions he is going to take, or to confute his opponents' actions, in terms of that theory. And then, just because the theory evokes interest and discussion, the pseudo-scientist thinks it has all the magic power it claims to have. He exalts it, instead of putting it under his microscope and testing it for what it is.

When "ideas" in full cry drive past, the thing to do with them is to accept them as an indication that something is happening; and then search carefully to find out what it really is they stand for, what the factors of the social life are that are expressing themselves through the ideas. The thing to do is to try to become more and more exact, not to outdo the vagueness of popular speech. What Dicey owed us in this book was a quantitative analysis of public opinion in terms of the different elements of the population which expressed themselves through it. He owed us an investigation of the exact things really wanted under the cover of the "opinion" by each group of the people, with time and place and circumstance all taken up into the center of the statement. In other words, he owed us a social dissection, which he was eminently prepared to offer, and not a rhapsody. Not accepting that task, he has succeeded in reducing his system of interpretation to an absurdity; but if his book leads other students to a recognition of the pitfalls of the "ideas," to avoidance of the evils, and to a search for real factors of explanation, it may, perhaps, in this way offer compensation for what it itself failed to accomplish.

CHAPTER III

SOCIAL WILL

There is a form of naïve social interpretation which is not nearly so troublesome as the interpretation through individual feelings or ideas, which has indeed for the most part signified a distinct progress toward a coherent interpretation among those who use it, but which nevertheless must be arrayed along with the others as amounting at bottom to nothing more than a poor make-shift or stop-gap. I refer to the appeal to the social will, the social mind, the social consciousness, and the other social psychic entities, unities, or personified processes of that type—it matters not at all just what one calls them, since the very best and most careful distinctions that have ever been made between the various terms amount to nothing more than word-splitting.

The good point about the "social will" in social interpretation is that it signifies a breaking loose from the hard and fixed individual, as the unit of explanation, and that it points toward a recognition that a real social material is before us for investigation, and not merely a fictitious, external, now-you-have-it-and-now-you-don't set of institutions which can only become real when given a sharp reference to individuals who bear or create them.

The bad point is that in putting the emphasis on the personified society itself, it makes all social interpretation an equation of identical terms. When we talk about social choices, we may distinguish between content and process, and we are interested in understanding both, or, better said, we are interested in understanding the given phenomena from both points of view. But beyond content and process there is nothing at all. So that when we personify the choosing capacity of society, we are putting a spook behind the scenes, or, what is the same thing, in other words, we are emphasizing a tautology as a cause. To say that "the social will does" something or other is at bottom merely to restate the problem. To talk of the will of the state is nothing more than to talk abstractly of the state itself. We can learn just as much about "social choices" without using the phrase as with using it. The word "will" and similar words have had a certain meaning in individual psychology, legitimate enough so long as the individual was studied with his social setting unknown or ignored. But to transfer them from the individual to society is not to help matters, but merely to transfer a faulty point of view from an application in which it had some value, to an application in which it has no value. The use of the phrase "social will" gives us, in exchange for all the little tautologies which we found in the feelings and ideas, one huge tautology. But if we believe that it carries us to the explanation of social happenings, we are simply lulling ourselves to sleep with a huge draught of the "psychic" opiate.

Now this social will appears in many forms. We find it varying all the way from the schematic mysticism of Mackenzie to the more practical, but also more self-contradictory, assertions of Ross. As a curious development of it we have a Novicow, who, needing an "organ" to carry the will—for how absurd to have a function without an organ—places it in the élite, in other words, in "our best citizens," where it finds a happy home.

By Ward the social will is described as the form or process through which the feeling forces work in certain high stages of social organization. But his tendency is to make it very concrete, and to rely upon its aid as a cause in his interpretations, instead of holding fast to it as process and studying directly what is passing through it. He states it frequently as a sort of welfare-seeking institution; thus he makes the modern democratic state embody the social will, and says it "has but one purpose, function, or mission, that of securing the welfare of society."[1] By making the social welfare concrete and the social will which is seeking it also concrete, he of necessity abandons the useful statement of will as a form of social process. Moreover to agree with Ward one would have not only to accept the feelings for the work he puts on their unhappy heads, with all the infinite loopholes to error

[1] *Pure Sociology*, p. 555.

they bring with them, but in addition one would have to admit the greater prevalence of this social willing process in modern over earlier societies; one would have to be ready to admit that there was quantitative increase in it, and that more things were accomplished by and for society through it now than formerly. To all of which there is most grave objection.

An elaborate attempt to utilize the social will in interpreting society is made by Professor C. A. Ellwood in a series of articles in Vols. IV and V of the *American Journal of Sociology*. His position is frankly based on Professor Dewey's psychology, which he lifts up bodily in its main categories and applies thus straightway to social facts. I can use his articles to show briefly the fundamental weakness of the social will for practical use in interpretation.

Professor Ellwood holds, to start with, that the real proof of the existence of "socio-psychical processes" is that social groups "act."[1] But he makes no attempt to absorb the idea process in the action so as to use it to give the action meaning at every point. Instead he holds the action sharply distinct over against the social mind. The social action seems to be for him a part of the physical world, the so-called objective world. The social mind is subjective, and directs the performance. It does not direct the whole performance, or rather he does not pretend that he can explain the whole performance in terms of the social mind. He puts the social mind's subjective interpretation alongside of an objective interpretation which shows what part rivers, and mountains, and ore deposits, and microbes, and so forth, play in society.

An objective interpretation is necessary beside a subjective interpretation, he tells us, because

there are many physical phenomena of land and climate and many physiological phenomena of race and population, which are not less than psychical facts to be taken into account in a complete interpretation of society, but which social psychology as such cannot consider.[2]

He calls his study "functional psychology,"[3] yet he makes the subjective and the objective interpretations "supplementary"[4]

---

[1] *American Journal of Sociology*, Vol. V, p. 104.

[2] *Ibid.*, Vol. IV, p. 658.   [3] *Ibid.*, p. 808.   [4] *Ibid.*, p. 658.

to each other. For instance, he thinks he can give us a subjective interpretation of revolutions, and then supplement this by an objective interpretation, and so put all our curiosity to rest.

He transfers Dewey's categories of co-ordination, adaptation, and habit to the social whole, and tops off a definition of law as follows: "Laws are formal expressions of social habits which have come into consciousness."[1] I will not criticize that here except to say that the laws we get into contact with are anything but "formal;" they are the social habits themselves, as mediated by government; and if those laws only are law which have got into "consciousness," whatever that may really mean, it will be hard for anyone who has ever gathered enlightenment from the school of Sir Henry Maine to accept the social will for practical use in his studies.

"Society," the writer tells us, "selects ideas and individuals upon the basis of their utility in building up or maintaining its co-ordinations."[2] There we have that generalized social welfare which takes the murderer up with the avenging public into one social whole; which is a unity in expressing itself. So long as murderers exist to give meaning to laws against murder, the social welfare as a whole expressing itself in laws against murder will be a fiction, not a fact. The theory of the social will does not allow for this—in actual interpretation—whatever its advocates may say about it when the ink and paper are handy and the writing co-ordination is well set.

In this way Professor Ellwood wants to found a social psychology "upon the fundamental principles and categories of a functional psychology of the individual."[3] It is significant that he finds it easy to discriminate between individual and social psychology, but he has some trouble in showing how the social psychology is different from sociology.[4] No wonder. Nor is it any wonder that some years later, with his theory no doubt well sunk into his habits of thought he can still find time and interest to discuss with some of his colleagues such questions as the nature of

[1] *Ibid.*, p. 816.
[2] *Ibid.*, p. 821.
[3] *Ibid.*, p. 822.
[4] *Ibid.*, Vol. V, p. 101.

"psychical unity," "inter-individual psychic processes," "object-ively organic unities," and other angels-on-the-point-of-a-needle questions.[1]

Leaving the definitions, the hair-splitting, and the fine-drawn logic out of account as insignificant, there are certain things we need to know about a social mind, if we are to use it concretely in social interpretation; if, for example, we are going to try to make it help us in understanding why some particular law or type of legislation is adopted.

One is as to its substantiality.   Can we get hold of it anywhere? Can we handle it by itself before trying to put it to work?   Have we any tests of it?

Another is as to the amount of the social-mind process.   Is there more of it in one society, or at one stage of a society, than at another?   Can we estimate societies in terms of this so-called consciousness or conscious process, and depend on them to mani-fest it in a way that helps us to understand things?

As far as the first question is concerned, the second part of this book will show how in the processes of government where it is supposed to be most characteristically manifested the only thing to do with the social will is to ignore it, as a separately existing "thing," and analyze to the best of our ability what is actually happening.   Except by way of challenging anybody who believes in its substantial participation in social life to locate it somewhere —not humorously as in the élite, but seriously—I will drop that question here, with only a reiterated general denial that any such factor can be put to work concretely in our interpretations.

As for the other question, a few illustrations and comparisons will be useful.   We are told that society is becoming conscious of itself, that it is progressing in ability to construct itself, that it is gaining in freedom to make itself what it will, and so on.   We are offered a picture of the benighted horde or tribe or barbarous nation, bound in custom, helpless, driven hither and thither, and told to contrast it with our modern nations boldly initiating wonder-ful things and manipulating their own destinies, conscious to great

[1] *American Journal of Sociology*, Vol. X, pp. 666 ff.

extent of what they are about. It is an arbitrary, artificial contrast, that falls before the first touch of fact.

In what sense can we Americans say that we created our own government? Certainly we did not create ourselves as a nation. It was the nation, the people with common interests, however far they recognized the full truth, that made the Revolutionary War possible, that expressed itself in the war. There was no separately existing self-consciousness in that. We certainly did not set out to gain independence; it is well enough known that we were driven into independence against what we call our expressed desires and our better judgment. Did we even make our own form of government? One cannot say yes while the beginning of our federal institutions can be traced back in the long history of the British monarchy, while some of the most important characteristics of the relation of the governmental powers came from the forms of the colonial governments as matured in the thirteen states. Were we more self-conscious than, say, the Phoenicians were when they built up the institutions of Carthage, or the Peruvians when they established their "paternal" government?

The most striking feature of our government is generally set down as our Supreme Court with its unique control over the laws through its tests of their constitutionality. Can anybody point to any self-consciousness, any deliberate creative act in that feature of our Constitution?

Is there more originality in our president than there was in Rome's transition from king to consuls? in Sparta's elevation of its ephors?

When one of our states holds a constitutional convention is it taking more intelligent heed to its ways than Rome did when it appointed its decemvirs?

When the old tribal system broke down in Greece and in Rome a territorial basis of government was established. Do not the demes which were then established in Athens and the wards in Rome show as much of deliberate planning as anything we can offer?

And before that time, when we consider the tribal structure at Athens, with its four tribes, each with three phratries, each with thirty gentes; or at Rome, with its three tribes, each with ten curiae, each with ten gentes, do we not see society's formulation of its own institutions—to use that phrasing—as plainly as we could wish? And this whether the established numbers of gentes and phratries were full all the time, or ever? Somebody or other, somehow or other, had been hammering things into shape with as much deliberate plan as even our most pigeonhole-headed moderns can boast of.

Or let us go still farther back. It is unquestioned that there have been many transitions from maternal to paternal descent and clan organization. When the time of change came, individuals, for reasons, we may say, of many kinds, began to break away from the old system and take to the new. But that is not the full statement. At some time the group ceased to punish the innovators. That is one of the essential things. There must have been many a palaver of the ancient worthies. The change shook the old social organization, we can say without exaggeration, to its very foundations. Do we talk of our own greater social will and self-consciousness in contrast to such a change, when we want to introduce a trifling institution like the referendum or direct primary and have to spend decades making a beginning?

Or let us take specific acts. The Spartans used to select their boldest helots for assassination to insure the preservation of order. Were they less deliberate and self-conscious than we are when we adopt—or fail to adopt—some new method for suppressing anarchists?

The names we still use for the days of the week were allotted perhaps four thousand years B. C. in Egypt by a most complicated process of astronomical reckoning, designed to show planetary influence. Is it probable that we today can show any institution or custom more consciously created?

Pharaoh filled his granaries for seven years' famine? Are we often as full of foresight?

Rome under Augustus adopted the Lex Julia et Papia Poppaea. Are we passing from our excitement over divorce and race suicide to more calculated action?

Read of an Indian tribe's council of the chief and sachems, and question whether, up to the full measure of the situations they had to face and of the problems that they had to decide, they did not act with a consciousness which equals anything our parliaments can show.

In our recent American rate legislation, how many of our people today honestly think they know what the results will be? Is not the great proportion of blind striking at a head that needs a blow easy to see?

When we base our laws on moral principles, do we not cut the ground out from under the modern social mind, quantitatively lauded, as much as we think we cut it out from under some old society when we speak of its unconscious custom?

We have a reign of graft, and some graft-cure operations. Will the factors of social will and consciousness appear prominently on either side, however we may twist the facts to find them?

I do not pretend that such haphazard illustrations as I have just given prove anything positively. But they certainly do challenge the upholder of self-consciousness as a growing quality or force or power, to show with exactness what he means. I do not want to be understood as denying point-blank that the processes of modern society are not possibly more complex along those lines that are meant when the word consciousness is used than were the processes of earlier stages of society. That is an open question which anyone may prove who can. I do deny that that proof can be drawn from any manner of comparison between so-called individual and so-called social psychic process, or from any admiration of the marvels of present-day intellect, or from any study that has yet been made of such social achievements or such social organization as modern science and modern representative government. It is a greater complexity of psychic process, remember, that has to be proved, and there is simply no proof at all in the fact that it is easy to assume complexity of process to explain complexity of results. Within the slight range of difference between our highest and our lowest societies, the whole of organic evolution being taken into account as background, the conclusion simply does not follow from present evidence, and it will take exceedingly delicate tests in the end if it is established.

CHAPTER IV

POLITICAL SCIENCE

Set opposite to all these various forms of so-called psychical interpretation, we have a dead political science. It is a formal study of the most external characteristics of governing institutions. It loves to classify governments by incidental attributes, and when all is said and done it cannot classify them much better now than by lifting up bodily Aristotle's monarchies, aristocracies, and democracies which he found significant for Greek institutions, and using them for measurements of all sorts and conditions of modern government. And since nobody can be very sure but that the United States is really a monarchy under the classification or England really a democracy, the classification is not entitled to great respect. Nor do the classifications that make the fundamental distinction that between despotism and republics fare much better. They lose all sight of the content of the process in some trick point about the form.

When it is necessary to touch up this barren formalism with a glow of humanity, an injection of metaphysics is used. There will be a good deal to say about civic virtue or ideals or civilization. It makes a very pleasing addition to the work, but the two parts have no organic unity, not even in the hands of a Bluntschli.

After compounding the formalism and the metaphysics, political science adds works on practical problems of the day or on the higher politics to suit the taste. These works are sufficiently detached to be capable of preparation in almost any form, and they can be manufactured as well by rank outsiders as by the experts of the science to which they are supposed to belong.

Your political scientist thinks he is going a long way afield and that he is meritoriously portraying "actual" government when he inserts in his work some remarks on the machine, the boss, and the practical virtues and vices of men practicing politics. He is quite right in this but only by contrast with the writers—I do not say on constitutional law, for these are doing their proper work in their proper way—but those who take the fictions of constitutional law and pretend thereby to give a real picture of society in the process of governing itself.

But the boss himself is almost as formal an element in a political science as is the president or governor. When you state him you have not stated the living society. You must still go behind to find what are the real interests that are playing on each other through his agency. A discussion of the work and defects of a state legislature carries one nowhere as long as the legislature is taken for what it purports to be—a body of men who deliberate upon and adopt laws. Not until the actual law-making is traced through from its efficient demand to its actual application, can one tell just where the real law-creating work is done, and whether the legislature was Moses the law-giver or merely Moses the registration clerk.[1]

There is hardly anywhere a work on political science that does not, when it examines the phenomena of public opinion, either indulge in some wise and vague observations, or else make a frank admission of ignorance.[2] And yet what can there possibly be to a political science with the very breath of its life left out? He who writes of the state, of law, or of politics without first coming to close quarters with public opinion is simply evading the very central structure of his study.

[1] Professor Giddings has made some observations on private associations as the real law-formulating bodies in America, but so far as I know has not attempted to get the full meaning out of what he has observed, nor have the facts been utilized elsewhere. See *Democracy and Empire*, chap. xv.

[2] Jellinek, *Das Recht des modernen Staates*, Vol. I, "Allgemeine Staatslehre," p. 93, gives part of a page to describing public opinion and concludes: "Die Bildung, Feststellung, Bedeutung der öffentlichen Meinung im Detail zu untersuchen gehört zu den interessantesten Problemen der Socialwissenschaft, zugleich aber auch zu den schwierigsten, da es sich hier um massenpsychologische Vorgänge handelt, deren Objekt mit Hülfe unserer wissenschaftlichen Methoden schwer zu beobachten ist." Cf. Preuss, *Schmoller's Jahrbuch für G.V. und V.*, Vol. XXVI, p. 579: "Jenes undefinierbare, jeder rechtlichen Erfassung spottende, und doch in lebendigster Realität existierende Etwas das man öffentliche Meinung nennt."

We have in this world many lawyers who know nothing of law-making. They play their part, and their learning is justified by their work. We have many law-makers who know nothing of law. They too play their part and their wisdom—though they may not be able to give it verbal expression—is none the less real. But the practical lore of neither of these types of men is a scientific knowledge of society. Nor by putting their two lores together do we make an advance. It is they themselves we must study and know, for what they are, for what they represent.

CHAPTER V

SUMMARY

I have written the preceding chapters to prepare the way for the chapters that are to follow. I have wished to make it clear why the method of interpreting society which I am about to set forth is justified, and why the irruption into it of any unassimilated factors of the kind I have been criticizing would only serve to distort it.

What I have thus far said amounts to about this: that the "feelings," "faculties," "ideas," and "ideals" are not definite "things" in or behind society, working upon it as causes, but that they are—or rather, that what is meant by them is—society itself, stated in a very clumsy and inadequate way.

I am aware that many refined theories exist which state these psychic elements not as "things" but as process. I am not concerned with such theories, but with the practical use made of the elements themselves in interpretations of society; and in that use they always present themselves as "things," however much that fact may appear to be veiled. Their very statement as phases of individual life throws them concretely into opposition to the society which they are used to explain, and makes concrete causes out of them in the bad sense.

To avoid misconception let me emphasize afresh some of the things I have not said.

I have not denied the existence of a real, living, intelligent human social material which is indicated when feelings and ideals are mentioned.

I have not denied that this feeling, thinking, ideal-following material is the stuff we have before us in interpreting society.

I have not denied that the ordinary statement of this material from the individual view-point, in terms of our current vocabulary, is fairly adequate for the purposes of everyday life. I have no more desire to interfere in that region than I have, for instance, to deprive some unhappy being of the anthropomorphism that suits his needs.

I have not denied that this same ordinary statement has an aesthetic value, any more than the physicist would deny color when he studied wave-lengths. That form of statement has a clear value for fiction and poetry—and for painting and music too—which for all I know, or care, it will retain forever.

What I have denied is that the separation of feelings and ideas, looked on as individual psychic content, from society or from social institutions or from social activity, is a legitimate procedure in the scientific investigation of society. I have insisted that such a separation, when built up into a system of interpretation, collapses of its own defects, and brings down the whole system in a crash. I have insisted that such a separation in fact exists wherever feelings or ideas are given independent value as factors in interpretation, even though the interpreters themselves enter a most vehement formal denial. I do not for an instant claim that the point of view I am taking is novel, except perhaps so far as the manner of its presentment and emphasis is concerned. On the contrary—I shall return to this in my final chapter—I conceive that every advance step that is taken in the analysis or understanding of society, whether in history, in ethnology, or in sociology, involves, tacitly at least, this point of view.

But, of course, even though the feeling and idea system breaks down, the feelings and ideas still have a meaning in the social interpretations in which they are used, and fill there a function. They are used because they bring a certain amount of order into what would otherwise be a chaos.[1] In casting them out we must be very careful not to cast out that meaning, that order, with them. It is with them much as it was with Zeus in early Greek thought. He answered a real purpose. He held together the various personified powers of nature and of social life in a system. When

[1] Professor Small points out that Adam Smith used the "sympathies of the impartial spectator" in just this way, and indicates what those sympathies are equivalent to in modern sociology. See Small, *Adam Smith and Modern Sociology*, p. 39; cf. also, pp. 50, 92.

we cast out Zeus we must be careful to retain the practical realities of our lives which he has symbolized. We are justified in casting out Zeus only when we have reached a better way of stating those realities. Indeed until then to cast him out would be impossible.

What are the practical realities for which these feeling and idea factors stand?

If we take the feeling elements in everyday speech we readily see that they stand for certain regularities or tendencies in activity stated as individual conduct. For instance, if a child is kind to its cat it is apt to be kind to its dog. We indicate the tendency by calling the child kind hearted. A man's habit with regard to truth-telling, or with regard to stealing, is similarly made his quality. Among boys who pass examinations with honors in one set of subjects we believe we find some tendency to stand high in other subjects, and we say they are smart. A man outraged at the fate of the Boers is apt to be outraged at the fate of the Fili-pinos. Here we are getting over into the regularities denoted by the ideas. We find part of the people getting the suffrage and the rest probably tending toward it: the men have it, and the women follow after—perhaps. We observe a government we call a democracy in one land, and probably we see a tendency toward a similar democracy in a sister land: we talk of the domina-tion of ideas. We find legislation regulating the meat industry following swiftly on railroad and insurance legislation, and we attribute it to the development of something or other in human nature. We get half a dozen liberties and we state a lot of other things we want as liberties also; and we say that it is the ideal of liberty that is guiding us. We appeal to a difference in feelings and ideas to explain habits and customs different from our own; for why should not other individuals and nations act just as we do, if they are not fundamentally different in some way? The very complexity of social fact drives us to the individual feelings. as interpreters; and the appearance of "chance" in history, the prominence of conspicuous persons at critical moments, seems to give the explanation in terms of individual character added force.

In this way individual men are not only distinguished from one another, as I have pointed out before, but, what is the reverse side of the same process, regularities of character are made intelligible. And beyond this the regularities in the institutional side of life are also brought under the same system of explanation. Their unity and coherency are emphasized; the adaptations of men to each other in society are given a passable statement; each man is brought into relations to the mass of men.

However, while these feelings and ideas put themselves forth to be definite dependable things, experience proves that they only conform roughly to the actual activity that can be observed. We may put this differently by saying that from the standpoint of the feelings we can observe nothing more than unreliable, poorly defined tendencies of activity to correspond to them. Kindness to cat or dog is not accompanied by kindness to snake or mosquito. Truth-telling has many different standards, according as friend or foe is addressed, according as "business" or pleasure is in view. The "smart-boy" tests prove their narrow limitations when the tests of the practical world are superimposed on them. We see on further inspection that it is the exception rather than the rule for men to be enraged similarly over the fates of the Boers and Filipinos. And so with all the others.

When we get to the application of these feeling and idea elements to social interpretation, our difficulties become greatly increased. The whole working process, regularities and tendencies and all, is what we must study. But we find the feelings we are using breaking down under our hands. We find it necessary to make them ever more and more specific, or else ever more and more generalized, if they are not to become admittedly inadequate for the work we put upon them. And similarly with the ideas. We must make them so exact and definite that they fit the facts of the case like shadows, or we must make them so highly generalized that there is no more substance to them than shadows. And in either case, at either extreme, we thus bring them to vanishing points. When a feeling is so definite as, say, the love of theater-going, or when an idea is so definite as, say, some detail of ballot-law reform which we are on the point of adopting, it becomes the same thing as our activity itself, for all the good it does us as an aid in interpretation. And when a feeling becomes so general as, say, virtue or vice, or an idea so general as, say, democracy or liberty, it is necessary to fill it full of social content in order to give it any meaning at all. And that content is the social activity itself. In either case the feelings and ideas vanish into the activity. They stand naked before us as impotent inferences from activity.

This is equivalent to the point I have repeatedly made in the preceding criticisms that nowhere could the feeling and idea factors be located for themselves as apart from the activities they were appealed to to explain—nowhere, that is, except in the speech-activities of society. There they must be studied, of course, with great care and their meaning and value allowed for on lines which will occupy us for a considerable time in the chapters which are to follow.

Parenthetically I may admit that feelings and ideas as tags or labels have a certain practical utility for scientific investigation which may continue even after a more satisfactory system of interpretation is in use. We may name particular feelings and ideas in order to mark out tentatively fields of phenomena for investigation. Here they serve as symbols of the unknown quantities of our reckoning. Probably also they can be used conveniently to this extent in the preliminary descriptive work which prepares the way for the more careful description which is interpretation. And possibly, though at much risk, they may be employed as a sort of shorthand expression in indicating briefly causal connections we have already worked out, which would take many words to state otherwise. But the minute we go beyond these uses, the minute we plant ourselves on feelings and ideas as solid facts, that minute we open the way to all confusions.

Let me next give a more theoretical statement to the position I have taken. No matter how highly generalized or how specific the ideas and feelings are which we are considering, they never lose their reference to a "social something." The angry man is never angry save in certain situations; the highest ideal of liberty has to do with man among men. The words anger and liberty can easily be set over as subjects against groups of words in the predicate which define them. But neither anger, nor liberty, nor any feeling or idea in between can be got hold of anywhere except as phases of social situations. They stand out as phases, moreover, only with reference to certain positions in the social situation or complex of situations in the widest sense, within which they themselves exist.

It has long enough been established that there is no "outer world" except in idea. This is not deep philosophy, but plain common-sense; for it amounts merely to saying that we do not know any outer world except the world that is known to us, or, what is the same thing, as it is known to us. But it is equally well established that we ourselves, ideas and all, are a functioning part of that very outer world.

Now, when we attempt to separate an idea or a feeling as such from that outer world, do the best we can, we cannot help taking up a large part of that outer world into it, for that outer world is felt idea. To succeed in this attempt at separation is just as impossible as to find an outer world that is not "known" to us. And when we strive to interpret any phase of that outer world— say, some phase of society—by the aid of feeling or idea, we inevitably have society itself contained in our alleged "cause;" and this in the double sense—or, better, from the twofold point of view— that the idea or the feeling is social, and that the society is reflected in the feeling or the idea. This admitted, it follows at once that the individual as the definite, firm, positive, foundation for individualized feelings and ideas, is a highly abstract social idea himself, and in the way in which he is put to use, fictitious. All depends then for the success of our interpretation in terms of such feelings and ideas as built up in speech for practical uses and carried over into science, on how well our interpretation actually works—on its practical scientific efficiency.

But we may well expect difficulty with interpretations based on a fundamental split between the idea and the outer world. If we throw emphasis on either one of the two to the exclusion of the other, and deny the complement, we are constructing a world out of stuff that has definition only in terms of the very opposition we attempt to deny. If we take both concretely—the subjective and the objective—and attempt to function them together in a causal system, we are putting two halves together which never possibly on causal lines can make one whole; for the excellent reason that the original analysis which produced the two parts was not made on adequate causal lines.

I do not want to be understood as placing any special reliance on reasoning of the kind I have just been using. It has a certain incidental use in helping to define the position I am taking, but it lacks the direct control of facts, and anyone who lets himself be hypnotized by it is lost. With that warning, I think, the little of it I have indulged in here can do no especial harm.

To get back to our immediate subject, which is the meanings and values in associated human life which are represented by feelings and ideas, and the possibility of preserving them after the feelings and ideas in their concrete statements are cast out, we can get a little more light on it through the distinction between process and content, which is, of course, merely a distinction of point of view. The meat of this book has to do with the process of government, but that process itself would appear as social content, if the point of view chosen were that of individual psychic process. I have at no time any quarrel with the point of view of functional psychology, but I want it scrupulously adhered to for its own purposes, so that whenever psychic "states" are taken full of social content, the point of view in interpretation will change to correspond. The psychic process may correspond admirably to brain physiology, but concreted "chunks" of brain will not serve on crude causal lines to explain "society," since society is itself—to adopt that phrasing—just brain "chunks" and nothing more. One does not lift himself by his own boot-straps anywhere else, and there is no evident reason why he should attempt it here.

With this understood, I think it will be apparent that in casting out the concrete feelings and ideas we are not necessarily casting out the values and meanings they represent. These meanings and values long ago read themselves into the feelings and ideas for

certain practical purposes.   If we can read the values and meanings into another manner of statement which will aid us to interpretation where the concrete feelings and ideas prove themselves
incoherent, then we suffer no loss while making a very great gain.

Instead of values taken from very limited view-points—as
with the feelings—or of values taken from slightly wider, but still,
in comparison with the whole social range, very narrow view-
points—as with the ideas—we must seek for values and meanings
which will work coherently throughout all society; so that, instead
of making society a patchwork of feeling and idea view-points, a
mosaic with lines of unreality all through it, we can grasp it more
as nature presents it to us in its mass effects, with its lines of differentiation and opposition, such as we must insert in it to hold
it under comprehension, better corresponding to the reality.

We must deal with felt things, not with feelings, with intelligent
life, not with idea ghosts.   We must deal with felt facts and with
thought facts, but not with feeling as reality or with thought as
truth.   We must find the only reality and the only truth in the
proper functioning of the felt facts and the thought facts in the
system to which they belong.

PART II

ANALYSIS OF GOVERNMENTAL PRESSURES

CHAPTER VI

THE RAW MATERIALS

The student of government, like the student of any other subject, must make his investigations upon a mass of raw materials. What are the raw materials of government?

The morning paper tells me that the Standard Oil Company has been indicted on some thousands of counts for violating the federal laws. A few months ago it told me that many employees of one of the executive departments of the government were scurrying over the country gathering facts about the way in which that company had conducted its business with the railroad companies. Before that it told me of a resolution put through Congress ordering such an investigation. Still farther back I could have read of the excited activities of many men which came to a climax in the passage of the law under which these indictments have been found. If I wait a few months more I shall read of the trial in the court, of the punishment which will perhaps be imposed, and in part of the effect which the punishment has, or, alternatively, which the indictments even without punishment have, on the company's business methods. I have reason to think also that I shall soon hear a certain leader of a great portion of the people announce fresh steps to be taken toward the introduction of improved methods of controlling such corporations as the Standard Oil Company; and that this will sooner or later be followed by a renewed assertion by another popular leader that the present methods of control will be applied so vigorously as to secure the desired change in conditions without further legislation. If I care to I may read many criticisms of everybody and everything concerned, both in current periodicals and in books of all degrees of remoteness from the hottest spots in the conflict.

Here is some of the raw material for the study of government. There is no other kind.

It is first, last, and always activity, action, "something doing," the shunting by some men of other men's conduct along changed lines, the gathering of forces to overcome resistance to such alterations, or the dispersal of one grouping of forces by another grouping. The writing and talking and speech-making are activity just as much as any of the other facts I have mentioned.

Always there are many men involved, a few directly and very many more indirectly. But the distinction between direct and indirect is not fundamental. It is a practical distinction made for convenience in describing currently to one another what is happening; made so that it will not be necessary to tell the whole story over again with each new incident. For our purposes, as we shall see in due time, it is an arbitrary, and not an edaquate, distinction.

The raw material we study is never found in one man by himself, it cannot even be stated by adding man to man. It must be taken as it comes in many men together. It is a "relation" between men, but not in the sense that the individual men are given to us first, and the relation erected between them. The "relation," i, e., the action, is the given phenomenon, the raw material; the action of men with or upon each other. We know men only as participants in such activity. These joint activities, of which governmental activities are one form, are the cloth, so to speak, out of which men in individual patterns are cut. The "President Roosevelt" of history, for example, is a very large amount of official activity, involving very many people. Any other "President Roosevelt" of public life, physical, temperamental, moral, is but a limited characterization of certain phases of that activity.

These collections, or groups, of men are composed of thinking and feeling actors. They act through a thought-and-feeling process. "Ideas" and "feelings" are words we use to emphasize certain phases of men's participation in the actions. Ordinarily we regard these "ideas" and "feelings" as concretely existing individual possessions. Of late years they have frequently been spoken of as socially existing. From either point of view it remains true that we know nothing of "ideas" and "feelings" except through the medium of actions.

This last sentence will be misunderstood if it is taken to mean that the ideas and feelings are "there," and that the action is "merely a medium." We must be on guard against such false interpretations of current language. It is akin to the lowering of activity to a mere abstract relation between given men. In fact, the action is what we have given us. It is our raw material. The ideas and feelings, as such, are not given facts; they are not fixed points from which we can start to argue. They are ways of talking about the facts; they are hypotheses, very useful in their way for the practical purposes of everyday life; but by us always to be employed only with the interrogation mark after them; always to be abandoned whenever and wherever they are not useful. The talk itself—comprising all the speaking and writing activities—is, of course, never to be abandoned. It is to be reckoned with in interpretation for just what it is, like any other form of activity.

The "ideas" and "feelings" serve to give the individual man his orientation in the social activity in which he is involved; they serve, so to speak, to define him as an individual. There is no idea which is not a reflection[1] of social activity. There is no feeling which the individual can fix upon except in a social form. He can define it only in terms of language which myriads of men have built up. He knows what he feels, and indeed even that he feels, only in terms of other men's lives.

The "ideas" and "feelings," as set apart concretely, serve to indicate the values of the activities which are our raw materials. We are not able to take up for consideration any activity as com-

---

[1] I see no reason for offering definitions of the terms, reflect, represent, mediate, which I shall use freely all through this work. They indicate certain facts that appear directly in the analysis of social activity; the very facts indeed that I am especially studying. My epistemological point of view is admittedly naïve, as naïve, I hope, as the point of view of the physical sciences; I nowhere lay any stress on the difference between the conscious and the unconscious, save as a minor variation of technique in the group process; and even that variation can much better be brought out without the use of the two terms than with it.

plete in itself. If we attempt it we have a corpse, or rather a fragment of a corpse, in our hands, and that is poor material for study. The activities are interlaced. That, however, is a bad manner of expression. For the interlacing itself is the activity. We have one great moving process to study, and of this great moving process it is impossible to state any part except as valued in terms of the other parts. This is as true of the talk activities as of any other activities. Take the indictments against the Standard Oil Company. The only way we can state them adequately is in terms of eighty million people, more or less; and indeed that even may not be a sufficiently comprehensive statement for purposes of study. The meaning of the indictments, their values, extend to the activities of people who live far beyond the confines of one country; extend, indeed, very nearly to all parts of the world. But where the values become too trifling we can profitably ignore them; rather, we must ignore them if we are to make any progress in scientific study.

It is of crucial importance in handling our raw materials to give them a statement which will yield the best range of values for our purposes. And, it is almost needless to say, our purposes, when we aim at scientific study, will vary materially from the purposes of everyday life with reference to which these phenomena are ordinarily stated and defined. We must attain a statement, a valuation, which will neglect none of the important phases. When the best available statement has been made, the scientific study will have been carried to the farthest possible point.

Now the trouble with "ideas" and "feelings" when they are taken up just as we find them floating around is that they give values to our activities which may be, and which indeed usually are, very different from those we must reach even at the very starting-point of our investigation. Here is a city with a bad street-car service and two million dissatisfied citizens. The situation breaks into political life in the form of a municipal-ownership movement. The "ideas" and the "feelings" flash over the field of action at white heat. Municipal ownership, in and for itself, takes the pulpit and yearns to burn at the stake all objectors. In its vocabulary one set of citizens become boodlers, and another set the purest patriots. Altruism, as a matter of rhetoric, damns selfishness. Selfishness, almost convinced that it is selfish, sneers at altruism. If one can pass through the fiery furnace without being consumed, one can get many hints as to the values of the activity before him. But if one attempts to reach an understanding of what is happening by adding brand to brand, "idea" to "idea," and "feeling" to "feeling," one can never reach the goal. The confusion grows worse, the more faithful the arithmetic.

And yet there is not a shred of all the activity which does not present itself as an affair of feeling and intelligence. It cannot be stated with these phases left out. It cannot be stated with these phases erected into other "things," and set over against it. It can only be stated as purposive activity (in a very broad sense of the word purposive), as the doings of wanting-knowing men in masses. It can only be analyzed and its parts can only be valued in terms of all the rest of it. It cannot be analyzed in a structure of "feelings" or in a structure of "ideas" taken apart from it. We must get our raw material before us in the form of purposive action, valued in terms of other purposive action.

Let me restate all this in a different way, with special reference to government. The raw material of government cannot be found in the lawbooks. These merely state the method by which certain participants in government proceed, or claim they proceed, in their part of the work.

It cannot be found in the "law" behind the lawbooks, except as this is taken to mean the actual functioning of the people—in which case law is an important aspect of the raw material, but by no means a complete statement of it.

It cannot be found in the proceedings of constitutional conventions, nor in the arguments and discussions surrounding them. Hints and helps are there, but only minute fragments of the raw material.

It cannot be found in essays, addresses, appeals, and diatribes on tyranny and democracy. All that the world has ever produced in this way cannot do more than point out to us where the raw material may be found.

It cannot be found in the "character of the people," in their specific "feelings" or "thoughts," in their "hearts" or "minds." All these are hypotheses or dreams. Whatever truth or other importance they may possess, they certainly are not "raw material," but instead highly theoretical.

The raw material can be found only in the actually performed legislating-administering-adjudicating activities of the nation and in the streams and currents of activity that gather among the people and rush into these spheres.

The people striking at somebody or something along lines that tend to produce purer food, safer insurance, better transportation facilities, or whatever else—that is the raw material of our study. That is the "simple fact" given us to examine, not the "complex fact" for us to build up in interpretation out of "simple" facts which we hold behind in our hands. Motives? They may be as complex as you will. And the more you deal with them the more complex they become. And with them you go into the labyrinth, not into the light.

The "ideas" and "feelings" appear on the scene, I have said, not for themselves, but in the form of words. Spoken and written language (signs and expressions included) is supposed to convey them from one person to another. This language is one form of activity. It is prominent in government and politics. We all know the sea of words in which political movements swim. We must not neglect it. On the other hand we must not overvalue it.

When we follow everyday theories and set the "feelings" and "ideas" off by themselves as the "causes" of the activities, we arrive at once at an enormous overvaluation of the forms of activity which appear in words. To the words are attributed a sort of monopoly of intelligence. Ideas, creeds, theories, and other such abstractions, all of them appearing actively as words, are supposed to rule the world, other things being merely ruled. One can get anywhere from primitive magic to "laissez faire" or a theocracy by this system.

It is no doubt because that particular form of activity which consists in the moving of the larynx or the pushing of a pencil has a direct value relation with such a very large proportion of all our activities that it has gained this extravagant attribution of importance. And then, too, the pencil-pushers naturally value their own activity most highly, and, as they have by far the best opportunities to make their valuation known, they have set a fashion of speech about it.

Language is surely a technique of fundamental importance. But nevertheless it is what is reflected in language that demands primary attention. Language must be regarded as a differentiated form of activity, and the only way we can handle it with any approach to scientific accuracy in studying social phenomena is by valuing it, not with reference to some theoretical idea or feeling content, but with reference to other activities directly.

The language activity is simply one case of the organ-within-an-organism problem. I consider it futile to discuss it in terms of organ and organism, mainly because when we use those terms we are desperately endeavoring to explain the better known by the less well known. And that is never profitable. But if there is any difference in principle between the language activity as differentiated from other activity, and any other form of the differentiation of social structure, I have failed to appreciate it. Observe, I am not here discussing quantities or relative importance, but simply the nature of this differentiation of activity.

When our popular leader—to revert to the Standard Oil illustration—gets upon the platform and tells us we must all rally with him to exterminate the trusts, we have so much raw material for investigation which we must take as so much activity for just what it is. If we start out with a theory about ideas and their place in politics, we are deserting our raw material even before we take a good peep at it. We are substituting something else which may or may not be useful, but which will certainly color our entire further progress, if progress we can make at all on scientific lines.

Now the speech, plus its thousands of printed reproductions, backed up by the excited audience that heard it and by the large part of the population that reads and approves it, is certainly a most significant factor in the political life of the country. But just as the speech itself is a differentiated bit of activity—we have it in no other form, remember, unless we consciously or unconsciously bolster it up with a theory made in advance and dragged in by violence—so this whole set of speaking-writing-indorsing people is a differentiated bit of activity. It is a group activity that has taken on, temporarily or with some permanence, a fairly definite form—definite enough, at any rate, for us to handle, describe, and value in terms of other activities. But if we are going to handle, describe, and value it with the greatest measure of success, we must be careful not to insert into it a theory of the importance of ideas any earlier than we have to. We shall find theoretical tangles set for our feet all too soon at the best, and we must insist on getting first of all a view as objective as possible of the talking-indorsing group of people to see how we can place it with other groups or group activities, also observed by us in the simplest, most direct manner we can bring ourselves to use.

If we label this group the "trust-busting group of August–September, 1906; Bryan, leader," we have something definite that we can take in hand and study. If we took merely the idea it purports to follow as our material, we never could get beyond our noses, without finding ourselves far out on the tangent that leads to infinity. If we took instead the set of conditions, economic or other, which we assume will decide the fate of this group, as our material, we might or might not get to the goal, but we never should follow the course. And the "course" in this case is just what we have to explain. It itself is our raw material. We must stick to it.

I want to make it clear that this "trust-busting group," "ideas" and all—for without the idea phase we could not define it—is much such a differentiation in social activity as any other group or organ or structure, whatever term we may use in discussing these things. Suppose we compare it with our federal Supreme Court, meaning by that term the justices who sit together and react upon certain people who come before them in certain ways. Now this is an extreme case, by no means the easiest for purposes of comparison, since the Supreme Court is an established body, presumably having no demands of its own, while the "trust-busting" group is so insistent in its demands that demands seem to be about all that it consists of. The Supreme Court is a relatively definite region in the configuration of social activity, itself brought to its present condition as the result of the pressure upon each other in the past of just such groups as the "trust-busters" represent today.

Both in the "trust-busting" group and in the Supreme Court a speaking, thinking, feeling process is observable. In both alike there is reasoning: it is purely arbitrary for us to set one down as reasoning and the other as vociferating merely on the basis of our personal sympathies. Each has structure, that is, each has a structural aspect, and it is only for limited temporary purposes that we are justified in calling the court group organization, and the other group public opinion or something similar with the emphasis on the opinion. From the most rarified reasoning circles to the most definite organization circles we are dealing all the time with a process identical in quality at every stage, a process of human activity.

"Trust-busters" and Supreme Court alike can be stated effectively only as activity, only in terms of their values for other groups. If "trust-busters," being by hypothesis in the minority among the people, work up too much steam, so that they become a nuisance, they will sooner or later perhaps conflict with the Supreme Court, supported by the majority of the people (I simplify the illustration to a mere counting of heads, leaving out other elements of strength), and a change will thereby be brought about in their lines of activity. Or, being in the majority, directly or indirectly, they will in time be working their will through the agency of the Supreme Court.

The point I have been striving to make is that the talk activities, the planning activities, as we actually find them among our raw materials, are differentiated activities of groups of men in society, with no more mystical, no more mysterious, no more fundamental, no more "causal" character to be assumed in them, than in any other groups or differentiated sets of activities. Just what their relations are with other activities, that is, just how the whole complex can best be stated to bring out the value of its parts, is something to be proved through investigation, not to be assumed in advance on the basis of any psychology whatever.

These talking, planning activities will have to be examined with great care as this work progresses. Any analysis of leadership or of public opinion, fundamentally important phases of all forms of government, must deal in great part with them. At every step we must regard them as activities and as nothing else. We must hold fast to what we can observe and examine and not prop them up on hypotheses until we are sure the hypotheses are of a kind that are useful to us. An inadequate vocabulary may occasion now and then sentences which seem to desert this position. In such cases leniency must be asked for the language and fair judgment for the thought behind the language; this very sentence, indeed, cries for mercy in just this respect.

It is now necessary to look a little closer at a specimen of this activity with its thought-feeling coloring; we must try to get a cross-section of it under the microscope. We have no microscope of glass and brass; we must make one by concentrating attention at the right spots.

If we limit the term activity to the motions of the body—the hands and feet and so forth—conceived of as more or less detached from the "man himself," and external to him, we do not get good material to study. Even such "external" activity as this cannot be understood as merely external. It must be regarded as the activity of the human being taken as a whole, as a person in society, and even then it must be valued in terms of thousands, or rather of millions, of individuals, if it is to have meaning as activity.

Suppose now I call such "external" activity manifest, or evident, or palpable activity. To it then must be added under the same term, activity, certain forms which are not palpable or evident to the same extent at the stage of their progress in which we have to search them out. They are activities which can perhaps be pictured by the use of the word "potential." Or, again, we may draw an analogy between them and molecular motion, in which case the palpable or external activity corresponds with molar motion. One way of stating them is to call them "tendencies of activity." This contrasts them seemingly with the external activity and is a half-compromise with everyday speech. It will only be tolerable if we remember every time we use the words that these "tendencies" are activities themselves; that they are stages of activity just as much as any other activity.

Suppose we should try to state the activity merely as the bodily motion, and then say that the tendency was the interior brain motion. There would be a certain utility in the statement, but we should probably find ourselves soon falling into the error of the natural scientist who carries his points of view with all their crudities into a field in which they will not apply at all adequately till their crudities have been greatly diminished. We should soon be following the error of everyday speech, which the natural scientist inevitably follows, and treating these brain motions concretely as feeling things, making them crude causes of outside happenings. This, however, would not do at all, both because of the logical collapse of all such theories and because, as I have previously shown, the whole structure of the outside world is presented to us in this very feeling-idea content, which is in this hypothetical way of speech supposed to be set over against it in opposition. We are driven back to a statement in which we give the brain motions value only in terms of bodily motions, which they mediate, and which are themselves (taken in the social mass) the creative or constructive phase of the whole world, social and physical, as we know it. I hardly need to add that I am not making this "activity" something different from or superior to any other experience; I am treating it simply as the view-point from which the unity of experience can best be appreciated, or, in other words, as the view-point from which our interpretation of society can best proceed and with which it can best make progress.

In the few pages immediately following, which are devoted to illustration of this use of the words, I cannot pretend adequately to justify my position. For such justification the whole of this book must be brought into reckoning, since this use of the words itself rests upon and is the outgrowth of the studies which fill up the rest of the book. I shall not later attempt to deduce anything from what I am here saying. I am merely trying here to indicate roughly how the great social processes work through the individuals, not transforming themselves from objective to subjective and back again to objective, but remaining always coherent and consistent activity. I do not strive at an interpretation of society in terms of qualitatively uniform activity because of what I am saying here, but I merely take the position I do take here because I find it is possible to interpret society in that way. If anyone deems it absurd to subsume these "tendencies" of which I have spoken under activity, I may perhaps refer to Zeno and his inclusion of rest under motion. Zeno is being rehabilitated in the latest mathematical thought, and the need of getting a coherent statement of rest and motion is no greater than the need of getting a point of view with reference to society from which we can look straight through the chains of activity without any breaking over into other worlds on the way.

Tendencies that are suppressed, checked, inhibited, postponed, are the most difficult to illustrate. If it is hard to see that there is a stage of activity that is not "palpable," but that still is activity, it is much harder to see that we have still to do with activity when there is an inhibitory process which to all appearances cuts our material off from any manifest bodily motions with which it can be directly connected. I will move from the simpler to the more difficult case in this exposition.

Now, of course, in everyday life the interpretation of the phenomena to which I am directing attention is made by the aid of the hypotheses of everyday psychology. A network of ideas, feelings, and motives is built up, set a-creaking, and made to explain the results. That ordinary psychology comes itself straight from observation of activities through the use of language for practical purposes. The word anger, for example, indicates certain contortions of the face and violent motions of the hands, with certain further tendencies of action. The ordinary psychology (I mean that psychology which we ordinarily find used in social interpretation) assumes an anger state or condition of the soul which produces those contortions and violent motions; and word and psychological hypothesis combined link together various varieties of anger activities for ease in description. But neither word nor psychological hypothesis ever get beyond the activity. They are limited strictly to the bringing-out of its meaning with reference to other activity. My own knowledge of my own anger states has just that much validity and no more.

Certainly no man has any direct experience of the feelings or other mental states of other men. He may make very useful, or very slipshod, inferences in terms of those feelings, and so forth, of other men; but the practical merit of his inferences, whether good or bad, is not in question here. For myself, my observation indicates that so far from having direct knowledge of the soul states of other men, the truth is I have next to none of my own. I know myself, so far as I have any knowledge that is worth while, by observation of my actions, and indeed largely not by my own observations, but by what other people observe and report to me directly or indirectly about my actions. These observations about myself are not different in character, so far as I am aware, from the observations about other persons or things, which I use as material of study or for practical guidance. There is no greater certainty that they are correct by practical tests. So far as I have observed other people they get their knowledge about themselves in much the same way.

Whatever physical phase, therefore, there is to "anger," and whatever shorthand paths of expression may be used about it, it is, as it is concretely known to us, supported on a skeleton of language dealing with observed varieties of action in ourselves and in others.

If we should follow this anger activity backward in time, we should find it a complex of certain other activities, which, when stated with sufficient completeness, would state the anger activity itself with no need of any soul-plus to add to it. But we do not here want to follow it backward, but rather, taking it as an activity roughly indicated by the word anger, to follow it forward. It is sure to be found intertwining itself in other activities, with greater or less need of new descriptive words to help us to place it. The outcome will be noticeably different, for example, according as my anger evolves around the office boy, around a drunken prize-fighter, or around my own knotted shoelace. Wherever and however it works, we can state it fully in terms of various activities. However addicted we may be to the use of psychological terms in causal senses, we can still with a little practice succeed in stating simple "soul states" in terms of activity.

But now we come to the suppressed, checked, blocked, post-poned, or inhibited activities which will probably seem not "tendencies to action" but rather "tendencies" which have no clearly evident action following after them. It is here much harder to get the focus on the facts. Suppose our angry man "dissembles." That also is a way of action. The anger activity which was working toward a blow with the fist now stops part way, and pauses, perhaps waiting a more fitting time for the blow. The man will tell his confidential friend about the situation, perhaps in terms of anger, perhaps in terms of hate. We, however, unwilling to erect a word into a "soul state" and explain things by means of it, must try what we can do by getting all the activities that are involved stated as fully as possible. We find literally the man's body, the whole man, not merely his abstract "soul," but all of him, poised as if to spring. He is directed toward some further activity which will be more palpable, but no more truly activity. As placed in his social world he will have many tendencies working through him at the same time. There will be not merely the immediate irritation relation, whatever it was, but also various other relations, such as those with the spectators, with broader activities, or with the law, all these being commonly indicated by the use of terms such as motives. These various phases of activity, these relations, are working in a system of conflicts and adaptations (I will discuss the system phase in the next chapter), and a palpable activity results which involves all of them, however definitely for practical purposes in everyday speech we may identify it with a single one.

If we state the full situation in terms of all the activities entering into it, we give values to the man's present attitude, and we get the meaning out of it in a way in which we can handle it. Our statement will be too complicated and cumbrous to serve the turn of the man and his friend in their talk about his fit of anger, but it will be much more adequate for our purposes of further investigation. If we want to simplify the statement for any special need of our own investigation, we shall then be free to choose such a method of simplification as suits our ends. We shall not be tied down to the current psychological simplification, which almost inevitably would lead us into bogs and quicksands where we should lose sight of our very task itself, even before we get well started toward its achievement.

The cases I have been discussing are simpler to use in preliminary illustration than would be the kinds of social activity with which we shall be most concerned in studying government. But actually such cases as this are very much more complicated when we try to state them in terms of activity than are the ordinary social facts with which we have to deal. There is too much which we have no possible chance to observe, or even to learn of at second hand, in the activities involved in an individual man's anger. The biologist can tell us a great deal that is important about earthworms, but if we demand of him an explanation as to just what factors bring it about that two chance earthworms, as individuals, vary in this, that, and the other particular, we should be asking something that he could not usually even attempt to answer. He has nowhere to turn for the material for his answer.

Let us now transport ourselves into the directors' room of an individual corporation, in order to see whether the procedure that takes place there can be stated on a basis of activity or whether we need the mechanism of concreted ideas, feelings, character, knowledge, motives, and so on, to enable us to state the facts.

If we made use of such a mechanism we should say that the directors had knowledge of the affairs of the corporation in varying
degrees; that they varied in character with respect to their honesty,
eagerness for large dividends, and scruples as to improper business methods; that they represented varying interests outside
of the corporation's interest, which alone they are supposed to
represent, and that they varied in their degree of business acumen.
We should combine these factors and say that a proposed policy
for extending the corporation's sphere of operations was adpoted
or rejected as the result of all of them taken together, and we
should almost inevitably pass judgment upon the wisdom or unwis-
dom of the decision in accordance with our own view-points.

This way of stating the situation would be very useful if we
were attending a stockholder's meeting and preparing to cast our
votes on the election of new directors, or if we were passing judgment on a question of policy, or if perhaps we were preparing to
preach a little public sermon on directors and their duties.

But suppose we wish to place that corporation in the industrial
life of the country. It will then be primarily the activities of the
corporation as they are reflected and guided through the directors'
meeting to which we shall give emphasis. There may be two
policies competing for adoption. We can state these in terms
of the corporation's contacts with the world around it, in terms,
that is, of its opportunities. The different directors will reflect
these opportunities in different ways. That sentence is misleading
but it cannot be helped. If the reader will take the emphasis off
the disreputable grammatical subject which makes all the trouble
by its pretense of independence, and try to see the corporation
activity streaming right through the directors toward realization
on one line or another, he will see the social facts, the given raw
material, without the misleading structure of hypothetical psychology in which it is ordinarily stated. The corporation is nothing
but men. Its activities are nothing but the specialized activities
of those men. Its factory wheels turn, its products stream out
under the hands of those men. It stretches its activities out in
this direction or that like the pseudopodia of an amoeba; there

may be a pulling or hauling, a strain between the activities; one gives way, another prevails. And it is just the same when the activities have not yet carried themselves through till they show signs visible to the outer world; it is just the same while they are still under debate in the directors' room. The two plans, the two tendencies of the two factions of the directors, reflecting two contacts with the surrounding world, two opportunities, fuse and break away and fuse again till the corporation activities move definitely forth on a positive, clear, visible line. But it is not the plans as abstractly stated, as idea, that thus conflict or coalesce. It is the active groups of men, for whom the plans are but symbols or labels.

The whole situation can be stated in such terms. It can be stated much more adequately than it can be stated by the psychology of verbosity fresh drawn from practical life. It can be stated in a way in which all the physical world—the environment—can be taken up into the human activity, and in which all the troublesome human soul states can be reduced to terms of human activity. It can be stated so that a fair chance will be given to explain the whole complex of social activity with the corporation activity in the midst of it, and thereby to get a fairer start toward the interpretation of the structural lines of activity of the whole society.

For the present one other illustration must suffice. Suppose we have a corrupt city government under consideration, and want to reach a statement of the phenomena involving corruption which will help us in analysis and in comparison with other similar phenomena. We can use the word "corruption," to begin with, as a rough indication of the field of phenomena we are to explain, without committing ourselves thereby to any special principle or set of judgments, moral or other, about it. Now, the usual method of statement used, for example, in the newspaper editorial, tells us that certain corrupt acts have been committed because corrupt men have been in office or have controlled officials or both. Put in men who are not corrupt, the argument runs, and you will not suffer from corrupt acts. There is, of course, a certain measure of truth and a certain practical value in this form of statement;

otherwise it would not be used. It is a very useful statement, indeed, for campaign time. But it will not carry us very far for our purposes. There are too many questions about the special forms which the corruption takes, about the extent to which it is carried, and about its appearance at one spot and not at another, which cannot be answered in such terms. If we explain the facts in terms of "corrupt men," we find ourselves merely erecting a set of problems in the background corresponding identically with the problems in the foreground, but not throwing any light upon the latter, when closely examined. Moreover we involve ourselves in a mass of contradictions, and stimulate contradictory forms of statement which still further heighten the confusion. The statement in terms of "corrupt men" is, in short, much too crude. It generalizes along limited lines and does not take nearly enough of the factors described as "environment" into consideration.

What is necessary for us to do in a case like this is to forget the crude mental and moral qualities for a time, and stick close to the acts that are actually performed. We must study these as they come, in as full detail as we have capacity to handle; we must bring them into relation with the acts of men in other phases of the same city, and with similar acts in other cities. It is not moral "qualities," remember, but actual activities, that we must compare. To do this we must find out what circles of the population those activities most directly represent in each case; we must get them stated in terms of the opportunities for activity in the different cases; we must work them out in terms of other circles of men whom they affect, or injure, and we must get some measurement of the extent of the injury. This cannot be done without including a statement of the technique that exists for reaction against injuries of these kinds. When all this is done with sufficient painstaking we shall find that we no longer need crudely to attribute municipal corruption to "bad men," while on the other hand we have not neglected any of the human-nature facts referred to by the terms which describe "badness," but rather have comprehended much more of the mass of such facts. We shall have the human nature and the environment comprised in our very statement of the activities themselves—the actual happenings. We shall not have "bare" activity, but very rich activity as material for further theorizing.

As a matter of fact, just this sort of thing is actually done both in popular agitation and in theoretical discussion as it now exists. For instance, when municipal corruption and public-service corporations in private management are brought into connection, the solid structure of the argument rests on a direct correlation of activities as found by observation. And this remains true, however vaguely the process is comprehended at the time, however much it is overshot with statements in terms of mental and moral qualities. The important thing is to make such statements as these not accidentally, but deliberately, not partially, but exhaustively, not in a medium of extraneous ideas and feelings, but with the idea-feeling shadings thoroughly taken up into them at their practical value.

I have said incidentally above that the environment itself can be taken up into the statement in terms of activity. On this point some further explanation is necessary. Ordinarily we treat the environment as external and as sharply separated from the men who by means of certain qualities that characterize them are supposed to act upon it. That does very well for current conversation about our experiences. It also does very well for preliminary description of certain phases of our activities. No one wants to eliminate geography from our scientific knowledge. Only, even here, it is necessary to remember that for any studies of society we may make this geography is a very far-away, very external, description of certain phases of human activities. It is all right by itself, but for a study of society it must not be so much used by the latter as taken up into it.

Let us look at the physical environment, say, of the people of the United States. There is not a factor of it that has any importance or any meaning whatsoever for a study of government, or for that matter for any study of social activity, save as it is a part

and parcel of men's activities.   In other words, it is not the environment we have to use, but certain special activities of men, which
can only be stated, environment and all.   That is our raw material.
Our national domain, the fertile land ready for immediate use,
which was available until recently for our expanding population,
is a good illustration.   Given no increasing population, no improving transportation, that land would have had little meaning for
our country.   Given a population of different activities, it would
have a different meaning.   By taking the land plus the knowledge
of its use we can get a half-way statement good enough for some
purposes.   But the knowledge factor is full of pitfalls as we have
to use it; and no combination of part statements gives us anything
more, or indeed nearly so much, as a definite statement of our
actual doings and tendencies of doing.   Gold in the ground is
a cipher for a study of society so long as we are doing nothing and
not tending to do anything in connection with it.   Gold that does
not exist is an important factor when we are in a turmoil of chasing
for it.   Mountains have various meanings, according as we are
fighting, railroad-building, food-hunting, cattle-raising, or health-
seeking.   It is not the mountains at all, but the "meanings,"
the practical, actual, uses that form our material of social study.
The silver mines, as such, had nothing to do with the campaign of
1896, but certain silver-mining men did.   Bad weather for crops
abstractly stated is negligible, but men with changed activities
according as granaries are full or empty are never negligible.
Mosquitoes twenty years ago and today are negligible, but men
angry at little pests twenty years ago, and men fighting yellow
fever and malaria today come upon our scene in different valua-
tions.   This is so evident that it may possibly seem not worth
emphasizing.   But it makes a great difference in many phases of
the study of government whether the environment, abstracted
from the human activities which contain it as part of their structure, is dragged in for itself alone, or whether it is treated as the
raw material presents it to us—a phase of the activities, not as
something external "plus" the acting men.

   Suppose we take such a social fact as the struggle of the coal miners for a 5.5-per-cent. increase in pay, with many variations in the terms of their demand in different mining districts where different kinds of coal are produced and where different processes are used. The whole comes to an adjustment, and one can, of course, indicate the lines of adjustment to some extent by describing the different mining fields as so much physical nature. But at every stage of the process it will be not the mines objectively, but the mines in terms of the men who are working in them, who own them, and who use the product, which must be taken into account, and all the factors are reducible to terms of groups of men, in which terms they get their best and richest statement, with the fullest values, the most complete "relations," brought to light.

We can get further light on this fact, even at this early stage of our analysis, by aid of a reference to that absurdity which is now and then seriously discussed—the "social environment." This social environment must be by definition a something plus the men who are members of the society; otherwise one cannot get out of mysticism in talking about it. But the society is itself composed of all of these same men. Hence it should be clear that if one is really discussing the given social facts, the raw material for our study, one cannot possibly deal with a social environment. The social environment is merely one aspect of the raw material, itself a social fact. It is only when one makes a fixed starting-point with the individual man, A, that one can put meaning into the phrase, "social environment." But if one does that one is not really studying social facts as he finds them. He is settling his whole study in advance by a whole mass of assumptions about the individuality of the man, A, assumptions which no doubt are all very well for their proper purposes, but which cut the ground out from under our feet in this place. Such a study is merely a systemization and dignifying of A's little outlook on the world. It has no value beyond the A variety of world-reflection, from which it starts, and to which it is forever bound.

And along with "social environment," I may add, the "social heredity" that is frequently heard of must also be driven out as an impossibility. It also has meaning only in terms of the fixed individual to which it is referred. If we get a truly social statement, then the heredity phase disappears, because the whole material is the social material just as it stands, and the addition of a heredity idea is meaningless. In other words, while it is natural, from an individual's standpoint, to talk of a "social heredity" of the customs and habits and speech forms passed along from the individuals of one generation to the individuals of the next, nevertheless if we take a view-point that sweeps across individuals, that takes them primarily in masses, we shall see the social facts, the raw material, not merely spread out in space, but extended in time through the ages; and the use of the word heredity in this connection will at once show itself to be superfluous and, since superfluous, misleading and harmful. What is true in this way of the past is equally true of the future in social interpretation, from the same point of view. It is not the individual's "future," but the social fact in time which we have before us.

This consideration of environment brings us back to that distinction between subjective and objective which we have already discarded so far as any value it has for social interpretation is concerned; for the physical environment makes up a great part of that objective over against which the subjective is placed. Indeed, the old distinction and, for that matter, every distinction between mind and matter, as obverse and reverse, or however put, is a very crude metaphor; and, one may say, it is little complimentary to human ingenuity that such a metaphor has been made to do service so long. All distinctions between wants, and the men who want, and the external acts of these men, and the institutions, or things done by them, and the external world in which these things done are supposed to exist, when made concretely and treated as different kinds of "things," are very crude. We do not get in them different parts of a machine; but instead, different phases of a process which, while serving certain practical ends, will certainly not serve interpretative purposes. Likewise any distinction between the conscious and the unconscious, made concretely, and not merely as different shadings of the process through which a common material passes, is equally crude. Society rests on the whole nervous system, and indeed on the whole physique, and not merely on certain crudely described "states" in the higher brain centers.

We shall find as we go on that even in the most deliberative acts of heads of governments, what is done can be fully stated in terms of the social activity that passes through, or is reflected, or represented, or mediated in those high officials, much more fully than by their alleged mental states as such. Mark Twain tells of a question he put to General Grant: "With whom originated the idea of the march to the sea? Was it Grant's or was it Sherman's idea?" and of Grant's reply: "Neither of us originated the idea of Sherman's march to the sea. The enemy did it;" an answer which points solidly to the social content, always in individuals, but never to be stated adequately in terms of individuals.

It is the same with all other forms of invention and discovery. We shall find that the forces and pressures at work are great masses, groups, of men. From this starting-point we shall come to the same position that we reached when, starting from the environment a moment ago, we found that it had to be stated in terms of masses, or groups, of men before it got any full meaning in social interpretation. We shall find in the same way that that similarity in the character of differentiation which I tried to illustrate some pages back as between talk groups and organization groups, holds for all the so-called socially psychic features of society as well as for all the institutional features; and that from the point of view of activity all these features can be valued in terms of one another, the customs and social classes and subclasses and the knowledge and religious factors and all that we come into contact with.

If any such view of the raw material of our study as I have outlined sacrifices anything whatever of the mental and moral qualities, of the feelings and ideas, of the motives and wisdom, or rather of the real meaning of all these factors, which appear in ordinary talk of social life, then the view I have taken is a false view, in the sense that it is inadequate. It is to be rejected, not accepted. My own attempts at the study of social facts have shown me no such sacrifice whatever, but rather, as I have insisted before, a great increase in completeness of statement.

I do not point to human mental and moral qualities in the form of concrete feelings and ideas, definite, fixed causes which produce results, effects at the same time of other causes, forming links in a long series of causes and effects of which society is made up. But then who can point to such feelings and ideas in the actual material he uses, without regard to his initial theories about it?

Each man is a feeling, thinking being. That much I can admit without making any objection to it, but without having any special use for, or interest in, the statement. It may be, for all I know or for all I care, that this fact, or position, or inference, or whatever it is, has the germ of eternal truth in it; it may give meaning some day to an interpretation of the whole universe in some peculiarly satisfying form. Whether it does or does not, it is certainly none of my business here; and I conceive that it is none of the business of any man who is settling down to study the phenomena of government from the raw material. A purely functional psychology from the individual view-point is, of course, legitimate, but that again is not our problem here.

Leaving then this question of the self-existent soul states to its own devices, we are concerned, so far as the feelings and ideas go, with not losing any of their value in our social interpretations. Intelligent actions, emotional actions, linked actions, trains of action, planned actions, plotted actions, scheming, experimenting, persisting, exhorting, compelling, mastering, struggling, co-operating—such activities by the thousand we find going on around us in populations among which we are placed. There are many systems of interpreting and valuing them found with them; and such interpreting and valuing is a phase of all the activity we find, while here and there it appears in such differentiated forms that it seems to stand for itself alone. If we can get the activities analyzed we may be very confident that no feelings and no ideas will get lost in the process. One man's work may be deficient in the analysis, and do violence to some of the fact that is meant when certain feelings and ideas are referred to in ordinary speech. But that man who fails will have his work corrected by others who get more adequate results than he. No doubt when an adequate analysis of social activity in any line is made, there will be "feelings" and "ideas" standing outside, lifting up their voices in wailing at their neglect. No matter. If such unfortunates cannot show themselves as representing important phases of the activities that we are studying, they have no claim to consideration. They may cheerfully be permitted to wail themselves into oblivion.

One more question remains as to this raw material for the study of government. Ought we not to draw a distinction in advance between it and other varieties of social activity, so that we can have our field of study defined and delimited at the outset? The answer is No. Many a child, making paper toys, has used his scissors too confidently and cut himself off from the materials he needs. That is an error to avoid. Instead, we shall plunge into any phenomena or set of phenomena belonging to the roughly recognized field of government, be it Congress in session, a town meeting, a murderer's trial, a ballot-box manipulation at election time, or a mass meeting communicating the oracles of the age. If any of these things lead us to interesting paths we shall be prepared to follow them, heedless of definitions. Who likes may snip verbal definitions in his old age, when his world has gone crackly and dry.

CHAPTER VII
GROUP ACTIVITIES

It is impossible to attain scientific treatment of material that will not submit itself to measurement in some form. Measure conquers chaos. Even in biology notable advances by the use of statistical methods are being made. And what is of most importance, the material the biologist handles is of a kind that is susceptible of measurement and quantitative comparison all the way through. The occasional recrudescence of vitalism in biology is not irreconcilable with this statement. It simply indicates that from time to time some investigator directs his attention to phases of life, ever lessening in extent, which, he holds, are not measurable by present processes, and which, it pleases him to feel, will remain unmeasurable.

In the political world, the dictum, "the greatest good of the greatest number," stands for an effort to make measurements. Sometimes, of course, it is simply the rallying-cry of particular causes. If we take it, however, where it pretends to be a general rule of measurement, we shall find that it applies itself not to what actually happens in legislation, but merely to what a thinker in some particular atmosphere believes ought to be the law; and this, no matter what systematic content of "goods" is pumped into it. I hope to make it clear later that even such a generalized social theory as this is nothing but a reflection, or an index, or a label, of some particular set of demands made by some particular section of society. It is not a measure of social facts which we can use for scientific purposes, and it would not be thus useful even if logically it could be regarded as a standard of measurement, which, of course, it cannot be without further specification.

Statistics of social facts as we ordinarily get them are, of course, measurements. But even after they have been elaborately interpreted by the most expert statisticians, they must still undergo much further interpretation by the people who use them with reference to their immediate purposes of use. As they stand on the printed page, they are commonly regarded as "dead," and they receive much undeserved disparagement. But by this very token it is clear that they do not adequately state the social facts. People who are in close connection with all that rich life-activity indicated by the "feelings" and the "ideas" feel that the heart of the matter is lacking in them.

But, now, the idea and feeling elements, stated for themselves, are unmeasureable as they appear in studies of government. This is a fatal defect in them. Any pretense of measuring them, no matter with what elaborate algebra, will prove to be merely an attribution to them of powers inferred from their results. Usually they appear in social discussions with wholly fictitious values, in support of which not even a pretense of actual measurement is presented. The measurements of experimental psychology are not such measurements as we need. They are measurements of activity looked upon as within the physical individual. The social content is incidental to them and is not measured.

If a statement of social facts which lends itself better to measurement is offered, that characteristic entitles it to attention. Providing the statement does not otherwise distort the social facts, the capability of measurement will be decisive in its favor. The statement that takes us farthest along the road toward quantitative estimates will inevitably be the best statement.

In practical politics a large amount of rough measuring is done. There is measurement with the sword when one nation defeats another in war. South American revolutions, which answer to North American elections, also use the sword as their standard of measure. Under Walpole the different elements in politics sought equilibrium in great part by the agency of gold coin and gold-bearing offices. In an election at its best in the United States, the measurement goes by the counting of heads. In a legislative body, likewise, the counting of heads appears. A referendum vote is political measurement.

This measuring process appears in various degrees of differentiation. In a battle the social quantities, and the measuring of those quantities which is taking place on the spot, are fused together, so that one has to make an effort to consider them separately. But in a vote in the federal House of Representatives differentiation appears. Here a much more complicated measuring process is carried through, which appears finally in a simplified form in the announcement of the vote for and against the project by the tellers. The student of political life has some hint of the measurements in the figures of the vote; but it is necessary for him to measure the measure, to go far back and examine the quantities that have been in play to produce the given results. The best of these practical political measures are indeed exceedingly crude. The practical politician himself is estimating quantities all the time; indeed his success is in direct proportion to his ability to make good estimates. He may show a preternatural skill. But his skill is of little or no direct use for the scientific student. The practical politician will never under any circumstances consent to make a plain statement of his estimates; indeed it is rare that he knows how to tell, even if he should wish to.

The quantities are present in every bit of political life. There is no political process that is not a balancing of quantity against quantity. There is not a law that is passed that is not the expression of force and force in tension. There is not a court decision or an executive act that is not the result of the same process. Understanding any of these phenomena means measuring the elements that have gone into them.

If we can get our social life stated in terms of activity, and of nothing else, we have not indeed succeeded in measuring it, but we have at least reached a foundation upon which a coherent system of measurements can be built up. Our technique may be very poor at the start, and the amount of labor we must employ to get scanty results will be huge. But we shall cease to be blocked by the intervention of unmeasurable elements, which claim to be themselves the real causes of all that is happening, and which by their spook-like arbitrariness make impossible any progress toward dependable knowledge.

I have used the word activity or action thus far to designate the point of view from which an adequate statement of the phemomena must be sought. The activity is always the activity of men. I might have said "men" straightway at the beginning, instead of activity, but "men" has too many implications which it was necessary to keep from creeping in where they would give rise to misconception. Perhaps now, however, I can discuss the same subject in terms of men direct.

Human society is always a mass of men, and nothing else. These men are all of them thinking-feeling men, acting. Political phenomena are all phenomena of these masses. One never needs to go outside of them. One must take them as they come, that is in the masses in which they are found aggregated. In some cases and for some purposes this is easy to do. At the time of the Russo-Japanese war it was easy to take Japan in one mass and Russia in another and watch them react upon each other. It is easy to take one of our American states as apart from some other, say California as apart from New York, though the interactions which would require our taking them in this way are very rare and usually negligible. It is easy to take the mass, "New York City," and separate it from the mass, "New York State outside the city." Similarly in some societies one can take a family group and hold it fairly distinct from surrounding family groups, for purposes of examination.

But in the complex modern state it is seldom that our problems involve masses as sharply separated as these. Take, for example, New York City and New York State. The state includes the city. In many political problems involving the two we must hold the New York City people as city residents, apart from those same people as state residents. We must keep them distinct in their two functions. We find them in two groups, which must be separated in our analysis. The same physical men are among the components of both, and perhaps they find themselves in one group pulling against themselves in another group. It is exceedingly hard, indeed almost impossible, to hold such groups apart in terms of logic—witness the hair-splitting of the lawbooks over state and federal citizenship.   Fortunately, it is much simpler in terms of facts.

Still the difficulty of picturing the nation as made up of groups of men, each group cutting across many others, each individual man a component part of very many groups, is by no means inconsiderable.   But the difficulty disappears as practice shows us how to concentrate attention on the essential features and to strip off incidental points which appear to have extravagant importance because of the prepossessions as to the nature of human individuality with which the task is approached.   With increased facility in thus observing society we find we are coming to state more and more adequately the raw material of political life.   If a law is in question, we find that our statement of it in terms of the groups of men it affects—the group or set of groups directly insisting on it, those directly opposing it, and those more indirectly concerned in it—is much more complete than any statement in terms of self-interest, theories, or ideals.   If it is a plank in a political platform, again we find we can state its actual value in the social process at the given time in terms of the groups of men for whose sake it is there: a group of politicians and a number of groups of voters holding the prominent places.

The whole social life in all its phases can be stated in such groups of active men, indeed must be stated in that way if a useful analysis is to be had.   Sometimes the groups, although not territorially distinct, gain a marked separation, so that two opposing parties may face each other with well-closed ranks.   Then again all is seemingly confusion, and the crossed lines of different groups seem too tangled to be followed.

What a man states to himself as his argument or reasoning or thinking about a national issue is, from the more exact point of view, just the conflict of the crossed groups to which he belongs. To say that a man belongs to two groups of men which are clashing with each other; to say that he reflects two seemingly irreconcilable aspects of the social life; to say that he is reasoning on a question of public policy, these all are but to state the same fact in three forms.   How was it with a cattle-raiser during the campaign for the passage of a meat-inspection law by Congress in the spring of 1906? All cattle-raisers had interests both as producers and consumers (I will presently return to this use of the word interest and justify it). Some reflected their producers' interest so strongly that it quickly dominated; they arrayed themselves with the opposition to the bill. Others, a much smaller number, it is true, reflected their producer's interests on broader lines, or reflected primarily the consumers' interests of the country, and found themselves lined up with the group behind the President. It is not the set of reasonings put forth by men on either side, but the position that they assumed, which had its roots—for the mass—much deeper than the reasonings, that is the vital political fact. The reasonings help us in the analysis, but only as indicating where to look for the facts; and one token is that in most cases the reasonings, at least the elaborate reasonings, come long after the assumption of position on the question, and as supplementary to it, and explanatory of it.

When one hears a loud public outcry against "corporations," it is easy to prove logically the folly of the outcry, but such proof is irrelevant and immaterial for genuine study of what is happening in society. The outcry, just as it is heard, indicates certain very real group facts, and these facts are themselves the vital facts of the process. The people afflicted with "corporationphobia" are much better justified in sneering at their intellectually arrogant critics than are the latter in sneering at them.

It is possible to take a Supreme Court decision, in which nothing appears on the surface but finespun points of law, and cut through all the dialectic till we get down to the actual groups of men underlying the decisions and producing the decisions through the differentiated activity of the justices. In most cases this substantial basis of the decisions does not readily appear, because of the foundation of habitual activity on which the facts rest. But in exceptional cases, as when the court strikes out on a new line of precedent or gives a decision of a kind which, say, ten years earlier it would not possibly have rendered, the analysis can be made with comparative ease.

There is ample reason, then, for examining these great groups of acting men directly and accepting them as the fundamental facts of our investigation. They are just as real as they would be if they were territorially separated so that one man could never belong to two groups at the same time. They lose nothing in reality because one man may belong to two conflicting groups and may be tossed up and down for a long time before he settles for the final steps of the process with one group to the exclusion of the others. They are vastly more real than a man's reflection of them in his "ideas" which inadequately interpret or misinterpret to him his course; which, as speech activity, help to reconcile him with the groups he deserts, and which help to establish him firmly with the group he finally cleaves to. Indeed the only reality of the ideas is their reflection of the groups, only that and nothing more. The ideas can be stated in terms of the groups; the groups never in terms of the ideas.

Every classification of the elements of a population must involve an analysis of the population into groups. It is impossible—at least, for any pending scientific problem—to make a classification so comprehensive and thorough that we can put it forth as "the" classification of the population. The purpose of the classification must always be kept in mind. This is because of the limitless criss-cross of the groups. It would only be in a rigorous caste organization of society, or perhaps in a very severe slavery in which one race held another in subjection, that the groups would so consolidate in separate masses of men that a classification—as, say, into white masters and black slaves—would serve for all the leading purposes of investigation. In nearly all cases of government with which we have to deal, and, I think I can say in practically all cases in modern society—excepting certain extreme cases of war, and these are more apparent than real—the varying sets of interests will not so settle or consolidate themselves upon masses of men as to make any one classification adequate for all interests. To illustrate, even in the case of our American Civil War, with North arrayed against South, there was a great array of groupings on other than war lines which cut across the war frontier. These reasserted themselves as soon as union was achieved, and would have reasserted themselves, though with more effort and less manifest result, had disunion been the outcome.

Perhaps I may be permitted to offer a geometrical picture of this mixture of the groups, under the assurance, however, that no proof depends on it, and that it pretends to be nothing more than a crude attempt at illustration. If we take all the men of our society, say all the citizens of the United States, and look upon them as a spherical mass, we can pass an unlimited number of planes through the center of the sphere, each plane representing some principle of classification, say, race, various economic interests, religion, or language (though in practice we shall have to do mainly with much more specialized groupings than these). Now, if we take any one of these planes and ignore the others, we can group the whole mass of the sphere by means of an outline or diagram traced upon the circle which the plane makes by its intersection with the sphere, and by partition walls erected on this outline at right angles to the circle. Our principle of classification may include the whole population, or it may have to allow for a section of the population indifferent to it; but the latter case can equally well be allowed for in the diagram. Similarly, by means of some other plane together with partition walls perpendicular to it, we can group the whole population on a different basis of classification: that is to say, for a different purpose.

Assuming perhaps hundreds, perhaps thousands, of planes passed through the sphere, we get a great confusion of the groups. No one set of groups, that is, no set distinguished on the basis of any one plane, will be an adequate grouping of the whole mass.

In case the planes should revolve till a great proportion of them came to coincide, we would possibly, though even then not certainly, be able to take a single grouping as roughly giving us "the" grouping of the mass. A very rigorous caste system, as before said, will somewhat answer to this condition, or two nations in war time, where we ignore the "habit background" on which the war is fought and a lot of other factors which still exist, though little vociferous, despite the war.

In great modern nations we are indeed often told that such a mass grouping, such an all-embracing classification, does actually exist in the form of the classes that enter into the class war of socialism. No socialist or other person has made an analysis, however, which can in any sense be said to prove that this hard grouping exists; nothing better is offered than emotional assumptions and class "ideas." Moreover the observed reactions in our societies are not such as would follow from such a grouping in which the criss-cross had disappeared, and sharply defined outlines were traceable—the war in fact is not to the finish, the socialism that extends itself to large portions of the population is, wherever we know it, a socialism that ends in political compromises. And compromise—not in the merely logical sense, but in practical life— is the very process itself of the criss-cross groups in action.

A classification into farmers, artisans, merchants, etc., will answer some purposes in studying our population, but not others. A classification by race answers some purposes, but not many unless it is fortified, as it may or may not be, by the coincidence with it of the planes of many other group classifications. One would be hard put, for example, to justify emphasis on a distinction between Germans and English in treating the local politics of a city like Chicago. And the same would be true of other races, Italians, Poles, or any that are present in no matter how large numbers, regarded as groups to be distinguished from one another by the race test alone, and acting as such in the political field. "Representation of the race on the ticket" and to some extent, also, a difference in attitude toward the liquor problem, would be about all that one could find in the way of lines of activity, and even that would probably be exaggerated out of all proper proportion by those who talked about it.

The great task in the study of any form of social life is the analysis of these groups. It is much more than classification, as that term is ordinarily used. When the groups are adequately stated, everything is stated. When I say everything I mean everything. The complete description will mean the complete science, in the study of social phenomena, as in any other field. There will be no more room for animistic "causes" here than there.

But it is not our task in this work to make an analysis of the groups that operate in the whole social life. We are to confine our attention to the process of politics, and the political groups are the only ones with which we shall be directly concerned. And indeed, our task even here concerns the method of analysis, not the exact statement of the groups that are operating at any particular time or place.

It would at first sight seem that the political process could not be studied till the process of the underlying groups had been studied, for political groups are built up out of, or, better said, upon, the other groups. Political groups are highly differentiated groups reflecting, or representing, other groups, which latter can easily, and I believe for most purposes properly, be regarded as more fundamental in society. The political process goes on, so to speak, well up toward the surface of society. The economic basis of political life must, of course, be fully recognized, though it does not necessarily follow that the economic basis in the usual limited use of the word is the exclusive, or even in every detail the dominant, basis of political activity.

Nevertheless, it is my conviction that political groups, highly differentiated as they are, can well be studied before the other groups; and that indeed one has better chance of success in studying the political groups first than in studying the other groups first. The very fact that they are so highly representative makes it easier to handle them. They are in closer connection with "ideas," "ideals," "emotions," "policies," " public opinion," etc., than are some of the other groups. I would better say, they work through a process of ideals, etc., more plainly than do the deeper-lying groups. And as the same psychic process, including all its elements, is involved in the facts which enter into the interpretation of all forms of social life, we have better prospects of successful work in a field in which we can get it, I will not say in most direct, but in most manifest, most palpable, most measurable form. If I may be pardoned a remark from my own experience, I will say that my interest in politics is not primary, but derived from my interest in the economic life; and that I hope from this point of approach ultimately to gain a better understanding of the economic life than I have succeeded in gaining hitherto.

We shall confine ourselves then to the groups that appear in politics, and as they appear in politics. Now the political groups can never safely be taken to be the same identical groups that we would analyze out in studies of other phases of the social life. The political action reflects, represents, the underlying groups; but the political groups will have different boundaries than the other groups; there will be splittings and consolidations; and even if as regards the persons belonging to them they are ever the same, even then they will have different ways of reaction, different activities; and since the activities *are* the groups, they cannot properly be called the same groups under exact discrimination. I do not mean at all that political parties, the Democratic, Republican, Prohibition, Socialist, and so on, are the essential groups for a political study. These are certain of the political groups, but we have to strike much deeper than their level. We have to get hold of the lower-lying political groups which they reflect or represent, just as in turn these lower-lying political groups reflect other groups, which are not properly speaking political. The "properly speaking," here, has merely to do with the particular plane of discrimination, the standard or test on the basis of which the group analysis is made. We shall have to take all these political groups, and get them stated with their meaning, with their value, with their representative quality. We shall have to get hold of political institutions, legislatures, courts, executive officers, and get them stated as groups, and in terms of other groups. The presidency, for example, is an institution that includes a considerable number of men in and out of office—ignoring for the moment constitutional theory on one side, and a little crackle of arbitrariness at the pinnacle on the other—and we must state it in terms of party and in terms of the nation, or rather in terms of those portions of the nation stated not in party but in deeper political groupings, which it represents at any moment or in any period. We shall have to get all the ideas and policies and selfishnesses that enter into current talk or specialized political talk stated in the same way, as differentiated activity, as the reflection of lower-lying activity.

When we have done all this in a preliminary manner, when we have our raw material in hand, then we shall be ready to set up theories about the relations of the activities. And so we can pass to a new and more adequate statement and at last to an interpretation, if we have fortune and perseverance, that will stand firmly the test of application. I do not mean by this, of course, to be outlining the path of this book, but to be outlining the long road on which the book is, I hope, taking some steps.

The term "group" will be used throughout this work in a technical sense. It means a certain portion of the men of a society, taken, however, not as a physical mass cut off from other masses of men, but as a mass activity, which does not preclude the men who participate in it from participating likewise in many other group activities. It is always so many men with all their human quality. It is always so many men, acting, or tending toward action—that is, in various stages of action. Group and group activity are equivalent terms with just a little difference of emphasis, useful only for clearness of expression in different contexts.

It is now necessary to take another step in the analysis of the group. There is no group without its interest. An interest, as the term will be used in this work, is the equivalent of a group. We may speak also of an interest group or of a group interest, again merely for the sake of clearness in expression. The group and the interest are not separate. There exists only the one thing, that is, so many men bound together in or along the path of a certain activity. Sometimes we may be emphasizing the interest phase, sometimes the group phase, but if ever we push them too far apart we soon land in the barren wilderness. There may be a beyond-scientific question as to whether the interest is responsible for the existence of the group, or the group responsible for the existence of the interest.   I do not know or care.   What we actually find in this world, what we can observe and study, is interested men, nothing more and nothing less.   That is our raw material and it is our business to keep our eyes fastened to it.

The word interest in social studies is often limited to the economic interest.   There is no justification whatever for such a limitation.   I am restoring it to its broader meaning coextensive with all groups whatsoever that participate in the social process. I am at the same time giving it definite, specific content wherever it is used.   I shall have nothing to say about "political interest" as such, but very much about the multiform interests that work through the political process.

I am dealing here with political groups and other groups that function in the specifically social process, and not extending the assertion that the words group and interest coincide, over all groups that on any plane can be analyzed out of masses of human beings.   One might put the blonde women of the country in one class and the brunettes in another, and call each class a group. It may be that a process of selection of blondes and brunettes is going on, and it may perhaps be—I am taking an extreme case— that it will sometime be found necessary to classify some phase of that process as social and to study it along with other social phenomena.   I am not expressing an opinion as to that, and I have no need of forming an opinion.   Whether that attitude is taken or not will depend upon practical considerations upon which the investigator himself must pass.   I would not say that such a "group" for other than social studies could properly be described as having a blonde or brunette interest in the meaning here given to interest.   It would not be a social group, and probably the equivalent of the interest could be better specified without the use of that particular word.   But that is neither here nor there.   The essential point is that if ever blondes or brunettes appear in political life as such it will be through an interest which they assert, or— what comes in general to the same thing, when the analysis is fully made—which is asserted for them through some group or group leadership which represents them.

In the political world, if we take the interest alone as a psychological quality, what we get is an indefinite, untrustworthy will-o'-the-wisp, which may trick us into any false step whatsoever. Once set it up and we are its slaves, whatever swamp it may lead us to. If we try to take the group without the interest, we have simply nothing at all. We cannot take the first step to define it. The group is activity and the activity is only known to us through its particular type, its value in terms of other activities, its tendency where it is not in the stage which gives manifest results. The interest is just this valuation of the activity, not as distinct from it, but as the valued activity itself.

In using the term interest there are two serious dangers against which we must carefully guard ourselves. One is the danger of taking the interest at its own verbal expression of itself, that is to say, the danger of estimating it as it is estimated by the differentiated activity of speech and written language which reflects it. The other danger is at the far extreme from this. It is that we disregard the group's expressed valuation of itself and that we assign to it a meaning or value that is "objective" in the sense that we regard it as something natural or inevitable or clothed in oughtness. If we should substitute for the actual interest of the activity some "objective utility," to use the economist's term, we should be going far astray, for no such "objective utility" appears in politics at all, however otherwise it may be attributed to the men who compose the society. It is like the undiscovered and unsuspected gold under the mountain, a social nullity. A man who is wise enough may legitimately predict, if he is addicted to the habit of prediction, that a group activity will ultimately form along lines marked out by some objective condition which he thinks he detects. But the interests that we can take into account must lie a good deal closer to the actual existing masses of men than that.

If we cannot take words for our test, and if we cannot take "bed-rock truth," one may say we are left swinging hopelessly in between. Quite the contrary. The political groups are following definite courses. They may appear erratic, but hardly ever to anyone who is in close enough contact with them. The business of the student is to plot the courses. And when he does that—it is the course of only a single step, not of a whole career, that he can plot—he will find that he has all together, the group, the activity, and the interest.

The essential difference between interest as I am defining it and the psychological feeling or desire qualities should be already apparent. I am not introducing any suppositional factor which can be taken in hand, applied to the social activities and used in the pretense of explaining them. I am not taking any mental or other possession which the individual man is supposed to have before he enters society and using it to explain the society. I am not dealing with anything which can be scheduled to any desired extent as a set of abstract general interests, capable of branching out to correspond with the complexity of the activity of the social world. I am not using any interest that can be abstractly stated apart from the whole social background in which it is found at the moment of use.

The interest I put forward is a specific group interest in some definite course of conduct or activity. It is first, last, and all the time strictly empirical. There is no way to find it except by observation. There is no way to get hold of one group interest except in terms of others. A group of slaves for example, is not a group of physical beings who are "slaves by nature," but a social relationship, a specified activity and interest in society. From the interest as a thing by itself no conclusion can be drawn. No fine logic, no calculus of interests will take us a single step forward in the interpreting of society. When we succeed in isolating an interest group the only way to find out what it is going to do, indeed the only way to be sure we have isolated an interest group, is to watch its progress. When we have made sure of one such interest, or group, we shall become more skilful and can make sure of another similar one with less painstaking. When we have compared many sets of groups we shall know better what to expect. But we shall always hold fast to the practical reality, and accept the interests that it offers us as the only interests we can use, studying them as impassively as we would the habits or the organic functions of birds, bees, or fishes.

Such interest groups are of no different material than the "individuals" of a society. They are activity; so are the individuals. It is solely a question of the standpoint from which we look at the activity to define it. The individual stated for himself, and invested with an extra-social unity of his own, is a fiction. But every bit of the activity, which is all we actually know of him, can be stated either on the one side as individual, or on the other side as social group activity. The former statement is in the main of trifling importance in interpreting society; the latter statement is essential, first, last, and all the time. It is common to contrast conditions in India or elsewhere in which "the community is the political unit," with conditions in our own society in which "the individual is the political unit." But in reality such a contrast is highly superficial and limited, made for special purposes of interpretation within the process. From the point of view here taken all such contrasts fade into insignificance except as they are "raw material" when the special processes in connection with which they are made are being studied.

When we have a group fairly well defined in terms of its interests, we next find it necessary to consider the factors that enter into its relative power of dominating other groups and of carrying its tendencies to action through their full course with relatively little check or hindrance. As the interest is merely a manner of stating the value of the group activity, so these factors of dominance are likewise just phases of the statement of the group, not separate from it, nor capable of scientific use as separate things.

First of all, the number of men who belong to the group attracts attention. Number alone may secure dominance. Such is the case in the ordinary American election, assuming corruption and intimidation to be present in such small proportions that they do not affect the result. But numbers notoriously do not decide elections in the former slave states of the South. There is a concentration of interest on political lines which often, and indeed one may say usually, enables a minority to rule a majority. I cannot stop here to discuss the extent to which majorities are represented by minorities under such circumstances, but only to note the fact. Intensity is a word that will serve as well as any other to denote the concentration of interest which gives a group effectiveness in its activity in the face of the opposition of other groups.

This intensity, like interest, is only to be discovered by observation. There is no royal road for scientific workers to take to it. Catchwords like race, ability, education, moral vigor, may serve as tags to indicate its presence, but they are of little or no help to us, and indeed they are more apt to do us positive harm by making us think we have our solutions in advance, and by blinding us to the facts that we should study. Mere vociferation must not be confused with intensity. It is one form of intensity, but very often the intensity of the talk does not correctly reflect the true intensity of the group. This must be allowed for.

Besides number and intensity, there is a technique of group activities which must be taken into account. Blows, bribes, allurements of one kind and another, and arguments also, are characteristic, and to these must be added organization. A group will differentiate under fitting circumstances a special set of activities for carrying on its work. We must learn how these specialized activities vary under different forms of group oppositions, how the technique changes and evolves. We shall find that the change in methods is produced by the appearance of new group interests, directed against the use of the method that is suppressed. If violence gives way to bribery, or bribery to some form of demagogy, or that perhaps to a method called reasoning, it will be possible, if we pursue the study carefully enough, to find the group interest that has worked the change. That group will have its own technique, no more scrupulous probably than the technique it suppresses, but vigorously exerted through the governing institutions of the society, or possibly outside those institutions.

Technique will of course vary with the intensity of interest, as for instance when assassination is adopted by revolutionists who can find no other method to make themselves felt against their opponents. Number also has intimate relations with both technique and intensity. In general it is to be said that there is no rule of thumb which will point out to us any particular lines of activity in which the most powerful groups can inevitably be found. We may sometimes find the greatest intensity over matters that still seem to us trifles, even after we think we have interpreted them in terms of underlying groups, and again we may find slight intensity where we think there ought to be the most determined effort. It is solely a matter for observation. And observation shows, here as before, that no group can be defined or understood save in terms of the other groups of the given time and place. One opposition appears and adjusts itself and another takes its place; and each opposition gets its meaning only in terms of the other oppositions and of the adjustments that have taken place between them.

I have been talking of groups as so much activity capable of definition, each group for itself. When we analyze a group in a fairly satisfactory way, we usually give it some kind of a name, and set it off with a certain individuality; the individuality it has is, however, nothing more than the definition of its activity.

At the same time I have said that no group can be stated, or defined, or valued—I have used various words in this respect—except in terms of other groups. No group has meaning except in its relations to other groups. No group can even be conceived of as a group—when we get right down close to facts—except as set off by itself, and, so to speak, made a group by the other groups.

I have also made preliminary mention of the way in which some groups represent others, and have indicated the importance of this representative relation for our further study.

I have not called these group activities forces nor said anything about forces involved in them. The word force can be used, no doubt, even in sociology, to indicate phenomena for study, but it is too apt to drag in some metaphysical suggestion, and in social studies it connotes almost inevitably the isolated, metaphysically posited, individual feelings and ideas, which hypothesis places at the bottom of social life as its causes. Moreover we have little need for it. If we say activity, we have said all.

Now, as the points I have just reiterated imply, the activities are all knit together in a system, and indeed only get their appearance of individuality by being abstracted from the system; they brace each other up, hold each other together, move forward by their interactions, and in general are in a state of continuous pressure upon one another.

If we take a little different angle of vision we shall be tempted to state each group activity, not directly in terms of such and such other group activities, but as resting in a great sea of social life, of which it is but a slight modulation. We shall get the conception of a "habit background" in which the group activity operates. The chapter on law will bring us to close quarters with this phase of the social process, but the ground must be sketched in advance before proceeding farther here.

Suppose, for example, we take a modern battle, and note that it is fought, not with complete abandon, but under definite limitations which forbid certain cruelties, such as the poisoning of springs, the butchery of the wounded, firing upon Red Cross parties, the use of explosive bullets, or the use of balloon explosives. Or suppose we take a political campaign, and note that in one country the contestants use methods which are not used in another. The Cuban liberals used methods against President Palma which are not resorted to in the United States; Tammany uses methods when it can in connection with the New York City police force which no political party uses in London, and which would be injurious to any party that tried to use them. There are "rules of the game" in existence, which form the background of the group activity. There is no savage tribe so low but that it has rules of the game, which are respected and enforced. I hardly need to add that a large part of this habitual activity is commonly discussed in terms of moral factors.

The habit background may usefully be taken into the reckoning as summing up a lot of conditions under which the groups operate, but reliance on it is apt to check investigation where investigation is needed, or even become the occasion for the introduction of much unnecessary mysticism. By appealing to the habit background we must not hope to get away from the present in our interpretations. Just as ideas and ideals are apt to give us a false whirl into the future with our investigations, so in somewhat the same way the habit background is apt to carry us back into the past and thus away from our raw material. We set up "tradition" as established, and then we are apt to think that by appealing to tradition, and by tracing the methods of tradition, we are explaining some social phenomenon that we have in mind. But indeed if tradition is anything at all, it is an affair of the present. If we ever handle it except as a thing of the present—that is, of the particular date under consideration—we trust to it as a false support. Long, in point of time, as may be the trains of activity which we must follow, we never grasp them except at some present moment. The flight of an arrow will serve for illustration. We may plot the curve the arrow follows, but we must study its flight at each moment in terms of the forces in play at that moment. No arrow "tradition" will serve any good purpose.

If we have a form of activity traced down from a remote past—of the kind, say, that is usually called a belief—we have got to value it in terms of other activity at each moment of its career which we study. The question is always what other activities does it represent "now"? What relations, including oppositions, does it have with other activities? What are the underlying interest groups? It is certainly true that we must accept a belief group of this kind as an interest group itself. A totem group, imposing a certain duty as to the eating or the not eating of the flesh of the totem animal, is an established interest; it reflects certain other interests, probably involving the food supply, certain diseases, demons in the air or forest, or all of them together. If those other interest groups change in any way, the effect on the totem activity will be corresponding, whether it is an effect which an outsider can observe or not. It has a different meaning, a different value; in other words, it *is* a different activity. We cannot carry the belief up into the present out of the past and be effecting anything in our work beyond a rough sketch of the surface appearance. Nothing but the "present" can enter into a scientific balance of the group activities against one another to show their tension and cohesion and lines of development.

Another difficulty which may arise from a misuse of the conception of the habit background needs mention. It is easy to generalize the background so much that one thinks he finds in it a "social whole" which he can treat as an active factor in his interpretative work. We are often told that social interests or social welfare demands this thing or that thing; that this custom or that institution has survived because it furthers the welfare of society. I do not want to go beyond my proper range in discussing this difficulty, but for political phenomena I think I am justified in asserting positively that no such group as the "social whole" enters into the interpretation in any form whatever. Where we have a group that participates in the political process we have always another group facing it in the same plane (to revert to the illustration of the sphere). It is true that if we have two nations at war we can treat for the purposes of the war, though only to a certain limited extent, each nation as a separate group; but it is clear that under such circumstances neither nation is the "social whole;" it takes the two together to make the society whose processes we are at the time studying. On any political question which we could study as a matter concerning the United States, for example, alone, we should never be justified in treating the interests of the whole nation as decisive. There are always some parts of the nation to be found arrayed against other parts. It is only by passing from the existing, observed, actual interests to the "objective utilities" I have mentioned above that we can drag in the "social whole," and there we are out of the field of social science. Usually we shall find, on testing the "social whole," that it is merely the group tendency or demand represented by the man who talks of it, erected into the pretense of a universal demand of the society; and thereby, indeed, giving the lie to its own claims; for if it were such a comprehensive all-embracing interest of the society as a whole it would he an established condition, and not at all a subject of discussion by the man who calls it an interest of society as a whole; except again when it is idealistically "objective" but humanly impossible. It is easy to say that it is to society's interest that airy, light lodgings should be provided for all the citizens. But it is plain that what is meant is that from some particular group's point of view, this "ought to be to society's interest;" for it is very clear that the actual interests now existing do not include it either among all tenants or among all landlords. It is easy again to say that "murder is against the social interest," but even if we ignore riot-suppression, police work, judicial executions, wars, and so forth, this "social interest" that is appealed to is not actually the interest of all the people. For besides the continually recurring crimes of passion, and the murders by professional thieves, there is a vast amount of homicide in routine features of our commercial life, such as railroad operation, food manufacture, sweat-shop clothes-making, and so on. And such murders answer to existing interests. All assertions of this kind need very careful qualification in any uses; and indeed need to be abandoned entirely to get any approximately exact statement of the processes under way for scientific investigation.

It may seem overstraining the point to say that in any community of Australian savages in which the main totem rules work continuously without a breach, in any Indian village in which crime is unknown for years at a time, it is wrong to speak of an "interest of the whole." But here the "interest of the whole" would be simply a statement of the established social habit, and whatever change came about in it would be brought about by changing conditions, or in other words by changing group interests; indeed should we go under the surface we could no doubt find a powerful and very definite group interest sustaining the habit by effectively suppressing diverging tendencies.

In the case of the totem tribe we might envisage the community of men and women as in opposition to the demon community, which is a very real social factor, however much the schoolboy may laugh at it; but the demons themselves would prove to have their meaning in terms of groups of the population. In the case of the Indian village, it may be that a very simple community under very favorable conditions of life—I mean food supply, instruments of production, etc.—shows the disappearance of certain tendencies which we, from our own experience, think ought to be present. In that case we might say that the tendency or interest was not present simply because the condition at which it is normally taken by us to be directed was not present. On these questions we need not pass judgment here. I have let them come into the text merely to broaden the issue.

As for political questions under any society in which we are called upon to study them, we shall never find a group interest of the society as a whole. We shall always find that the political interests and activities of any given group—and there are no political phenomena except group phenomena—are directed against other activities of men, who appear in other groups, political or other. The phenomena of political life which we study will always divide the society in which they occur, along lines which are very real, though of varying degrees of definiteness. The society itself is nothing other than the complex of the groups that compose it.

CHAPTER VIII

PUBLIC OPINION AND LEADERSHIP

Leadership and public opinion are two fundamentally important, interlinked phases of the group process in government. They appear in all degrees of differentiation, from the leader who springs forth for the moment, from the public opinion which is an expression of the work immediately in hand, up to organized, firmly set rule, up to definite policies and programmes with complex theoretical statement. They connect at either end with what has been called the habit background, from which they spring, into which they lead.

Leadership is not an affair of the individual leader. It is fundamentally an affair of the group. Pomp and circumstance are but details. Leadership by an individual leader is not even the typical form. It is only a minor form; or, what comes to the same thing, leadership can most often be given an individual statement only from certain minor and incidental points of view. The great phenomena of leadership are phenomena of groups differentiated for the purpose of leading other groups. One specialized group leads certain other groups in a special phase of their activity. Within it are the phenomena of individual leadership in various grades.

Public opinion is also a phenomenon of the group process. There is no public opinion that is not activity reflecting or representing the activity of a group or of a set of groups. There is no public opinion that is unanimous, none indicating the existence of any "social whole," such as we have considered and rejected in the preceding chapter. The unanimity of opinion is as much a myth as the individuality of leadership. Sometimes public opinion appears in differentiated forms in which it stands out very clearly as itself group activity; at other times it is less specialized, less easy to grasp from this point of view, but it is none the less activity.

Public opinion, public sentiment, and public will are three phrases which are at times distinguished from one another, but they all indicate the same group activity. The difference in the shading of the words is not a difference that we meet with among social facts. The three words, opinion, sentiment, and will, are the products of individual psychological analysis, not of direct analysis of social phenomena at first hand. If the term "public opinion" were not so well established one of the others might better be used, as indicating more closely the activity which the word "opinion" but crudely describes. However, it is best to take it as we find it.

Leadership and public opinion can properly be given their preliminary discussion in close association. Public opinion itself has leadership and is leadership. From the opposite point of view leadership is found sometimes working directly through widely organized public opinion, and in all other cases it is connected directly with the public opinion of a narrow group, and indirectly with the vaguer public opinion of larger groups. The justification of this joint treatment must appear as we proceed with this chapter. After we have discussed in detail the group process in government (chaps. x to xviii) we shall seek in chap. xix a more comprehensive statement of the phenomena in terms of discussion groups and organization groups.

In considering leadership I am not going to pay any attention to differences from the individual point of view. The studies that have been made by others on those lines have a recognized value. My object here is of another nature. It is to show how all forms of individual leadership require statement in group terms, and such types as I give emphasis to will be chosen solely from this point of view. I shall discuss in turn, but without endeavoring to hold them sharply distinct, leadership of group by group, "boss" leadership, demagogic leadership, and the leadership of the ruler or mediator.

There is plenty of group activity in society without specialized leadership. But a political group is, by the very fact of its differentiation as political, itself a case of leadership, and within it in turn we shall find organized leadership, probably in several degrees.   For example, let us take the organization of a national political party.   The leadership of the chairman in the executive committee, of the executive committee in the party, of the convention in the party, of the party among the underlying groups and interests which it represents—all these kinds of leadership are not phenomena of different, but of the same, nature, when one cuts down to essentials.   The party gets its strength from the interests it represents, the convention and executive committee from the party, and the chairman from the convention and committee.   In each grade of this series the social fact actually before us is leadership of some underlying interest or set of interests.

Or take the case of any government organ, as, say, a legislature. It is a specialized group, itself an activity, representing other group activities among the people which are organized through it.   It gets all its power, all its meaning, from those other activities. Within it again there is leadership of several kinds, as seen in the speaker, in the party floor leaders, perhaps also in the "boss" in or behind it.   This leadership gets its meaning from the legislative body, and ultimately from the interests behind that body.   The phenomena are not dissimilar, but closely related.   At every stage we are dealing with the differentiation of activity.

The leadership which one group performs for another or for a set of other groups is not dependent upon the express adhesion of the full membership of the represented groups.   Dissent by a member of the group may not take him out of the ranks.   Under some circumstances it will, or rather it represents his actual transfer to another group position; but under other circumstances dissent may be a wrong expression of group position, and the dissenter may be actually arrayed in co-operation with his supposed opponents, and lending force to their movement.   One must not put a false stress on every declaration a man makes about himself socially, any more than on the traditional "woman's no."   I have diagnosed more than one case, for example, in which men who dislike Roosevelt and denounce him bitterly in all their spare time are actually being represented and led by him, and are lending him their support in fact, though not in profession. So radicals and even revolutionists are actually represented in many of their interests by the very government which they are denouncing and which they think they are trying to destroy.

The socialists claim to be representing the entire proletariat as one group. Now suppose there really is such an actual effective group as the proletariat, the socialists will draw a certain amount of strength from the parts of it which do not affiliate with them, or even tolerate them. This proletariat interest must be, remember, not an "objective utility" or "ought to be" on the one side, and not mere vociferation on the other, but a substantial activity tending toward palpable results. The socialists are a "danger" just as they have such a group underlying them. Their policies, or rather concrete portions of their policies, are gaining recognition even from self-styled unfriendly sources on that basis. I am not planning to abuse this point by making arguments rest upon it, but merely calling attention to a possible situation.

Let us take a less disputable illustration. It is common for cities to prescribe the width of wagon-wheel tires in proportion to the load carried, so as to save the pavements from the injury caused by narrow tires and heavy loads. In a city in which such a regulation does not exist, but where conditions make it important, a movement for it is begun. Some of the taxpayers will organize. They will lead the others. These others, however, although actually suffering in equal degree will be indifferent, and often really ignorant of the fact that any such movement is under way. Common speech will say they do not "know" their own interests. Success will not be easy to achieve, for the team-owners will strenuously resist the adoption of the regulation. Nevertheless the movement, or some substitute for it, is bound to win after a greater or less time. It will win because the organization that leads it genuinely represents the mass of indifferent taxpayers. It will win because it will be clear that those indifferent taxpayers are potentially comprised in the group activity. There is a tendency to action among them. If sufficiently goaded they will certainly come to "know" their own interest. The movement will win before all taxpayers are enrolled in it—long before then—and it will win in part by the strength of the unenrolled. In the arguments that strength will masquerade under some such phrase as a "just cause," but it itself will be the justice. In attributing strength to leadership from such a source as this we must, as ever, be cautious not to jump at conclusions. The only way we can discover it is by actual observation. "Objective utilities" and mere verbal adherence are not proof. In each case we must get to the bottom of the conditions by hard work in investigation.

There is no essential difference between the leadership of a group by a group and the leadership of a group by a person or persons. The strength of the cause rests inevitably in the underlying group, and nowhere else. The group cannot be called into life by clamor. The clamor, instead, gets its significance only from the group. The leader gets his strength from the group. The group merely expresses itself through its leadership.

This is not to say that there is no difference between man and man in the capacity for leadership. Nothing is more evident than that there is in fact just such a difference. Some adult men, just as one finds them, will fit certain group needs of leadership, and others will fit other group needs; some will answer best at one time, others at another; some perhaps will not do at all as leaders in any group activities which we are apt to have under investigation. Given a specialized group in a special phase of activity, and A will answer its purposes better than B. The group will probably secure A for its leader. If instead it secures B, its activities may suffer to some extent. When we are superficially writing superficial varieties of history we tend to tell the whole story in terms of A or B. We heap imprecations on their heads or we glorify them. Perhaps there is a certain correctness within the limits of such history in making events turn on leaders, but it is within limits that have very little scientific interest. The "fate of a nation" may indeed in some rare cases turn on a leader's fitness or unfitness, but the kind of a "fate of a nation" that does turn in that way is a bit of sensationalism, with even less relation to the mass of matter we need to study than a yellow newspaper's headlines have to the news-matter that follows them, or to the facts which that news-matter is supposed to describe. The individual leader counts only because he is a part of the human mass, and as a part of the mass. His very personal qualities, which are often so highly emphasized ·as causes, are themselves in the main merely group facts—they mark his reflection of special phases of the society around him, and they can better be stated in terms of the groups they reflect than as purely personal capacities. The differences between men in their capacity of leadership, even more clearly than elsewhere, are typical social differences.[1]

Let us turn now to the kind of leadership typified by the American political "boss," remembering that we are not concerned with the content of his service, with his merits or demerits as valued by himself or others in the midst of the process, but solely with the process itself. We must examine this kind of leadership under several aspects. First there is the boss as leader of the political machine. Then there is the boss taken together with his machine as leader of a large portion of the voting public, the rank and file of his party in his territory; but since boss discipline is often very severe inside the machine, we may sometimes for our practical purposes best treat the boss himself as leader of this section of the voting public. Finally there is the boss-led machine, in control of the organs of government, as leader or ruler or mediator for all or many of those groups of the population which are working through government.

Underlying the political machine of the American type we need the two-party system, resting on a certain great complexity of national life, which involves a marked political grouping of the population along the lines of many intense interests; and also a complex set of government activities, so poorly adjusted that they provide many rich opportunities for profit. When many interests are synthesized for political purposes in one political party, which

[1] Speaker Reed is generally recognized as having been a "strong" man; Speaker Henderson, as a "weak" man. Yet Reed had one session in which his power was greatly weakened; while in Henderson's term the power of the office increased in several important respects.

is a group that represents other groups, and when this party faces
another party of similar character, we observe as a matter of fact
that a strong leadership group organizes itself within the party.
This leadership group attains a very intense interest in self-maintenance. Given the special conditions which are summarized in
the phrase, "great opportunities for profit," then the leadership
group presents itself as a "machine." As a machine it is dependent for existence on its success in leading the party, and on its
ability to keep some other machine from ousting it from its leadership, the two factors being related in various ways not necessary
now to point out. The machine is in some respects a hostile band
of marauders in a fertile, but—for the time being—seemingly
helpless country, despite the fact that it holds leadership in the
very country in which it is encamped. The type of leadership
which the boss exercises in the machine grows out of the nature
of the activity itself, and we find strict discipline, arbitrary decisions, and personal loyalty tested in the outcome by the alternatives,
complete authority or else complete overthrow. I am, of course, not
attempting to describe all American political machines, but merely
picking a characteristic type of leadership for illustration.

The power of the boss lies in his machine. The power of the
machine lies in the boss only to the extent that the given boss is
superior to the next best man (not in any attributed mental or other
ability, but as a definite given man under the circumstances); and
this superiority is much less than it is apt to be declared to be by
close onlookers or by conversationalists of one sort or another.
Now the activity of the boss represents the combined political
activity of all the machine members, even when he hardly gives ear to
any lieutenant. Whether he holds consultations or not is for
our present purpose a technical detail. With or without consulta-
tion there may be factions of the machine that feel they are not
adequately represented, in other words that they are not getting
"fair treatment." When a boss is overthrown it is apt to be by
discontent, conspiracy, and revolution inside the machine. The
relations of the machine to the wider groups it represents have a
good deal to do with the overthrow. They make overthrow easy

at times, even when they do not stimulate it, but the technique inside the machine will probably be what I have indicated.   Weak leadership is primarily the outcome of quarreling interests, not vice versa.

The relations of the boss to the machine typify one form of leadership. It should already be clear that the boss phenomenon cannot be more than roughly stated without putting it in terms of the machine itself.   Any short cuts which talk about the bad character of men who fill bosses' positions, or about the indifference of the individual voters who allow bosses to be elected, and any generalizations, such as those concerning the decline of the society which tolerates bosses, are useless until a more complete statement is given to the facts they indicate.

But this is only one phase of boss leadership.   There are also the leadership by the boss of the party outside the machine, and the leadership by the machine in the organized government in which all groups are in tension. In both these aspects the boss loses some of his dictatorial attributes, and becomes more the representative in the formal sense, namely a man intrusted with a certain right to exercise his judgment, being in turn judged for the use he makes of his powers by the men who have given him his position: and this often at the very moment when he is being reviled as a dictator.   When he loses elections or falls below what is expected of him, he is judged as undesirable in the party group. When he abuses public office too grossly, wastes too much public money, tolerates too much injurious discrimination between citizens, he is judged by large sections of the citizenship in subparty group-ings, and with him his party is judged, so that the subparty interest dominates the party interest in a certain proportion of the out-lying party members, leading to a desertion at the polls by the "independent" vote, and to possible loss of a good part of their power by both boss and machine.

In all this we have nothing but group process, first, last, and all the time. It is of course not so stated in the attendant dis-cussions which are a part of the process to be discussed a few pages farther on.   But all the morals and the ideas in which the discussion is clothed are but symbols for these group forces. The essential point is that all this activity, whether envisaged from the point of view of the boss, or of the machine, or of the party, or of the public (a general name for masses of groups at certain stages of the process), has its value and meaning only in terms of the group opposition. Each group phase of it comes to light in contrast with some other phase, and all phases together get their definition at each stage of the process in common. Their transformations, their surgings and subsidings in their manifest or palpable forms, go on in terms of each other. They are phases of one common process, which again for its part can only be stated as the sum of them all.

With this ever-pending accountability, whether immediate or remote, first to machine, then to party, and then to "public," the boss will hold himself and his machine in check to some extent to keep from overstepping the danger line. But at the same time he is apt to feel his way carefully and to venture as close as he deems safe to the danger line. Here he is allowing for "public opinion," as we say, or, in other words, he is performing, however meagerly, his leadership duties for certain subgroups which have perforce trusted their causes to his organization. It is a matter of common observation, though not worked out by comparison of carefully analyzed cases as it needs to be, that under ordinary circumstances a boss under pressure of strong interests directly behind him, will tend to creep farther and farther forward until some day he finds he is too far across the danger line to retreat. The pressure of the machine interest and the interests the machine directly represents is much more continuous and intense than that of the subgroup interests, or even than the party interest, and it finds its way forward till checked by sharp punishment. So the process goes on, gradually changing in its content and in the limits set for it in the habit background.

Pass now to demagogic leadership. If the implication of insincerity were inevitable in the word demagogue, then that word would not be well chosen here. But there is ample justification

for resorting to the older usage in which the term demagogue is
equivalent merely to a popular leader.   In this sense the word
lends itself well to technical use for a special form of leadership.
Insincerity, as applied to the motives of a leader, like any other
interpretation in terms of individual motives, has but trivial importance in the group process.   If we can take a sound word like demagogue, strip it of that quality, and use it in the sense in which
Demosthenes would have recognized himself as described by it,
we make that much pure gain.

The demagogue stands in a very different relation to his following from that of the boss to his, although in both cases the leadership
can be explained only through the groups that are led by it, and
gets all its meaning from those groups.   The demagogue reflects
his group through a different technique.   As current speech has it,
he operates not through wire-pulling, but through appeals to the
passions with more or less accompanying reasoning.   (Wire-pulling, appeals, "reasoning" are, of course, the activity itself, not
something different from it.)   He may do this by proxy, as in one
present-day specially notorious American case, but that is only an
interesting instance of the very common phenomenon of syndicated
leadership, already discussed in substance, though not by that
name.

Nevertheless, as leadership, demagogy is a differentiated
activity representing or reflecting the group.   The demagogue's
group will be vastly larger than the boss's immediate group, the
machine, and the relationship of the demagogue to the group's
members will be in appearance much more direct and even more
simple.   The machine hierarchy is commonly not found, or is
found only in traces; the group member feels his inspiration
coming direct from the lips of the leader, and is most apt to regard
himself as an unselfish patriot, whereas the machine henchman
operates in good part on a tacit, or sometimes even admitted,
assumption of self-interest.   But this question of motives, I repeat,
has very little value for us, and gives us but trifling help in finding
our way through the group process.

The group which the demagogue leads is as a rule highly

complex. As a group, that is, it reflects or represents the interests of a lot of subgroups which may be very different in character from each other. It gains for itself a simple enough statement in a demand for some reform, or some related set of reforms, as, for instance, free silver, or a set of "pure democracy" projects, but underlying it is a kaleidoscopic field of economic and other non-political or semi-political groups. The demagogue's group has its own activity and tendencies, its own interest. It has its life-history. But this life-history cannot be stated except in the most superficial way, without putting it in terms of subgroups, which the demagogic group leads, which it represents, whose interests it reflects. The life-history of the demagogic group is the history of the co-operative activity in group form of those subgroups, or fractions of them, at a certain stage in their career. One can state the demagogic group in terms of the subgroups, but never the subgroups in terms of the demagogic group.

The demagogic group is not apt to have a long history, and it is not apt to complete its activity along the lines of its declarations, though it may do so in part. As it approaches success its subgroups are apt to assert themselves more and more forcefully, and combine into new political groups that reflect their varying interests more closely. For instance, suppose an "annihilate-the-trusts" campaign, and assume that it carries a critical election. We may confidently enough predict that we shall soon find the various subgroups that have been reflected in this demagogic group splitting apart from one another, perhaps on the question as to which trusts are to be annihilated first, or as to which phase of trust activity is to be annihilated first; and the resulting action will be modified thereby; and this entirely apart from the opposition which the defeated minority representing the trusts will bring to bear, an opposition which of itself will modify the lines of operation very materially from the declared policy.

Despite subgroups and the transformations they occasion, the demagogic group is itself an interest group and an activity, which we must be careful to study and estimate at its actual value. We must trace the modification of the subgroups, due to their co-operation, and we must follow the activity lines into the next demagogic group that appears. To a certain small extent platform planks and catchwords will help us, but in the main we must get below these to the interests underlying, and get the statement throughout in terms of them.

In comparing boss leadership and demagogic leadership it is easy to find certain tendencies of transition between them. The machine and the boss are most apt to establish themselves upon the basis of past demagogy. Demagogic leadership, once in political power with a task that requires time to complete, will tend to transform itself into boss leadership. Rank bossism is sure to produce after years or centuries, as the case may be, rank demagogy. In Russia the bureaucracy, which is bossism, now faces the most terrible, though sometimes the most necessary, of all demagogy, the revolutionary uprising of the people. Revolution of this type is to be distinguished from Spanish-American revolutions, which are merely primary elections, waged between rival machines by the aid of a form of violence now abandoned in English America. The Russian revolutionary movement is an interest group, demagogic in form, representing subgroups that include the greater part of the population, working with poor technique against a minority group of great intensity and highly effective technique. All through history we find the specialized group which has been called in to keep order, that is, to represent a lot of subgroups in a common differentiated interest, transforming itself in time into a hierarchically organized, more or less aristocratic, machine of government, and in turn stimulating against itself demagogical group movements, with operations prescribed by the available technical methods.

Demagogic leadership carries us directly over to the discussion of public opinion, but before taking up that latter subject a few words should be added on the kind of leadership that is found in the ruler or mediator. We have seen something of this in certain of the functions of the boss, but the boss is not a good illustration, because in talking of him we think so largely of his representation of certain special interests that we forget the function he is playing all the time in connection with larger groups of interests. We cannot analyze any bit of government very deeply, no matter where and no matter what its abuses, without becoming aware that it is holding the balance between conflicting interests, that it is enforcing restraints on their activities in the political field, that it is standing between them and acting as mediator at the same time it is acting as ruler. We have the mediating functions in a certain limited range specified in the courts of justice. This same function, however, is exercised everywhere in government—in legislatures and in executives as well. It also is leadership, and, like the other forms of leadership, it also can be interpreted in terms of groups and must be so interpreted if we wish to get its full functioning value. I cannot go into this here for its complexities are many and it will occupy much of our time later on. Before I get done with it I hope to show in a satisfactory manner that there is not a single function of government of this kind which is not supported on a powerful interest group or set of groups from which it gets all its strength and social effectiveness. In every such case where two opposing groups have their conflicts adjusted or controlled through a ruler we shall find that that ruler is in reality acting as the leader of an interest group or set of groups more powerful than those in immediate conflict, and that the adjustment and limitation which we observe is dictated by that more powerful group.

Public opinion bears something of the relation to government that talking bears to the full-mouth activities. Lip says, "I am," and positively and arrogantly declares to Mouth its primacy, indeed its uniqueness, in the organism. But Mouth goes right on attending to business, eating where and when it can. The situation may be compared with that of the man who declares with intense conviction, "I am a vegetarian," but who confesses that he eats meat every day, and who explains his meat-eating habit as a triviality, a mere external circumstance forced on him by the conditions of life and not affecting in any way his true existence as a being of thought and feeling, a real vegetarian. When the world agrees to call such people vegetarians then public opinion may be admitted to rule the world, but not till then.

We shall be compelled to reduce public opinion to its proper place as activity, reflecting or representing other activities. But we must do it with caution, for if in the process we lose any of the realities for which public opinion stands, and which it represents, our last state will be worse than our first.

The public-opinion process has been involved in the discussion of the demagogic form of leadership, and it has been less directly involved in boss leadership. We are not passing into a new field when we turn from leadership to public opinion, but making the analysis from a different angle. It is a case of obverse and reverse, but our business is to pierce clear through the coin, and not be content with the pretty pictures on the two surfaces.

There is no use attempting to handle public opinion except in terms of the groups that hold it and that it represents. Public opinion is an expression of, by, or for a group of people. It is primarily an expression of the group interest by the group itself, but where it has become a differentiated activity representing an underlying group we may say it is expressed by the opinion group for the underlying group. As always we must be exact in our analysis of the representative quality in cases that we describe as "for the group": we can know nothing there except by intelligent, carefully controlled observation.

A public-opinion that is supposed to be made up of a certain collection or fusion of the thin, colorless "ideas" that you read about in your psychological textbook cannot be found by any process I know of in social life. The abstractions, the ideas, all by themselves, cannot be found. I admit that we often read or hear such sentences as, "Municipal ownership is good." But what we have there is a speaking, writing, printing, reading, hearing activity. It remains to discover by actual observation what, if any, connection such a phrase or its reiteration has with the possible later appearance of municipally owned street cars in a given city. To say "municipal ownership is good" implies something further, namely, "we want it," or, "we ought to have it," or, "we are tending to get it," three variations of the same thing. Our "opinion" is a pushing process in all its stages.

When we examine this public opinion with its onward tendencies, we find that, besides being borne in a group, or given differentiated expression for a group, it always is directed against some activities of groups of men. It may specialize in expression against an individual man, but it concerns even then some group activity, representative or direct, in which that man participates. Municipal ownership, for instance, is not any remote thing, to be discovered apart from men. It does not exist in the cold of interstellar space. It is a method of activity. The movement for it is directed against the activities of certain private owners of quasi-public enterprises, such as, for example, the street-car lines, who have been acting in a way that interferes with the activities of the citizens who became believers in municipal ownership. The demand for municipal ownership does not take its birth out of nothing at all. It rises out of certain definitely felt evils among groups of the population.   Inadequate street-car service, illiberal treatment of patrons who are compelled to patronize the lines, the corruption of city governments in connection with franchises, all these are facts which precede any theories about governmental functions or any public opinion favorable or unfavorable to municipal ownership. They themselves grow directly out of group oppositions and opportunities in the existing state of society, and they inevitably result in an effort to do away with the evils.

It often happens that street-car owners, for the sake of a few thousand dollars additional revenue, will refuse to give the traveling public some privilege or convenience, which, if one could estimate its money value in terms of added facilities, might be worth millions of dollars to them. It is solely because of the privileged, exclusive position of the company that it can and does take this attitude. The group reaction of the populace, which otherwise would attain an adjustment through ordinary competitive process, now concentrates to strike for relief through the governmental agency. It strikes at the privilege which clinches the evil fast beyond ordinary means of removal. Reaching out the hand to seize is a simple act. That is the municipal-ownership tendency, nothing more, nothing less. It is the removal of group irritation. It is a typical act of government, all the "theories" of the limits of state activity to the contrary notwithstanding. How that tendency actually works itself out is a matter for observation to discover; the form of group opposition, the methods, and the limitations of methods, all rest on the habit background at the given time and place. It is all a question of conflicting activities.

But now if this is the nature of the municipal-ownership movement in fact, how about that "municipal ownership" which one hears vastly more about, the opinion, the theory, the creed? It is clearly a differentiated activity, consisting of talking, writing, printing, and so forth, and it clearly has something to do with the process of municipalizing certain industries in fact. But whether as excited talking or whether as reasoned theory, for it appears in both forms, it is only a group activity reflecting other group activities; it does not control the fates of society, but its fates are dependent on what society, that is to say, the complex of active groups in the case, proceeds to do. Those groups may find on meeting the obstacles in their paths that they can work most effectively along some other lines, and this they may proceed to do, leaving the theory group and the agitation group which gave them expression high and dry. Or again, those underlying groups may actually push their process through into municipal ownership as a fact without having given rise to any excited groups of talk and belief at all. It is solely a question of the particular process, of the channels it must follow, of the condition as given, in short of group struggle, and of group leadership of group.

What value has this public opinion in society? It has just the value of the group that is given expression by it. What tests have we of it? None except in the examination and analysis of the group or groups behind it. What is it then? Precisely a differentiated group activity, expressing, or reflecting, or representing, or leading, as the case may be, a group activity, or subgroup activities still lower down in the social mass. It would appear, then, that, not for any ulterior purpose, but simply for the needs of scientific examination of the raw material of the social process, the group method of interpretation strips off the mystery of public opinion, and lays it open to analysis and eventually even to measurement, on the same plane with other social facts. If this point is clear there will be no difficulty in the further analysis of public opinion as group expression that must now be made. If the point is not clear that analysis will be meaningless, and indeed if it does not become clear as we progress, the whole discussion of leadership, with its further elaboration in the following chapters will fail of being understood.

We must examine public opinion under various aspects. We find it in various grades of differentiation. Again we find it in various degrees of generality and intensity.

Ordinary public opinion, such as we most commonly refer to when we use the phrase in American public affairs, is very highly differentiated. Take for example the condemnation of the insurance "grafters" in 1905–6. We saw a highly specialized condemning and denouncing activity. It appeared more or less strong in the editorials of almost every newspaper in the country, in a large part of the sermons, in the casual conversation of friends and of chance acquaintances alike. It was very definite as a social fact, a differentiated activity; and this even though every logician, every political economist, every political scientist, and in general, every "wise man," should make sport of it for vagueness and confusion of thought and hypocrisy. It had a small specialized vocabulary of catchwords of its own. It lasted for a while and then gradually disappeared, having thus as an "opinion-group" activity a traceable history.

Ranging from this organized public opinion down to conditions of tacit acquiescence or blind restlessness, which are not called public opinion at all in current speech, we have the grades of differentiation of this one type of phenomena. If sane Persia accepts its sovereign's rule for centuries, so far as we see without any debate or organized critical thought except among court cliques, it offers a tacit, undifferentiated public opinion favorable to the rule. A Russia, passive under a milder phase of autocracy, an American city, indifferent to its bosses' use of power, show in various degrees of differentiation the same thing. Perhaps starting at the bottom with a condition in whch we can hardly find a trace of public opinion in a differentiated form, we may ascend to a higher stage in which a simple approval or disapproval of complicated official acts will be cheered or growled out; thence still higher to the germs of organization of opinion outside the official activity and during its progress; thence again through a growing perfection of organization of this opinion to an "initiating" opinion, which finally takes such highly organized forms as we find in the present-day United States with its thousands of organizations, often under clever leadership, all working in most specialized forms as activities, reflecting, representing, leading other activities of society. This is a mere schematic statement of the gradations intended only to indicate the progress, but not claiming the authority of fact, an authority which can come only from a thorough study of the materials and which can be conveyed only by offering the mass of analyzed materials in proof. What I am here saying must be taken as merely preliminary to the further examination of the organization and discussion phases of activity in a later chapter.

In addition to degree of differentiation the degree of generality and the intensity of public opinion must be considered. Just as one can nowhere find a "social whole" as a factor in society, so one can nowhere find a unanimous public opinion which is the opinion of the whole society, of every member of it. There will be group arrayed against group and opinion group against opinion group. The opinion activity that reflects one group, however large it may be, always reflects the activity of that group as directed against the activity of some other group. Each group will try to show that its own opinion activity reflects the activity of the "whole," or at least of all of the whole except some loathed minority. Each group will claim that its opinion is "public" opinion. It will bolster up its claim on an elaborate structure of reasoning and

assertions of "objective utilities" and of natural and other rights.
A plausible case can often be made out under cover of the complexity of highly differentiated opinion groups which reflect the activities of a large number of lower-lying groups. Many different groups may adopt one policy, that is, become part of an opinion-activity group which reflects all of them, and which takes on a so-called individuality different from any of them. In current psychological language we say that the men who hold the opinion hold it for different reasons. When we talk of their reasons in this way, we, of course, make a very abstract statement of the truth, in a form so limited that it will never carry us far. When we go down to the group statement we get down below mere reasoning to the very basis of reasons.

The intensity of expression which these opinion groups give themselves in their various forms, from loud clamor to dogmatic assertion and cold proof, will, like all intensity in social phenomena, be a factor of the particular occasion, of the group process as given. The group struggle and the solution of struggle is under way in every bit of the social process. Sometimes it works through a friendly suit in a court and sometimes through a bloody revolution. The manner and intensity of expression which public opinion assumes depends entirely on the character of the conflicts, on how deeply they are splitting the groups apart, on how well they are controlled in the habit background, on how well fortified the groups are which are being attacked, on what technical facilities the attacking groups have at their command. It is again entirely a matter for observation.

One very complex opinion group is the big party of the American political system, the Democratic or the Republican of our generation. If anyone still feels confusion about the propriety of calling opinion groups activity like other groups, perhaps a consideration of the political party will help to clear up the trouble. The party is from one point of view organized public opinion. This is true whatever differentiated leadership groups and whatever dictatorial leadership it may show. It is true in the same sense that it is true that all government is the organization of public opinion,

and in the same sense that it is true that even the most abstract
reasoning is activity. The party occupies an intermediate positon
in which its activity and its so-called opinion features can better
be seen in their unity. We could not discuss parties at all save as
political activities. They would melt away into thin air if we
ventured it. But no hard line can be drawn between the formal
party and even the least formal of the other manifestations of opinion. And no fundamental differences exist between the representativeness of opinion groups and the representativeness of
structural organization of society. "Manifestation of opinion"
means a group activity, however we take it. We know no opinion
that is not manifested. We can trace evolving differentiation
between the different stages of the activity, we can watch it pass
farther and farther along in its course, nearer and nearer to those
stages which we call in current speech the results of the action.
But there is never a point from beginning to end at which we can
stop and say: Behind us lies opinion, before us lies action. The
activity ever goes on. Here actions conflict; at once opinion groups,
opinion activities appear: these pass on, transforming themselves,
organizing, reflecting various subgroups, combining groups, passing into new stages of activity. Never is the process abandoned
for a moment. When I have said opinion groups, I have merely
made a concession to current language for the sake of more easily
indicating the particular kind of activity immediately under consideration. It is a special form of group activity only as phenome-
nally observed, not as answering in a different way to some exterior
test applied to our social phenomena.

Taken as activity, our groups will embody the biggest ideals
that may be floating around in society and the most petty, most
"selfish," policies of the smallest fractions of the population.
Moreover they will embody them at their true value, not at any
mystic claim of value; a true value to be discovered by observation. The group that holds the ideals will be located. It will be
watched at work. The subgroups underlying it will be studied,
and their tendencies toward activity along the lines of the ideal
group will be very carefully examined. The persistence of all

the groups, big and little, modest and pretentious, will be tested. Liberty and equality groups must take their place with other groups, and stand the same tests.

It is safe to say in general that we shall find that the largest opinion groups and the most pretentious are in most continuous need of being interpreted at every step in terms of subgroups, or layers of subgroups, which are reflected with more or less completeness by them. With public opinion that is precise, limited, driven home, that amounts to an expression merely of what social groups are actually in the process of doing, we can often afford to let the opinion groups stand as factors, summing up, or expressing in shorthand, groups of factors. But with the vaguer, wider, larger groups, we shall find ourselves sailing the empyrean when we trust ourselves too much to them without reducing the statement at every step to more exact terms. As we proceed with this method of interpretation we shall get continually a better understanding of the meaning of the much abused terms, organ and function. The opinion group that is most insistent upon itself as a "reality" will present itself to us as the analysis becomes more intimate in the guise of a process, and often a not very essential process at that, but a mere by-path, so to speak, or at times a short cut. For every different group position that we personally adopt for the time being as we look out upon society, different activities will appear to us as the realities, and different activities as mere functioning. For every different position we take there will be a different "truth." It will be only as we get all the group activities together, and all valued in the terms of each, each valued in the terms of all, that we shall be able to set up a scientific truth; and even then our results can claim to be truth only in the sense that they will "work" for more cases, for longer lines of activity, with more exactness, than the group "truths" we have relegated to lower rank as mere processes.

One other point remains to be made before passing for the present from this subject. In the foregoing pages I have had nothing to say of interest groups, and have hardly used the term interest at all. It has been better not to let the current speech-contrast between interest and opinion force itself intrusively into the discussion. Opinion groups, however, are merely one variety of interest groups. Like all other groups they must be stated in their interest terms. No interest group exists which cannot be reflected by an opinion group, but for many we find no organized, differentiated opinion group in our material, merely because activity in that form is not called for, does not in fact appear, as the social process happens to be working at the given time. Nothing turns on the distinction between interest and opinion. All turns on the observed and observable facts as to the activities in their values and along their lines of development. What interest groups are most active, what are dominating, what are absorbing others into themselves to their increased activity, what are the representative relations between them; all this, as a matter of plain fact, is involved in the scientific question about society. This when answered will give as much knowledge of the scientific kind as is obtainable about the social process.

CHAPTER IX

INDIVIDUAL ENDOWMENT AND RACE TYPE

It may be said that the groups I have been describing are themselves "up in the air;" that, even though they consist of the actual activities of actual men, they are floating free, when they ought to be pinned down to the endowments which the individual men who are the members of the group bring to it in advance. I have said a good deal that bears on such objections already, but I am going to take the time and space to say more, especially as the discussion will lead up to the question of race type, concerning which we should be at rest before proceeding to the further analysis of the institutions of government.

The alleged individual endowment presents itself to us either as physical or as psychical; or rather, to be more exact, it is discussed sometimes as the one, sometimes as the other; for the line in such discussions is not well drawn in fact, even when it is presumed to be in theory, and the argument is apt to shift at critical moments from one set of terms to the other in a way that is not conducive to trustworthy conclusions.

So far as the individual endowment regarded as psychical is concerned, I have surely said enough in Part I to make it unnecessary to go into details here. I will only recall that psychical factors regarded as causes proved to be mere shadows of what they were supposed to explain. Certainly, now, if there is any validity at all in my argument, one cannot hope to bring the social groups down from their alleged floating position "up in the air" by trying to hitch them on to any individual endowment of this nature. We must remember that in one sense all science is "up in the air." It does not have absolute validity. It is the construction of the scientist's mind, to use the current phrase; it is all conception, not perception, to take another similar way of phrasing. To give our groups the appearance of being "pegged down" by using fictitious pegs will not give them any more scientific validity. I am not asserting that never, nor in any way, a more than scientific truth will be reached through the study of human social living. I am asserting only that I am not after such results myself, and that within the range in which I am working there is no utility in demanding such absoluteness. It is at any rate the duty of any-one who thinks he can increase the substantiality of the groups by any such means to prove his point, not assume it.

Turning to individual endowment regarded as physical, we have a form of statement which so far as it goes is much more trust-worthy, but which goes only a very little way. In speaking of instincts in chap. i, sec. v, I forecast what is to be said here. The illegitimate use of instinct, the psychic use, is found when one localizes an instinct somewhere in a low form of soul and makes it "explain" the instinctive activities. The legitimate use is found when one comes to close quarters with the facts and studies the instinctive activity directly. But here all depends on how far the instinctive activity, as one finds it in its specific form, can be traced forward into the network of social activities, and shown to persist just as it is.

Note, however, that activity of this kind, the physical endow-ment of the individual, is material identical in kind with that which I myself insist on using as the exclusive material of our study. The only difference is that it is put forward as capable of individual statement, whereas I believe I find as a matter of fact that most of it is capable of adequate statement only in terms of masses of men living together under given conditions. It is strictly a question of fact between the two methods of statement as to which is the most useful, or rather as to the exact range of cases in which each is the most useful. I will admit without argument that wherever any investigator isolates a definite manner of reacting in the individual in society, a manner of reacting so definite that it stays clear and distinguishable through whatever reasonable range of variations in the environment it may be followed, so definite that it can be passed on from father to son without any greater variation on the average than is found in the inheritance of the color of the hair or eyes, the height, or the shape of the skull, there we will be provided with a statement of the facts that is simpler and more useful than the group statement I am urging. But as to the possibility of bringing the groups down from that alleged position "up in the air" by connecting them with individual physical endowment, it is evident that this will result only where and when the individual statement is more adequate than the group statement. And that is to be shown only by the practical test.

Suppose now we examine certain phases of activity which are capable of individual statement, and see how far that statement remains useful for all social facts in connection therewith. Man is, for instance, an eating animal. The physiological side of this eating activity can be studied in the individual organism. However, even the biologist must look for answers to many of his questions about it in the species regarded as a whole. If we take the food supply operations of society, we find certain limits set to them by the physical side of the individuals as we have just been stating it. Some materials cannot be digested; other digestible materials are poisons. But within the limits there is wide range for alternatives, and food customs and techniques are built up in society which cannot be stated merely in terms of the environment, nor merely in terms of the individual physique, but which can only be stated in terms of the activities of men in the groups in which they are found. Starting with the endowment of stomach and mouth you cannot possibly build up an interpretation of the economic activities of society.

Then there is sex. As the given fact, human beings are bisexual and the two sexes can be traced back in the line of evolution far beyond the point at which one first finds social phenomena in our human sense. Also as the given fact, there are customs and institutions in society in which sex plays a prominent place. But sex is by no means all there is to marriage, and indeed I should want proof before asserting that sex was even the dominant element in marriage, save perhaps in the most ephemeral unions of savages and of the gilded circles of civilization where divorce is easy. Marriage is a forming, a shaping, an organizing of social material of which one very important and characteristic element is sex, and our question of social interpretation has to do just with these forms of organization. Why does the sex relationship appear in organizations of one form here and other forms there? Clearly sex as a presocial endowment of the individual is not going to answer that question, nor is even a very specifically stated physical human sex going to answer it.

Consider next the power of the individual organism to resist disease. We know how a people may grow immune to such diseases as consumption, and how the capacity to endure city life may be acquired by a race. We know that while a disease is running its course in a society it may change the amount of the human materials, and may sometimes change very radically the character of the interest groupings. But we cannot build any of our social facts up out of the disease and resistance facts themselves. These underlie society like the oxygen of the air, like light and heat and gravitation. In interpreting society we must deal with the interest groups, perhaps as modified by plagues, perhaps as reacting against plagues through government. This is true even when our quarantine and sanitation is intrusted by us to experts at the seat of government, a phase of the subject which will be discussed later in its proper place.

Or perhaps it is a question of the physical subjection to intoxication, and of a theory—which apparently rests on a number of confusions even in its physiological statement—that society will never get rid of drunkenness till men become unintoxicable, or constitutionally unwilling to drink to excess. No matter. We have to observe how groups of men, actually using intoxicants in given social forms and ways, reflect their interests through other groups, rouse group opposition, and work in the social structure along certain lines. We have to observe just what course the groups take toward each other, what their group power of resistance and attack is, and what groups survive and how; and all this regardless of any theory as to when the end of intoxication will be reached. The activity of the man with the theory is itself a social fact which must be noted, but only for what it actually is. Just so far as the theory is the sign or the mark of a group activity will its importance grow in our study.

In all these cases we find the social institutions growing up within the limits of the range of ready adaptability of the individual's physical characteristics; and hence not to be interpreted as due to the existence of those characteristics broadly stated as such.

By all means the most important phase, however, of the physical endowment of the individual has to do with the nervous system. We may properly say that such human society as we know would be impossible without the developed nervous system, without brain. And yet brain does not explain society. The brain facts, or more broadly, the nervously mediated facts, *are* the social facts, and no emphasis placed on brain as such helps materially to the analysis of the facts from the social view-point.

I have indicated (chap. i, sec. i,) the nature of the difficulties, almost unsurmountable, which one must face in any attempt to isolate brain capacity by itself either in individuals or in races as apart from achievement as social fact. The case of the idiot is clear, and so the case of the dog when the special activities of human society are under study; but even when one takes as low a people as the Bushmen, it is not at all clear how the analysis may be made; and when, to note merely one abuse, an anatomist attempts to portray the fates of the negro on the basis of a study of 103 negro brains, the procedure becomes ludicrous.

I am not denying that there may be actual differences in nervous complexity (and so capacity) between physical races of men just as there may be between individuals. I am not denying the significance of the skulls of Pithecanthropus and of the Neanderthal man. The whole point concerns the interpretation of social activity and organization in terms of such differences. Against the exaggerated emphasis that is placed on slight shadings of capacity stated in anatomical or physiological terms, I am appealing to a whole world of social facts, and asking their analysis on their own merits.

Perhaps the point will become clearer by considering for a

moment animal societies.   Everyone knows of the complex social organization of the hive bees and of social ants.   Everyone knows also that these animals have but meagerly developed nervous systems.   It is true that a clearly defined physiological differentiation of the individuals into two or more classes is a very important characteristic of their societies.   But over and above this phase there is a vast deal of social life in the hive and in the anthill in just our own sense.   So significant is the functioning social equilibrium in bee societies that one writer, M. A. Lane, in his *Level of Social Motion,* has felt able to use it as a guide in estimating the tendencies of human social equilibration.   Or consider the beavers. They are mammals by no means high in brain development.   Yet they have societies organized on the compound system of both social group life and intra-social family life.   It was not "brain" that created the bee societies and the beaver societies, and it is not "brain" that keeps them functioning in their complex processes.   Their social activities are mediated by nervous process, of course, but one cannot even by the aid of a most desperate prejudice succeed in correlating the degree of social organization with the degree of nervous differentiation, whether one compares these animals with other closely related animals, or these animal societies with human societies.   Such intelligent animals as elephants and monkeys have very rudimentary social forms.   Human societies show all degrees of complexity, many of them far below, and from one point of view all of them below, the bee society.   What can one make of it ?

It must be remembered that animals even without any nervous differentiation at all show all the typical reactions of animals with nervous systems, as is proved by Jennings in his work on the *Behavior of the Lower Organisms.*   From the bottom of the scale to the top we have a qualitatively uniform "activity" for our material.   With the differentiation of the nervous structure there is an increasing complexity and completeness of the reflection in each specialized activity, of the surrounding world (that is, of surrounding activity).   This greater complexity of reflection, or representation, is unquestionably of the very highest importance.

But here is the rub. If it is so exceedingly hard to find any way to correlate this nervous differentiation and complexity with social differentiation and complexity in the long scale of vital evolution, how are we justified in dogmatically placing an assumed correlation of this kind at the basis of our interpretations of society, where the differentiations on the physiological side are in comparison infinitesimal, and where the social differentiations are so strikingly great ? Certainly a dogmatic correlation of this kind is not justified. Just as certainly a dogmatic assertion that there is no such correlation would not be justified. Any full and careful proof of any such correlation will be welcomed, for just what it is worth, and just to the extent that it is carried. But the presumption is in favor of an interpretation in social terms directly—in terms, that is, of masses of men; and the probabilities are that interpretation in terms of nervous differentiation will serve merely as a control on the other interpretation at special points, not as something that can replace it.

Recalling the argument of chap. v, I can restate this as follows: It is not "brain power" as such which we find, but "brain at work;" it is "brain at work socially;" in this "brain-at-work-socially" material the abstracted "brain-power" phase is of minor importance, so far as giving us light on the material goes; it is not the brains which set the social tasks, but rather the tasks socially set which busy the brains.

Suppose now someone should attempt to interpret an increase of brain power, stated as such, in terms of natural selection. In this decade, of course, the inheritance of acquired characters is not to be mentioned. Whether the variation from which this interpretation started was regarded as fortuitous or not, it would remain true that the only kind of variation of nervous structure that could be selected would be one that functioned better than others in the given social life at the time of its appearance. It would have to win in the struggle also as against many other physical conditions of survival, such as insensibility to pain, muscular strength, resistance to disease, and so forth. We should have an infinitely rich field of social phenomena set over against minute brain-power variations, which themselves would require statement in social forms in order to make it possible to study them. We have therefore a fine field for study on the social side, but a very defective field on the individual side. Should such an interpretation of increasing brain power be given, we should not be much better off because of it, since all depends on how that power is used, on what work it does; and this we must continue to get on the social side, and nowhere else. The case is the same whatever variation of the brain-power theory we are considering; whether it be a question of higher average nervous capacity, or of the more frequent appearance of men of exceptional capacity, or finally of top points of capacity appearing which were never reached before.

Race endowment or race type is another manner of speech by which coherency is given to the social facts, but it will be very easy to show that it is actually "up in the air" to a very much greater extent than are the groups I have been using, even at first appearance. In his *Races of Europe*, Ripley tells us that "race denotes what man is; all these other details of social life denote what man does." Then he proceeds to describe the three physical races in which "the shape of the human head is one of the best available tests known," and in which all other tests are like unto it; and he proceeds to demolish the various attempts to prove that the variations of social life depend upon these race variations. I think I hardly need to argue that all the things that man does give us just as good a knowledge of what he "is" as the shape of his skull gives us. The physical races are admitted. The work of Ammon and his followers has been admirable on the side of physical measurements, but "Ammon's law"[1] in all its forms is merely a hypothesis at long range, and not even a plausible hypothesis. It is so far from being proved that it needs no further attention here.

Race type as we commonly meet it is a very different thing. It is stated almost exclusively in psychical terms. It is a seductively bright-hued clothing of endowment, conceived of as the property

[1] See especially *Revue internationale de sociologie*, Vol. VI, p. 173.

of all the individuals of the race. It makes interesting reading and is not hard to write when one gets the trick. It does not require any of the close, hard, careful study that other methods of interpreting society require. The plain citizen on his travels writes home a good bit about race type. The statesman on a vacation is interested in it, much more than he is when he is at work. The fiction-writer on a lecture tour takes his turn at it. The pompous quack of sociology is sure to find in it materials suited to his needs. And occasionally a hard student of social facts nibbles in its green fields, finds the freshness and flavor a relief from his troubles, and is seduced into wasting himself in the vain attempt to make definite and calculable that which by its very nature is the foe to definiteness, the glorification of illusion, the veil over the real world.

The English are thriftless, the French thrifty, the Germans are phlegmatic, the Spaniards volatile, the Corsicans vindictive, the ancient Hebrews religious, the Greeks artistic, the Romans legal minded, the Red Indians cruel, the East Indians lost in the mists of speculation, the native Australians theatrical, this people individualistic, that communistic—it does not make much difference what you call them or how you combine the adjectives, except that the nearer home you come the more cautious you are for greater danger of being laughed at. One would think that the Jews never waxed fat and wicked, that Greeks never went forth to trade nor had a religion worth mentioning, and that the Romans had pure law without any content of social activity at all.

When once one has built up a race type in this way out of such materials he can use it to suit his purposes. By proper admixture of elements he can make the race type a plausible explanation of whatever is. Yet all that he gets is verbosity.

The trouble with race type in such uses is that it reflects not the life of the people supposed to be described, but something of the historical value they have, or have had, for us. Such race type is a mere extension of psychological terms from their use in the practical distinction of man from man to an application to whole peoples where they have no practical purpose. The terms are carried upward, losing their merit for ordinary everyday purposes, and keeping all the misconceptions that go with them. They do not distinguish race from race at all.

The way to find out how a thing works is to take it to pieces and examine the parts, not to sit down and draw clever pen pictures of it. Just what are the parts, just how are they brought into one system, what is the functioning of one with reference to the other; such are the questions that must be answered.

It is true that all distinctions of race type are not so bad as this. There are many degrees of naïveness among them.   Von Jhering, for example, in his work on the Aryan, laughs out of court many of the worst varieties of race character, such as the alleged "love of wandering" which made the Germanic ancestors go a-roaming. He seeks always to reduce such innate, inborn characters peculiar to a people, to characters which they have acquired through the conditions in which they have lived, and which any other people under similar conditions would similarly have acquired. But he nevertheless retains many of these race propensities, not merely as actual activity, but as psychically stated characteristics, as, for example, when he discusses the non-gambling character of the Semites, which, in contrast with the Aryan love of gambling, has persisted through the ages. Here the statement in terms of activity is good just as far as it applies, but the statement in psychic terms which pretends to be something superior to activity is just as bad as the "Wanderlust" itself.

We will be able to test results which are as good as any that can be reached by the use of mental type in race if we examine Professor Dewey's article, which has proved stimulating to many writers, on the "Interpretation of Savage Mind," in the *Psychological Review* (May, 1902). With his functional psychology Dewey should be little apt to fall into the crude errors of the use of mind states as causes.

Like Arthur Bauer and Demolins, Dewey lays great stress on "occupations." He sets forth that mind has "a pattern, a scheme of arrangements in its constituent elements," and that "so fundamental is the group of occupational activities that it affords the scheme or pattern of the structural organization of mental traits."

Taking the Australian natives, who are hunters, he tries to show how in a hunting community "the mental pattern developed is carried over into various activities, customs, and products, which on their face have nothing to do with the hunting life;" he looks forward to getting an "important method for the interpretation of social institutions and cultural resources—a psychological method for sociology."

Illustrating with his Australians, he strives to show that their art, the corroboree, is just of the character one could expect among hunters who, unlike agriculturists, have always the direct satisfaction, the food itself, in immediate view.   So with their religion with its ever-insistent animism; so with their war games, and so also with their marriage institutions.   Now while Professor Dewey gives us comparatively plausible interpretations in the first three cases (though even here there is trouble because the "hunting pattern" is not so clear, so definite, so firm a point of support as he makes it out to be), when he comes to marriage he is not plausible at all.   Australian exogamy is much too complicated to discuss here, and much too complicated for anyone to discuss in a few sentences of comparison with hunting activities.   Professor Dewey thinks the natives get just that dramatic excitement out of it which comports well with hunting life.   But when one thinks of the exceeding complexity of the system and the rigid discipline and self-control it involves, not merely in tense moments, but steadily every day, one might just as well compare it with the "mental type" of the agriculturist.   However, that is neither here nor there.

The point is that the "mental type" is here nothing but a convenient phrase to cover certain similarities of activity which the investigator observes, or thinks he observes, and that it does not stand for any factor in the proceedings.   All these interpretations, so far as they have value, might just as well be made in terms of activity direct.   What one needs to do in order to interpret is not to depict a mental pattern or type, but to take the activities, to analyze them as they come, to break them down into group relations, to compare them when thus broken down with similar sets of group relations among other peoples, and thereby strive in the usual manner of investigation to get a more adequate statement of each of the two sets of groups that are compared. When that is done one will have types of activity, and not interjected mind types. Professor Dewey's article makes a distinct advance over ordinary methods of treating the savage, by looking at him much more nearly from his own center of activity (I do not say "point of view," because that would imply the savage's own statement of himself, which is not in point here). All it needs is to keep the psychic process but drop the concreted mental type.

What then are we to understand by race? First, we have the physical or, much better, the anatomical race. But all attempts to identify the characteristics of this in detail with social race activities have been painful failures. Then we have the social race facts, the peoples and sets of peoples as they actually exist and act. In each people we have an elaborately built-up group formation, and in each set of peoples we have a type of group formation which can, for certain purposes and to a certain extent, be contrasted with the type in another set of peoples. These race facts are very real, positively existing, social facts. You cannot change a group complex or type by breathing on it, or poking a finger at it, or praying to it, or "educating" it. Each has built itself up under conditions—which are mainly to be found in its own masses in their given locations—and, given a change in the conditions, there will be a definite enough change in the facts.

In interpreting government we have to do with given kinds of activity among given peoples: in such cases race simply is a name that indicates roughly the complexes of groups. We have also to do with race facts inside governments, where two "races" are both under one rule, or where they come into contact in neighboring governments. In these cases it is usually necessary to split the race facts down into group facts which can much better be described under a different terminology. Discussion—public opinion—will usually be carried on in terms of race, but the underlying groups which the opinion represents usually need a very different statement. Sometimes when color of skin distinguishes such "races," the race division strikes deeper, and we have something akin to what in later chapters I shall call "classes," that is solidified groups, firmly set with many cohering interest lines on one plane.   They are comparable also with castes.   But in these cases as in all others we are dealing with interest groups, in the terminology I have already established.   Maeterlinck has an essay on "The Latin and the Teuton Races," which may profitably be read by anyone who thinks the race distinctions are more fundamental than I make them.   As an artist he paints a picture of the contrasts between Flemings and Walloons, but he judges his own picture to be superficial, and finally says that "it seems very positive that the Fleming and the Walloon are of exactly the same value."

What I have said of races I might say also of psychic "character" classes, if it were worth the trouble to elaborate.   But I will leave that as a corollary.   It applies to Patten's clingers, sensualists, stalwarts, and mugwumps; Giddings' forceful, convivial, austere, and rationally conscientious; Ratzenhofer's interjected set of fearfully and wonderfully made "Individualität" and "Interesse" classes: Bauer's classes, so far as they are distinguished on this side (he, however, mixes many points of view in his tables); Novicow's élite; Lecky's reactionaries, conservatives, liberals, and radicals; Fouillée's "sensitifs," "intellectuels," and "volontaires," and many others.   Such efforts merely restate the social facts "psychically," but get nowhere.

CHAPTER X

GOVERNMENT

I have set forth our raw materials as consisting entirely of the group activities of men; activities that always embody an interest, that never define themselves except in terms of other group activities of the existing society, that in many cases are differentiated in such a way that they become representative of other group activities; and I have made a preliminary examination of leadership and public opinion, important elements of the governing process, to show that they are themselves only to be understood as such representative group activities. By these steps the way has been prepared to take up systematically the phenomena of government and study them in group terms.

The phenomena of government are from start to finish phenomena of force. But force is an objectionable word. In the first place, it is apt here, as in the natural sciences, to lead its users into metaphysical quagmires. In the second place, it is too closely identified with so-called "physical force," and too apt to be understood as in opposition to non-force factors of a sympathetic or moral or ideal nature; and this even while these latter factors are actually being treated as themselves very powerful agents in social process.

I prefer to use the word pressure instead of force, since it keeps the attention closely directed upon the groups themselves, instead of upon any mystical "realities" assumed to be underneath and supporting them; and since its connotation is not limited to the narrowly "physical." We frequently talk of "bringing pressure to bear" upon someone, and we can use the word here with but slight extension beyond this common meaning.

Pressure, as we shall use it, is always a group phenomenon. It indicates the push and resistance between groups. The balance

258

of the group pressures *is* the existing state of society. Pressure is broad enough to include all forms of the group influence upon group, from battle and riot to abstract reasoning and sensitive morality. It takes up into itself "moral energy" and the finest discriminations of conscience as easily as bloodthirsty lust of power. It allows for humanitarian movements as easily as for political corruption. Groups exert their pressure, whether they find expression through representative opinion groups or whether they are silent, not indeed with the same technique, not with the same palpable results, but in just as real a way. The tendencies to activity are pressures as well as the more visible activities.

Political phenomena have no peculiar technique of pressure not possessed by other social phenomena; that is, no technique qualitatively or fundamentally all their own. They have, of course, specialties of organization which are themselves technique; but these, from the present point of view—pressure itself—are merely a special forming or working-up of the common material. The technique varies greatly from age to age, and sometimes even from day to day, in accordance with the character of the interest groups that are involved; and indeed political progress is often sketched by writers about it in terms of the development of technique from some abhorred form toward some idealized form. But murder may break through at almost any time as one technical process, even in our biggest and most pretentious governments—as, in the United States, now in Colorado, now in Alabama—while again results may seem to be achieved through a pure "love of mankind." Of course, what is process from one point of view is content from another, as when political murders and lynchings are taken in hand and suppressed, but that is a double-sided characteristic of all the phenomena with which we shall have to deal—merely a difference in group activity on different planes of grouping.

The term political phenomena does not square exactly with the term government. From one point of view the former is the broader, as when we talk of certain party or subparty activities as political, but hesitate to include them under government proper.

From another point of view, however, government is much the broader term; this is where political is limited in its meaning to activities having to do with the organized government, and government is given a still wider meaning. I wish next to describe three senses in which the word government may be used, not because our study has to do equally with all of them, but because they indicate different ranges, or types, of the pressure process between groups; because similar specific contents of activity may be handled in all of them and make clear transitions from one to the others; and because we cannot get an adequate understanding of the particular facts we shall have before us, without taking a glance at them in their broader setting. I shall call these three senses of the word government simply the broadest, the narrowest, and the intermediate.

In the broadest sense—a very broad sense indeed—government is the process of the adjustment of a set of interest groups in a particular distinguishable group or system without any differentiated activity, or "organ," to center attention on just what is happening. We must recognize that there is such a thing as genuine government in this very broad sense, because societies showing adjusted interest groups without a differentiated "government" are actually found in corners of the earth—their government is called "anarchy" by political scientists who find it in primitive communities; because an immense mass of such adjustments not mediated by the government organs underlies the work of the differentiated government in our familiar societies—this is the habit background already discussed; and because interest groups, identical with those that are adjusting themselves or that have become fully adjusted in the ways just described, work through the differentiated government, and give that government its characteristic forms and movements, whether that government be despotic or "pure democracy;" or, in other words, whether it is as near to what somebody thinks would be abstract despotism or pure democracy as can be found. I shall return to this sense of government, to illustrate it, in a moment.

In the narrowest sense—except for the British technical use

of "the Government"—government is a differentiated, representative group, or set of groups (organ, or set of organs), performing
specified governing functions for the underlying groups of the population.   I may well say now, and be done with it, that "organ" is
merely an inept word to indicate a peculiar kind of representative
group, and that if I occasionally lapse into using it, the word has
no other meaning than that.   Government in this sense is not a
certain number of people, but a certain network of activities.   The
most absolute monarch that ever ruled does not himself under
exact analysis enter as a physical man entirely into the government;
he always takes part in many activities that are not governmental.
Nor is he ever under exact analysis all by himself the whole of the
government: he always is a part of it, a most spectacular part, of
course, but still a part.   And so with other official personages,
no matter what the type of government.   It is always their specialized activity that is the government itself in the present
sense.

Now between the broadest and the narrowest sense of the word
government there lies an intermediate sense to which we must
attend.   We get to it when we have clearly passed beyond the
limits of the differentiated governing activities, but are still among
phenomena that are specialized with reference to the government,
or, let us say, among political phenomena.   A particular form of
political party may or may not be regarded as part of the government in the narrowest sense, but even when it is not it is decidedly
a phenomenon of government, that is, of the governing process.
And behind that are organized movements of a political nature,
or tending toward political activity.   We cannot shut them out.
The directors of a corporation may finish their ordinary business
and turn at the same meeting to discuss the part the corporation
will take in the next political campaign.   Their activity, which
a moment before was industrial or economic, then becomes at once
political—a part of the governing process of the country—and is
to be studied specifically as such.   Moreover, the corporation as
activity will be represented through its members, along with other
corporations, in various organizations, which operate in the political

field; and the activity of all these organizations is part of government in the intermediate sense.

I might, indeed, add a fourth sense to this list to cover cases in
which differentiated governing activities are found in organizations of men which are not of the kind we call political. Such, for
example, would be the government, or administration, of a large
corporation. Such government is, however, to be assimilated in
type to that of government in the narrowest sense, above; the distinction concerning rather the field, or content, of the activities
with which it has to do. I shall be interested in it here only so far
as it furnishes illustrations presently to show that political government is not unique in its methods and technique. As it does not
come within the direct range of our studies, it would only bring
confusion into the distinctions above to arrange them so as to allow
specifically for it.

It would be very difficult indeed to draw a precise line to mark
where the activity that is economic ends and the activity that is
political begins. It would be just as hard to draw a precise line
between the activities that are part of government in the intermediate sense and those that are part of government in the narrowest sense. Fortunately no such lines need to be drawn in our study.
Our failure to do it at the start need not handicap us any more
than the biologist's failure to draw a precise line between vegetable
and animal life handicaps him. Fine-spun theories will not help
us. Quite the contrary. We must wait for gradually increasing
knowledge of facts to enlighten us. We have the economic and
other underlying groups, we have their given adjustments, we have
their political tendencies, we have their representation through
various organizations and opinions ranging up to the political
party, with technique ranging from violence and corruption to
"statesmanship," we have their representation in the differentiated
political activities, in the executive, the legislature, and the courts.
For the present we see three general senses in which the word
government is used, and for the present that must content us.

It is natural, I think, to call the differentiated government "the
government," or the "governing body," and to embrace the inter-

mediate range of activities in the term "government," without the
article, or in the phrase, "the process of government," or under
"political phenomena." The very widest meaning of government
will rarely recur in this work, after we have done with some illustrations a few pages farther on. Without any attempt at exact
definition, I shall aim to indicate in all doubtful cases the exact
sense I have in mind by qualifying adjectives, even at the risk of
cumbersome phrasing.

If now I had any occasion to use the word "state" in this work,
I think that word could probably be well defined as the sum of the
activities comprised within the intermediate sense of the word
government. All those activities which together make up the
whole process would correspond fairly well to "the politically
organized society." But the only advantage in this would be that
we should be holding these activities under a logical classification
apart from those that fall under government in the possible
fourth sense above, and the evil involved therein would be at
least as large in amount as the good. The "state" itself is, to the
best of my knowledge and belief, no factor in our investigation.[1]
It is like the "social whole": we are not interested in it as such,
but exclusively in the processes within it. The "idea of the state"
has been very prominent, no doubt, among the intellectual amuse-
ments of the past, and at particular places and times it has served
to help give coherent and pretentious expression to some particular
group's activity. But in either case it is too minute a factor to
deserve space in a work covering as broad a range as this. Nor
need the state, as "the tyranny of the minority over the majority,"
concern us. We are not conducting a propaganda. Of course

[1] If an effort were being made here to restate theoretical political science it
might be a serious question how far the exclusion of the term "state" would be
justified. Since the object is a very different one—namely, to illustrate the possibilities of the application of a particular manner of statement or scientific method
to the material—I am convinced that the gain is vastly more than enough to
offset the passing inconvenience to persons accustomed to starting their trains of
thought from the word "state" as they define it. From such persons I ask only
the recognition that I am adapting my verbal tools in what I conceive to be the
best manner to the task immediately in hand.

an American state, such as Massachusetts or Louisiana, must be mentioned at times, but in this special sense the word needs no definition.

I may add here that "sovereignty" is of no more interest to us than the state. Sovereignty has its very important place in arguments in defense of an existing government, or in verbal assaults on a government in the name of the populace or of some other pretender, or in fine-spun legal expositions of what is about to be done. But as soon as it gets out of the pages of the lawbook or the political pamphlet, it is a piteous, threadbare joke. So long as there is plenty of firm earth under foot there is no advantage in trying to sail the clouds in a cartoonist's airship.

As for a very common mode of expression, which puts the state and the phenomena of government in general in a class all by themselves with sanctions peculiar and distinct from those of other forms of social organization, it is perhaps needless to add that we shall have no use for it here. The state as "compulsory" or "involuntary" organization may be distinguished from minor groupings as "voluntary": to the one may be attributed power to punish, which is denied the other. But this can be done solely from a limited view-point. Voluntary and involuntary are artificial distinctions. The penalties the state inflicts are simply special forms of a great class of penalties imposed by all social organizations. Similarly, the state and the minor groupings need to be assimilated to one another, rather than sharply contrasted. Indeed a kindergarten acquaintance with the facts of government, as apart from the halos, the hero-worship, and other sensationalism, should suffice to put an end to 'any such approach to the subject.

Let me next discuss a few illustrations of government considered as the adjustment or balance of interests. All of these illustrations are of phenomena which are apt at any time to be regulated through "the government," but I want to ignore for the moment that phase of the matter and show how as institutions they themselves embody a balancing of interests, and, in some of the cases, how they have differentiated governing organs, which are all of a piece so far as process goes with the process of "the government."

Take the marriage institution. Just as we find it in society, lying sometimes apart from, and sometimes in part mediated through, "the government," it is itself a phenomenon of the adjustment of interests, and not of interests that may adequately be described as "individual," but of social group interests. I am not talking about anything that goes on inside the family, taken as a society for itself: I do not mean, that is, that the husband governs the wife, or that either husband or wife or both govern the children, but I am thinking of the marriage grouping as embedded in society. In human society at all stages—and to a certain extent among many mammals, whatever may be the truth about the pairing that is so frequent and permanent in the unpenetrated world of the birds—marriage is an arrangement of social order, a balancing of conflicting interests, a forming and shaping of these interests along lines which eliminate certain disturbances and violent struggles and soften down others, a substitution of a new technique for the adjustment of interests in place of an older technique become objectionable to dominant elements of society. And it is an adjustment of interests which can never be comprehensively stated in terms of individual men and women or by any process of adding A to B, to C, and to D, as individual persons, but which, instead, requires the recognition of group interests for its statement even in its simplest manifestation.

At the bottom, of course, there is sex; that is to say, all the individuals have sexual activity. Moreover they are discriminatingly, not blindly, sexual; this is about what the disproof of the theory of primitive promiscuity amounts to. By discriminating I imply nothing more than the choosing or pairing fact, which is open to direct observation in the acts of members of low societies; it is not necessary to go behind it as a given fact. The discriminations of the individual members of the society conflict with each other, and there is settlement of the discriminations in various simple ways. There is a governing process in the widest sense a process of balancing interests, going on already. Then according as the little society is composed of more or fewer members; according as it is settled in a village from which its members move to but short distances, or as it is migratory; according to the relative permanence or changeableness of the individuals in the little society; according to the manners of getting a living—all of them factors of group arrangement within the society—these sexual discriminations and adjustments of discriminations from being process become content to large parts of the membership of the group. That is, certain phases of what is going on which are regarded as incidental by the primary actors become most important phases to the larger group of bystanders. And the bystanders begin to interpose. It is entirely indifferent for present purposes whether one talks of custom or of conscious choice. In the forest, two bucks fight it out, but no deer group forms with interests to intervene. But in the crowded village community, two youths get into a feud; they disturb their elders' peace, they may draw their elders into the feud against the elders' will, they may keep the village awake all night, they may wreck the fishing boat, bungle the hunt, or bring defeat in tribal war by mischance of their quarrel. A group shuts off some part of their technical procedure, and we have a marriage institution on the spot. The old women around the fire in the Iroquois village dispose of sons' and daughters' hands, and thereby keep the peace. The household community sometimes comes to require marriages outside of it, and we may have one form of the clan. The adult men and the newly initiated youths may organize against each other and we have a trace of the class division inside the clans. We may have sex group against sex group, trade against trade, or rank against rank. There is no philosopher's stone to assure us of the outcome. What we observe we observe, and that is all there is to it, except as we compare and analyze it. Once given an organization of the interests, held in position by effective groups, and with no clashes with changing group interests, then that organization may persist indefinitely. There is no reason why it should not be continued—which is just another way of saying that there is no interest group in action powerful enough to alter it.

Or let us jump to modern society, passing over intermediate marriage forms. Is mobility of individuals increasing? Are income conditions changing? Are important new group relations forming among women, or including women? Are nuisances and dangers growing out of disjointed families? Then there will be a shoving aside of the old ordering of the interests, and an establishing of a new ordering, with groups of all grades of depth, of all degrees of representativeness, functioning away in a great whirl. There will be a busy talk group whirling around high up, with much to set forth about social crimes and the rights of women and men; and another talk group denouncing the first talk group as though social order depended on it. They are highly superficial—significant, but incidental except as process. Order is bound to result, because order is now and order has been, where order is needed, though all the prophets be confounded.

I do not for an instant want it thought that I am attempting to interpret marriage. That is a task that even for a single attempt, in a single stage of the institution, would involve some thousands of times the labor I am giving it here. I only want to indicate how the interest groups are fundamental in the institution, and how the ordering of the groups is a type of government in the widest sense.

For another illustration, let us take the church. The mediaeval church was a differentiated government alongside of political governments. The modern church daily complains that as a differentiated government it has been or is being discarded, which is equivalent to saying either that the interests which it formerly regulated have transformed themselves until they are outside its structure, or that they are now being regulated through some other differentiated government, or that they are now balanced in such a way that they do not need the differentiated organ to do any adjusting for them. All of which possibilities may in greater or less degree be true—that is a question of fact. But whatever the interests may be or have been, or whether they are stated in natural or supernatural terms, which is from the present point of view a question of detail, the church and organized religion are phenomena of government in the widest sense from start to finish, and sometimes of government in a differentiated form akin to "the government," the state.

A corporation is government through and through. It is itself a balancing of interests, even though it presents itself in many of its activities as a unit. It has been forced into corporate form by the struggling of the interests upon one another, by the struggling of wider groups with the intra-corporation groups. It functions in the political government, and at the same time it has its own interests functioning in it, with a differentiated government evolved from their adjustment. Possibly there are as many forms of corporate government as there are of political government, and possibly those corporate government forms can ultimately be classified on the very lines used for the classification of political governments. I do not know that they can be, I only suggest it. Certain technical methods which political government uses, as, for instance, hanging, are not used by corporations, generally speaking, but that is a detail. Corporation activities often put people to death by carelessness or by parsimony: this is not a judgment upon the corporations, but merely a statement of fact. The difference in technical methods, the fact that political government controls corporations, even the fact that corporations sometimes control political government, does not suffice to throw their processes out of the range which must be included in the same word that is used to cover the phenomena of political government.

Or consider a labor union. We can find everything of government within it: locality interests, rank interests, strict economic interests, autocracy, revolution, boss rule, representative institutions, the referendum, judicial processes, punishments, terrorism, corruption, self-sacrifice, loyalty, and a thousand other things, all capable of statement in terms of the balancing of group interests of the same kind that goes on in political government.

I do not intend to discuss in the remaining chapters either the balance of interests without a differentiated governing agency, or the governing agencies that appear in organizations outside the political field. I shall confine myself to political government (in the narrowest sense), and to the related processes by the aid of which the underlying groups of the population make themselves effective through the government (government in the intermediate sense).

All phenomena of government are phenomena of groups pressing one another, forming one another, and pushing out new groups and group representatives (the organs or agencies of government) to mediate the adjustments. It is only as we isolate these group activities, determine their representative values, and get the whole process stated in terms of them, that we approach to a satisfactory knowledge of government.

Let me give two or three illustrations, chosen from primitive societies, so as to avoid dragging in the conflicts of our own times, which show the kinds of interests that function through government. An Arab sheik at the head of several tribes has as one of his most important duties the ordering and assigning of pasturing districts; he is the agency through which this adjustment is made. In the Code of Manu we read of rajahs fixing every five days the price of merchandise; here we have a people different in its industrial life, and consequently with different group interests to adjust through government. It may be said that the rajah's exactions made his services come high, but that is a, question to decide not from our point of view, but from the very group tensions as they existed there and then. In China under the Chow Dynasty almost all the officials were occupied with agriculture. Again the group interests were dominant; it was a society with no idle land, with no land speculation, and with no "single-tax" issue in any form. Among the Australian natives elaborate rules for the division of food exist, forming an important section of the "law," mediated in part through the government, and in part lying outside in the realm of government in the broadest sense. The Spartan ephors once reprimanded a Spartan because he was growing fat, and threatened him with banishment. It does not matter that we may perhaps think today that such a regulation is "ridiculous;" it had a very real meaning in terms of group interests at the time. Tacitus tells us that the Suiones had a strong ruler who

took their arms away and locked them up under a guard ("arma
. . . . clausa sub custode"): the ocean protected them from
invasions and they were very prosperous. It is easy to see what
group interests worked through that strong ruler and gave him his
strength to do what he did. I cannot refrain from adding just one
illustration—though out of place here—to show how a similar
mediating function is found in those representative activities we
commonly describe under the name of ideas. Consider the worship of Adonis or Osiris, gods of vegetation, as set forth by Frazer.
The gods, stated as such, did not make the crops grow; but the wor-
shiping activity kept the population keen to its agricultural duties,
and was therefore functionally the representative of agricultural
activity. It helped to keep the bulk of the people in community
life from suffering from the bad habits of the sluggard and frivolous
elements of the population, and helped to keep the system working to
the support of the priest and warrior castes where those were found.

When we take such an agency of government as a despotic ruler,
we cannot possibly advance to an understanding of him except in
terms of the group activities of his society which are most directly
represented through him, along with those which almost seem not
to be represented through him at all, or to be represented to a
different degree or in a different manner. And it is the same with
democracies, even in their "purest" and simplest forms, as well
as in their most complicated forms. We cannot fairly talk of
despotisms or of democracies as though they were absolutely
distinct types of government to be contrasted offhand with each
other or with other types. All depends for each despotism and
each democracy and each other form of government on the given
interests, their relations, and their methods of interaction. The
interest groups create the government and work through it; the
government, as activity, works "for" the groups; the government,
from the view-point of certain of the groups may at times be their
private tool; the government, from the view-point of others of
the groups, seems at times their deadly enemy; but the process
is all one, and the joint participation is always present, however
it may be phrased in public opinion or clamor.

It is convenient most of the time in studying government to talk of these groups as interests. But I have already indicated with sufficient clearness that the interest is nothing other than the group activity itself. The words by which we name the interests often give the best expression to the value of the group activities in terms of other group activities: if I may be permitted that form of phrasing, they are more qualitative than quantitative in their implications. But that is sometimes a great evil as well as sometimes an advantage. We must always remember that there is nothing in the interests purely because of themselves and that we can depend on them only as they stand for groups which are acting, or tending toward activity, or pressing themselves along in their activity with other groups.

When we get the group activities on the lower planes worked out and show them as represented in various forms of higher groups, culminating in the political groups, then we make progress in our interpretations. Always and everywhere our study must be a study of the interests that work through government; otherwise we have not got down to facts. Nor will it suffice to take a single interest group and base our interpretation upon it, not even for a special time and a special place. No interest group has meaning except with reference to other interest groups; and those other interest groups are pressures; they count in the government process. The lowest of despised castes, deprived of rights to the protection of property and even life, will still be found to be a factor in the government, if only we can sweep the whole field, and measure the caste in its true degree of power, direct or represented, in its potentiality of harm to the higher castes, and in its identification with them for some important purposes, however deeply hidden from ordinary view. No slaves, not the worst abused of all, but help to form the government. They are an interest group within it.

CHAPTER XI

LAW

Law matches government every inch of its course. The two are not different things but the same thing. We cannot call law a resultant of government. Rather we must say it *is* government—that same phenomenon—only, stated from a different angle. When we talk about government we put emphasis on the influence, the pressure, that is being exerted by group upon group. When we talk about law we think not of the influencing or pressure as process, but of the status of the activities, the pressures being assumed to have worked themselves through to a conclusion or balance. Of course, the pressures never do as a matter of fact work themselves through to a final balance, and law, stated as a completed balance, is therefore highly abstract. Law is activity, just as government is. It is a group process, just as government is. It is a forming, a systematization, a struggle, an adaptation, of group interests, just as government is.

There is nothing mysterious about law; but the task of unraveling its group intricacies without indulging in an appeal to mysteries is as difficult as any task we have to face. One trouble with the analysis lies in the many kinds of facts the word law indicates, in the many meanings it has, even when no attention is paid to any meanings other than those found in connection with the phenomena of government. We are better off, however, in English with our word law than we should be in other languages with their distinctions between "jus" and "lex," between "Recht" and "Gesetz," between "droit" and "loi." "Jus" and "Recht" and "droit" have been the "open sesame" to the door that leads to the world of mysteries. We have the words right and justice, but we have not abused them so badly. We may be thankful that we have escaped the double terminology.

It is with law just as it is with government. If, in studying

272

it, we at any time desert the observable activities of our social groups we shall be off on a tangent with any destination possible. There are a myriad fine-spun legal theories to every fine-spun political theory. Sovereignty is, indeed, but one legal theory grown luxuriant. However, the legal theories dance along the path of the legal process in a way for which the political theories find comparatively little opportunity. We cannot set the legal theories aside as insignificant, as was possible with the theory of sovereignty. We must keep the legal theories inside our inter-pretation, as having a continuously important representative value. Our way of going through them will seem to the theorist himself very much like cutting the Gordian knot. But then Gordian-knot cutting is just what is actually happening in society all the time, even up to the very inmost chambers of the Supreme Court, after it has been flooded with the finest of all fine theroies. So that if we do cut the Gordian knot in the right way, we are merely presenting the social truth.

Because of the different points of view involved in the words law and government, the "senses" which we can discriminate in the use of the word law will not correspond exactly with the senses we found for the word government. The phenomena are all one, the fields into which the phenomena are divided are the same, but where we had to force the word government a little in one direction to cover them, we should have to force the word law even more in other directions. Fortunately, nothing turns on the words except simplicity of expression, and that we have long before this been compelled to sacrifice. I will merely indicate the way the two words, law and government, correspond and differ in their applications, before going on with the analysis of the facts.

Corresponding accurately with the field of phenomena I have called "government in the broadest sense," we have also a law in the broadest sense. The dictionaries tell us, however, that the word law is obsolete in this sense, and that the word custom has replaced it. This field includes all the established, socially enforced, modes of activity, not mediated through a differentiated governing body. It involves, or rather it is one form of statement of, the equilibration of interests, the balancing of groups. I shall not deal with it directly in this work for the simple, practical reason, that if I succeed in interpreting the more complicated processes of the equilibration of interests through representative groups, I shall at the same time have provided the basis for the interpretation of the less-complicated cases without further words.

Corresponding to government in the narrowest sense, we have law in the narrowest sense, namely, our ordinary law of the statutes and the precedents. It is that part of the habitual social activity which is either formulated or enforced, and most commonly both formulated and enforced, through a differentiated governing body. (Customary law as applied by courts is not technically formulated, and international law is not technically enforced, by a differentiated governing body, but we need not consider those distinctions here.) It may seem that law in this sense is something "beyond" the governing body; but it will be remembered that I have insisted that the government itself can only be interpreted, or adequately stated, in terms of the interest groups it represents; and law is merely another manner of statement of those same interest-group facts, so that the correspondence is in fact exact. The interests that function through government, and that are government in the sense that the governing body is only their instrument or tool, are the same interests that hold law in place and bring changes in the law.

As government in what I have called the "intermediate" sense is a process which from the practical standpoint of the actors is not complete, but incomplete, we have corresponding to it, not law, but rather projects of law. As for the possible fourth sense of government, the government of minor organizations, such as corporations, the law aspect will readily be recognized in the constitutions or charters, and in the by-laws and the enforced customs and methods of the organization. I will just add, to avoid misconception with reference to all this comparison between government and law, that while government includes many specific acts (or individual acts), and while law seems to imply the generalized rule, there is no fundamental difference between the two; the distinction lies rather in the character of the representativeness of the activity, partly with reference to the extent of the groups, but more especially with reference to the duration of the activity in time.

We have now to proceed with the analysis of law as it is mediated through differentiated government. Hereafter wherever the word law is used, it is this kind of law that is meant. Let us first make a list of the activities which have to be taken into account in connection with the law process. They include:

The written rule printed in statute book or volume of precedents, accompanied most often by written interpretations handed down by the courts.

The plaintiff and the defendant.

The activity of one portion of the population, probably very large, along the lines prescribed, or, better said, described, in the written text.

The activity of another portion of the population, probably very small, along lines conflicting with those described by the written law.

In the background, the activity of some law-registering body, legislature, or court, our authority for the text.

The activity of a set of officials, including public prosecutors, who seek with greater or less energy the persons whose activity deviates from the line set forth in certain parts of this law and who bring them before courts.

The activity of certain persons, the lawyers in private practice, who represent persons who do conform to the habit in the effort to penalize others who do not conform; also the activity of those same lawyers in representing those who do not conform.

The activity of a set of persons, the judges, who measure conformity or non-conformity, declare it in formal terms, and impose penalties.

The activities of a set of persons who execute penalties or enforce decrees.

The activities of a set of persons who, placing themselves at various points in the process, and allying themselves with various groupings, reflect or represent the tendencies of the groups in various degrees of completeness through spoken or written language.

Needless to say, none of these groups is exclusive of others. Some of them have a personnel which for fixed periods of time cannot be altered; but that very personnel may belong simultaneously to several other groupings. So a sheriff may at the same time be a criminal, a plaintiff in a civil suit, and perhaps also a lawyer in practice.

In listing these groups, I have not gone behind the legislatures into the group process there represented, for the reason that I am here confining myself in the main to the consideration of the law phase of the process, as abstracted from the further governmental phases. Nor have I complicated the statement to include "dead-letter" law. We shall give that special consideration in due time.

Suppose we ask ourselves: "What is the law?" meaning not what is the meaning of the word, nor what is the best expression of what lawyers say about it, but what is the solid ground for our study of the law as it exists in the life of social men.

Certainly the law is not the attested document offered us by the secretary of state or by the clerk of the court. That is a definite enough thing, but it only indicates to us what to look for and where.

Certainly the law is not the theorizing activity of any group or portion of a group of men: that is, it is not the verbal or written arguments of the men who take part in its processes within or without the differentiated governing body. "Such is the law," may end neatly a speech or argument, but it merely indicates a tag or label of the law, an activity representing other activities and still others at possibly a great degree of removal.

The law is not primarily what the governor does, nor what the sheriff does, nor what the judge does, nor what the lawyer does, nor what the bailiff does, nor what the criminal does, nor what the man who varies from the prescribed (better said, described) rule in civil cases does.

The law at bottom can only be what the mass of the people actually does and tends to some extent to make other people do by means of governmental agencies. (I repeat. I am not speaking as the lawyer speaks when he looks out of his window upon society. I am speaking of society with the lawyer included as part of the process.) The law, then, is specified activity of men—that is, activity which has taken on definite social forms—embodied in groups which tend to require conformity to it from variant individuals (these themselves appearing in groups and having their variant actions valued and judged only as affecting groups), and which have at their disposal, to help them compel these variants to adapt themselves to the common type, certain specialized groups which form part of the governing body of the society, that is, certain organs of government.

With this formal statement, however, we are by no means out of our difficulties. Rather our difficulties have just begun. We must follow this statement of the law as activity through many intricacies and show that it is adequate, which means both that it is a useful working statement, and that it ignores no phases of importance to us. We shall have to test its application to different kinds of law; we shall have to reckon with "dead-letter law," with survivals, with law-making, with the systematic side of law, and with all the "theoretical" phases of law interpretation and law enforcement. These questions will be illustrated and discussed in general terms in this chapter, but they will accompany us all through the rest of the book.

In taking up different kinds of state-enforced law for purposes of illustration, I shall pay no attention to the distinction between criminal and civil law. It is not a distinction that is useful here. Indeed it is a distinction of a kind which is very important for us to break down and obliterate. It is a lawyers' distinction, having to do primarily with "process" in the technical legal sense, and while it is an important distinction practically, even in the law-books it breaks down theoretically on the test of penalties, and on every other test as well. From our point of view there is no law that is fundamentally more "public," none that is more private, than any other. The most insignificant suit between two petty disputants over a contract is dealt with socially on the basis of great group interests which have established the conditions and the bounds for it. All law is social. Every bit of law activity may, it is true, be stated as a sum of individual "acts;" but every bit may also be stated in group terms, and this latter is our method of statement here. We do not ignore John Doe's doings, but we state John Doe's doings just as they are given to us, with all their social meanings, values, and realities.

I proceed now to illustrate this position on law facts of two kinds, which I will only roughly distinguish between by designating, first, those in which, at a given time and place, any individual may potentially be involved as defendant; and second, those which, at a given time and place, are directed only at a given section of the population, as say at some particular trade or profession. The distinction is rough, because in the latter case any individual may potentially go into that defined section of the population, and because in the former case all individuals are so specified themselves as bits of society that what we may call their "potentialities" are not identical for any two of them. It answers, however, our present purposes.

As an illustration of laws of the first kind, let us take the law forbidding murder, limiting our consideration to the taking of human life in those rough forms, such as by direct act, by direct agent, or in a limited degree by gross negligence, which almost alone we have thus far undertaken through government punishments to suppress.

Even in Sicily, where the proportion of homicides is, I believe, greater than in any other civilized region, the common habit of the population is "not-killing." In the United States perhaps one person in 10,000 commits homicide each year. In the greater part of Europe the proportion is very much less than that. Sometimes it is only one in 100,000, or in 150,000. And yet possibly there is not a single human being in all these stretches of the world who could not, on sufficiently close analysis, find tendencies in his life toward the use of murder as a technical means to attain certain of his ends. ("Means and ends" is merely common speech to indicate the killing activity in its earliest stages, where it is more or less promptly inhibited.) Every person is, in short, potentially a murderer.

The definition of murder is, of course, not uniform. Different conditions produce different killing reactions and produce different "crime" judgments upon them by society. Nor does the dictionary definition of the crime correspond necessarily with the actual social habit of crime and crime punishment. In Sicily certain forms of feud killings are eliminated from murder as it appears in the real law of the land; the letter of the statute may cover them, but the actual maintenance of a non-killing activity through governmental agencies is not seen. In certain mountain districts in Kentucky, Tennessee, and neighboring states, in the same way, certain feud killings cease for considerable periods to be murder as actually reacted on by government. In our large cities conditions arise, that is, certain sets of interest groupings arise, which at times come near to eliminating special forms of murder from the legal reaction. Indeed, apart from the formally "justifiable homicide," there are nearly always more or less definite classes of murders which are actually excluded, as, for example, often the killing of a seducer. I mention this unenforced "law" only to postpone its consideration for a few pages.

Now, the fact that every person, roughly speaking, is potentially a murderer, so far from operating to prevent the development of actual law against murder, is just the basis on which that law appears. Of course, merely because every person may use murder as a method, it does not follow that every person will carry his activity through on that line. There are many alternative lines of action. But enough murder is committed so that—I merely register the fact—a great interest grouping develops which reacts on murder not as a mere bit of technique but as an objectionable content in the social living. It specifies certain forms of killing for its attack and it strikes at them by various means which in the end take the form of our judicial process through the differentiated governing group or organ, with the continuing possibility of the use of lynching or the sheriff's posse or vigilance societies under special conditions. Lynching, it may be noted, is from one point of view an embryonic governmental activity itself, while from another point of view it is an offense against the government; each point of review represents a group attitude, and according as conditions cause one or the other attitude to prevail does lynching spread, or is it suppressed.

We find in society at this stage on the one side the murdering activity, and on the other side the non-murdering, murder-sup-

pressing activity.   This is a division merely on the particular
plane of murder in the limited scope of the word given above.   We
cannot go behind it into the hearts of men or above it into the idea
of justice to explain it.   We must recognize at the same time all
the countless other groupings or other planes, and from them we can
feel our way to interpreting the form of the murder grouping at
any given time, and the intensity of the reactions.   These other
groupings are shifting, and, as individual men find themselves
placed among them, will, now one, now another, emerge into the
murdering group and receive the reaction, through the governing
body, of the non-murdering group.   It is true that even in our
most disorderly societies today the murdering group is very greatly
reduced in numbers; and this reinforces our ordinary modes of
speech so that we come to regard its members strictly as individuals,
acting strictly with individual responsibility, and to discuss it as an
individual phenomenon.   But the group nature of the activity
struck at by law appears whenever we appeal to statistics, whenever we talk of the "good example" or "moral effect" of punishment, and indeed whenever we mention murder at all, for murder
is a special form of life-taking definitely marked out by the reacting
group.   It is impossible to try a murderer purely as an individual.
The ordinary speech points to the murderer as an individual and
to the law as a generalized social rule, but actually the murderer,
that is his murdering activity, is just as much generalized, just as
much "social," as is the rule, and apart from the murdering and
non-murdering activities there is no rule, save as a differentiated
phase of the governing group and of the various kinds of representative "opinion groups."

Turn now to law which directs itself against some phase of
activities which are segregated in a particular trade, profession, or
section of the population.   Here the case is not so simple.   How
are we to state the facts here in terms of a group habit tending to
extend itself ?   Suppose we take the Sunday-closing law governing
saloons.   The activity against which the law is directed is the
selling of liquor in saloons on Sunday.   Now, if we should isolate the
saloonkeeper and describe the whole activity in terms of him as

an individual, or even in terms of saloonkeepers as a class, we should have difficulty. For manifestly we cannot find a great saloonkeeping population closing its doors on Sunday and trying to make the doors of a few open saloons also close. But such statement is little more than a caricature of the social fact. Whenever the saloonkeeper hands a glass of beer over his bar there is another human being on the other side of the bar who is taking it. While these are thus engaged, there are other people passing along the street in front of the building, perhaps on their way to church, witnesses of what is happening, in other words participants in the action to the extent that their church-going activity is disturbed. Later in the day there will be a certain number of drunkards on the streets, brushing against men and women who thereby participate in the total activity. Also there will be a certain amount of noise in the city and a certain distortion of the activities of people for whom this noise is a disturbing element. Mix in a few fights, a few wife-beatings, a few empty larders at a new week's beginning, a certain increased amount of various other activities known as "vice" and whatever other ingredients exist, and you have the total of the open-saloon-on-Sunday activity at which our assumed law is hitting. Out of all this you get a Sunday-closing interest group in the political field, and it is this group which hits at the open-Sunday group. The open-Sunday group, for its part, is made up of a large number of persons who do not own saloons, as well as of all, or nearly all, of the saloonkeepers, brewers, and distillers. As formulated by the governing body, the law will specify the saloonkeepers for the observance of the rule and for penalizing in case of non-observance, but the law as a social habit of action involves the largest part of the population as acting and enforces itself upon the other part. The saloonkeeper stands at the center in the place of prominence merely for technical purposes. Our point of view, then, does not fail to cover the facts here, any more than in the case of laws like those against murder.

In the case of legislation governing life-insurance management the analysis goes on similar lines. Here there is a large, well-defined group of policy-holders whose interests have been hurt at certain points. There is a small group of insurance-company managers (with their outside allies) who have been doing the hurting in certain ways. There is, let us assume, a resultant law specifying forms of policies and modes of management. We may contrast the groups involved by the catchwords, the safe-policy group and the unsafe-policy group. The safe-policy group, including policy-holders, agents, and managers, predominates, then, and strikes through government at the unsafe-policy group phenomena wherever they appear. It might be that all managers appeared on the unsafe-policy side and all policy-holders on the safe side. That would be a transitory phenomenon, highly significant for concrete interpretations while occurring, but nevertheless not the most significant line of division for getting down to the bottom of the law activity as we find it existing. This illustration like the others has been treated here right in the bed of social habit in which it lies, without any attempt to go far in comparing the given groupings with groupings on other lines in the given society. That phase will get attention later.

Should we take even such a detail of commercial law as, for example, the proper phrasing of a promissory note, we must regard it also as a way of acting tending to impress itself upon variants, and penalizing them through government functions, when they do not conform. This is the most complete statement of the law to which we can aim. All the other characteristics, which for certain purposes (which is the same as saying from certain group points of view) are often held up as fundamental, slip down to their proper proportions and allow themselves to be stated as incidental to this characteristic group activity which itself is the law of the society.

If we take up now the question of laws that are not enforced we can see better what place they occupy in society. Suppose it is a question of a blue law which forbids the selling of goods, including, say, milk, on the Sabbath. Milk is habitually sold by all the milk dealers to all or nearly all their patrons seven days a week. Yet the words can be found on the statute book which forbid it.

If the law is to be defined in terms of the statute book, then such a law exists. But if we turn to the activities of the people, we observe at once that there is no such law in existence at the given time. There is no non-milk-selling-and-using group tending to require conformity from any would-be milk-selling and milk-using group. At most there is a little inchoate material from which such a group might develop. Nevertheless the situation in society is not what it would be if that law in so many letters were not on the statute book. Any proper local official, no matter what variety of interest he represents, has it in his power to function as though it were a law, and so in very fact to make it law again, or rather to start the process of making it law again. His activity may be checked, almost certainly will be checked, and he will be overthrown if he persists. But that is neither here nor there. What we observe is that there is a track or a technical means by which milk-selling on Sunday can be suppressed without the issue passing through the legislature. Should a vigorous anti-milk-selling group ever develop it can push its activity with fewer obstacles than if the old blue law had been repealed. Here is observable fact, free, or at least free so far as my understanding goes, from the implications and coloring of any particular group-made theory about the law, about the Sunday-observance ideal, or about social life in general. We observe as fact that just as an easier technique is provided for changing a statute than for changing an article of the constitution, so an easier technique is provided for making law in the field of dead-letter law than for making law in the ordinary legislative field.

Incidentally, we can now get light on the question whether a majority of the population must always be discoverable on analysis as standing behind each law, that is, whether the group having the habit and tending to extend the habit must comprise a majority of the population of the society in question, in order to entitle its activity to rank as law. The distinction between majority and minority now comes to appear as a rule of thumb and not as crucial at all. Majority and minority are simply a bit of technique—a very important bit, of course, which becomes vital content at some stages of the governmental process—and they are used as tests mainly in certain stages of the legislative part of the government work.   They cannot be transferred to this portion of our analysis with any claim of validity, and indeed they are practically not needed.   Anywhere along the majority and minority lines we may expect to find a law-making struggle going on.   We may indeed say that it is invariably possible to decide by direct inspection whether a bit of formal law is or is not actual law.   Actual law tends to run well up toward general observance so swiftly that we hardly have a chance to notice it at the minority and majority dividing line.

"The law of a society is something beyond the sum of its laws." What that common manner of statement means is merely that the process of summation is not the process which will give us an adequate picture of the whole body of the law.   And the reason summation is inadequate lies in the abstract, and hence artificial, nature of the components which it is attempted to add together. It is not merely laws but rather systems of law with which we actually have to deal.

Now my previous illustrations in this chapter have been, as I have noted, abstract in just this sense.   I have mentioned particular laws without carrying the analysis back into the whole system in which they are placed.   Each particular law rests in a great habit background of law, that is, has its place in the system.   The value of each law, its meaning, is known only in terms of the values and meanings of the other activities which taken all together make up the system.   In the instances above we were concerned with tracing roughly for purposes of illustration the immediate activity groups which support—or, better said, which are—the law, but not with getting their full values.   If these groups were not themselves taken by us as immediately given phenomena just as they appear in the complex social grouping with its great habit background assumed we should go wrong.   That is, if we attributed any force or power or value to the groupings behind their immediate operation in the law, we should be tangling our feet.   But error of that kind is not made here.   It is necessary, however, to complete the picture by considering the system of law and what it means.

Now it is in the fact that the law is thus a great system to which such a term as "coherent" can be applied; it is just in this fact that much of the mystery and metaphysics of current legal theories develops. But if we hold to the view that all law is itself activity, we have no reason for wandering off into the mysteries, or preferring the least stable to the most stable elements in our explanation. It is of the very definition of activity that it is systematized. Even the simplest motion with which the physicist deals is part of a system of motion. When the geometrician gives position to a point, he admits system. In living beings there is no function that is not systematized. Behavior is a word biologists are now using of the very simplest reactions of the simplest organisms, and except as system it cannot be comprehended at all. All the actions that enter into the behavior of an idiot are correlated, much more all the activities of a mentally competent person. True enough, we can choose many special points of view from which we will say that a certain lot of activity is not systematized, but here we are merely adopting a group's position as our own position from which to view the world, and we are judging along the lines of that group's activity; and the denial of systematization so uttered is a limited denial of a limited form of system, no matter how vehemently or how absolutely phrased. It is a representative activity, reflecting certain group interests along certain lines, but not capable of elevation for use in broader fields.

The common fault in overemphasizing the system characteristic of law, and contrasting it with assumed unsystematized activity outside it, is seen in the giving to a system of law of a certain individuality or personality, and treating it as though it developed by its individual and personal power, and as though capable of interpretation in that way. Such an attitude represents a certain amount of truth, which we must be careful not to lose. But its emphasis leads us to error far greater than the bit of truth involved.

What we have then is not a series of laws, or, I may say, law activities, disconnected from one another like so many pebbles in a pile, to use a common illustration. Instead, we have these law activities so knit together in larger groups that by analysis on a different plane we can point out what we may call a single group activity representing a whole set of laws. For instance, the particular kind of disturbance which produced the group reaction against murder may be examined on a plane on which it will be found to be assimilated with a lot of other disturbances, all producing or tending to produce reactions. That is, the social situation in which the reaction against murder occurs will perhaps show reaction against minor assaults, against brawlings, and against sex violence. Where there is a reaction against one form of offense against property there will doubtless be reactions against other forms. A code of commercial law will show not merely a group activity for each item in it, but a group activity for large portions of it; perhaps one group activity can be found for the whole or nearly the whole of such a code, perhaps several will cross one another in it; that is a matter for direct observation to decide. Thus, likewise, when we find municipal ownership of street railways, we may or may not find federal ownership of steam railways. In a highly representative discussion group, this assimilation will almost certainly appear; but I am not considering that now, but the deeper-lying groups which support the law.

It is always a matter of direct observation and of nothing else to show what law groups can be analyzed out of the mass. If perhaps the whole mass of law in a given society can be interpreted in terms of a set of groupings, which bring it in contrast with the whole mass of another society, resting in another set of groupings, that also will be a matter of observation. And the fundamental point for us to notice in connection with this systematization of the law is that our reasonings upon it in large masses cannot extend farther than the facts of our observation; we cannot make any progress toward building the law up out of reasonings of that kind any more, for instance, than the student of the evolution of animal life could build up the succession of forms except by studying the facts of the pathway that life has followed. Within their great systems of facts both biologist and student of law can bridge gaps, supply missing links, and work over the material to a very limited extent. But the student of law like the others must stop there, even in his study; much less has he the right to attribute to the system as such any self-realizing capacity.

It may have occurred to some readers while I was discussing majority and minority aspects of the groups that sustain the laws, and also while I was discussing dead-letter law, that I did not make sufficient allowance for the power of "the government" itself, and that it would be much simpler to attribute results to this power directly, than to attempt to put through the analysis in terms of groups. It would certainly be simpler, but not simplicity of the helpful kind, for our problem is to analyze this very power itself. Similarly, it is simpler and easier to say that the weight of the "whole society" is back of the law than to make a painstaking analysis of that weight.

Government itself, like the factors indicated by "ideas," is organization, and its representative activities in themselves add to the effectiveness of the process at various stages. With the question as to what increase of pressure may be attributed to them we shall have to deal in due time. What we can see here from the point of view of law as system is that complexes of groups, working together through the government, combine their pressures. There is nothing absolute about the combination. It does not conform to any theory, and even the best theory only poorly conforms to it. But where we have it, we have it; and at certain transition stages between adjustments, it seems to stand out as an independent factor. That "seeming" however need not mislead us here.

From this point of view we get the meaning also of the statement often made that law tends to spread, to generalize itself. The spreading, the generalizing, is dominated entirely by interest-group needs, and this whether the spreading is from one people to another, or from one phase of a given people's activity to another phase. If a system of law as a whole spreads, it is because of similarities (we may say, system) in the groups as they stand. The greatest case of all, that of the influence of Roman law on continental Europe, needs just this interpretation. The facts that Rome was no longer existing (in the ordinary, concrete sense) and that the influence had so wide a range, do not add any more mystery to the process.

Each law, then, is a habitual activity, maintaining itself through organized government, and resting in a great bed of such activities, in which, because of the many planes of grouping of the population, it can be found arrayed with other laws, systematized with them, depending therefore on them from one point of view, while from the opposite point of view it itself is part of the bed or beds of habit in which each of the other law activities rests. The system characteristics are themselves reducible to activity, just as are the laws separately considered. The whole is matter of observation, as activity, at every stage and at all stages of development and operation.

To avoid misconception I have postponed to this stage the consideration of the perfectly valid assertion that all law strikes at something. That something will inevitably be human activity. This is only to put in other language the principle of the group interpretation itself. Any classification of laws into those which hit at evils and those which work constructively for public welfare is fundamentally wrong, or, rather, it pretends to be fundamental, when actually it is superficial. This is true of, I care not what, laws. Suppose we have quarantine regulations "to promote the public health": they strike at certain objectionable activities of men. Take a campaign by the state to protect crops against some insect pest: it proceeds by striking at certain careless activities of men, and this whether it works by penalty of by propaganda, a difference which is one of technique. Revenue-raising is a stage in a great complex of striking processes. The scientific investigations of a government department of agriculture can be envisaged from the same point of view. There would be no law, even in the most extreme socialistic state, without this quality. Criminal law, commercial law, all law setting forth government activities can be looked at in the same way.

I do not want to be understood, however, as saying that this is the only point of veiw, or for all purposes the best point of view, to take of the phenomena. Activity is very positive from the point of view of the actors. The striking done by the law is not anything negative which exists merely for striking's sake. But it is never, on the other hand, a pure matter of everybody's welfare. However much any of it may be ennobled and glorified in the speech that accompanies and represents it, the conflict phase can be found when the whole range of the society in which it exists is taken into account. For its interpretation the discovery of this phase is essential.

This analysis of law activity is, however, not even yet complete. There is still necessary a showing in outline of the processes by which the various activities of the population are represented through courts, legislature, and executive. Law-making and law-sustaining pressures are the same, and in some of the preceding illustrations we have already touched on the law-making phase. Here we must consider both directly. We have to observe how it is that even when the representative group appears to be taking an independent initiative, it is still the group activities as actually observable in the populace that carry forward, support, and *are* the law. In connection with this the activity of the legal theorist will, I trust, appear at something like its proper value in the whole process.

The chapter on leadership and public opinion contained a discussion of the representation of group by group, but we must get here to even closer quarters with the process. If a political party has carried an election and secured the passage of a certain law, we can readily see how the maintenance of that party in power sustains the law, and further how the continued existence of the underlying groups which potentially can call that party into life again or call up a new party with the same policy or give the same policy to some existing party will sustain the law long afterward.

But the party that won the victory on the particular issue has much other work to put through the government; or, what comes to the same thing, the governing body, as it stands after the party victory, has many tasks to perform not decided explicitly by the vote at the poles.   It goes ahead and uses its "discretion;" that is, to use a current distinction between terms, it acts as a representative as distinguished from a delegate body.   What are we to say of the group activities as underlying the law in the case of law promulgated by the governing body under circumstances like this ?   The governing body, of course, is a group, an activity, itself, and as such has its interest.   But this special group interest is not nearly so prominent as it is often made out to be.   In a bureaucracy it appears perhaps more strongly than anywhere else, and here it concerns matters of technique which may be annoying, but which nevertheless permit almost anything in the way of dominant underlying group interests to pass through, however faultily.   Usually when emphasis is placed upon the government's own interest, it is due to confusing the governing activities as such with the class activities of the persons who are most prominent in, or who make up, the governing body.   The practical value of the confusion for the participants at certain stages in the political process is not to be denied, but nevertheless our analysis must distinguish the governing activities from the underlying activities, even in the case of a feudalism, in which the land-holding interest forms a hierarchy which step for step is identical, so far as personnel goes, with the governing hierarchy.

Now, leaving the "government's own interest" to one side for the present, we find many activities carried through the governing body without the direct appearance on the scene of the underlying groups through representation by differentiated activities of a political character.

And yet those underlying activities are actually supporting and indirectly "making" the law that results.   And what is more, however indirect the process of making may seem to be, through whatever complicated technical elements of representation or control it works, the law once made is just as much as in the former case supported by the group activity and group interest.   It has no meaning without reference to that activity, and it is fundamentally that activity's creation and that activity's legal functioning, whatever its technical mediation. To make this clear we must come closer to the individual psychic process than is usually necessary in social interpretation, but only in order to remove misunderstandings and preconceptions involved in the ordinary reports of what is happening in a legislature, a court, or an executive office, such as we read in the newspaper dispatches.

Take an official functioning in the government group. A neat illustration from the day's news is Secretary of War Taft as he proclaims himself provisional governor of Cuba, announcing meanwhile that all Cuban institutions and laws will stand during his tenure, save those which must yield to the intrusion of an executive selected by other than the constitutional methods, that is to the intrusion of himself. We read from day to day of Governor Taft's "decisions" and orders. These come to us as though they were qualities of the man, marks of his wisdom, elements of his genius or incapacity, as the case may be. There is no objection to such a statement for its own purposes, but for our purposes it merely indicates crudely what we must look for. Every "decision" he makes will be really the pressing through to achievement of some element of the Cuban population. The technique is very different from what it would be with a smooth-running republican government, but the concrete showing of results will be much closer to what it would be under such a government than to what it was under the crumbled Palma administration, or to what it would be under a revolutionists' conquest. To state the law situation of the succeeding six months or more in terms of the intellect of Taft or his successor as governor is a puny trifle compared with a statement of it in terms of the Cuban interest groupings, Taft entering as technique. And this is true without for an instant taking away any of the actual value of the Taft-governing-body in the interpretation. In photographing the surface of Cuba today, Taft looms large; but in dissecting the country, Taft is merely a ganglion, and it requires trained eyes, technical instruments, and measuring rods to place him exactly. This is true even when we take into account the fact that Taft embodies an American technique of adjustment, and that he has the force of our army and navy behind him.   The only assumption I make is that Taft's proclamation sets forth the whole truth about the interest activities involved, and that no further "United States interests" will force themselves into the field.   In the latter event the ultimate outcome might be very different, but even then the value of this illustration would not be destroyed, for we have to do solely with process, and the process which we are considering here would be the same in both cases.

It is so with every public official in every function.   Perhaps he has little discretion and we can easily watch the pressures operating through him.   Perhaps he has great discretion, and we have difficulty to keep ourselves from being led astray by his prominence as a technical process.   But in either case we must push the analysis down to the groups represented, and in either case we shall on the test find that our fullest and richest statement of the law is in terms of the group activity tending to spread itself, with allowance for the differences of technique in the governing organ through which it functions.

In all this, of course, I am not taking sides with one interest or another.   My "anti-plutocratic" friend will tell me that because some "plutocratic" measure exists and maintains itself as law the interest groups are not expressing themselves.   It is because he exalts "objectively" the groups for which he is a mouthpiece activity, and contemns those which have found expression, that he makes his complaint.   Let him decry the "hard heart."   Either there is no heart at all in the process we are trying to study, or else it is all heart.   But that is a mere trifle of verbiage.

Of the habits of activity which seem socially indifferent I will add just a word, because they may seem stumbling-blocks to some critics of this point of view.   It is very common in extra-legal life and not uncommon in law activity to find an established habit maintaining itself where one has great difficulty in putting his finger on any interest groupings which sustain it that do not seem purely formal and called into existence to support the theory.   So, for instance, certain rules of the law, concerning negotiable instruments when they are just at the transition point between the condition in which there was an interest to create them, and the condition in which they have become such a nuisance that they must be swept away. This period of indifference may last indefinitely. It all depends on the shifting of the activities underlying them. Fundamentally there is no reason why a thing should be done one way rather than another, except as we find it in the very activities themselves. The person accustomed to our marriage laws looks upon them as "natural," and thinks other nations' laws are "queer" and needing explanation. Our own he accepts as though they did not need explanation at all. And yet no outside test will give one the advantage over the other. The test must be in the activity itself. Now if a law establishes itself and works along smoothly furnishing a course of conduct, not perhaps the one that would be made afresh, but at least one which is not troublesome, we find as a matter of fact that it usually maintains itself, call it from inertia, stupidity, conservativeness, or what you will. This seemingly indifferent activity is a real group activity, even though the abstracting of an interest, a value, a meaning, in terms of other groups, seems difficult. It is a law activity like any other; the difficulty is only in the use of words to make it seem positively worth while in common speech; in other words it is no difficulty at all when properly approached.

Besides the representative determination of incidental issues in law, there is also a process of filling in details, which is carried out by the various portions of the governing body. Here also we may treat law as the habitual activity of the society, sustaining itself and extending its range through the agency of the governing body. For example, we have a group activity in the commercial world following certain law lines. Continually this law is being worked up and expanded by the courts to fit variations in circumstances. Or it may be a case of executive judgment which fills in the details of some line of activity. "Municipal ownership of some enterprise" may be the general statement of a policy, but the selection of alternative methods to secure it may fall to the executive of the municipality. Here again the executive represents the great interest grouping, acts for it, or at times for minor groupings within it, and so works out the plan. The law itself rests in the interest grouping of the population.

Where we have the law worked out in the courts, as in the case of the English common law, we find special cases leading to interpretations and precedents, and so filling out a system of law, which in the course of generations solidifies itself till it conflicts with newly growing interests, which then modify the old precedents, or, alternatively, create a new technical channel through which they can effectuate themselves, and this technique again enlarges itself into a system superimposed on the old. This process is observed historically in both the creation of new courts and the introduction of new writs. Usually a dominant interest group modified by other such groups can be located, sometimes the interest group of the lawyers must be referred to in interpretation, and very much more rarely the peculiar interest of the court group as such. For a sluggish or weak court, for example, technicalities may provide an outlet which saves it labor and anxiety, but the precedents accumulated in this way may become a disturbing factor, requiring reaction from injured interest groupings as time goes on. However, the sluggish or weak court is itself capable of explanation in interest-group terms.

Now in this court process of filling in the details of the law, and of working it up, we can see the place of law theory better than in any of the illustrations given before. As the various interests present themselves in the courts, they are represented for the special purpose by the advocates' activity, and the advocate specializes on working out the whole law situation from the point of view of the interest he represents. As he reflects the legal world from this point of view, he works out a theory of it. The theory of course is most often put before us as though it were a purely psychic phenomenon abstracted from the action to which it relates. It is never that, but always itself an activity, reflecting in a particular way the underlying activities. The courts make this theorizing a dignified portion of their work. But they do not decide cases purely in the highly rarified atmosphere of such theorizing. They decide them by letting the clash of the underlying interests work itself out, and then making the theorizing follow suit (not crudely, remember, but as a representative process). Within fairly broad limits theories will be found available for either apparent alternative of activity. When this theorizing activity gets away from the lawyers and away from the judges, it works itself up into a philosophy of law which is still more remote from the underlying interests, which reflects them in even paler tints, but which, the paler it becomes, is the more insistent on proclaiming the absoluteness of its truth. In a later chapter I hope to show how the group interpretation such as is here used is itself a group activity reflecting the social process at long range; not reflecting merely the legal activity phases in limited statements, as do the theories of law themselves, but instead reflecting wider and deeper groups with the law groups imbedded in them and carried by them.

What I have been saying of law is true also of constitutions. For constitutions are but a special form of law. They are specially guarded habitual activities of the society, enforcing themselves on all would-be variants. In England, the constitution cannot be separated from other law, except by subject-matter. It is found in charters, statutes, and precedents. In the United States, constitutions have a special technique, different from statute law, but in subject-matter they overlap at many points. When the letter of the constitution is dead, then we have a constitution only from the constitutional lawyer's standpoint, but not from the standpoint of the student of society. The British privy council, prominent in the lawyers' constitution, is almost nothing in ours, while the prime minister, who was never formally recognized by the king for what he is before Campbell-Bannerman's accession, has long been very prominent in the constitution that students of government have studied. The American method of electing the president is one thing in the written constitution, and another in the actual constitution. Russia has a constitution as much before revolution as it can possibly have after. If one means by the constitution the written instrument, then of course the revolutionists are fighting to get a constitution. But if one means a certain part of the established, specially enforced, activity of the society, then the movement in Russia is merely to change the constitution, and to provide new structures, new technique, to preserve the changes for the future. Other organized activities besides political government also have constitutions in the same sense. We could find in the Koran, for instance, the constitution of Mohammedanism, so far as the written words were adequately representative of the activity. The constitution is always what is. Ferdinand Lassalle put it admirably, though of course only for his limited temporary purposes, in his address to the working-men of Berlin, "Ueber Verfassungswesen," when he said: "Sie sehen, meine Herren, ein König dem das Heer gehorcht und die Kanonen—das ist ein Stück Verfassung . . . . die grossen Industriellen—die sind ein Stück Verfassung." King, cannon, noblemen, capitalists, all are parts of the constitution—and working-men as well.

But one more remark needs to be made before leaving this general discussion of law, and even this has been anticipated. It is common in many quarters to say that physical force at bottom underlies the law, and often this physical force is referred directly to the force in control of the organized governing body, to the "Staatszwang." The latter view is inadequate. Even in Russia today in its revolution it is not merely the physical force of the autocracy and its army that preserves the old order. Organized as it is, the autocracy with its armies would fall before a unanimous people, even unorganized, which means poorly organized. The population is clearly split even yet, and the government represents enough of it so that it has a great force behind it in addition to its physical force as represented by the army. The broader view, namely, that physical force in general lies at the bottom of law, has a certain measure of truth. It is true in the sense that the appeal to violence is often the ultimate technique when all other forms of technique fail. Sometimes violence is resorted to long before we think other methods ought to have failed; that is a matter of the particular organization of the government at a particular stage and place. But we have only to look around us to see pressure in thousand-fold forms actually at work. When we reduce all pressure to physical violence, we are introducing a hypothesis which is not useful. The other pressures do not represent violence. They are, many of them, as primitive, as "natural," if one will, as violence itself. They are given to us in our material. In the illustration of Taft in Cuba used above, the Taft régime rests, it is true, on the physical power of the United States, exerted through its army, but it rests on much more than that. The limits of physical force are better indicated by the case of Spain and its army in Cuba. Physical force must be relegated to the position of one among many forms of technique, and the pressures must be taken at all times for what they are—very richly human, not abstractly "physical."

CHAPTER XII

THE CLASSIFICATION OF GOVERNMENTS

Every schoolboy today knows that the presence or absence of a hereditary monarch is not a test which will give him much knowledge of the characteristics of a government. He knows roughly how the English monarchy and the United States republic resemble each other; how the two republics, the United States and Venezuela, differ, and how the two monarchies, England and Russia, differ. Perhaps he has been interested in watching Norway in its effort to decide whether it will get enough incidental benefits from a king to make the luxury worth while.

The reason why the presence or absence of a monarch is not a good test of the nature of the government is that under twentieth-century conditions it gives very little evidence as to the manner in which the interests of the country are mediated through the government, the manner in which the group activities function politically.

When Aristotle made his standard classification of governments into monarchies, aristocracies, and democracies, with their normal and perverted forms, he was fortunate in combining both a fair practical classification of the governments he knew most about, with a logical principle (that is, a verbal method) for distinguishing them as simple as one, two, three—the rule of one, of the few, of the many. True his normal governments could rarely, if ever be found, and his abnormal forms, in varying degrees of abnormality, were the only ones he really knew; but, for all that, his method of handling his material was excellent; so excellent indeed, that it succeeded in perpetuating itself in that form of activity which consists in writing books or making speeches about government, long after it had ceased to represent well the facts and after its further utility had disappeared. This is too evident to need discussion.

It was on the basis of eighteenth-century facts that Montesquieu drew the distinction between monarchy (law regulated) and despotism (arbitrary), and made these two, together with the republic, his three types of government. His classification was a good one for his purposes and within the range of his material.

The facts of the present age have directed attention to parliamentary and other methods of controlling the central governing body; and along with this the historical stages of governmental organization have come more clearly to view. In many recent classifications there is to be observed a decided tendency to make the fundamental distinction that between absolutism (despotism) on the one side, and democracy (republicanism, the "legal state") on the other. Classification within these divisions takes many lines for different purposes, as in distinguishing degree of civilization, methods of distributing powers, checks and balances, fields of activity, and so forth. In contrast with these there are classifications of a more concrete nature, designed to show the evolution of the state, such as Letourneau's. Also we find a number of hopelessly inexact distinctions which arise from bumptious rationalism, such as Ostrogorski's between mechanical and personal government, and another occasionally met with, contrasting theocracies with democracies, law as duty with law as right.

I do not propose here to attempt to offer any classification of governments of my own, or even to indicate a preference between existing classifications. I conceive that there is a very large amount of very hard work ahead before a classification can be established which will be of practical service to the full corps of investigators in government fields, and that for the present the best classifications are those of special groups of governments, consciously limited to special uses. What I propose is merely to set forth some of the underlying similarities which exist in the process of government in states which are sharply separated in many of the current classifications, and further to indicate certain lines of discrimination I have found useful at one stage or another in the present work.

First of all it is necessary to become clear as to what kind of facts we are classifying. As follows from what I have said in an earlier chapter, it is not the "state" as such that furnishes us our material. The state as discussed in political science is usually the "idea of the state," and that is not good raw material for an investigation. What Professor Burgess so admirably studied under the name of the "state behind the government," is from my point of view nothing else than government itself. It is a part set off by fairly definite characteristics, with a technique that ranges from very little to very marked differentiations; but there is nothing about it qualitatively different from any other government. The same interest groupings, in other words, which show themselves in administration, legislation, and the courts show themselves in constitution-making and constitution-sustaining.

Primarily it should be the institutions of government, all those differentiated activities which make up the governing body and mediate the deeper-lying interest groups of society, which we should attempt to classify. But no sooner do we attempt to study these than we find we must take into account the various grades of political groups (government in the intermediate sense) which function through them. These range down from the political parties as organized in "the government" through the parties organized outside of the government, to policy organizations, citizens' associations, and political adaptations of non-political groups, with no sharp dividing lines between them. We are forcibly reminded that the governing body has no value in itself, except as one aspect of the process, and cannot even be adequately described except in terms of the deep-lying interests which function through it. It therefore appears hopeless to attempt to classify governing bodies as abstractly stated by themselves. An institution, or even a set of institutions, which in formal statement seems to be identical with or at least comparable to an institution or set of institutions in another society may have an entirely different value because of different interest groups which work through it. An Aztec "king," an Indian maharajah, a Russian czar, and a British king are not easily comparable as functioning parts of government. So important indeed are the interest groupings in classifying governments, that practically they are allowed for more or less consciously in all classifications.

But now, in reacting against too superficial a statement of governments in attempts at their comparison, we must be careful not to fall into an error at the opposite extreme. There is a temptation to center attention strongly on the adjustment of interests as such, and try to find the basis for comparison and classification in the relative perfection of the adjustment, in the degree of smoothness or friction in the governmental process. Should we do this we should soon find ourselves outside of the limits of scientific treatment, in other words giving a statement not capable of sufficient generality in its application. We should inevitably be applying our own group point of view as the test of that perfection, and at the same time we should be apt to give too much weight to the process as it appeared in discussion terms, too much attention to vociferation. We should fall also into the related error of bringing all governments wherever found into one long series from the point of view of perfection, attempting to assign to each its relative rank in the series.

As a matter of fact there is no necessary connection whatever between degrees of perfection of adjustment and the types of government as they appear in the ordinary classifications. Aristotle assumed for each of his forms of government a normal, or perfect, form; the test of its perfection being, in his phrase, how far it was carried on "with a view to the common interest," in other words, an entirely arbitrary test. A primitive anarchy, a tribe with no crime, some despotisms, some republics may be said from some points of view to approximate this condition. China, one may well believe, has approached it over wide territories and for long periods. On the other hand, just as Russia is fearfully out of adjustment today, so is the same thing true in that "best of governments," the American republic, though here we shall probably carry through our readjustments by technical methods that avoid copious blood-shedding. It is all a question of the existing interests, the rapidity of the change in them, the methods they have found for harmonizing themselves.

We know that where activities are relatively simple and uniform a very high degree of adjustment may exceptionally be reached without the use of a specialized governing body, or with but slight traces of such specialization. We can conceive that even a large population, if its interest lines could work themselves out sufficiently, and if no disturbing factors entered, might dispense with a large part of the activities of its governing bodies. But we do not know as a matter of fact any large population that has reached anything like this stage, and—peace to the philosophical anarchists —we do not see any indications that such a time is in fact coming. What we do observe is that the interests as they stand find many methods of adjusting themselves, and in different combinations can reach relatively high degrees of adjustment by different methods.

It follows from this that we must not expect practically to be able to put all societies in one collection and run a scale of high and low across the whole lot of them. Rather any standards of perfection, of high and low, that are applied must be applied only within the range of the particular type of interest groupings. It is easy to see for example, how old Peru can be allowed a higher development, within its range, than any great modern nation's government has within its range. And so with many tribal and village community governments. But all such judgments are essentially inexact, for the limited group point of view from which they are made is never overcome by them.

Now what all this comes to is that if we are going to get any substantial basis for the classification of governments we must on the one hand take pains to get the institutions of the governing body out of their abstract statement all by themselves, and to get them reduced to terms of the group interests which in each case are functioning through them; and on the other hand we must avoid letting any system of standards of good whatsoever serve as a test, except so far as those standards are merely the direct and immediate reflection in each particular case of the group process within it. We must get all our values for comparison out of the governing process stated in each case with its full representative meaning.

Let us take a look at two or three of the characteristic differences in interest-group formations of the kind which are especially important for our present purposes; remembering as ever that there is here no pretense of comprehensive investigation, but merely of the analyzing and illustrating of typical phases of the process.

One of the first such distinctions which will be thought of is that between the city-state and the nation. If the groupings form themselves within the compact boundaries of a city wall, among a comparatively limited number of people, we shall have a series of successive governmental forms not identical with those found among nations which comprise city and country on fairly equal terms. The evolution of forms, so far as we can speak at all of such a thing, will be very different in most respects. It is true that a little ingenuity enables one to compare the Aristotelian evolution series with European governmental evolution. But one must be very cautious with such comparisons. Centuries for the Greek cities were longer than thousand-year periods for Europe. Forms that occur in Europe did not occur at all in Greece. The whole staging of the group process is different. One contrast in governmental technique is known to everybody. It is the presence or absence of the representative system in the ordinary limited sense of that term, very much more limited, remember, than the sense in which I use the word through the greater part of this work.

Again we find an important distinction between interest group formations with reference to locality. Sometimes they rest very largely on locality, and at other times the groupings are not locally distributed. Morgan's range of studies, for example, led him to draw a fundamental distinction between the tribes organized in clans (socially organized) and the politically organized peoples resting on territorial areas. Genuine territorial interest groupings, however, are, I am inclined to think, exceedingly rare. That is, territorially stated interests can in most societies be better studied when they are broken down into deeper-lying groupings, since the special political technique that rests on their being territorially consolidated is not prominent enough to center attention upon it.

We might say that Hungary, or rather the Magyar part of Hungary, was opposed on a locality basis to the other nationalities within Hungary and to Austria, but this has more the marks of a race opposition, and so would fall under the next line of discrimination to be considered; and more than that, whether as race or as locality, it is necessary to reduce it for the greater part to economic groupings. There were locality oppositions resting on different economic tendencies, as between North and South, or on commercial rivalries, as between large and small states, in the early United States, but today locality oppositions are very small. Some we find between cities and rural districts, but inside the cities or inside the rural districts, locality plays little part, save for administrative convenience, and for the division of spoils. In the legislative field the locality basis is mainly a survival, lending itself to abuse, and serving little positive purpose. A San Francisco anti-Japanese movement is a mere flash in the pan, so far as arousing locality oppositions goes, however violently troublesome it may seem for the moment. Even the "solid South" is more a surviving form than a substantial element in our politics, and its future as a locality group will strictly depend on the future of the negro problem.

A third line of distinction has to do with the extent to which interest groupings are consolidated in different classes in the community. We can use the word class, holding fast to the essential elements of its popular meaning, to describe any set of groupings so consolidated in a particular set of persons as to make that set of persons, as a whole, come into opposition in a great majority of their activities to one or more other classes which are likewise sets of persons, embodying similarly consolidated groupings. We must persistently ignore, or reduce to incidental details, all the trivialities of class distinctions which are often grossly over-emphasized in excited discussions. The caste is a good example of the word class as here used. The middle-age "Stände" functioned in this way. The Jews with their physical heredity running back everywhere but to Palestine, have kept themselves socially distinct as a class, though they do not function in that way in America today. "Race" is most often a class of this kind, and we can see how the negro class in the South has modified methods of government in southern states. The socialists insist that the proletariat forms a separate class in modern capitalistic nations, but what they have to show in nations in which socialists are numerically many is not a class political activity, but a normal group activity, becoming less class-like even in its talk, the larger it becomes and the more fully it enters into the political process. Class as a fact of talk is often very different from class as a fact of men in masses.

Suppose now we take a general formation of interest groups, such as we know in our existing European and American countries; countries, that is, on a large scale, with a great complexity of interest groups which manifest themselves in politics, with more or less marked territorial and class distinctions, but without either territorial or class distinctions as the dominant elements of government, however prominent one or the other of such distinctions may seem at certain stages of the process. It is evident that within this range of nations the tripartite division into monarchies, aristocracies, and democracies has absolutely nothing whatever to bring to us in the way of making our material better capable of analysis and study. We must examine these governments with reference to the ways the interests work through the government, with reference to the technique they follow, and to the special kinds of groups, or organs, which exist to reflect them and to harmonize them. It becomes a question of the amount, efficiency, and variety of the machinery that exists both to bring to expression those interests that assert themselves directly in politics, and also to give recognition to those interests that are represented only indirectly.

By way of approaching the governmental process here let us first mark out abstractly and hypothetically two extreme types of government within this range of nations. Let us set up, say, at one end the hypothesis of a government consisting of an individual who passes personally on every group antagonism at its very inception and allays it by appropriate action. At the other end let us set up the hypothesis of a government in which every interest would be able to find a technique for organizing and expressing itself in a system in which every other interest was equally expressed on "fair" terms, so that in the final course of action all interests would get their "due" weight. It is manifest that the very hypotheses of such governments are absurd. And yet I do not know what pure despotism and pure democracies would be except these very forms of government. Could we find them, they would both come to the same thing in legislative and administrative results—that is, government would follow concretely the identical lines, were one or the other practiced in a given society. Actually there is always an immense amount of organization in any government; actually there is always much discretional representation in any government; actually there are always interests that are not able to get expression in the government without disproportionate exertion, and actually the transformations of the interests are always making trouble in the government, to greater or less extent.

In the range of governments we have under consideration the variation in the technique provided for giving expression to the interests is very great. In Russia, for example, where the czar serves both to hold together conflicting localities in one system and to permit certain classes to exploit the others, there is just at present no available technique for the most depressed groups but violence or a show of violence. In the United States, with its fixed four-year presidency and its Supreme Court with powers over consti-tutional questions, we break through into violence at times, but we can nevertheless count on running pretty steadily without it. In England, with its parliamentary system, there is a still swifter and more effective technique for the adjustment of such conflicts as at the present time come before it. And in a Swiss canton, with its referendum or possibly annual assemblage of the people, the technique is even more effective.

But there is not one of these forms which can inherently be said to furnish a smoother adjustment of interests than any other. It all depends on what the interests are. In the Swiss canton the groups are little strenuous, little crystallized, and little antagonistic, and within the range of the canton's activities, the government that there exists tends to keep them from coming into sharp clash. In England the test is yet to come. A method which, within the limits of one large range of dominant interests permits the oppositions to adjust themselves smoothly, may or may not yield to a new-appearing set of interests which antagonizes all those which have functioned in the previous process of adjustment. In the United States we see the resisting classes giving way even in their strongest seats of power. In Russia the same government that is an agent in holding together the empire has identified itself so strongly with one cross-section of the empire, that now it is blocking those very portions of the populace for which the czardom at one period of its history most strongly stood.

All these governments are but the interest groupings wrestling with one another. In all of them we have interest groupings finding their leadership in portions of the government. In some of them we find a stratification of the interests more firmly established than in others. Some of them we believe will prevent the interests from stratifying better than others, that is, they will produce earlier adjustments as the change in the groupings develops itself. But we can in no case assuredly state that the method of the one will serve as the method of the others. And the method itself we observe to be always the resultant of the previous conflicts. Only as we are given the extent of the stratification of the interest groups and their range and intensity can we follow out their methods of expressing themselves.

Let us next take a look at certain of the technical methods by means of which groups operate through the government and keep its activities in line with their tendencies. We find the groups, first, ousting the person of the ruler; second, dividing him up into two or more institutions; and third, exerting a direct control over some of his specific activities while he remains in office. We find these technical methods in all stages of combination.

Heredity, election, and lot are technical methods having to do with the person of the ruler. Heredity may be broken in upon by revolution and expulsion, either of an individual or of a dynasty.

Election may be for a dynasty, for a life, or for a term of years. It also may be broken in upon by revolution. What is true of election is true of lot. While I am not engaged in interpreting these particular institutions, I think anyone may see for himself how closely they correspond to the interactions of the interest groupings, whether consolidated in classes or functioning freely and easily as groups of rapid transformation; one may even estimate something of the possibilities of lot along just these lines.

It has frequently occurred, however, under particular kinds of relations between groups, that there has been pressure enough to modify the activity of the ruler without ousting him, in such manner that the basis is laid for a permanent division of his functions into two or more institutions. One simple way of doing this is to make him bind himself not to do certain things. The early English charters are in point. While in form limitations of the king's power by himself, they actually gave the barons a certain definite corporate standing in the general government with the right to intervene at certain points. The development was very marked later on.

This division of a ruler's powers has given us, on one side the courts as independently organized, and on the other side the legislatures with their chambers. Each such development, and each stage of such development, has been the result of very distinct group (usually class) pressures. Legislatures and courts as we commonly know them are by no means the only agencies that have thus been formed to represent group activities in government. There have been many varieties of such institutions with all sorts of values, and having all degrees of permanence in their representative work. But these two are the ones which have established themselves most solidly and shown the most efficiency as tools. What the value of any such institution is depends entirely, as we shall later see more clearly, on what the pressures are that are working through it.

Another common division of a ruler's powers is territorial. Provinces are interest groups themselves, and they compel, as such, a differentiation in rule from time to time, whatever the terminology of motives is in which the developments are ordinarily described. The division of powers between central and local governments is to be interpreted in the same way. I am, of course not reducing this to the results of a class struggle in the usual limited sense, but stating it in terms of that wider process of the adjustment of interest groups, of which the class struggle is but one phase. Thus the federal and state governments in the United States rested at the foundation on different ranges of group interests, and the later discussion of states' rights reflected differences in interests, getting a large part of its vitality from the slavery question, for which it, as a discussion activity, meant a technical means of operating in the federal government.

But now, even after the ruler—I am of course merely using him as a shorthand designation of the government—has been, so to speak, split up in time and split up in space in these ways, there still remain the technical methods for direct group control of him just as he stands at any given moment. It will be understood that when I say direct control, I mean control by a differentiated technique; for in the wider sense all government of whatever kind, as representative of group interests, is under control, and is itself nothing but control, so to say, personified. As the group process continues, we find developed by it in the government all the different forms of the differentiated suffrage, of party organization both inside and outside the government, as the expression goes, of parliamentary technique, and of the referendum. All of these are direct functions of the group process, resting on the mass of the society, on facilities for contact and communication, and on the varieties and intensities of the interest oppositions.

In this sketch of the technique I have, however, thus far only in part indicated the working of the group process. I have been speaking about the groups in opposition to "the government," but it is necessary to supplement this by pushing the analysis farther and showing "the government" itself at every stage, even in the most extreme despotism, supported on groups, or classes, of the population. I will postpone this for a moment in order to take a glance at two or three systematic classifications of government with a view to seeing what value may be atrtibuted to them at the present stage of our analysis.

In distinguishing between the "militant type of society" and the "industrial type of society," Herbert Spencer is really "framing conceptions of the two fundamentally unlike kinds of political organization." These are his own words in the first sentence of the first of the two chapters of his *Sociology*, which discuss this distinction. As contrasted with most classifications of government, Spencer's effort makes a distinct advance because it gets away from the verbalisms and formalisms, and tries to go down to interests of a certain kind. Unfortunately, however, Spencer's "interests" are not the real interest formations that exist in societies and that are read directly out of them, but instead they represent Spencer's own middle-class English groupal view-point, made coherent by statement in terms of his own fictitious "feeling" elements. Take almost any page in these chapters at random, and it will appear that what he has in mind is gospel-truth liberty, the individual owning the state, and the state owning the individual, and all that sort of thing. Therefore, while in one sense Spencer is on the right track, his actual results are utterly worthless, except for the propaganda purposes of his own "liberty"-loving followers.

Of classifications of the formal nature consider first that of Jellinek in his recent work, *Allgemeine Staatslehre*. Governments are for him either monarchies or republics. Monarchy is the state guided by the will of a single person. Republic is every state which is not monarchy. Applying this he tells us that at the very least a monarch must be able to prevent any change in the constitution without his consent. Therefore he finds that England is a monarchy. The veriest tyro knows, however, that in the last resort the interests will inevitably express themselves through the House of Commons, not through the crown, nor through any combination of crown, lords, and commons. Jellinek's line of division may indeed have a certain limited value if interpreted as mere technique for the interests, but it becomes an absurdity when made a matter of formal law in the way that he understands and applies it. The interest groups of the nation function in England through a single organ, or group activity, the House of Commons, and in very truth the king changes with each change in "the government"—the king, that is, not as such and such a man, Edward by name, but as an official policy and government activity carried out in Edward's name.

Take Bluntschli. To monarchy, aristocracy, and democracy he adds a fourth kind of government, ideocracy, which includes all states which rest on some ideal element, such as religion. What little reference to the underlying interests there is in the tripartite classification disappears almost entirely in this fourth member. We could indeed work up some kind of a statement of the way groups expressed themselves through various belief activities, but it would not be a good means of discriminating between organized governments in any case, and it could not possibly enter the same classification as the other three forms of government, which are discriminated by a numerical test.

Ratzenhofer offers an elaborate classification which, despite all that he says of "Interessenvertretung," is based, both in general and in detail, on arbitrary distinctions. First of all he makes a fundamental separation between the state and the government. Then he classifies states into absolute and legal ("Rechtsstaat"). So far as this is taken to mean that in certain governments there is no organization provided for getting behind the ultimate decision of a single individual while in others there is, it has value. But to make it a fundamental classification of states "as such" overlooks the facts that there is no monarchy so despotic that it is not imbedded in custom; no ruler so powerful that the governing machine he leads is not more active than he; and that both ruler and governing machine must be themselves interpreted in every case in terms of class interests. The fundamental opposition between absolute and legal state is impossible both because the absolute ruler is imbedded in law, and because the legal state invests its officials with great discretion. Inside of each of these kinds of "state" Ratzenhofer groups governments in an empirical manner, aiming not to specify typical activities, but to get a certain range of states thrown roughly into a limited number of pigeonholes.

One recent writer, Leacock (*Elements of Political Science*), throws a handful of modern states into a despotic class, and calls all others democratic. Within the democratic states, he distinguishes as to whether they are limited monarchies or republics, as to whether they are unitary or federal, and again as to whether they are parliamentary or non-parliamentary. His first distinction between the despotic states and democracies has, as we have seen, its germs of sound meaning, not properly developed. Within the democracies his first distinction turns on what is often an incidental detail; his second concerns territorial groupings, which are important, as having to do with the way governing activities are distributed in space; and while his last distinction is on a solid foundation, it cuts across all the others and could stand entirely independent from them, if more adequately stated.

Hobhouse in his *Morals in Evolution*, an even later work, well illustrates in its worst form the theoretical distinction between despotisms and other governments. After first setting aside clan and tribal government as one division, he then distinguishes between "despotism—the principle of force and authority" and "the principle of citizenship, the common good and personal right." I only mention it to show how this distinction ultimately lands in "principles" at the maximum distance from facts.

In all this work there is of course much that is substantial in the way of analyzing governmental structures. Professor Burgess' canons of distinction in his chapters on the form of government, for example, get really to close quarters with the facts and give good aid toward classifying types of governmental activities, even if they do not go farther than preliminary steps themselves. And so does Jellinek's further elaboration of the same distinctions. The work of Hammond, a follower of Seeley, in his *Outlines of Comparative Politics*, should also be mentioned. He classifies primarily aggregates of men, "political bodies;" whether simple, as tribes, city-states, nations, or composite, as empires brought together by force and voluntary confederations. For each aggregate he contents himself with indicating some trait of government to be expected, but beyond that he does not feel justified in going. He lays great stress on the class process where it occurs, especially in ancient and middle-age governments, and gets good preliminary results by this method, but he does not follow the group process into later governments, and consequently even with his class interpretations he falls short of what is necessary. What he has accomplished is, however, of marked value, and his lack of dogmatism is by no means the least of his good qualities.

I proceed now to discuss at length the question of despotism, especially with reference to its class basis, for it is of the greatest importance. Let me first give a few quotations which are in point. May, in the introduction to his *Democracy in Europe*, says that public opinion "is potent everywhere" and that "it controls the will even of despotic rulers." Freeman, in his *Comparative Politics* (chap. v), writes: "In all times and in all places power can have no lawful origin but the grant of the people." De Tocqueville, in his *Democracy in America* (chap. viii), comparing the power of the king of France with that of the president of the United States, says: "The supremacy of public opinion is no less above the head of the one than of the other." James Bryce, in his essay on "Flexible and Rigid Constitutions," says:

No monarchy is absolutely despotic, and least of all perhaps in the ruder ages; for monarchs are always amenable to public opinion, and most so when they are the leaders of a tribe or people in arms. The real distinction is between a government checked by religious sentiment consecrating ancient usage and by the fears of insurrection, and a government checked by well-established institutions and legal rules.

Frederick the Great wrote: "Le souverain bien loin d'être le maître absolu des peuples qui sont sous sa domination, n'en est lui-même que le premier domestique." Consider also this from the *Coutume* of Bayonne (about 1273): "The people is anterior to the lords. It is the people, more numerous than all others, who, desirous of peace, has made the lords for bridling and knocking down the powerful ones." Or this old Persian inscription: "A great God is Ahuramazda . . . . who created Peace for man, who made Darius king." And this from Sadi:

> The people are the roots, the king the tree;
> As are the roots, so strong the tree will be.

Some of these quotations express aspirations rather than observations, and some go rather to the limited monarchies than to the despotisms. I do not use any of them as authorities, but all of them to point to the dependence of the despot as well as of every ruler on his people.

Suppose we are classifying despotisms and other governments separately, calling the latter perhaps democracies. Can we then say that the despot has "absolute" power? Surely not, without giving a technical and closely limited meaning to "absolute." It is not the despot, but despot plus army, or despot plus land-holding class, or despot plus some other class, that dominates, wherein despot appears merely as a class leader and it is not despot but class dominance that is characteristic of the government. The despot's personal discretion is exercised within class-established limits. Moreover, it is never necessary—except in the extreme event, under abnormal conditions—for the ruling class to have physical force actually superior to the ruled class. If we offset as equal in physical force a certain minority well armed and well trained, and a certain majority poorly armed and poorly trained, nevertheless we shall usually find that the rule is being exercised by a minority smaller or weaker even than this. And when this happens it inevitably means that the minority is not merely the master, but also to some extent the servant, the representative, of the majority. If the weaker group governs, it is because the interest groupings in the stronger party to some extent support it as their government.

We can state this truth in this way that, except in the case of a subjected population immediately under the heel of the conqueror under conditions of most primitive oppression, the ruling class is to a certain extent the chosen (that is, the accepted) ruler of the ruled class, not merely its master, but also its representative; and the despot at the top of the system is representative both of his own class, and to a smaller, but none the less real, extent of the ruled class as well. If this is true we clearly are not justified in making a fundamental opposition between despotisms, let alone all monarchies, and other governments. For we have found a process of representation in despotisms which is inevitable in all democracies, and which may be distinguished by quantities and by elaboration of technique, but not in any deeper "qualitative" way.

Or let us regard despotism from the standpoint of the individual's arbitrary will. Leaving aside the trimmings of despotism, personal vices, pomps, and crimes, which are incidental, it is clear that the despot must pass much the same content of group needs and demands through his "brain" that would pass through a representative assembly. He must get his information from other people, which means at least the rudiments of an organized representative system for at least one class of the population, and possibly for others. He must leave an immense mass of detail work to his lieutenants to perform, which means at least the rudiments of a division of power, by locality, by function, or by both at once There will be established lines on which these functions will be conducted. There will be limits to the activity of bureaucrats and despot alike, which cannot be exceeded without penalties. The setting of custom in which government exists never disappears. We must not let our peculiar ideas as to rights distort our judgment. We put emphasis today on the sacredness of human life and not on the sacredness of symbolic acts of worship. But just because some petty despot is free to slaughter, but not to omit his religious functions, we must not make the mistake of thinking that his authority is "unlimited" in any peculiar sense qualitatively different from our president's. We have got to get the right balance by observing facts—each side from the other side's point of view. Russia is most often classed among despotisms in the extreme abstract sense, in forgetfulness of its bureaucracy, its organized religion, its "grand-ducal clique," using that phrase as symbolical of a mighty class force, and in forgetfulness also of what is of much less importance, the "fundamental laws of the empire," mentioned by James Bryce in the passage from which a quotation was above

given, the law declaring the sovereign's autocratic power, that requiring him to be a member of the orthodox church of the East,
and that fixing the rule of succession to the throne. Assuming
that the czar may alter these fundamental laws, and is indeed
the only constituted agency for altering them, it would nevertheless
be foolish to think he could do it arbitrarily. His activity would
be participated in by a very large number of very energetic
bishops, noblemen, land-holders, and bureaucrats.

Despite all this, there is a very real basis to the emphasis that
is put on the despotism as a distinctive form of government.
The real distinction is, however, merely one of technique in the
adjustment of the interests. Let us develop this a little farther.
There have been despots that have supported themselves on the
"people" as against the aristocracy. They are, however, exceptional and transitory. They illustrate interest pressures as well
as other despots do, but we may pass them by for the more common
case of the despot who leads the great land-owning class and
represses the "people." We find in this latter case a well-organized
system for bringing the interests of the aristocracy to expression.
Personal favoritism will be prominent in it, but then that is prominent in any American legislature today. Other classes of the
population will have much greater difficulty in expressing themselves. They cannot organize permanently, and lack political
labor-saving devices. It is only in their greatest needs that they
can make themselves felt. A wealthy subject class may perhaps
succeed by bribery. A poor class must resort to violence, and
then only can accomplish anything under the pressure of direst
need. Probably it will aim at ousting the despot from his throne.
This accomplished, it will have no organization ready to realize
for it the goods it has desired, and it will permit another despot to
take the place of the last, hoping from him a better representation
of its interests. Or, even if defeated, but still strong enough for
possible revolution later on, it may be granted voluntary concessions. These will be a very real political achievement on its part,
but, of course, only at enormous cost.

Suppose now a second class has asserted itself sufficiently to get a formal method of access to the sovereign. It will need guarantees for its method of access, not being able to trust to the chance that it will not be crowded out in a neglected moment by the old monopolists of power. As soon as two classes have entered directly, even though on very unequal terms, we have a new organization, a new type of government. The old kind of absolutism may seem to prevail, but the channels by which the class interests flow through it have stiffened somewhat, and we have the beginnings of a more complex organization. Perhaps the class that has struggled to expression may secure a charter or guarantee of certain rights, whereby the despot agrees to limit himself in certain activities. Here we have the beginnings of the constitution, in the ordinary sense, or, using the word constitution more broadly to include the whole structure of the government, we have a change in the constitution, with a specified point of leverage upon which the resistance of the injured class can work. But what we have is not really an absolute monarchy becoming limited. Rather it is the establishment of new methods or channels, which make it simpler for the old interests to express themselves in the government, and which in effect raise one class which formerly had very poor approaches to the despot to something approximating equality with the position of the former specially favored classes. By watching what classes, and how many, have secured organized methods of keeping themselves fairly in the attention of the despot, and by indicating the methods they use, we can classify or rank the new form of government with reference to the old form of single-class dominance.

In whatever way the development proceeds, the process will be much the same. A legislature may be attached to the monarch; the old council may have an additional chamber added to it; the control of some portion of the finances may be specialized in hands other than those of the monarch; certain courts, perhaps minor ones, may be carefully segregated from the monarch's intervention. A bit of the governing institutions may differentiate so as to allow for the activity of an additional class. Or a bit of class organization outside the government may solidify itself, and in time be taken up into the government as a part of it. Such developments have been going on for thousands of years and they are going on today in our most developed societies, in terms of group pressures, even where the harder class distinctions have disappeared so far as their manifest influence in the government is concerned. That peculiarity of structure in the federal House of Representatives, seen in its scattered appropriations committees, is the structural after-effect of just such a conflict.

To come back to the despot, we can now view him in a phase in which he shows us two different forms of leadership which need to be understood together. For the class which he immediately represents, he is the ordinary leader of the organization type. But at the same time he may fill the function of mediator as between other classes. He can do this, however, only by virtue of the group or class force behind him. Sometimes, as general of an army, the despot will hold the balance between provinces which tend to conflict. At other times he may mediate between classes not on a locality basis. In all cases what he actually accomplishes will be the direct resultant of the various pressures which enter into the system.

I have been giving my attention almost exclusively to the "internal" conditions as opposed to the "external"—that is, as opposed to war dangers from abroad. These war dangers may be among the factors in maintaining the despotic leadership, but that does not take us beyond the field of group pressures. The despot is there because he is needed, but this is only another manner of saying he is there because the groups as a matter of fact form themselves under the given conditions so as to maintain him. I am, indeed, inclined to think that these external dangers as factors in the maintenance of despotisms are commonly greatly exaggerated. The home group formations are, in other words, vastly more important than the direct foreign pressure. We can easily point to modern nations which exist perpetually in the face of heavy pressures of this kind from without, and yet are very far from needing to resort to established forms of despotic rule. I may add that so true is it in all stages of the social process that the home pressures are vastly the most important in interpreting the process of government, that in my illustrations I have generally ignored the foreign influences entirely. These latter can easily be allowed for in the method as minor variations of the group process. This is not to say that the content of the governing activity in most nations is not immensely affected by the war dangers of the time; but instead, to say that we can only interpret the process by making the statement primarily and mainly in terms of domestic groups.

As it is the process, as such, of government which concerns us here, I have not been introducing any material as to the nature of the group interests that are in play, nor as to their origins. They are, of course, the very material of society; their activities are to be comprehended only with reference to one another; and the intensity of their struggles, or the relative smoothness of their adjustment, will always be capable of direct interpretation in terms of what they actually are. In other words, where classes are very nearly balanced against each other the outcome will be very different from what it is where one has a decided preponderance. Great inequalities will bring still different results.

If we should go back behind the governments in the range of which I have been speaking to the simple tribal organizations, we should find a group process going on inside the tribes, but not a solidification of the groups into what I have called classes. We should there find leadership and governmental organization corresponding to the needs of this functioning of the groups. Should we advance to larger societies with compacted masses of people, we should quickly find them divided into classes, and whether these classes were castes, or land-holding aristocracies, or whatever, we should find easily recognizable phenomena of class rule manifesting themselves in the leadership and governmental institutions. The political history of the Greek city-states, and the history of Egypt and of Rome as well can only be interpreted if the classes are brought into prominence. At every stage we find ourselves tempted to say that the greater the intensity of the class oppositions, the more certain there is to be found a strong leadership of the dominant class called into existence to preserve the balance. If we advance still farther to societies in which the classes, both locality and other, are found to be breaking down, and the process of freely changing groups to be appearing in their place, we find again a change in the governing institutions. We may sometimes get closer to leadership of the old tribal type, but always when the group divisions begin to solidify and class oppositions to appear, we find stronger leadership called into existence for the work to be done. At all stages in the process we find representation of interests, the government as such resting always on certain classes, or alternatively on groups of groups, and representing indirectly the others. We find representation sometimes through single individuals, and sometimes through large bodies, whose members have each their own constituencies. We find the various operations of government differently distributed between different organs. But wherever and whenever we study the process we never get away from the group and class activities, and when we get these group activities properly stated we come to see that the differences between governments are not fundamental differences or differences of principle, but that they are strictly differences of technique for the functioning of the interests, that they are adopted because of group needs, and that they will continue to be changed in accordance with group needs.

Except as a difference of technique is meant, itself directly to be interpreted in terms of changed interest groups, there is no abandonment of "absolute" power in England or the United States today, even as compared with England in the reigns of William the Conqueror or the Tudors. There was no "absolute" power then any more than there is today. Both statements are true. The English cabinet can today do things which the earlier sovereigns would not have dreamed of doing, and the early sovereigns had powers which the cabinet of today cannot exercise. The American president can be invested with a most tremendous representative force, or reduced to a nonenity, all within a year or two, and without changing the "Constitution," merely according as the group pressures work successfully through him or through other branches of the government.

If I have indicated in this chapter why, and how, the comparison of governments must be carried underneath the surface forms into the group process, I have done all I set out to do.

CHAPTER XIII

THE SEPARATION OF GOVERNMENTAL AGENCIES

It is common in America to say that there are three "powers" of government, the legislative, executive, and judicial. This manner of dividing them is incidental to our Constitution. For reasons already made clear I shall not here use the word "powers." It is too mystical. The word "agencies" much better expresses the facts. We certainly find the three agencies named above in American government, and in many other governments. But we do not find them in all governments. They are not the only agencies we find in American government. And finally, there is no theory of powers that I know anything about that will serve to define the actual work of these agencies—that is the actual agencies —closer than a rough approximation.

In opposition to the threefold division of powers it is proper to emphasize the unity of government, but only in the sense that all government is one common process. It is hardly necessary here to argue that all these agencies of government are involved in one common process, any more than to argue against the idea that there is any unity in government other than that of process. The preceding chapters have given the proof over and over again. It is desirable, however, before taking up a consideration of the different agencies of government in detail to sketch roughly the facts of their relations.

Any governmental process, no matter what, is an activity. It is also group activity. Does the president of the United States put a paragraph in his annual message urging legislation in regulation of railroads? It is a very different thing from the case of a private citizen writing the identical words and putting them in a book or from the president writing them and locking them up in his desk without putting them in the message. It matters not how much the paragraph is discussed in terms of the president's ego, the given fact is a little, differentiated activity growing out of past group activity, having all its reference and meaning in group activities and looking forward to more group activity. In other words, it itself is group activity. "President Roosevelt" does not mean to us, when we hear it, so much bone and blood, but a certain number of millions of American citizens tending in certain directions. The czar, the speaker, Campbell-Bannerman, Jean Jaurès, the judges in their chambers, all are activity.

Confining ourselves now to government in the narrowest sense, that is to the governing body, we find that that body, in other words that specialized set of activities, can usually be separated into two or more parts, according as different sets of persons take part in them. This test, the difference of the sets of persons participating, is at bottom the only fundamental test there is between different functions or powers of government. It was by observations of groups of men functioning officially, that Montesquieu prepared himself for his discussion; and his analysis holds good there, and there only, where men are actually acting in groups which can roughly be described by his three terms. Where men do not so act, the analysis does not apply, and theory has no further word to say.

If it were essential that the individuals making up these special sets of activities should never participate in more than one set at a time in order to justify a classification, no classification would ever be made. The sets are not exclusive. And nevertheless the whole classification depends upon the men in the groups, not on any theoretical functions or powers. Such is the nature of the social process. We find a cluster of men carrying out one line of activity here, which we can contrast with another cluster carrying out another line of activity there. Some of the activities of many of the men in each cluster bring them into intimate association with some of the men in the other cluster, so intimate that for many purposes we classify activities as running across the combined clusters. But this only means that the distinction between the two great groups is the biggest one we can make, the distinction on the biggest lines, the one which separates the groups of men most adequately. It means that it is an approximate division, but the best approximation obtainable. Even when a theory of powers is set up to go with each group, the theory itself breaks down at a thousand places—as books on constitutional law, or, better still, court opinions on cases involving the powers of officers, will quickly show. It is groups of men that the judges tend to follow, and only lines of reasoning so far as the reasoning adequately reflects groups of men.

Taking now the actual groupings of men met with in the governmental process, as the agencies of government, we find, as I have already said, that it is necessary to make varying classifications of the agencies in varying nations or societies. There are governments, with the three agencies, executive, legislative, and judicial, well defined; there are governments that have the judiciary as a subordinate branch of the executive, as is still to great extent the case in France and Germany; there are governments that have the executive and legislature consolidated, as in England. There are governments in which a classification on such lines cannot even be made "theoretically" without the greatest straining, as in Russia, where a czar, a class council, and a bureaucracy may be called the divisions of government, with a duma struggling to co-ordinate itself with them. There are governments in which political parties have organized themselves in such complexity and power that they cannot well be treated otherwise than as a fourth branch of government along with the other three, as today in the United States. Again there is often a very real division of activities between localities and between central and local governments, a division just as worthy the dignity of a theory of its own as is the Montesquieu classification. Finally there is the division of powers between numerous co-ordinate officials, all nominally executive, as in American counties, but really as much entitled, for many purposes, to separate classification as any governmental activities. This list does not pretend to comprehend all the varieties of divisions of powers we actually find, but only to show how the most pretentious of them all has a place merely as one among many.

Suppose we take the case of a Greek tribe with its typical organization of king, council of elders, and assembly of the people. Certainly no one studying it would ever come to make a classification of powers into executive, legislative, and judicial. Aristotle's deliberative, magisterial, and judicial elements were analyzed by him in governments of a much later type, and at that they approximate only roughly to our modern classification. The differentiation of the agencies of government in the tribe was on entirely different lines. Nor can one drag such a standard of classification into the facts with success. It is futile to say that custom represented present-day law, and was unchangeable, and that the government was purely administrative. The government decided questions of policy, and plenty of its acts would be as hard to classify as the typical ordinance of a modern American city council. As for judicial and administrative acts, we find them passing through the same groups of men by similar processes and with similarly registered results. Evidently the agencies of government were just king, elders, and assembly, and that is all that can be said about it.

With the stratification of the population into classes, and with the community growing in size, new groupings of governmental activities will form, new agencies will appear. Often the army must be put down as a special agency, and not subsumed under any other. Sometimes perhaps the diplomatic work may seem so important as to be allowed co-ordinate place. In a despotism the actual division of labor is what counts. Under a feudal government the feudal structure itself is the "distribution of powers." In a league or confederacy the distribution is indicated by the very name. And so with the rest.

Among continental writers, especially among Germans, one is apt to find these agencies of government classified under three divisions, which differ from the Montesquieu classification in essential things simply because the observation has been made upon German governments and not upon England. We are told of the ruling power, and the legislative, and administrative powers —the "Regierung," the "gesetzgebende Gewalt," and the "vollziehende Gewalt," or "Verwaltung." Here the judiciary is subsumed under the administrative branch, and the "Regierung" is set apart as something very much greater and more magnificent than the mere executive of our own constitution. You cannot put these two classifications into opposition and say one is right and the other wrong. It is all a question of the particular government one is talking about, in other words of the actual activities, the agencies as they present themselves to observation.

In England today it is surely artificial and inexact to make a sharp distinction between executive and legislative functions. Parliament devotes itself to administrative matters much of the time. Not to speak of the budget which occupies the center of the parliamentary stage and which is strictly administrative work on a theoretical division of our customary kind, there is the continuous interpellation of the "government" on administrative questions; and on such questions a ministry may even fall. The cabinet is both the head of the administration and the initiating force in legislation. The judiciary is a much more sharply separated agency of government, despite its culmination in the House of Lords, and despite the political character of one or two of the highest judicial officers. But if we wish to divide the rest of the government into distinct agencies we must do it by naming the electorate, the House of Lords, the House of Commons as organized in parties, the cabinet, and possibly in addition the civil service.

In the United States we certainly find executive, legislative, and judicial agencies. They are set up with walls built between them, each taking up its work at a certain stage, using certain methods, and continuing its work to a certain further stage, and each entering into formal relations with the others only at specified points. Actually the interactions occur at many presumably forbidden points because the same groups of pressures are working through all of them and seeking always to find their smoothest courses, wherever they may flow. But in addition to these agencies we find others. First, there is the constitutional convention, which we have developed into a regular instrument of government in frequent service. Then there are the organized political parties, which lie outside the personnel of any one of the three branches named in the Constitution, but which are just as definite portions of the governmental structure as are executive, judiciary, and legislature.   The question as to whether the parties shall be regarded as a special agency of government indicates clearly the nature of the tests that are needed.   If the party is a fugitive thing, showing itself inside the legislature, we can hardly make of it a separate agency.   Even if strongly organized with its main strength in the legislature we shall not make of it a separate agency.   But if it is strongly organized outside the legislature, if it has its own leadership apart from the leadership of the legislature in which its leaders may perhaps not even be members, then we shall for many purposes find ourselves literally forced to regard it as a separate agency; and we shall be justified in this to the extent, and to the extent only, that it is a consolidated organized body.   Again, the electorate itself is sometimes seen to function separately as a differentiated activity in so marked a manner that for some purposes it is proper to add it as another distinct agency of government.   Constitutional conventions, executive, legislature, judiciary, parties, and suffrage are all on the list of agencies in America; and at that the six words by no means adequately set forth the extent of the differentiation.

For practical purposes probably the best test as to the agencies of government is to be found in the method of control by the people. "People" is a word not lightly to be used, but here I may employ it perhaps without confusion, by way of shortening the statement.   Wherever we find a separately organized responsibility we may name the agency a separate one.   In an old New England township with its horde of petty officials, each one was really a separate power or agency of government.   In a nation in which, by current modes of speech, the monarch is "sovereign," and the popular assembly is a comparatively unimportant body, we find the organization for the control of the monarch to rest mainly in occasional revolution, and to be different from the organization for control of the popular assembly, which will be by ballot.   In England there is no different control over the executive from what there is over the legislative work.   The control is a control of parliament by people, of cabinet by parliament, or sometimes better by people direct, and of judges by process of appointment and impeachment. In the American government judges, executive, and legislators are controlled by separate elections, or by separate forms of appointment and removal, while parties have been, as Professor Goodnow has shown, subject to very imperfect control, and consequently the centers of a disturbing energy, which is only now commencing to be subjected to the popular check. So far as parties have controlled executive, legislature, and judiciary in one consolidated process, the effect has been to break down to some extent the constitutional separation.

There is one method of classifying the "powers" of government which seems definitively to abandon the observed groups of functionaries and to set up a line of distinction concerning "functions" which do not rest directly on corresponding "organs," but instead cut across the organs. This is the distinction between the expression of the will of the state and the execution of the will, as it is set up, for example, by Professor Goodnow in his *Politics and Administration.* Here the judiciary becomes part of the executing function. The executive as we actually find it is admitted to have many expressing functions, and the legislature as we find it to have many executing functions. But the two kinds of functions are nevertheless held to be clearly distinguishable and adequate as a foundation for the theory of the governmental process.

Such a test too readily accepts a distinction of individual psychology as a standard for classification. The "will" and the "act" are taken from their use with reference to the individual and applied to the state, where, indeed, we are often told that they appear in more distinct forms than they do in the individual life. But a closer look at the facts would discourage this mode of treatment. To take an illustration once more from the immediate political life of the day in this country, there is President Roosevelt's activity with reference to the western coal lands. Some of these lands have been fraudulently secured from the government and the ownership of much of the coal property, whether rightful or fraudulent, has been grossly abused. The President has therefore withdrawn the remaining coal lands from entry, he has taken steps to secure the cancellation of the fraudulent entries, and he has prepared plans for a lease instead of a sale system for the disposition of the land. Retaining the term "will" as used in the mode of classification under consideration, is this activity of the President's an expression or an execution of the social will? It would take the most refined casuistry to answer. Expression here is execution, and execution is expression. Casuistry is of no service. We have facts to watch and our business is to interpret those facts by getting them into relation with other facts, but a distinction between expression and execution of will does not answer.

Moreover, the very use of the term "will" is an admission of superficial treatment. It is society with which we are dealing and nothing else. The social will then is synonymous with society itself. If we are to make progress in study it must be by analysis of the society, not by duplicating its existence under the name will. We find the social activity moving through various stages. We find interest groups, and these reflected by political groups, and these organized in parties, and all working through the other agencies of government, now placing a statute on the books, now rushing a malefactor up for trial, now declaring the validity or invalidity of this immediately expressed "will" (the statute) in terms of a broader "will" (the Constitution); but always and everywhere there is action and always and everywhere there is a meaning to the action; never is the meaning found apart from the action, never the action apart from the meaning. So the distinction between expression and execution will be of value just so far as we can find definite groups of activities differentiated from others. It is by actual representative activities, not by an abstract distinction between expression and execution of "will," that we must group our material and aid our investigation.

One question remains. What of the theories of the separation of the powers as we actually find these theories functioning in society? Do they or do they not guide the organization of the government? This is merely a new form of an old question we have repeatedly discussed before.   Our "theories," whether they appear in all the arrogance of purity at constitutional conventions or whether they present themselves garbed in the subtleties of the law courts, are always aids in the actual process of arranging and rearranging the shape of the governmental agencies.   They are of aid just so far as they reflect correctly the given grouping and permit unassigned activities to take easy running positions in one or other agency.   They serve as a sort of practical shorthand on the borderland to aid us in the quick application of one or the other agency to a new piece of work, in proportion to its fitness for the task.   They do not guarantee fitness.   They do not create the agencies.   They only serve to help the assignment and they always stand ready to slink into obscurity the moment it appears that they have not properly reflected the facts of the developing situation. Later on it will be shown more completely how this process works in similar cases in other fields.

CHAPTER XIV

THE PRESSURE OF INTERESTS IN THE EXECUTIVE

In this and the three succeeding chapters (to which the first part of chap. xviii may also be joined) I propose to follow the workings of interest groups through the various agencies of government. From what has been said in the preceding chapter it will be clear enough that the division of the discussion into the sections indicated by the chapter titles is made for convenience, that it does not claim more than an approximate correspondence to the various phases of the complex governmental process, and that it rests not upon hypothetical functions of government, but upon the actual separation of governmental agencies, each agency being accountable to "the governed" or to some other agency of the government through a special technical process in greater or less degree peculiar to itself. It should also be clear that these agencies are not all found coexisting in all societies, nor even in the majority of societies, and that there are some societies in which none of the terms correctly designate any of the existing agencies. It is purely for convenience in treatment that this division is used here, the convenience arising from the fact that the societies to which most attention will be given have agencies in general in these forms. The order in which the chapters occur is also a matter of convenience in treatment.[1]

Before taking up the executive, even in the form in which it unites the whole governmental process in one agency, a few paragraphs may be given to societies to which the term executive will even less accurately apply. Suppose we take a society in which

[1] In the historical illustrations in these chapters I hope no substantial errors of fact have crept in. I wish, however, to say frankly that I am writing without detailed verification, and with no pretense of having made such exact studies as would justify me in speaking positively of the strength of the various group pressures which in each instance have been in play. In the interpretation of any particular bit of history such exact study is, of course, an absolutely essential pre-

the interest groups are comparatively few, comparatively simple, and comparatively well adjusted.   Within our range of observation such a society must be a small one living under conditions which, when stated as environment, must also be simple.   Suppose it be a Homeric Greek tribe, or an Iroquois tribe in the stage described by Morgan.   The government will deal with local peace and order, with some economic questions such as the distribution of crop land, the harvest, and the taking of wild animals or fruits, and finally with war expeditions.   Many of these group oppositions will, in part at least, be well adjusted through religion or otherwise without passing through the process of the differentiated governing body itself.   So far as they pass through the differentiated government they come much closer to adjustment through the process called reasoning than would be probable in more complicated societies.   In other words, we have it as an observable fact that the most intense interest will be that of the whole tribe in opposition to some outer tribe, while the intra-society groupings will have less intensity and will consequently subordinate themselves and adjust themselves by argument.

The king, elders, and populace arrangement is typical here, and it makes little difference whether the civil and military chieftainships are separate or combined, or just what measures for the selection of the chief are used.   Even if the chief is hereditary in some degree, he will be under close popular control.   Similarly, it is a matter of detail as to just how the elders are chosen, whether they are heads of families, clan representatives, selected old men, or what.   We find the lines of activity formulating themselves freely throughout the society, and moving freely along their full course.   The elders formulate a proposal and submit it to the

requisite.   Here, however, I am not attempting to throw light on historical occurrence, but to use such rough knowledge of history as we have to throw light on the group method of interpretation.   The group method is for its part only of value so far as it can be used in specific interpretations.   But we must proceed step by step, and I am only taking one short step here.   If there is any of the material of the governmental process which is not capable of statement by the method I propose, then I am open to serious criticism, but not if I have merely made errors of fact in illustration.

assembly of the people.   But as they formulate it, they both take account of the whole complex situation as they reflect it "for" the people, and of the popular reflection of the situation, that is of the public opinion, as it percolates in to them.   Neither they, nor the chief, are at any stage of this process intrusted with full representative discretion.   The popular approval, by applause or otherwise, is a great part of the process.   When the activity proceeds farther, say into warlike expedition, the point of view of an epic poet may give the chief the appearance of great arbitrary power, and may reduce the populace to the semblance of a mere echo; but even then the chief is only expressing his following in a very immediate way.   He is only filling in little details of their activity by his own commands.   I am tempted to call this kind of a government very highly developed in contrast with our great modern states, but such a way of putting it would easily give a false impression, and, moreover, it is a type of judgment which one should be most cautious in making.   It is, of course, not true in the sense of complexity; but given the existing range of interests in the societies that have it, it expresses them with the greatest facility.   There is enough structure to prevent confusion at each stage of the developing activity, but at no stage is the structure able to misrepresent large elements in the society or to block the activity.   For the development and perpetuation of such a government there is necessary not merely the simplicity of the interest groupings, but perhaps also freedom for the splitting of the society in two, and for the emigration of one part to an independent neighborhood.

For a very different type of government in the tribe we may turn to the kinglet of tropical Africa, with all his ferocious brutality and established terrorism.   The group conditions are of course in reality very different from what they are in the tribes we have just discussed.   It is not my province here to go into them, but such factors as food supply, the amount of labor needed to supply daily wants, surplus energy, thickness of the population, and available slave markets all enter into the account.   These groupings have ended by adjusting themselves very crudely through a form of absolutism, in which copious blood-letting is the technique both for the control of the people by the petty despot and for the control of the despot by the people.   Order is maintained by terrorism which sometimes takes the form of random arbitrary killings conducted by the kinglet himself.   The means for approach to him are very imperfect, and the decisions of the kinglet, while reflecting group interests, do so in no steady balanced way, but by rough and irregular approximations.   A circle of lordlings around the kinglet serves not to modify his vagaries, but to terminate them by assassination and by the substitution of a new ruler in extremity.   The whole system is hedged in by a thick growth of religious rites and ceremonial, that is by a habitual activity little flexible and reflecting crudely the great mysteries of the tropic environment, which is seemingly arbitrary and violent in its treatment of the natives beyond the arbitrariness of any but the wildest of kinglets. Should anyone be inclined to attribute the ferocity of such government to some inborn characteristic of the people, I have but to remind him of the many well-adjusted governments to be found among American Indian tribes, whose members could always show the most extreme cruelty to prisoners of war under certain circumstances, but who did not use cruelty under any circumstance as technique of government.   If the typical African kinglet government is to be contrasted with the typical tribe as previously described it may be by pointing out that the agencies of government have now been reduced to a single one, the kinglet, so far as ordinary activity goes, while the group of assassinators steps in on rare occasions to play a part which we may compare with a constitutional convention, and the populace rarely or never appears in any organized form. It is a government which is controlled by elimination of the ruler, not by altering the policies of a continuing ruler, and in which the technical means used by all parties is blood-letting.

We have had in none of these cases any proper distinction between executive, legislative, and judicial agencies.   We have had real agencies, and the whole social governmental process working in stages through them; but only an arbitrary application of the three "powers" or functions is possible, and that is undesirable and far from being helpful.

If now we pass to a great nation like China we shall find the agencies of government distributed on territorial lines, and if we treat the emperor as an executive it can only be as an executive who does the work at the central seat of government which executive, judiciary, and legislature together do in other governments. Under the provincial viceroys an "intellectual" bureaucracy holds office. Some years ago we had an interesting illustration of the way the interest groupings of the empire pass through a monarch of this character. The young emperor became infected with reform ideas, as current speech has it. In other words, a certain interest grouping in the empire secured its reflection through him. This did not come about through any organized mechanism, but through agencies which in contrast to organization would be called accidental. The reform group gained the emperor's ear. That group was itself highly representative, that is involving at long range groups that were reflected through it in several degrees. Being far enough away from practical life, it posed mainly as an idea activity. But as soon as the emperor proceeded with his activity along the new lines, he was put aside and the empress dowager, representing the old arrangement of dominant interests, reigned in his place. The viceroys were behind the empress dowager. But the interest groupings in China are rapidly changing with the development of Japan, the defeat of Russia, and the alignment of the other powers, and the central authority is reflecting them with the result that what some of us call progress, and what others call a menace, is reported. We have, therefore, in this despotism anything but arbitrary rule. We see a practical setting-aside of the ruler and his partial restoration, and know that the process can be described only in terms of the rearrangement of the interest groups of the empire. This is not to say that a supernatural photograph of the groupings could be taken, and that the emperor would be found exactly reflecting the balance of pressures, but merely that channels exist by which the interests may work themselves through him with more or less of accuracy, not merely as his own observation makes them clear to him, but as they can state themselves to him. We know that should activity on the propaganda level push itself through to some degree which conflicted with the groupings of the time on lower levels, the decree would remain "in the air" and it would not adequately state the lines along which the government would continue to work.

Turn next to Russia. We find in it today nothing but a monster spectacle of the conflict of the interest groups.[1] Once upon a time the czar represented the rest of the population against the Boyars. More recently, his policy has often been dominated by the huge land-holding interests of the empire. When the serfs were liberated he swung far to the opposite extreme under the influence of a clique of St. Petersburg bureaucrats who in effect represented the peasants in the process. Thereby he mortally offended the land-holding nobility, which had been strongly addicted to "liberalism" on lines that would not have been so hurtful to their own interests but that nevertheless, they thought, would have successfully staved off the threatened peasants' uprising. Since then, measure after measure for the relief of the land-holders has become necessary. Twenty years ago began the rise of a great mercantile and industrial interest, typified by Witte's policies. Along with it there appeared on the scene the laboring proletariat of the cities. The expanded empire and its great internal works have made the burden of taxation heavier and heavier. The existing technique of the government, maintained by class pressures, has not allowed ways of relief to be found. The Jew has thriven somewhat better than the Russian under such conditions. The peasants' wild cry for land, the socialism of the working-men, and all the revolutionary movements with all their riots of theories and of bombs, have appeared to express these suppressed groupings of the population.

Under these circumstances we have today a government which

[1] For the groups and classes involved in recent Russian history one may consult Maxime Kovalewsky, *Revue internationale de sociologie*, Vol. XI, pp. 476 ff.; also A. Aladin, *London Times*, January 16, 1907. The party alignments in the dumas are also of service. In Paul Milyoukov's *Russia and Its Crisis* the various dominant and dangerous interest groups can be discovered underneath his superficial, propagandist statement in terms of ideas. It is a task not without its amusing phases to pick them out and note how they often give the lie direct to the various "isms" which are put forth by the author as the true Russian realities.

is not by any means one of a single class, but instead, a government in which many groups are forced into marked class oppositions because of the wretchedly poor mediation which the czar is giving them.   The czar is primarily mediator for the provinces of the great scattered empire.   Backed by his huge army, he holds them together against dangers of attack and dissolution.   The bureaucracy is itself a great interest group in the empire, similar in many striking respects to the political machines in the United States, as in the free access to it, in its technique of corruption, even in the cross-relation of locality group and other group functions.

Every act of the czar and of the bureaucracy is an expression of some of these groups.   We see the large industrial and commercial interests solidly behind the autocracy because their technique of corruption is in good working order.   We see the rising manu-facturing and mercantile interests arrayed on the other side because they are at a disadvantage in this technique.   We see the prole-tariat at the extreme radical stage because they have so little repre-sentation in the government that almost any change will for them, they judge, be a change for the better.   Similarly with the land groups.   The peasants are divided according to their economic position.   So far as the large land-holders feel that they can preserve their interests better through a constitution, just so far they are for it—as has actually been instanced in earlier Russian history.   But the moment the present revolutionary movement takes a phase which tends toward the partition of their lands, that moment they line up solidly behind the autocracy.

So complicated is this struggle that it is natural for keenly interested observers of it to state it, entirely in terms of the various "ideas," liberal, socialist, and so on, that are prominent in the talk. But these "ideas" can with sufficient care all be reduced to mere discussion phases of the process.   Political parties have formed on the basis of interest groups always to be defined, of course, in terms of each other.   During the preparations for the first duma we watched great masses of the population adjust themselves in new groupings on the party level; that is, the shifting situation made them transfer their efforts at political expression from one political group to another. The history of the Constitutional Democratic party, for example, or of any other, could be written in such terms.

The autocracy is the center of the struggle, but only the center, inasmuch as it has proved an inadequate instrument for the expression of the changing group interests. Place a duma with substantial powers alongside the czar, or otherwise alter the agencies for the expression of the interests of the nation, and the struggle will continue through the new agency, perhaps reduced in violence, perhaps increased in violence, and it will then be a struggle not only of class against class, and subclass perhaps against subclass, but also a struggle of territorial divisions of the huge empire against each other. The classes cannot fly apart; the territories can, and possibly will. The classes must remain to adjust their interests and evolve, if fortune is such, into less antagonistic groups. Perhaps they can achieve it through the agency of such an institution as the duma, and perhaps they will require a new despotism, this time representing some other element than the land-holding class most directly. Out of it all, after time has passed and after more blood has flowed, will come a better-balanced governmental structure, with better channels for the adjustment of interest-group conflicts before they proceed to the most extreme hates and to murder as technique. Let the czar and his class suppress the revolution, and they have but two alternatives, either devastation and the reduction of the population to smaller numbers, or else a substantial yielding of much of what has been demanded. Or, in other words, through revolution, even though formally unsuccessful the interest groups will have made themselves heard. Just this latter process has, as is well known, played a great part in the history of English liberties.

In contrast to Russia we may examine, in the case of the Greek tyrannies, governments centralized in a single individual in which the class basis of the autocratic rule is simple and easy to analyze. There are plenty of incidents of the tyrannies, such as that of Theagenes of Megara, who slew the cattle of the rich that were encroaching on common land, which show where the tyrants' strength rested. To describe the tyranny as unscrupulous ambition is thin and meaningless, compared with a description of the work the tyrannies did, of the work they appeared to do. Their task was to overthrow the oligarchies, which must not be understood to mean merely to change the form of the government, but to set aside in the specific case a rule which had ceased to express a large and strong grouping of the population, and which did not give that grouping any channels through which to make itself felt. Here was need, not for some formally analyzed functions of government to be separately performed, but for a mighty group interest to push itself through to better expression in the face of obstacles; hence the tyranny, a single agency, without any distribution of the governmental activity through a number of different agencies. When the work of the tyranny was finished, then the interest groupings arranged their governing bodies anew, providing a number of agencies through which their activities might pass at different stages. And these kept on changing in more or less ready response to the changing of the groupings.

In Rome all the way from traditional kings to latest emperors we find the character of the executive strictly dependent on the kind of work to be done at each period, that kind of work itself being capable of adequate statement only in terms of group pressures, with the executive as group leader. The kings come upon our vision as elective rulers, and though we lack the material for their earlier interpretation, they were primarily war leaders of all Rome against neighboring communities. In time, consuls, who retained most of the royal power, succeeded them as the very clear result of group reaction against king evils, under circumstances in which the group reaction could take place without injury to the reacting group. The consuls were primarily patrician leaders against the plebs, more so than the kings had been. When all Rome had to react against surrounding communities under specially perilous conditions, the king was temporarily restored under the guise of a dictator. The struggle against the curule magistrates in the early republic was strictly a class phenomenon, and the outcome depended strictly on the given balance of pressures. When the tribunes were created they were class leaders and had just the strength of the plebs behind them and nothing more.   One can even trace group interests to some extent within the ranks of the patricians and within the ranks of the plebs.

When we come to the Roman emperors we have again full material for interpretation in terms of interest groups, only this time locality groupings on a huge scale were what counted.   The provinces were being brutally abused by the richer classes of Rome and the poorer classes were systematically bribed into assent.   The provinces were held quiet by the legions, but the legions were made up of provincials.   Caesar had a devoted army of provincials behind him.   The very moment that imperial authority was established, the provinces were more humanely treated.   The emperors were the direct representatives of the provinces and their appearance marked a great advance in the adjustment of interests within the government.   The ordinary description even of a Nero in terms of morals and personal character is a pitiable caricature.   Nero was beloved throughout the provinces and there was good reason for it.   The army was a sort of electoral commission, never a very perfect one, and, when the praetorian guard was in control, a most wretched one, but always it had a value in the government.   The whole development of the administrative system and the bureaucracy, the division of the empire under Diocletian, and indeed almost every stage in every imperial career, must be interpreted, not so far as its trivialities and sensationalisms go, but in all its main outlines, in terms of the existing group pressures of the empire.

I am no more here than elsewhere in this volume making an attempt to cover systematically the field of government, and I therefore offer no excuse for skipping from one type of government to another and omitting many.   Suppose we take a look at Germany as it is now organized.   The executive, that is, the emperor, is so very much more than mere executive that that word but scantily describes him.   One needs a term nearer to ruler, to comprise all his work.   His initiative in the matters that pass through the Reichstag is so great that that popularly elected body becomes little more than a vetoing agency, and indeed often it cannot veto when it would, but must merely protest. Both under Bismarck and under Wilhelm II the progress of socialist legislation, whether adopting socialistic projects or in antagonism to organized socialism, clearly shows the group process at work. It matters not that the emperor's brain lays claim to certain policies or programmes. Getting down underneath, what is happening is that certain of the groupings of the empire, including prominently the old consolidated agrarian class and the new "big business," are being reflected directly by the emperor as agency of government. The test upon which the fate of the present system of government will turn is whether the emperor reflects the strongest of the nation's interest groups well enough so that they will not push through to better agencies of expressing themselves. This does not mean of course that he must express them along the level of the talk groups in which they combine, nor that he must follow anybody's idea of what is ideally or "objectively" best for them, but that he must express the deeper-lying interest groups which function through the talk at one stage of their process, and which also function through him. So long as they find their way through to the later stages of activity with some approximation to their intensity in its ratio to the resistance they must face, so long the emperor as head of legislation will stand, and the Reichstag will remain in its relative feebleness. When the time comes, as it no doubt will come, that this emperor or some successor, is too poor a representative of the more powerful groups, then he must give way, and if he is too strongly identified with one class, he must see an agency expressly representing other groups of the population placed alongside of him, and perhaps ultimately he must be himself dispensed with or relegated to a trivial position in the governmental system. This process can be described in terms of royal personalities with a very vague approximation to the truth; it can be described in terms of theories and political platforms with somewhat greater approximation; but the royalties, and the theories, and the Reichstag, and all officialdom as well, will have to be reduced to terms of the underlying interest groupings, to get a statement that will really stand the tests as an account of the phenomena of the government. The whole well-known process by which the propagandist socialism in Germany tends to transform itself into a working legislative policy with the increase of the party in strength is a proof of an increasing representativeness in the propaganda activity. The underlying interests are coming to be better expressed in the policies and in the differentiated governing bodies at one and the same time.

In France the changes in the form of the government during the last century have been the direct consequence of the process of adjustment of the interest groups. French character will not serve to explain it, neither will the characters of the various rulers and chief officials. It has been always a question of the identification of the head of the government with some group of the people, a question of the less ample opportunities for functioning through the government allowed to other groups, and a question of the effort of these others to secure expression. The war with Prussia brought on the downfall of the last empire, but the war itself was in large part the outgrowth of the direct group conflicts in France. We must of course avoid being sensational in describing these changes of government, for they can easily be made to appear more important than they actually were. Moreover, we must not think to explain every detail of a shifting situation whose adjustment is in process of establishment as directly due to certain large groups as we define them for broad purposes. Many points which are most prominent in a "story" of what occurred are trivial to an understanding of the process. Such for example is often the personality of a ruler. A ruler may identify himself with some frivolity groupings of the population to the neglect of the groupings that are most strenuous in forcing their activity through its full course. He will disappear, but his fate will be a mere detail. Only when he has been identified with a strong element in the population, and his disappearance involves a material change in balance and notably new methods of adjusting interests, will the event be one of high importance.

The history of Napoleon, as indeed the whole history of the

French Revolution, is such a story of the struggling of groups, there solidified into classes, for expression through the government, complicated, of course, by the backing which foreign armies gave to certain of the French classes. The French government today is just such a process of adjusting interests, only now the interests are in less violent antagonism, and the conditions admit of greater flexibility. One might compare Napoleon with the present French cabinet, the former as a strong man lifting a huge weight, the latter as a team of jugglers keeping a lot of balls in the air at once. The interests are now more minutely divided; no one has so great a dead weight; there is a more elaborate organization for giving them pathways through the government. If a lot of them combine to turn out the personnel of the cabinet, they will not stay combined for action on a radical programme disadvantageous to the whole opposition group of interests. We have therefore many freely functioning groups, together with but little activity of the older, more sharply consolidated classes, and so less resort to violence in the government. The anti-clerical programme has been carried along year after year by a government resting on "blocs" of different composition, but without involving equally radical action on other lines at the same time.

When the president of France summons a new premier—and the same is true when a premier is summoned in England, or, with appropriate modifications, when a presidential candidate is selected in the United States—the process is very clearly one of group adjustments. We may talk about it in terms of the qualities of the man, but we do not have to dig deep to see that it is always a question of his "strength," whether in the parliament or before the electorate, and this is a question of the group support he can array behind him. The process is easy to study in the press dispatches whenever a new premier is selected in France; that happens so often that one has not forgotten the old groupings before the chance to observe the new arrives.

The history of English royalty is a history of class or group struggles and would furnish countless illustrations, both to show how the interest groups of the country worked through the government, and how they served, when checked, to cast up structures for a changed type of government. The political history of England may be written in terms of her insular isolation, which has been a most important factor in the actual group formations of the country at every stage, and of her classes with their later development into freer groups, so far as that process has yet gone. The alliance of the monarchy, sometimes with factions of the feudal landholders, sometimes with all of them, sometimes with the cities, and so down through the list, is the very essence of the monarchy itself. The forms of governing institutions that have been developed, even down to the forms of judicial procedure, all have their roots in these class and group oppositions. From De Lolme's time down, it has often been remarked that the explanation of England's liberties is to be found in the absolute power of her early kings, and this sweeping statement can readily be given its truer meaning in terms of the group oppositions that gave substance to that "absolute" power, and that evolved farther in and through it. The whole development is so manifest that I will not give it detailed discussion here.

The executive agency in England today is the cabinet, or perhaps rather an inner circle of the cabinet. But this inner circle is at the same time the legislative agency for the most important changes in the law, the House of Lords holding a limited, and the House of Commons an absolute veto on it, subject to appeal to the electorate. It will be more convenient to discuss the play of the interest groups through the English government in the next chapter, and the discussion will therefore be passed for the present, in order that I may proceed to a more elaborate analysis of the play of interests through and upon the executive in the United States.

The executive agency in the United States government is the president with his department heads and their subordinates; in the states it is the governor and his co-ordinate elective officials; in the counties, usually a number of co-ordinate officials; in the cities, a mayor with his department heads and their subordinates. How the president through his veto power, through his ordinance power, through his leadership of popular movements functions as a part of the law-making system is well enough known. How the Congress shares in the administrative work of the country by organizing the departments, by apportioning funds to them, by ordering investigations, and by controlling appointments and the conduct of appointees, is well enough known also. But my business here is not with these classifications of function, but with the play of interests through the presidency in all its functions, and incidentally with the play of interests through the minor executive agencies in the states and cities.

The creation of a presidency, senate, and lower house was a mere extension of a set of institutions familiar enough in England and in the colonies, though a mass of theory grew up around the organization, much like superstitions around a peasant's harvest field, to the effect that the Senate was to adjust certain supposed differences of interest between big and little states and also to represent cautious proprietorship of property, that the House was to represent the "people," and that the president was to give unity to the united colonies as against the outer world, serve as a check on the Congress, and execute the laws. The early presidents corresponded with the theory groupings fairly well, since no more pressing interests on deeper levels bore in upon them; and they confined their activities within close limits, holding their veto power in strict leash, keeping usually at long distance from Congress, and even refraining from active control of their own subordinates. In case of need, however, they acted as fully authorized representatives of the nation, as appeared especially in Jefferson's purchase of Louisiana.

But despite all this it was impossible even for Washington to keep from becoming identified to a considerable extent with certain elements or combinations of elements of the population, and almost from the start presidents were party candidates and party representatives, all of the technique of the Constitution's electoral system notwithstanding. The necessary unity for successful representation of this kind was found first in the congressional caucus and later in the party conventions.

The history of the presidency from that day to this has been the history of the interests which chose it as their best medium of expression when they found other pathways blocked. Without attempting further analysis, it is only necessary to refer to the combination of groups which in the party of Andrew Jackson gained power and through its leader used the presidency in a most aggressive fashion, both by initiating legislation and through the veto power; to the weakness of the presidency in the later days of the slavery struggle before the Civil War when the great class interests that developed were closely balanced in Congress; to the test of the Civil War which made the presidency a dictatorship under republican forms, and evolved the doctrine of the war powers; to the use of the presidency as the platter on which spoils were served when the lack of other vital issues allowed the interest of the organized political machines to dominate; to the identification of the presidency under McKinley with the most powerful faction of the Senate, representing the successful exploitation of the nation's industrial opportunities; and finally to the use of the presidency under Roosevelt to beat down the entrenchments of this same ruling clique, not only in the Senate, but in the House, and to a degree in the judiciary as well.

Let us observe in some typical matters how the presidency has worked under Roosevelt.   The background may be briefly sketched at its high points, for it is familiar to everyone, but at the same time is so essential to an understanding of what the activity of the presidency has been that it will not do merely to take acquaintance with it for granted.   It included: a system of court precedents built up while industrial enterprise was seeking to use its opportunities, while the use of those opportunities was not bringing notable immediate harm to any large groups of the people, and while there was in consequence little resistance to the tendency of the decisions; a population at last become thick enough to limit the opportunities for new enterprises and make them the subject of hot competition, so that their free exploitation came to be felt as injurious by large parts of the population who could not seize upon any for themselves; a Senate closely organized by a powerful party dominated by the opportunity-seekers, ravenous to create oppor-

tunities wherever they were restrained; a House centralized under
the control of a speaker and two lieutenants, rarely breaking out of
the leading-strings except in minor matters, and representing in
general the same interests as the Senate; a powerful party organization, apparently at the height of its power, but actually materially
weakened by the civil-service laws which had withdrawn from it
much of its daily food, and so many of its sure workers and voters;
a great mass of the population feeling its hurts, but as yet little clear
as to the what or the how of revenge and protection, cut off from
effective representation in the government, driven therefore to
"radicalism," but neither desperate enough as yet to rush blindly
forward against the government, nor sure enough of its ground
to force a peaceable way. This statement of the situation is very
superficial, inasmuch as it makes use of many words which involve
problems instead of giving reliable information in group terms, but
it will do for the purpose for which I put it forward—a mere indication and reminder of the background of group activity in which
the presidency has been functioning.

By the chance, then, of an assassin's bullet—chance, of course,
only from the point of view of our immediate examination, and of
its immediate moment in time—a president came to power identified not at all with what popular analysis nowadays calls the
"system," nor on the other hand with the noisy protest against the
"system," but at the same time on a deeper-lying level, identified,
through whatever personal history, with the great interest groups
not effectively represented in the existing government; a man fit
for maintaining himself in popular leadership, in executive administration, and in political manipulation as well. The bullet made a
difference of a few years in the arrival of such a leader in power,
perhaps also in the particular person who secured this power, and,
mainly because of the earlier date of accession, it made a difference also in the particular methods which have been taken to
bring the interests in question to expression. So far as one can
see, it will make little difference in the concrete outcome, or even
in the great stages of political process.

Roosevelt went into office with known sympathy for the movement for tariff reform. He also pledged himself to carry out the policies of his predecessor, who had just been testing the country with reference to one phase of tariff reform—reciprocity—and identifying himself with the movement for it, so far as a leader of that type ever identifies himself openly with anything. Moreover public attention was strongly centered (in other words, an active talk group could be observed which was centered) upon the operations of one or two of the great industries of the country then in process of consolidation, which were among the most prominent direct beneficiaries of the tariff.

Taking all the conditions, it would have been natural to expect that the tariff movement would have found a leader in Roosevelt, and have made a strong struggle through this aid, which, of course, is just what has not happened up to date. And the reason for this is exceedingly simple. It is not that Roosevelt "betrayed" the cause nor that he sacrificed it to the "trusts," but that under present conditions, despite all superficial appearances, there is not an intense enough and extensive enough set of interest groups back of the movement to make a good fight for thoroughgoing reform with reasonable prospects of success. I say this is the reason, but I do not make any pretense of having worked out this problem in terms of the groups involved so as to be able to give positive proof. I am interested here in illustrating the group process through the presidency, and I merely choose the most probable of the explanations of the special fact; it might on the contrary be the case that the tariff-reform groupings have been temporarily hindered by defects in governmental technique from expressing themselves through the government, in which case they will express themselves a few years from now in more emphatic form; or it might be that the issue has stepped aside for others of greater intensity in which case it will return to its due place with every indication of huge energy before long. But in either of these cases the group process offers the best and fullest statement of the facts, just as it does in the contingency I have deemed most probable at the moment of writing, in default of thoroughgoing study.

Roosevelt, or rather the Roosevelt leadership which we observe in process, is a highly flexible mechanism, capable of reflecting many varieties of group activities, with great exactness, both as to their lines of movement and as to their intensities. The groups can function through a Roosevelt much more rapidly than through a leader more firmly set in the particular group interests he especially reflects, and less flexible in reflecting others. The tariff battle was therefore fought and lost in Roosevelt's own person, with much the same outcome as there would have been had the fight gone through Congress, while in the meantime Congress has been an open channel for the settlement of many other issues in which Roosevelt has been at the front in behalf of interest groups which were big and strong enough to win out. It is just this flexibility and accuracy in representing group interests that makes the clever politician under such interest conditions as now prevail in American public life, and the indications are that we shall have use for very much more of it in the future as a labor-saving device.

The essential point in an interpretation of government concerns the great pressures at work and the main lines of the outcome. It is relatively incidental whether a particular battle is fought bitterly through two or more presidencies, or whether it is adjusted peacefully in a single presidency, so long as we can show a similar outcome. This is true because the vast mass of the matter of government is not what appears on the surface in discussions, theories, congresses, or even in wars, but what is persistently present in the background. It is somewhat as it is when twenty heirs want to contest a will, but have only a single heir appear in the proceedings, while the other nineteen hang back in the shadow. The story will concern the fight of the one; but the reality concerns the silent nineteen as well.

Observing the political ferment of a country organized with representative institutions, one may easily think that a mass of issues is more closely bound up together than is the case; the sweeping assertions of party orators in their campaign work or of other popular leaders at other times may strengthen the impression. And one may infer from an uprising of "the people" that any one of a lot of reforms could be put through by this single force were it

properly directed. So one may identify the tariff-reform movement at bottom with the anti-trust movement, and argue that both
have the same strength as resting in the "people."   But it is just
this confusion and vagueness which the method of analysis into
groups should enable us to rid ourselves of.   We can there find
out why, for example, the president cannot at a given time lead a
campaign against the excrescences of the tariffs, but can lead one to
success against certain railway rate abuses.   There was a time,
indeed, when the tariff and trust issues were more closely allied;
and the reason why the trusts were not then struck at through the
tariff had to do mainly with the lesser strength of and the greater
resistance to the movement along anti-tariff lines in comparison
with movements on other lines against the injuries felt by the con-
sumer as inflicted on him by large industrial organizations.   Since
then the group objectives have differentiated noticeably.   In
neither case have any abstract equities, or any specialized theories
as to the relation between the tariff and trust development been
decisive.   Political economy may reason, or it may rave, against
these popular movements, but it is only playing with the fringe
on their edges.   It is never a test for the movements; instead what
vitality it possesses it draws from the movements.   The man of
wisdom may laugh at the popular theories as to the connection
between prosperity and the dominance of one or the other political
party; but the political groupings that grow not out of the theories,
but out of the underlying economic groupings, are socially very
much more real than the wise man's scornful wisdom can ever be.
And so long as we find Roosevelt leadership letting the tariff-
reform issue lie idle, and Hearst leadership putting protection
among its most sacred democratic planks (whether Hearst actually
made a poll of the working-men, and found 90 per cent. of them
protectionists or not), we may follow the given clue in studying
the groupings of the people with reference to the conditions out of
which tariff issues are built, without fearing that we will be misled.

Turn now to the president's action in connection with the
anthracite coal strike, to observe a different phase of the group

leadership. There can be no doubt that the president's intervention lay very far outside of the presidential powers as known to constitutional law. There can be no doubt also that a large group, which can roughly be designated as the coal-consumers' group, had formed as the result of the strike, and that it had no other channel in the government through which it could secure relief except the presidency. There is no doubt that this group was behind the president in his action. While as a matter of fact the president exercised coercion on the coal operators, it is also true that had not this great group of people so heartily indorsed his intervention, he would not have succeeded, because the coal operators then could have ignored his offer of mediation. We find, then, the president not merely representing a great mass of the people but actually exercising a power which he would not have had, formally or actually, had they not been immediately behind him. Of course such a statement as this is true of every act the president takes, if we go deep enough into it, but here it is clear at a glance.

For his action the president of course suffered much criticism. And a favorite phrasing of this criticism was in regard to executive usurpation, in regard to the collapse of the Constitution, in regard to the peril to our liberties from executive power. Such reasoning, as we currently met it, represented inevitably the coal owners' side of the controversy. Not that no men could be found advancing it who were not personally free from any alliance with the operators' interest, but that whatever men of this type were found were merely transition phenomena. The central fact we observed was that men in the mass on the employers' side grew ever hotter and more intense with this argument, while on the consumers' side men in the mass swiftly came to disregard it entirely.

No constitutional argument, no attack of nerves, any more than any inordinate ambition of any man can effect the expanding or the shrinking of the presidency in our government. The constitutional-argument group stands as a fact, and at times it may be a huge fact, say with almost every individual citizen belonging to it. But it is a highly representative group on the level of talk, and the

minute the facts frame themselves up, that is, the minute the
deeper-lying group interests shift so that this talk group no longer
adequately represents them in fact, that moment the talk group is
doomed; and long before the talk group has shrunk to small proportions the action of the lower-lying groups will be rushing forward through the presidency toward its ends. If group interests
tend in a certain direction, and are checked in their course through
Congress, they will find their way through the presidency. If the
group interests take permanently a form which makes Congress
an inadequate agency for them, then the presidency will consolidate
its power. If on the other hand the shifting of the interests or the
change in Congress makes the latter agency adequate, then the
presidency's power will readjust itself accordingly. The key to
the whole situation is to be found in the interest groups, save only
as a fixed distribution of work between the agencies, maintained
for some time, will tend to maintain itself thereafter indefinitely
just as it has been adjusted, providing there is no positive reason
for altering it.

Another compact illustration of a great set of group interests
working through the presidency, this time to bring about legislation, a work which is supposed to be the proper function of Congress, is offered us by the beef-inspection bill of the spring of 1906.
If we should follow through the steps of this legislation we should
find them something like this: First, an initiative in which the
secretary of agriculture and his subordinates acting for the meat
consumers of the nation without their much knowing or caring
about it, urged legislation along substantially the lines that were
ultimately enacted. Here you have an act typical of the benevolent
despot, so far as the form of the representation goes. Next a
committee of the House of Representatives holds the draft of the
bill in its keeping indefinitely, giving public hearings now and then,
but making no progress toward reporting a bill. Here you have
organized representative forms, but actually a fixed group dominance, corresponding closely with the class dominance of many
harshly organized governments. Then comes a Congress which
never sees, hears of, or thinks of the bill. Finally comes the presi-

dent, backing up his secretary of agriculture, watching a favorable chance, but in theory having nothing whatever to do with any such legislation till it is put on his table for his signature. What then? There came a day when the president found his chance; the incident that gave it to him happened to be a book, but it might have been any one of a number of other things. He used his chance, proved on the spot that his judgment of the interest grouping of the population was correct, bullied the congressional representatives of the beef interests until they surrendered, and the Congress finally went through the forms of legislation. But to every eye directed at the facts it was the president who made that law, he alone serving as the real legislature, with the nominal Congress acting little more than as a bad-tempered recording clerk. The president was the legislative organ, through which the great group interest functioned in this case.

These illustrations may perhaps be said to be of exceptional character. But if we take the president in his "routine" work of administration, we still find him representing interest groups. It is very common to argue of law-enforcement as though all that was involved in it was personal honesty on the part of the executive and strict adherence to the letter of the law. But even apart from the discretion that goes with executive office, every American can see clearly in local government a phenomenon which is met with in just as real, if not in just as pronounced, a form in federal government, that sharply contradicts the accuracy of this method of talking. When a Maine sheriff is elected on an anti-prohibition platform, he is standing strictly on his function in our political system as a local check on central government if he allows the saloons to continue; and when a Chicago mayor ignores the denunciations of a comparatively small body of citizens and allows the saloons to continue open on Sunday in violation of the state law, he also may be honestly representing his locality, and indeed filling the place actually assigned to him by the constitution, even though he does ignore his duty to enforce the state law. Here is a dilemma created by the American method of distribution of governmental functions between state and local governments, and there is no possible method of "reasoning" our way out of the difficulty. It is a hard, tough fact, and nothing but Alexander's sword will make its way through it.

In the presidency, as I said a moment ago, this same situation appears, though not in so manifest a form. The president is continually a representative of groups of the population. Usually the statute law specifies both the group interest which the president must represent and also the lines of his activity in this representative process. There is, however, a great deal of "grand-stand-play" law on the federal statute books, which represents, or has at one time represented, the people on the mouth level, but not on the level of deeper-lying interests, and which no one, outside of some small groupings, really expects the president to enforce. There is also much dead-letter law, forgotten by the law officers of the government as well as by the people, which in the terminology of this book is not real law at all, but merely occupies a favored position, so that with less formality it can again become law if popular initiative or federal attorneys in a representative capacity choose to invoke it.

Suppose we take a case in which a group pressure has moved to a certain extent through Congress, and has produced a statute, but in which the opposition has not yet become reconciled to the changed status; or in other words, in which despite the statute, the status is really not yet changed. We may find one set of group interests represented in the Congress and another set in the presidency, or perhaps we may find the same set represented in both, except for the fact that the Congress has been forced to go through certain dubious forms of representing the other set. Take for example the Sherman anti-trust legislation, which so long remained on the statute books with no serious attempt to enforce it, or the anti-rebate provisions of the interstate commerce law. One may denounce—or, alternatively, praise—the presidents who did not enforce this legislation, but in either event such reference to their character or intelligence or public spirit, or what not, is a very feeble method of stating the facts, just as inordinate praise or blame of the personality of some president who did enforce it, is a very weak statement. What we must get down to is the group interests which the presidents and other officials respectively represented. Then the praise or blame, the moral outbursts, and the reasonings, all alike, show themselves at their true worth as phases of the group process. The enactment of the Sherman law represented a certain stage in a certain group struggle. The presidency stood aligned with the groups which opposed the enactment of such a statute—the fact that a president's signature was appended to the law does not alter this situation. It is incidental to our present consideration that the president's position was mediated through party organization; the fact we are after here is that he did represent certain groupings and not certain others. The courts also would have to be taken into account for a full statement, but that also must be postponed. As time went on, the presidency, through certain of the department heads, took gradual steps toward representing the interests in favor of the law. In recent years we have seen the law invoked more vigorously than before, till now we may say in this matter that the presidency is representing the groupings that favor the law much more than those against it. The more or less here comes into operation because of the complexity of the agencies united in the presidency. The interstate commerce law well illustrates this, for we have at times seen the presidency through the Interstate Commerce Commission representing the consumers, and the presidency through other of its activities representing the interest groupings allied with the railways.

Here is an illustration of another character. The regulation of steamboats on navigable waters falls within the province of the federal governmnent. If the government should attempt to suppress steamboats entirely, it would face an opposition of one group of men looking for opportunities for profit, and of another looking for transportation facilities. But such a thing as suppression—barring alternative means of transportation—is something government will never undertake. The governmental process is a group process, and this situation incidentally illustrates my previous position that there is no such thing as a totality group

in government. If the government should let steamboats operate
with full freedom from regulation, the activities just as they proceed would quickly stir into life group antagonisms, which would
fight for and against regulation. At one stage perhaps we should
find steamboat-owners arrayed against patrons in general. At
another stage we should find some of the steamboat-owners allied
with patrons against other steamboat-owners; that is, the owners
who saw in the better, higher-class patronage special profit opportunities would wish to regulate the poorer, cheaper boats which by
their frequent accidents brought discredit even on the best boats.
Out of the process come inevitably—that is as a matter of invariable
observation in a society like ours—laws providing regulation.
Given this situation, we have only here to watch the process of the
interests through the presidency as it is now organized. The
Slocum disaster in New York harbor a few years ago brought the
situation out in the clearest light. The steamboat interests had
secured representation through the presidency of such kind as
practically to substitute what they assented to, reduced to its
lowest terms, for the congressional enactment. The steamboat
patrons had lost their representation. This also can be fully
understood only as by-product in connection with the party organization of much of the presidential activity. But it cannot merely,
or justly, be described as a result of party organization. It was
essentially the representation of the interests in the presidency,
differing in content, not so much from the representation of the
same interests in Congress, as from the weight of the interests at the
time the law was enacted. The Slocum incident—any other
might have served the purpose—consolidated the patrons' groups
and put the owners' groups on the defensive. Also it put the party
on the defensive, but that again is another story, of a type to be held
for later consideration. The result was that the patrons' group,
showing the greater positive strength—in other words, the so-called
"popular will"—expressed itself first through the presidency direct
in the form of more stringent supervision of the inspection service, and secondly through the Congress in the form of a new
statute.

The Panama Canal project, with its sharply defined interest groupings, would furnish a good illustration of the direct representation of groups in the presidency; so would the history of civil-service reform.   And so also would thousands of the minor acts of the presidency in its ordinary operation.   But the few illustrations above must suffice here.

The sheriff of a county will be found representing group interests in what he does and in what he neglects.   Incidental reference to him in this respect has already been made.   The office of a city mayor is a very hotbed of interest representation, whether the council has been reduced to a subordinate position, or is still co-ordinate with the mayoralty.   Sometimes, indeed frequently, the interests that are organized through a party machine dominate the mayor, and other interests have difficulty in gaining expression.   Sometimes he represents opposition to these organized interests, but of course only by representing the interests of the opposition.   Whether in legislation, in law-enforcement, or the management of public enterprises, he is allowing interest groups a chance to express themselves through him, and whether he is strictly adhering to the letter of some ordinance, or using his discretion narrowly or broadly, it is a case of direct interest pressure.   Our large cities' police forces are in reality legislatures as well as executive agencies—they pay so little attention to many laws, construct so much of their own law, and choose so freely what statutes and ordinances they will deign to enforce.   They are part of the organized mayoralty, and when complaint arises against them it is always from groups which are not gaining representation, and which see in them the appropriated agencies of other groups which gain too much representation to suit the objectors.

What is true in these other cases is true in the case of governors and co-ordinate executive officials of states, save here the state officials are of comparatively little consequence.   A governor is very apt under present conditions to give specially marked representation to the railroad groups of the state, and if a La Follette comes along who establishes his strength on a different basis, he at once makes a spectacular figure. While representing the railroads on certain lines of group distinction, the governor will represent large portions of the railway patrons on other lines, but here again it will always be the groups that function through him more or less directly that count. They may function straight through the legislature and the governor, with the governor one stage in serial order, or certain groups may function through the legislature and subside there, leaving opposition groups to function through the governor, or again the initiative in the process may come in the governor's office, and the legislature may not be used at all, in the attainment of even very important ends.

Now to consider the position of our American executive in the government in more general terms, and to compare him with the typical despot, we may take up the examination on somewhat different lines. The despot functions in a huge mass of custom. Our executive functions within the lines of a constitution. There is no vital difference here. From special points of view, of course, there is a very great difference. First, because we can change our Constitution with more ease than a despotic monarchy can change its custom. Still the amendment of the American federal Constitution is no simple matter, even when there is very marked group pressure in that direction; and if distinction is to be made along this line, there is much less difference between an American executive and a despot than there is between the British executive and a despot. Again—a fact that stands out in spectacular form, and is indeed very important in the kind of industrial life we live—the despot has free to him certain technical methods of keeping order and running his government, such as arbitrary judicial procedure and punishment, which our executive cannot practically employ except in very limited range. An American executive may try to bully a court, but he is very apt to find that his success will be less than accrues to the cajolery or worse of the law-breaker whom he is opposing. So far as a limitation of powers in the executive agency along the lines of the threefold division is concerned, we have seen how, even upon a very partial application in theory, there is a systematic breakdown in practice whenever the pressures become strong enough.

The real distinction is as to the methods of approach that the group interests have to the holder of central power, which includes existence of alternative organs through which the groups may express themselves if one is clogged up. In other words, it concerns the technique the groups have for the control of the government. Do certain interests block the legislature ? Then the executive may be set free. And vice versa. Meanwhile there is a process through the courts checking both. Instead of conditions corresponding to class domination, we have in our organization of the interests conditions corresponding to the breaking down of set classes, and a technique which helps to keep free the avenues of group approach. We do not have by any means the most free. avenues of approach. Looking at a section of our history a decade or two long, one may easily be tempted to say we have a government which tends to favor class dominance. But despite some tremendously strong underlying group interests, we have nevertheless frequent evidences of the giving way of the fortifications of one set of groups at the assault of another, and the freeing of the executive from class domination. We have avenues of approach through the government such that the class tendency can only advance to a certain degree before being overwhelmed, and that degree one which probably falls far short, except in most exceptional temporary cases, of the degree in which a resort to violence as the only effective technique becomes necessary.

Executive discretion still exists, covering indeed a much larger field than despotic discretion ever covers. It is a phenomenon of group leadership. It is group leadership "within the government," but it always stands face to face with organized group leadership "without the government" (that is, without the government in the narrowest sense but within the political process I have called government in the intermediate sense). It is a discretion that is not rigidly attached to one set of groups. If too rigid for the moment, the strong leadership which opposes it from the outside will tend to displace it. It must yield or fall. If the executive yields to a group organization gathering force from without, before the legislature yields, it will gain in power as compared to the legislature, until the legislature yields in its turn. Its gain in power will seem a menace merely to those who are immediately hurt by it, never to those who benefit by it. That is not a weakness of human nature; it is rather the characteristic of what we mean by the word menace itself. And moreover the hurts and the benefits so loudly proclaimed are never permanent things; they are small in comparison with the deeper-lying benefits; and if the most powerful movement through the executive seems dangerous to the "liberties of the state" or to any other fiction, we may be sure that it will trickle away in driblets with access to power. For the very nature of the group process (which our government shows in a fairly well-developed form) is this, that groups are freely combining, dissolving, and recombining in accordance with their interest lines. And the lion when he has satisfied his physical need will lie down quite lamb-like, however much louder his roars were than his appetite justified.

We may put it thus: that if the group interests work out a fair and satisfying adjustment through the legislature, then the executive sinks in prominence; that when the adjustment is not perfected in the legislature, then the executive arises in strength to do the work; that the judiciary, on lines that will later appear, bears in these points a relation to the executive somewhat similar to that which the legislature bears, similar, that is, in quality, if not in quantity; that the growth of executive discretion is therefore a phase of the group process; that it cannot be understood in any other way, and that no judgment concerning it will maintain itself except through the group process and by the test of the group process.

CHAPTER XV

THE PRESSURE OF INTERESTS IN THE LEGISLATURE

Tested by the interest groups that function through them, legislatures are of two general types. First are those which represent one class or set of classes in the government as opposed to some other class, which is usually represented in the monarch. Second are those which are not the exclusive stronghold of one class or set of classes, but are instead the channel for the functioning of all groupings of the population. The borders between the two types are of course indistinct, but they approximate closely to the borders between a society with class organization and one with classes broken down into freer and more changeable group interests.

Neither the number of chambers in the legislative body nor the constitutional relations of the legislature to the executive can serve to define the two types. The several chambers may represent several classes, or again the double-chamber system may be in fact merely a technical division, with the same interests present in both chambers. The executive may be a class representative, or merely a co-ordinate organ, dividing with the legislature the labor of providing channels through which the same lot of manifold interest groups can work.

It lies almost on the surface that a legislature which is a class agency will produce results in accordance with the class pressure behind it. Its existence has been established by struggle, and its life is a continual struggle against the representatives of the opposite class. Of course there will be an immense deal of argument to be heard on both sides, and the argument will involve the setting forth of "reasons" in limitless number. It is indeed because of the advantages (in group terms, of course) of such argument as a technical means of adjustment that the legislative bodies survive. Argument under certain conditions is a greater labor-saver than blows, and in it the group interests more fully unfold themselves.

But beneath all the argument lies the strength.   The arguments
go no farther than the strength goes.   What the new Russian duma
will get, if it survives, will be what the people it solidly represents are
strong enough to make it get, and no more and no less, with bombs
and finances, famine and corruption funds alike in the scale.

But the farther we advance among legislatures of the second
type, and the farther we get away from the direct appeal to muscle
and weapon, the more difficult becomes the analysis of the group
components, the greater is the prominence that falls to the process
of argumentation, the more adroitly do the group forces mask
themselves in morals, ideals, and phrases, the more plausible
becomes the interpretation of the legislature's work as a matter of
reason, not of pressure, and the more common it is to hear condem-
nations of those portions of the process at which violence shows
through the reasoning as though they were *per se* perverted, degen-
erate, and the bearers of ruin.   There is, of course, a strong, genuine
group opposition to the technique of violence, which is an important
social fact; but a statement of the whole legislative process in
terms of the discussion forms used by that anti-violence interest
group is wholly inadequate.

To anyone who is emotionally bound up to the personified
social will as the only adequate clue to the legislative process, what
I have to say will be a folly, although all that this work aims to do
is to avoid too narrow a connotation for the term will, and then
analyze the willing process as it actually appears, instead of glorify-
ing the name.   Jellinek, the latest of the systematic political
scientists, discards in one sweep all the theories of law that rest on
might because they do not satisfy his desire to view law as the
"einheitlicher Wille" of the state.   He discards all analyses of
legislation into the representation of interests because they offer
to him "schliesslich nur eine Karikatur der Wirklichkeit."   To
views which define might or force abstractly and narrowly as
direct physical activity, and which define interests as merely selfish,
his criticism will apply, though hardly to as great an extent as a
similar line of criticism would apply to views which insist on the
unified will of the state as the thing to emphasize.   But with the

progress of the reduction of thought and morality factors into the deeper-lying groups which they represent and through which alone they have a meaning, this form of criticism must disappear.

I do not deem it necessary to say anything more about the simple tribal governments in this place, for no agency of government appears in them which can properly be assimilated to the modern legislature, and I have already discussed the way in which the group interests, fixed in customary forms, and there well adjusted to one another, function through assembly, council, and chief in making the further minor adjustments which from day to day and from year to year are necessary. In later stages these governments are affected in all their parts by the class differentiation that appears, and every activity we can find of the kind that we call legislative must receive class interpretation, whether we have alternating governments, first of the rich, then of the poor classes, or whether we have a balanced government with both classes represented in it directly, all or most of the time. Indeed the very presence of one or the other of these two forms of government is susceptible of interpretation in terms of actual differences in the group formations. The Greek city-states give us many illustrations.

In Rome what has already been said of the executive in terms of the classes can be repeated almost sentence for sentence with reference to the legislating activity. At the best stage of the republic the agencies of government were the magistrates, the senate, which controlled directly all expenditures, and the three assemblies, the concilium plebis, the comitia centuriata, and the comitia tributa. Any one of the assemblies had full power to legislate, but no one of them could have been called a legislature in the sense of our modern definitions, any more than that name would have been deserved either by the magistrates or by the senate. The assemblies included all the citizens, but differently distributed, so that the balance of power as between the classes rested differently in them, and each had the duty of choosing certain magistrates. Any one of them could be prevented from taking action, however, by some magistrate chosen by one of the others.   The barriers were stiff and the struggles harsh, but barriers gave way and struggles ended in compromise.   Under the emperors the system of jurisconsults was developed to provide adjustment of conflicts adapted to the vastly more complex society of the times, but the content of the decisions of the jurisconsults consisted of the various pressures of the groups, as much as ever the content of the governing process had been the class pressures in the days of the assemblies.

I have said enough in previous chapters as to the way in which government structures of the type of the modern legislature have been produced, or, so to speak, cast up, by the pressures of classes. If we take these legislative bodies as they stand today, we shall find in all of them group oppositions which form both body and soul of their activity.   In the present German Empire the Bundesrath serves to equilibrate the pressures of the various states that make up the empire.   In the Reichstag all sorts of groups and classes of the population are represented, though not on a basis properly proportional to their strength outside the government, if a counting of heads were the test.   But there are more important tests of strength than that.   The adjustment of oppositions through the Reichstag is not the main technique of adjustment in the German Empire, but nevertheless it is important enough, and there is not an issue nor a set of issues raised in the political field, which is not fought and settled on a basis of group strength under the given technique.   It is the same with the issues of colonialism and tariff as with social questions.

While the German Reichstag is a transition form between the legislature of the older type which represented set class interests against the monarch and the later type in which the whole process of mediating all the groups of the nation is found, the French legislature is clearly of the later type.   Its activities as carried on through the cabinet give us a much better showing of the group pressures of the country than do the activities of the Reichstag taken all alone.   Whether the fight is over the octroi on wine in an effort to strike at the consumption of absinthe and other liqueurs, or whether it is anti-clericalism, the dominance of the stronger interests appears in every case. It is as foolish to state the former of the two issues I have mentioned as a temperance movement in and for itself, as it is to state the latter issue as an "atheistic" movement. The whole group formation must be taken into account in order properly to interpret what is happening. In the anti-clerical struggle the strength of the two sides has been tested over and over again in elections, in parliamentary votes, in cabinet changes, and in both hidden and open splits within the cabinet, and the progress of the adjustment of the interests corresponds closely to the manifested strength.

If we turn now to England we find the Parliament composed of two bodies, one of which is still a class representative, and as such comparatively very weak, for it has little strength apart from that of the class behind it. The House of Lords has maintained its existence solely by yielding its demands or shading them down to what its strength has justified. Its very existence like its policies depends on the same process of group struggles, and if it does not yield in time of stress it will be ended or mended to suit the needs of the case. Representing primarily a huge land-holding interest— one-fifth or one-fourth of all the land of the kingdom—it is ultra-conservative in all matters affecting directly or indirectly its land rents and its related perquisites, but it is apt to be alarmingly liberal in matters which are opposed primarily by manufacturing or commercial interests.

The House of Commons on the contrary is the dominant organ of government because in it all sorts of interest groupings gain expression, or, at least, have an agency through which to gain expression. Its adjustments, once registered, will be very much closer to the balances of pressures outside of Parliament than adjustments registered by the House of Lords can in general be. It is true that its personnel has been mainly professional and commercial, but the party system, as organized in the House itself and outside, has served to make such a membership act as mediator between the interest groups of the country, rather than as a narrow class representative. If the labor party enters in force, and if the other parties break down into political groups in the current parliamentary sense, that will be a change of technique itself brought about by group pressures, but will not affect the process in the phase of it which I am describing in this chapter. How even such an issue as that of the pay of members of Parliament is decided on a group basis will be readily recognized at the mere mention of the labor members.

The British cabinet, whether in its executive or in its legislative aspects, whether regarded in its dominating or in its subordinated aspects with reference to the House, is part of the technique through which this interest process plays. The cabinet leads the Parliament, and leads its party, and leads the country, but in each case is part of the mechanism for the adjustment of group pressures.

In this brief sketch of the working of the group process through a few typical legislatures I have said little or nothing about the idea and theory activities which are always present. My further illustration will be taken in somewhat more detail from the United States, but even yet I must postpone the fuller consideration of the various talking activities and the real facts for which they stand to a later chapter in which I shall consider political parties independently.

Taking our American federal legislature as a specialized governmental agency on the lines of its personnel and its form of control (that is, in this case, its manner of election), we find it consisting of two houses. If the analysis were made on the lines of the customary threefold division of "powers," the president would have to be added as a third branch of the legislating agency, but for the reasons already indicated that is not the best point of approach to the phenomena.

When the Congress was constructed by the constitutional convention there was an interest grouping on a locality basis which was exceptionally active. I refer to the states with their jealousies, and especially to the opposition between the large states and the small states. We had there a genuine interest grouping, in the sense that these interests cut deep enough to force themselves far along the lines of activity at the time. This interest grouping worked itself out in that phase of the organization of the Senate which gives an equal number of senators to each state. This characteristic was clinched into the Senate so firmly that there it remains to this day and there it will remain indefinitely, although there have been so few activities in the actually working government which have shown group opposition along large-state, small-state lines, that I cannot call to mind a single illustration. The system of two senators to each state survives as a technical method of organization because it has not yet been enough of a nuisance to make it become the focal point of group oppositions strong enough to bear down the difficulties in the way of abolishing it.

The division of the Congress into two houses was a projection into the federal field of the habitual legislative organization of the colonies. In the colonies it had been partly a projection of the English organization, and partly an outgrowth of colonial class lines such as those between the proprietors and the emigrants. In Britain it grew out of class divisions, in the colonies it was sustained by the usually less marked interest groups, and in the federal Constitution it was a projection of the same organization, certainly not in contradiction to the group organization of the population, and probably directly commanded by the split of interest groups; though just to what extent it is to be attributed to positive interest groups at the time, and to what extent to a projection of habit, is a matter for exact study, not for the passing of a personal judgment.

The statement of the result in terms of theory at the time was that the Senate was to represent the states, and the House the "people," with the more or less express addition that the Senate would give the dominating planters of the South and merchants of the North a stronghold in the government. The manner of electing senators through the mediation of the state legislatures must be connected with the fact that a high property qualification then existed for membership in state legislatures. To state the opposition as one between wealth and not-wealth is too superficial. The wealth requirements were technical means of keeping rule in the hands of certain group interests, not to be exactly identified with wealth *per se*.   In the lower house the members were at the start elected in some states by districts and in others by general tickets.   The method varied in accordance with the need the states felt for strong expression of some particular state interest.   When Congress discussed the subject at length prior to the legislation of 1842, the states using the general ticket were mainly in the South. The establishment of the district system over the whole land may today be connected with the absence of any peculiar state interests, the districts themselves being artificial except from the point of view of party interests.

Now the story of the workings of the legislature, of the varying aggressiveness of the two houses, of the way the lower house took control of the presidency and then lost that control together with much of its own importance to political parties organized with machines and conventions, is well enough known.   It is most commonly pictured in its broad outlines as the increasing power of "the people" in the government for one long period, and then of the increasing power of great industries over the people through the party organizations.   But such characterizations are far too broad.   They have indeed a greater measure of truth than a picture in terms of equality and progressive inequality, but they need to be broken down into more exactly defined interest groups. To do that is not the present task.   But one thing may at least be noted.   With our fixed system, resting on a rarely summoned agency, the constitutional convention, for formal change, we have been compelled to function through agencies susceptible of comparatively slight structural changes; and for the most part, instead of continuously modeling a system of government to meet our needs, we have watched our interest groups play through the different agencies in balance with one another, shifting their weight now to this, now to that, in order to make progress.   We have therefore registered comparatively few changes in the appearance of the three constitutional agencies of government, but we have added a new agency to them outside the Constitution, and have twisted now one of them now another more in their temporary than in their permanent workings.   Even in the Civil War, in which a class split cut far down toward the roots of our social life, we only brought about a temporary exaltation of the presidency, and if legislation later followed to bind the hands of the presidency in the matter of removals from office, that too has disappeared without leaving a permanent impress.

We have then today both House and Senate organized on a locality basis, which itself represents actual interest groups which at one time existed. But these locality groups, so far as they function through the government, have to a great extent long since become of trifling importance, and they exist now as technique, rather than as content of the governmental process. It is true that a locality group, as composed of so many persons in a neighborhood, does often present itself with a definite set of demands upon the government, but as we shall later see, these fixed sets of demands are rather to be regarded as the formal product of this "artificial" locality grouping, than as the causes or the underlying warrant of it. The substance of their desires is mainly in the nature of spoils—federal buildings, river improvements, jobs— rather than of activities involving policies or legislation proper. It is true that in some phases of the tariff disputes underlying locality interests show themselves with vigor, that the negro question raises the South against the North, and that economic questions may sometimes bring the West into line against the East, while the seaboard will have separate, though rarely conflicting, interests, as compared with the inland regions. Perhaps the cities may have interests in the federal governmental process which conflict with the interests of rural districts, though certainly so long as a city like New York finds no need to secure other than spoils representation in Congress, it does not seem probable. But whatever these underlying locality interest groupings are, they correspond very roughly indeed with the actual locality organization of the Congress.

This needs further consideration. The senators come two from each state, but by a further arrangement it is common to have one from each end of the state, or perhaps one from the big city, if any, and the other from the "country." Each senator "represents" his part of the state to the extent of distributing jobs and looking out for appropriations of local interest, but nothing more.   The senators of the South are keen on the negro question, and those of New England on the tariff.   A few other group lines can be traced but for the most part all the senators are free for taking positions on public questions entirely apart from any special locality interest.

It is true that "policy movements," as, for example, a movement for railroad legislation, will be more advanced among the people of one part of the country than of another, from time to time, but with our present journalism these differences are much less than they appear to be, and certainly the time difference from a locality point of view between the front and the tail of such movement is materially less than the length of a senatorial term; so that senators hardly give locality representation on this basis.

In the House, despite the election of the congressmen from individual districts, there is very little real locality representation, apart from the apportionment of federal "plums,"   If all the congressmen should go home to their districts to "test the feeling" of the voters, when they came together again and made their reports, the listener would allow much more for the " personal factor " in the observations of the congressmen than for the locality factor. And he would be more surprised to find the congressmen from one group of states in practical agreement as to the voters' attitude in their section and in opposition to the congressmen from another group of states, than he would be to find congressmen of certain non-local affiliations differing in a body from congressmen of other non-local affiliations—barring, of course, a few of the issues mentioned heretofore as of sectional nature.

What we have therefore is a collection of congressmen and senators, coming from locality groups, which in comparison with the powerful interest groups that function through Congress are of a formal nature, answering more as a technical means of election than as any real embodiment of the strong existing lines of pressure. The groups that most prominently work through the federal legislature are largely occupational, or complexes of occupations, or they are varieties of peace and order and self-protection groupings, which differ little throughout the territory of the nation. It would be a matter for exact study as to how frequently locality groupings manifest themselves in the congressional votes; and while my own tests show surprisingly little of it, they are but tests, not proof. The general situation however, is evident enough.

In a condition of this kind the control of the representatives by the voters is usually weak, and it is not a sign of degeneracy in the character of the people, but rather a phenomenon to be normally expected, that in ordinary times the excrescence factors which grow out of the local political subdivisions often count for more with the voters than other factors on which no direct constituency test can be had. In this I am simply stating the fact of observation, not taking sides about it, or suggesting anything better.

We find then that the positive interest groupings which seek expression in Congress turn to the party organizations to mediate it, and by our two-party system we have a great framework erected, which holds all the localities together in a tolerably coherent system. The discussion of the methods by which certain of the interest groups have freer play through the parties than others must be reserved for another chapter. Here I wish, for what remains, mainly to illustrate the manner of the appearance of the pressures in Congress and to show how the enactment of laws can most adequately be stated in terms of such pressures.

Log-rolling is a term of opprobrium. This is because it is used mainly with reference to its grosser forms. But grossness as it is used in this connection merely means that certain factors which we regard as of great importance are treated by the legislator as of small importance and traded off by him for things which we regard as a mess of pottage, but which he regards as the main business of his activity. Log-rolling is, however, in fact, the most characteristic legislative process. When one condemns it "in principle," it is only by contrasting it with some assumed pure public spirit which is supposed to guide legislators, or which ought to guide them, and which enables them to pass judgment in Jovian calm on that which is best "for the whole people." Since there is nothing which is best literally for the whole people, group arrays being what they are, the test is useless, even if one could actually find legislative judgments which are not reducible to interest-group activities.   And when we have reduced the legislative process to the play of group interests, then log-rolling, or give and take, appears as the very nature of the process.   It is compromise, not in the abstract moral form, which philosophers can sagely discuss, but in the practical form with which every legislator who gets results through government is acquainted.   It is trading.   It is the adjustment of interests.

Where interests must seek adjustment without legislative forms, if they cannot get recognition through the ruling class or monarch, they have no recourse but to take matters in their own hands and proceed to open violence of war.   When they have compromised and made adjustments to such extent that their further process can be carried forward in a legislature, they proceed to war on each other, with the killing and maiming omitted.   It is a battle of strength, along lines of barter.   The process is similar process, but with changes in the technique.

There never was a time in the history of the American Congress when legislation was conducted in any other way.   One has but to recall the struggle over the location of the federal capital, and how the financial measures of Hamilton for the assuming of the state debts were carried by trading votes with the advocates of the Washington site.   Jefferson was a party to this "deal," and he was an expert at similar legislative work, as one can see in an interesting way, for example, in the story of the wire-pulling which resulted in the creation of the University of Virginia and the selection of its site.   Nowadays tariff legislation is plain barter, based on relative strength.   Our river-and-harbor and our public-buildings bills are carried not by any standards of genuine national needs, but by apportioning the favors to various states so as to secure the requisite number of votes.   From legislation in which two factions, as say farmers and grain dealers, contend, each giving way to some extent to the other, all the way along the line to the plain barter of cash appropriations or to the barter of a public building against a vote for a reform in the law, the process is the same at bottom. There is this great practical difference between the various cases, however, that some of them are nuisances and some of them are not; that some of them rouse against them very wide but very weak interests, and that from time to time the nuisance becomes so great that these wide, weak interests strengthen themselves till they can abolish the particular kind of deal in question. The wide weak groups turn the technical means into content of activity, and fight along the indicated lines.

Of course along with all this log-rolling in all its forms goes a great activity of reasoning, theorizing, and argument, and at times the argument seems to be the cause of all that is happening. In this latter case as in the others it merely provides a technical agency for the transaction. The difference is not in the trading process, but rather in the particular kinds of interests that are gaining expression; or sometimes in the stages of the process, whether fundamental oppositions are being adjusted, or whether details are being filled in. I hardly need add that in assimilating these various legislative processes, I am not defending any which have proved themselves such nuisances as to arouse group opposition.

There is another misunderstanding to which I may make myself more liable, and a word here to ward it off, even though it is mere repetition of what I have said in earlier chapters, is useful. While I am making this discussion in terms of group struggles, there is implied all the time the habit background in which the struggle proceeds. That is, there are limits to the technique of the struggle, this involving also limits to the group demands, all of which is solely a matter of empirical observation for the given time and country. Or, in other words, when the struggle proceeds too harshly at any point there will become insistent in the society a group more powerful than either of those involved which tends to suppress the extreme and annoying methods of the groups in the primary struggle. It is within the embrace of these great lines of activity that the smaller struggles proceed, and the very word struggle has meaning only with reference to its limitations.

Suppose, now, we take a piece of legislation like the statehood bill passed in the spring of 1906. It provided for the admission of Oklahoma and Indian Territory as one state, and of Arizona and New Mexico as another. If we sought our knowledge of what happened from the accounts in the various newspapers and from the *Congressional Record* and the committee reports, we should find in addition to a very large amount of reasoning as to why the territories should or should not be combined into two states, some personal material about Senator Beveridge's long study of the situation, similar facts about the way in which other members of Congress "made up their minds," a great mass of objectively stated facts about the territories, put forth as the basis upon which minds were to be "made up," and some occasional accounts of the activities of lobbies of Arizona mine-owners or other persons.

If we should proceed to reduce all this information to order, we should soon find ourselves compelled to infer a great deal about the meaning of different parts of it, or else go outside it or rather through and behind it to get its value in the legislative process. If we could not do this, we should have to wait for the outcome of the voting in the two houses of Congress to get an idea of relative strengths, and even then we should have but a superficial understanding of the forces.

Now in all this material there is nothing from the stump speeches to the votes on final reading of the bill that cannot be reduced to what it stands for in the term of groups of men, and there is no other way to get a unified picture of the whole process except by reducing it to such groups. I do not pretend here to state them completely, much less to apportion relative weight to the various groupings, but only to indicate, by way of illustration, how such a problem must be approached.

First of all there were the locality groups, the four territories. Next there were the organized party interests, Democratic and Republican, having a special eye to the senatorships to be created. Then came the Arizona mine-owners, possessing certain present privileges, and fearing their loss. Also there were transportation interests directly involved, because of the probability of controlling the senators who would be chosen from the more westerly of the two proposed states.   There was also a wider grouping of industrial interests looking toward a similar end, and finally a very widespread but comparatively weak interest of Americans in avoiding the creation of "rotten-borough" states, which heightened at spots into a more vigorous opposition to the introduction into the Senate of more "corporation senators" than were necessary.   To describe these groups I am using loose language in compromise with current methods of speech, but I have solely in view the group activities which were forging ahead through the political process.

Oklahoma and Indian Territory as locality groups quickly proved themselves weak.   Oklahoma had in rough figures only one Indian to thirty whites, while Indian Territory had one Indian to six whites.   There was some vigorous leadership of the locality groups in both of the territories, but it made little headway.   No strong allies were found, and the local demonstrations succumbed easily to the pressure of the Republican party interests, backed up by the wider anti-rotten-borough interest.

In Arizona and New Mexico the case was very different. Roughly, the proportion of Spanish-Americans including "greasers" in Arizona was 25 per cent. or more of the population, and in New Mexico it was 40 per cent.   But here, although the Republican party interest in preventing double statehood with double sets of senators was even stronger than in the preceding case, there were strong allies for the separation movement, and the locality interests presented themselves as the central point of the whole dispute. Just how much appearance and how much reality there was in this prominence of the locality interests would be a matter for exact research, but the fact that the group interests involved were very much larger and very much stronger than the locality interests is well enough established.

Now in Congress the issue was fought out on several levels. I will roughly name three of them.   First the investigation made by Senator Beveridge and his committee; secondly the argumentation, and thirdly the lobbying.

When the committee filled itself full of facts about the population, the resources, and the industries of Arizona and New Mexico, about the probable working of government over the larger area of the two territories combined, or about the relation between the territorial population and the population of the older states, it was doing nothing more than making itself the medium through which the various group interests could state themselves.   When it made its report recommending joint statehood it set forth the adjustment between these various group interests to the best of its representative ability.   Had this committee been the final, instead of a preliminary, stage in the law-enactment process it might not have reported as it did.   At any rate, it allowed a different group pressure to dominate in the report it made than was actually able to dominate through the whole Congress process.   It reflected the Republican party, anti-rotten-borough phase of the struggle, rather than the locality interest, Democratic party, mine-owners' and corporation-interest phase.   The committee members represented directly certain group interests, and other group interests were presented to them by men who appeared before them, but its findings were passed along to Congress where all these same group factors could express themselves in more elaborate ways.

Now, once out of the committee's hands, the argumentative stage, which was active enough before, took on a great accession of fervor.   At once we found discussion groups reflecting all the elements of the process through a technique peculiarly their own. We heard unlimited talk about the right of the people (of the people of the territories, that is) to govern themselves.   States'-rights methods of phrasing came back in swarms.   The changes were rung on rotten boroughs, wicked greasers, corrupt senators, scheming mine-owners, and any quantity of other points.   Just so far as these arguments reflected group positions, and served to develop them and make clear the lines of the contest, so far they may be said to have counted in the result.   That is they counted inasmuch as they furnished a technique for bringing the group struggle to a more adequate settlement.   But so far as the argumentation got away from existing group interests, so far, for example, as it dwelt on states'-rights elements, we can assuredly set it down as having been almost meaningless in the issue, except as a crude

symbol.   I do not mean to make this remark apply to any possible
use of the "states'-rights" argument, but only to its use in this case;
and this, no matter how vociferously some legislator may have
asserted he voted as he did because he believed in letting the will
of the people rule, or in letting state sovereignty prevail, or in
letting local government decide.   If we cannot reduce an argument
to group interest on its face, we may know we can reduce it to
similar interests indirectly, and make it appear but a mask for
those interests.   There is just one way in which such an argument
as that of states' rights could count directly today in the settlement
of such an issue as the one before us, and that is, if off on the out-
skirts of Congress somewhere a member or two could be found who
reflected factors in the national life which as group interests have
by this time become very feeble, and which bob up here and there
in the way we call accidental; and if, such members being found,
the vote in Congress was so close that they cast the deciding ballots,
then the argument would have direct meaning—that is it would
have directly indicated a group interest, and that group interest
under the particular circumstances would have been an important
factor, readily and exactly traceable, in the result.   But even then
its effect would prove only transitory, as future events would
show.

Finally from the argumentative process, let us turn to the
lobbying.   Underneath the flow of oratory, the group interests
were pressing toward the adjustment in Congress, and pulling and
hauling on the votes of the members to get representation.   Other
interest groups irrupted into this particular struggle, and by the
log-rolling process diverted some of the votes one way or the other.
In such cases we sometimes find a party organization interest
strong enough to force a caucus and make the party interest dominate, or again we find the party interest too weak to suppress all
other group interests, and we have insurgents to consider.   We
might perhaps trace the process through technical methods border-
ing on the forbidden, and in the end we might find the technique
becoming more important than the original content, so that a new
grouping would have to turn upon it and ruthlessly attack it.

Out of it all we come in the end to the voting, and there if our study has been full enough we can trace back the group interests, and even on the rough votes, each a crude lump of pressures, we can make our analysis with fair accuracy.

I have sketched this bit of legislation, not exactly as it happened, but in broad outlines, without tracing the lines of activity back very far, either into party organizations or into the "public-opinion" activities.   But it is enough if I have made clear how the coarsest phenomena, so to speak, the crudest, largest, broadest, are really the most important in social interpretation, and how instead of trying to reduce them into fine theoretical elements, we should always aim to reduce the fine-spun theories into them, if we want to get on the track of a reliable interpretation.   Such a bit of legislation could conceivably be worked down into its finest details, that is, into the smallest group pressures that affected it in its progress, but that is no more necessary in the analysis of government than in any other scientific work.   We need to know with utmost precision how the group process goes on, but we do not need to know in the case of any particular legislative act every single group that was involved, any more than we need to know in the case of a particular bodily organ every detail of the pressures inside the body which make it take on its peculiar size and form, or in the case of a particular man's muscle every detail of the exercising that brought it to its given structure and strength.   Our most powerful microscope must be directed on the feeling-thinking activity in the relations of its processes, but not on every minute particular of the individual elements which have given a particular social phenomenon its particular shape at its particular time.   The outlines of such concrete interpretations are, after all, the only thing that we can handle or make useful.

If instead of taking a single isolated project of law we should take some general tendency of legislation across federal and state governments, as, for instance, that concerning the free and compulsory education of the common schools, we should find the interpretation in terms of groups to be even simpler to make, when we once got on its track.   Education laws in this country, whether

they have forbidden education to black slaves, or tended to provide
education for free blacks, whether they have extended the range
of the common schools for the whites, or at times compromised
with parochial or other private schools, have all expressed at every
stage the group pressures of the society as they actually exist. We
have popular education where an efficient demand for it exists,
and that efficient demand is a group demand; and in studying
the process of government all that we need to do is to locate it where
it is. If our investigation took us behind the governmental process
and we wished to find the "causes" for the presence of that effective group demand, we should here as everywhere else have to
look for them in the relations between the various group activities
of many kinds actually observable in the given society, the influences of city life being by no means among the least. So far as
we could connect the various group activities by analysis and
comparison, we should have material for an honest social interpretation, vastly less pretentious and also vastly more dependable and useful than the current interpretation in terms of
ideas.

If we turn from the federal government to the cities, we shall
find plenty of illustrations of the group process through the council,
we shall find nothing that is not susceptible of group statement,
and we shall find that we get much more coherence by such statement than in any other way.

I watched, for example, not long ago the process of the city
of Chicago in doubling its saloon license fee, and in setting a limit
on the number of saloons in proportion to the population. The
saloons had fairly free scope in the city. The Sunday-closing
statute had been for decades ignored, and nothing more than a
small, though occasionally noisy, group demand for Sunday closing
could be found. A one-o'clock closing hour had succeeded a
nominal midnight closing hour some time previously and was
fairly well enforced except in the districts appropriated by vice.
The saloon interests were strongly organized, mainly with reference
to contests in the state legislature against local-option bills, but

also for legal proceedings against municipal administrative measures.   Normally a proposal to increase the license fee even by a small percentage, would have passed unnoticed, whether made in the council or out of it.   That was because the saloon group, with which the breweries as owners of a large portion of the saloons must be joined, was strong and alert, and no effective opposition to it could be found.   But there came a time when a number of atrocious crimes had been committed close together, most of which were traceable, or supposed to be traceable, to saloon loafers, and a very strong, if somewhat hysterical, discussion group directed against crime was formed.   This formulated itself more definitely in an opposition to the excessive number of saloons, many of them living a hand-to-mouth existence with the lowest kind of patronage.   At the same time the city was feeling acutely its chronic shortage of revenue;   or in other words, the city aldermen, under pressure from a lot of group interests which demanded improvements of one kind and another for which funds were lacking, were in their representative capacity especially eager for more income.   This pressure for revenue, itself the result of a complex of group pressures combined with the group antagonism to saloon abuses, took shape in a proposal to increase the license fee from $500 to $1,000. The fight, once started, was bitter, and it was not ended till after a primary election had given the aldermen some opportunity to test on a big scale the sentiment of their wards.   In the process there developed a distinct grouping of the people of Chicago along locality lines.   One set of wards as measured by majorities stood, we may say, "for more revenue and fewer crimes." Another set stood "for no reduction in our saloon facilities."   The districts were well defined on the map, with certain wavering wards where one alderman might be found on each side, and where each alderman took a risk of representing his constituents wrongly.   The result was a victory for the $1,000 license without compromise; and further legislation which as a compromise suited fairly well almost all parties followed directly, providing that no additional licenses should be issued beyond those in existence, till the proportion of saloons to population had been almost cut in half.   As a matter of fact the event proved that the existing number of saloons was but little reduced, and therefore that the hard fight for "the poor man's beer" had been waged on lines which in their verbal statement we would call "false." They were very real group fighting-lines, nevertheless, and among the realities of the political process. The way the aldermanic votes were distributed, the way the leadership in the fight was assigned, the way the issue developed into life, the way the occupation and the law-and-order interest groups formed, and the way finally that the locality groupings took shape at the climax, all send us to the study of masses of men for their analysis and adequate statement. The way arguments were made in terms of liberty, individualism, morality, decency, freedom, paternalism, and so on, all send us to the same kind of factors, if we want to get sure ground for our feet.

Every franchise grant given by a city is similarly a question of interests, whether some small compact interest group seeking financial profit succeeds by a technique of bribery, or whether an aroused, excited group of abused citizens paying a high price for poor transportation facilities turns the scale in the opposite direction. And from the franchises of great public concern, if we descend to the little franchises, the special privileges, and exemptions which are bestowed by councils on individual citizens we have the same thing. There is not an improper favor granted by a careless or corrupt city council which is not given as part of a system which involves the group organization behind the individual alderman, the group organization of the aldermen with each other, and over against it, gathering force perhaps for its suppression, the group organization of the non-favored. A free peddlers' permit which presents itself first as a personal transaction between the peddler and the alderman, and second as a personal transaction between the alderman and either the mayor or "aldermanic courtesy," as the case may be, is in reality a product of much pressure of conflicting interests and a stage in the appearance of other interests which will have their say in the ultimate fate of the custom of granting such permits.

I will leave the subject of interests in legislation at this point, in order to discuss the operation of interests through the judiciary; but only after the political parties have been studied with reference to the interests which function through them can we begin to have a complete picture of the legislative process in its full extent.

CHAPTER XVI

THE PRESSURE OF INTERESTS IN THE JUDICIARY

The storied judge whose reputation was that of a Solomon till one day he incautiously gave reasons for his judgment, has been reincarnated in a thousand forms; and he has deserved it, for he is not a jest but a truth. Told of an individual judge under circumstances to which the method of speech that puts things in terms of reasons most adequately applies, the story is indeed a jest, but the farther we get away from the individual judge and the nearer we get to a large view of the judicial process the more closely does it reflect not only the truth, but the whole truth. Through reasoning much of the process works, but the reasons are of the process, not its directors.

The organized adjustment of disputes between man and man can be traced up from private vengeance, through clan vengeance, intra-clan adjudications by the assembly of the clansmen or by the council of the elders or by the chief, and adjudication by a monarch or by his lieutenants, to adjudications by organized courts more or less sharply separated from the other agencies of government. The initiative of the individual which was itself the very substance of the rendering of justice at first is seen to subdue itself into a technical operation in the judicial process, and finally in criminal matters to yield place almost entirely to the initiative of an agent of the government. The penalty which was blind vengeance and then "limb for limb" in early stages is seen to transform itself into cash compensation, and finally in criminal cases is no longer paid to the injured party but to the state. The method of proof is seen to pass through many stages from the strength of the armed man and the religious ordeal, to the sworn opinion of fellow-citizens, and finally to the testimony of witnesses to the facts. And in the process the simple direct "lump" situations which once presented themselves for adjustment have grown enormously complex and elaborate, showing many forms of contact with many phases of life. In other words, a complex of group interactions has developed which has found a more or less accurate representation in law as theory in contrast to law as crude reactions.

These sentences of course make no pretense to furnishing a sketch of juridical evolution. I write them merely to indicate the range of phenomena within which we can see the group process at work, and with reference to which, from beginning to end, the group method of statement will be found most adequate for scientific purposes.

We may begin with a society in which the injured man takes his own vengeance. By contrast with our own complex law-administering structure one may say it is anarchy. But that is only a manner of denunciation from a strictly group point of view. In fact the primitive man who seeks his own vengeance while his fellows look on does it in fairly regular channels. The character of the offenses against which he reacts has been determined largely by past group process. The manner of seeking vengeance has already become definite. The spectators play their part like a simple public opinion. And if the limits are overstepped there may appear a new seeking of vengeance to check the encroachment. The whole process goes on in a great background of definitely formed custom. This is true in the simplest society, but it is still more true where an ordeal of battle is carefully regulated, and where preliminaries must be gone through before the contest. Even in the simplest case we have "justice" for the outcome. The issue is decided in a way which we call crude, but which nevertheless takes up into itself something of the strength of many men.* It is not a mere figure of a speech, but a very real fact that the strength of the group behind the avenger arms his muscle, and that the culprit is weakened from the same source. The outcome will not ever answer to everybody's views of justice, but then no outcome in any adjudication, even under our most delicate methods in the most favorable circumstances, will answer that test.

When clan vengeance is inflicted upon an outsider or upon the outsider's clan, we have a process varying from the case of individual vengeance mainly in the greater elaboration of the executing agency. The interests in action are substantially the same, but the common clan action gives them a fuller expression, both by giving a more complete possibility of vengeance to the directly injured man, and by allowing the connected interest groupings of the clansmen to control the process more precisely from beginning to end.

As viewed from the standpoint of government in the narrower sense there is a great development, now, when we pass to judicial process in which a third party appears to mediate between the contestants, that is, in which a relatively disinterested agency of government appears. In the broader view of government no sharp break appears, because all the interest groupings that were actively present before are present still, and they are still predominant in what is happening. Just as was the case when in the transition to clan vengeance a new technique for the expression of these interests was given, so now a better technique appears—better, that is, for the changed circumstances. The significant fact in the new device is that it is a differentiated governing agency of the general kind which we observe all the way up the scale of social development. As such it permits a fuller expression of the interest groupings, or in other words it permits additional interests to come to effective expression, or to more effective expression.

Without going into details we can easily see how new interest groupings on new planes can effectuate a transition from private vengeance to mediated vengeance. The society becoming more thickly settled, with more persistent routine industrial operations, may be in a continual turmoil through the operations of the private vengeance system. Then there may develop an interest grouping bent on suppressing the turmoil, and the outcome may be the mediating body. We can see just this process all the way up the course of judicial development, and we can watch it today in more regions than one. For example, we today have no established mediating bodies between nations. We nevertheless have an international law which controls, in fact, the processes of war, much as the environing custom controlled the processes of private vengeance. We have the Hague tribunal resting on a great cross-nation interest grouping, which feels strongly the injuries of war and is directed against that technical method of adjustment, making it the content of its opposition, and tending to substitute for it a different method of adjustment, for which the Hague tribunal dimly indicates the outlines. Interests on the old lines are present and will continue to be present, but a new interest grouping forces itself into the field and insists on modifying the process of adjustment. And similarly with regard to industrial disputes between employers and employees. Even when they are carried on in accordance with law and simple moral standards, we find them making so much disturbance for so many of the people that they arouse a new interest grouping—roughly to be styled the "consumers"—bent on suppressing the nuisance. And whether compulsory industrial arbitration becomes established or not, will depend, not on reasoning—although mediated through reasoning—but primarily on whether the nuisances become violent enough to compel a remedy. Anybody with an eye keen enough to analyze the interest groupings as they actually will make themselves felt can predict on broad lines the outcome of the movement for industrial arbitration—and nobody else can.

Now, to return to our mediating body, we may find the case of the assembly of the people passing judgment between two members. Perhaps one contestant will be banished with or without formal act of the assembly. Perhaps the payment of compensation will be imposed. But however informal or however formal the process, what we have is what we would have had previously under the personal-vengeance system, only with a more complete expression of the wider group interests of the community, which specify themselves at the given time and place so noticeably that we are justified in calling them new group interests, or group interests on a new plane.

If the work of rendering judgment is handed over by the community to a body of elders or chosen men, that fact will be the direct outcome of such group factors as the changing modes of living, including the number of members in the society, the manners of working, the distribution of the people, whether scattered or crowded, and whether permanently together or sometimes broken into hunting or fighting parties, and so forth. But the decision of the elders will have for its elements the same material that functioned through private vengeance, or clan vengeance, or assembly edict, as the case may be.

Now, of course, it is possible that from time to time we shall find a court of elders doing its work in a way to stir up opposition. This condition will most usually be one phase of class dominance in the community. Whenever the elders do not let all the interests function through them, when they get warped in their representative capacity, then inevitably comes resistance, which may in the given time or place be sufficient to produce a change in the system of administering justice. Perhaps the chief or kinglet will take over the work. It will be for the better functioning of the interest groups through him, with respect to their strengths. If "abuses" later arise through his administration, they also must be interpreted through the interest groupings that are at work. If such abuses maintain themselves indefinitely, it is only because they represent a dominant grouping in the community or because without the king and his abuses the situation would be worse than with them, as the members of the society actually experience it; alternatives which really come to much the same thing at bottom.

Not only the form of adjudication, but also the character of the penalties and the character of the proof can easily be reduced to similar group elements.

If we turn now to the developed nation and take it in its despotic form, we are apt to find adjudication of disputes appearing as one of the perquisites of the monarchy. And yet, however widely the bribery of judges may flourish, and however much the monarchy may draw profits from administering justice, there will be a substantial substratum of work done which will be a fundamental factor in the maintenance of the governmental system of the time. Not that the despot can easily be overthrown for bad administration of justice alone, nor that he is maintained for the substantial adjudication work he does alone, but that these things count in with the rest of the operations of the monarchy, and cannot be omitted from that balancing of groups which "is" the monarchy.

Somewhere in the development we shall begin to see signs of a differentiation between judicial proceedings which are initiated by some differentiated agent of the monarch directly and those which still have as their technical start the initiative of individual citizens. Perhaps offenses against the state, analogous to our treason, will be among the first which the monarch by his agent will himself cause to be prosecuted before himself as he is organized through other agents as a court. However this be, the prosecuting official who here appears will be a representative of those underlying interests which uphold the monarchy, differentiated for this special purpose. And again, however much the monarch "abuses" his power, the fact makes no difference in the nature of the process that is going on, although it does make a big difference in his personal fate, in the fate of some of his subjects, and in the development of new and improved technique for the better mediation of the interests.

Of much greater significance than this is the fixed differentiation that comes to pass in time between the courts and the monarch in his other activities. In part we have a division of labor compelled by the mere mass of the labor, with a certain portion, namely court adjudication, standing to one side for so many purposes that it gains a relative independence from the rest of the government. It stands to one side because the interest groupings which are going through it are separated to a considerable extent from the interest groupings which are going through the rest of the government. That would not protect it from arbitrary, if occasional, interference by the monarch, and only a well-differentiated interest grouping which insists on such protection can create it and maintain it permanently, even in moderate degree. This judicial separation may appear in locality forms when it can take strong roots as it did in England, or also in central forms in which again England is the best example. When this comes about, the public prosecutor gains in importance as the representative of the rest of the government before the separated courts. The interest groupings directly

represented by the monarch may break down the separation temporarily, but the variations backward and forward must be entirely
stated in terms of these pressures, whether separately or jointly.
The jury system, the "Schöffen," the life tenure, and so forth, are
various devices adopted either by specific pressure from underlying interests, or by the specification of vague pressures by the
representative central organ of government, for the sake of giving
the judicial system the measure of independence which is demanded
for it from the other agencies of government.

When we come finally to the United States, we observe that the
very measures which have been taken, according to common
theory, to separate the judicial "power" from the executive and
legislative "powers" have actually ended by bringing about a new
confusion of the "powers," however much the agencies remain
distinct.   The unique work of American courts in overriding legis-
tures and executives on constitutional points is well enough known.
This activity places the courts—or, more properly, the supreme
courts of states and of nation—as intermediate agencies between
legislatures and executives on the one side and constitutional conventions on the other.   We have in the United States but rarely
illustrations of the executive as representative of group interests
interfering directly with the judiciary, though an organization like
Tammany Hall can knit executives and judges together in a tight
system, and President Roosevelt has recently made one or two
vigorous attempts to bully federal courts.   But we have luminous
instances of the same group pressures which operate through
executives and legislatures, operating also through supreme courts
and bringing about changes in law in a field above the legislatures,
but short of the constitutional conventions; changes which no
process of legal or constitutional reasoning will adequately mediate,
but which must be interpreted directly in terms of pressures of
group interests.   And we are clearly on the road to witnessing even
more picturesque operations of the governmental process through
our courts in this respect.   I shall proceed to give some illustration of judicial process in America, and on the basis of these illus-

trations I shall try to show more fully than I have yet done how the legal reasoning and the legal science fit into the process.

The phase of American judicial history which stands forth in greatest prominence is the work of Chief Justice Marshall, of the federal Supreme Court, in upholding and broadening the powers of the federal government. We are often told that federalist "ideas" dominated the court in this important period; and we hear elaborate discussions of the constitutional theories on the basis of which the decisions were rendered. Now it is an easy thing and by no means wrong, to draw analogies between Marshall's work and federalist policies as proclaimed by federalist leaders; and assuredly the reasonings which were set forth as underlying the great court decisions have not only a deep professional interest, but are also essential to the scientific student as pointing out to him the way to some of the knowledge he needs. But when all this is admitted, it takes us but a little way, and we shall get a great deal nearer to an adequate statement of what was taking place if we analyze the great interest groupings of the country which were then active in the fields on which jurists had to center their attention, if we observe how these interest groupings made themselves manifest in the great cases that went before the court, if we note how these phases of the life of the nation were reflected in the personalities of the justices as well as in their reasonings, and if we thus get the cases and the theories and the precedents and the people all stated in one common set of pressures, every factor in terms of the others with exact reference to what it represented in the others, and what perhaps the others represented in it. This manner of statement does not do violence at all to the possibility that had another than John Marshall held the chief justiceship for all these years, say for example an appointee of Thomas Jefferson's, our legal history, and indeed much of the rest of our history, as it is written from a surface view, would have been different. It only insists that that surface difference would not have represented a deeper-lying difference in our development. On the basis, not merely of the Marshall decisions but of all the rest of our country's history which bears on this point, we may feel sure that the interests that underlay those decisions, if they could not have gained expression through Marshall, would have gained it in some other way. The power was not in Marshall, but in the interest groups he so adequately recognized and allowed to come so smoothly and speedily to their due dominance in the government. And per contra, if the interest groupings had been actually different from Marshall's reflection of them, his decisions would have been but temporary obstacles and would have been overwhelmed, not by any virtue in some other constitutional theory or reasoning, but by the power of the underlying interests which pump all the logic into theory that theory ever obtains.

Turn now to a concrete decision of the greatest importance handed down by our Supreme Court, the Dartmouth College case, which has been generally followed by the state courts. Here was a decision which might conceivably have gone the other way; certainly there was "reasoning" enough to support either side. But it is a question, if it had been the contrary of what it was, whether a way would not have been found later on to get around the decision and make the law in effect what it actually has been. This was a land of opportunities; and among those opportunities were all those in which the investor must have preliminary dealings with the government; and it was greatly to the interest of large masses of the people that certain of these franchise opportunities should early be utilized. Too great an uncertainty in the utilization of them would have turned the investor to other fields, leaving the fields in question to lie fallow, whereby a strong interest grouping demanding the grant of charters on fixed and certain terms would have developed, and by one means or another, whether constitution-making or representative judicial insight, the certainty would have been granted. I do not mean to pass a positive opinion on this, for I do not pretend to have studied the groupings of the population well enough to do it. Be it as it may, the important thing for us here is that the time came when the opportunities, once uncertain, had become bedrocks of certainty, and when group interests began to form, this time looking not toward the utilization of those opportunities but toward the control of that utilization where injuries were being inflicted. Thereupon the precedent of the Dartmouth College case was doomed: doomed, that is, unless the interest groupings which get aid from it prove to have such actual accumulated strength that they can maintain it with all that its maintenance implies—and there is nothing in my study of the group pressures of the country to indicate this to me— or unless, after the precedent has been broken down, new group interests develop for its restoration in some modified form. This work is now under way, though indeed not far advanced as yet. Around the country one can find in many state supreme courts decisions which after much prying have found methods, or rather excuses, for opening loopholes to public control at one point and another. Even in the federal Supreme Court progress in this direction has been made. I do not mean that the tendency has reached a point at which an overthrow of the precedent "in principle" has occurred; but that the position of corporations before the law is in fact rapidly being changed; while at the same time strong minority opinions against even the so-called "principle" are ever more frequently handed down. Just how far the work will be done through the courts and how far through constitutional conventions is a matter of detail, but that it can all be done through the courts is certain.

The slavery decisions of the Supreme Court are instances of pressures that have come into the judicial agency of our government in bulk, so to speak, rather than in neat, well-tied parcels of legal argument. So again, are the legal-tender decisions. The income-tax decision will not improbably face its Waterloo, not because of any growth in brain power or development of reasoning ability among the lawyers of this country, nor because of any greater comprehension of "truth," but because of the shifting of group interests as recognized by Supreme Court members and reflected by them in their decisions. So again it is not an impossibility that if the federal legislature decides to regulate life insurance —it refused to take up this task a short time ago "on constitutional grounds," a phrase which masks instead of adequately representing the nature of its decision—the Supreme Court will permit it, Paul vs. Virginia and all the other cases to the contrary notwithstanding. There will be nothing to this but interest groups functioning through the court, and in no other manner of speech can it adequately be described.

I will content myself with one more illustration on this point. Early in 1906 the Supreme Court at Washington handed down a decision with reference to the asserted " ninety-nine-year rights " of the Chicago traction companies, which the city of Chicago was contesting in the hope not so much of overthrowing them as of limiting their application. I have not the slightest hesitation in asserting, and I think few persons who know the case will deny, that ten years ago the court, though it had been composed of the identical justices, would have yielded the companies their claim.[1] Now, however, the decision was in favor of the city and some seventy million dollars' worth of franchise rights, more or less, were practically confiscated at the stroke of a pen, to the very great advantage of everybody concerned except those who lost their respectable piece of plunder. Now it took most considerable ingenuity in legal reasoning for a line of argument to be developed whereby this decision could be justified. Most of the ordinary legal argument went the other way, and few of the really substantial lawyers on the city's side dreamed they would get such a victory. But they urged their case most vigorously, they pushed to the front before the Supreme Court their advocates most learned in the voice of the people rather than in the rules of the law, and they allowed " public opinion " all over the country about all sorts of related topics, such as municipal ownership, government ownership, wicked capitalists, socialism, and what not to speak for them. And the result was that the Supreme Court laid down a rule of strict construction so infin-

---

[1] A somewhat similar remark upon another decision has attracted my attention since the above was written. In the *Atlantic Monthly*, December, 1906, M. M. Bigelow writes: "The Supreme Court of the United States decides that a corporation cannot hide itself behind the plea of self-incrimination, when called upon to produce its letters and documents. This no doubt is gain; there are lawyers who think it doubtful if the question would have been so decided a few years ago. The judicial indicator is beginning to turn to the pressure of the greater social force, the public."

itely strict that it not only chopped off collateral benefits but that it annihilated the very grant which the legislature had most expressly granted, which the governor had most vehemently and unsuccessfully attacked with his veto, which capitalists had most confidently invested their money in, and which had seemed the very bedrock of the whole situation between city and traction companies.

In this I am not criticizing the Supreme Court, much less insinuating anything against it or any of its members. On the contrary, speaking as a citizen with definite group affiliations, that decision gave me such intense pleasure that I was quite sure we had "a Daniel come to judgment." I do not mean that the justices consciously forced the law to fit the case, nor that they showed any traces whatever of demagogism or of subserviency to popular clamor. Quite the contrary. I am convinced that they all, or at any rate most of them, acted with the most single-hearted desire— if one must use such phrasing—to render justice in strict accordance with precedent. What I do set forth about them is that so far from being a sort of legal machine, they are a functioning part of this government, responsive to the group pressures within it, representative of all sorts of pressures, and using their representative judgment to bring these pressures to balance, not indeed in just the same way, but on just the same basis, that any other agency of government does, and that in this Chicago case they let a changing weight of group interests come very clearly to expression. And I do set forth further that in the legal arguments on neither side was there any merit or weight in bringing about this decision, save as they held the mass of group pressures in compact form for discussion purposes, as they let great masses of interests not directly in question keep their places without being thrown out of adjustment by the particular decision, and as they represented or reflected on the discussion level the actual achievement of the court process to all the groupings of the country that were interested in it.

In the matter of argument this case stood in somewhat the position that the railroad rate legislation of 1906 will stand if it comes before the Supreme Court for a test of the so-called funda-

mental principles involved.   I have marked closely the course of a
protracted discussion of the law points that will come before the
court involving the interstate commerce commission's "law-making" powers, and I have heard presented by the two sides to the
controversy trains of reasoning that lead inevitably, the one to
sustaining the commission's powers on each of the points at issue,
the other to the denial of those powers.   The reasoning on each
side is so cogent, so unanswerable, that as reasoning it simply
cannot be overthrown.   The Supreme Court will effectively use
whichever line of reasoning it wishes, to state and explain to the
country the decision which it will actually render on lines which,
although passing through reasoning, are reasoning's masters, not
its servants.   The most perfect of logical machines, set to the
Constitution and to all the precedents, would have pathways
through it which would deliver simultaneous contradictory judgments on the same point without the slightest shock to its mechanism.   Compared with the multiform irregularities of the pressure
of the interest groups in a highly complex society, the finest legal
logic is but a trivial fly-by-night, and the very essence of unreliability.

It is incumbent upon us, nevertheless, to recognize the work
that legal theory actually performs in the adjudication process,
and to gain as exact an estimate of it as possible.   To do this we
must follow the same procedure we have used elsewhere, and
reduce it to group terms, and thereby make sure of the manner
in which it reflects other and presumably deeper-lying groupings.
We find all this theory in textbooks, in judges' opinions, in lawyers'
arguments.   Most remote from the pressure of the interests
working directly through the courts is the "philosophy of law."
A little closer we find the "general principles" of constitutional
and legal argument.   Nearer still are masses of special theories
which are knit together more or less closely with the general
principles.   Then we come at last to the special arguments as
used in the pleadings, which reflect directly phases of the particular process that is going on through the courts.   All of these
are activities.   All of them are remotely or directly part of the

court process. Our philosopher of law, mirroring the process from his far-off distant height, may mirror it in part truly, and it may be that his activity will aid the interest adjustments where they are clogged to shape themselves better. If so, it is a matter for exact study to establish, and this cannot be accomplished by a mere observation of some general correspondence or of some partial correspondence between theory and developments as we look back upon them. Whether we note correspondence or divergence, it will be necessary to make sure just how far as a fact of activity the little active group of philosophers has really mediated the deeper-lying interest groups. Just so far as it has we must place it in the process, so to speak, at a central point, and so far as it has not we must regard it as an incidental product thrown off by the process at its periphery; and this, I repeat, whether we hold that philosophy to be "true" or "false" from the group point of view with which we identify ourselves when we make such judgments as that.

The group activity which we may describe as that of "general principles" is a discussion group in which large numbers of active practitioners participate, and which indeed all lawyers come into contact with to some extent. Perhaps we can find it affected to some little extent by the "philosophy" group mentioned above, but more probably we shall have to analyze it almost entirely in terms of groups still lower lying than itself. Almost repeating our previous words, we can say that so far as it accurately reflects pressures and at the same time mediates those pressures into better function where they are in any way obstructed, so far we may bring it directly into our interpretation, but that we must always be on our guard against giving it some mystical potency because of its mere color of "truth." How it has worked as one interest group mediating between lower-lying interest groups and reflecting them in the process can only be learned by exact examination.

Coming down next to the mass of special theories, we find them framing themselves with great variety in lawyers' and judges' activity, answering to the special cases, that is to the special differentiated interest groupings, that are at play. And still lower down, among the actual arguments in the court we find a greater variety still, with the special interest groups reflected in very specific forms. But even here again we observe that we have to do entirely with a representative activity, and that the whole process can be understood only in terms of the interest groups that are functioning still lower down in the series.

Of course I do not put forth this series of stages as one we can universally use in grading our groups for purposes of study, nor even as one I have found useful in any large number of cases. It is schematic and merely illustrative. In actual work the grades must be worked out on the material itself to meet the needs of the problem.

Another warning is also necessary here. I am not in this analysis segregating the interests at one end and the theory, under the guise of intellect, at the other. From the most rarefied theory downward, I am dealing entirely with interest groupings, and the entire process is an intelligent, felt process, as I have argued at length in an early chapter. What we have here to deal with is the differentiated discussion groups, and within them the differentiated "pure-theory" groups, and the whole problem is as to the relation between the activities at these various stages, and as to the amount of representativeness that can be observed in them.

When a case is called in court it furnishes a plane upon which we have potentially the entire population arraying itself in groups. Sometimes we can observe a case in which such a group splitting is represented by a very widely extended discussion group, or in case "public opinion" is divided, we have two discussion groups making themselves evident in opposition to each other. Usually, however, the discussion groups do not form, and the interest groupings of the population are represented more or less adequately by the organized judicial agencies of government. In addition to this split on a plane formed by the direct issue in the case, we find involved, potentially, a myriad of other groupings cutting across the population at all angles, any of which may come out to direct action, or may show itself in the discussion plane, either inside or outside the courtroom.

Now the gradations of theory represent, or aim to represent, interest groupings on lines of varying generality.   Just as we may have a lot of interest groups combining in a larger organization for certain ends, so we may have a theory, or rather a theoretical statement or argument, representing such a complex of interest groups.   In the progress of the trial of any case, or in preparatory stages before trial, or in the further stages as the whole social process moves forward, we get complexes of interests expressed in the form of theory.   We have the criss-cross of interests, not bound together by the theory, but represented by the theory as they actually are bound together in our observation.   Wherever, as I said above, the interests are blocked or clogged, and wherever under such circumstances the theory activity can enable them to function more freely, wherever then it aids in the parturition, so to speak, of interest groups manifesting themselves, there we must give it a sort of individualized recognition for just what it is. In very superficial speech we may there say that it creates a new grouping, in the sense, that is, that through it that grouping pushes itself farther along and more noticeably in the process.   But outside of this it merely represents the status of affairs; it speaks, so to say, for the absent interests—which are absent only in the sense that they are not emphatically manifesting themselves in conflict at the moment.   The theory therefore may be said to function as holding together the system of interests, and as furnishing a short-cut through which the interests that have balanced themselves once may escape being compelled to make their fight all over again and to work out the balance all over again at any and every moment in the process when their adjustment is threatened.

It is in this court process as in all other processes of government. Always in order to understand it we must cut down to the deepest-lying interest groups that we can find in the actual living population at the time.   How these interest groups are represented through agencies of government, how through discussion groups, including all the theory, how indeed some of the underlying groups represent others in gradation below those we have just mentioned, is a matter for actual observation and analysis made on the material itself.

There is one other phase of this court process to consider; that is the judiciary presenting itself as an organization with specified interest lines of its own, which must be looked upon at times, not merely as process for the interest content that is functioning through it, but as content over against content. I have already indicated how the judiciary under a class government may be directly controlled by one class to the exclusion of others. It remains to observe the judiciary as itself an interest group under a freely functioning group organization of society.

There is a mass of judicial procedure, which comes to our attention when it is interfering with us, under the name of the technicalities of the law, much of which must be referred to this judiciary's specialized interest. There exist lines of ease for the judge and lawyers which are followed and elaborated by them, short-cuts which when once established perhaps in very inadequate and poorly representative form, are not worked over, but instead are allowed to stand as precedents until they become such a nuisance that they arouse a fighting opposition. In the same way there are portions of the substantive law which represent interest adjustments of the past which are still held in position in the complex system of the law although the interest groupings on the specific lines of the particular law have varied materially, and which are effective only till the storm has blown up to overturn them. It is of the nature of representative agencies that they lag or hasten ill-advisedly, and that they themselves at times come into conflict with the very interest groupings, or portions of them, which are functioning through them.

It is here also that should fall a discussion of what is meant by talk of the independent development of the law as an "independent organism." What modicum of "individuality" would be left after the main lines of the function were traced in terms of interests pressing through executive, through legislature, and through courts, would be a subject for specific investigation in each case. That fragment of it which was not merely the "x" set by the limits to our powers of study and observation, might perhaps be called the individuality of the particular system of law in question, if indeed any such fragment remained. The case most apt to be mentioned, that of continental European law in the first half of last century, would, I imagine, easily yield to statement in terms of the pressures within a dominant class or set of classes.

CHAPTER XVII

POLITICAL PARTIES

With the political parties we come to phenomena which show us public opinion and leadership, the discussion and organization phases of governmental activity, in closer contact than we have at any time thus far seen them. But even this chapter will not take us to the bottom of the analysis of their relationship; it is only one more step on the way.

Whether the political party in its developed permanent form is or is not in formal classifications listed as an agency of government on a level with the three stand-bys is a relatively unimportant matter. The important facts to observe are that continuing parties, organized outside of the legislature, bear a relation to the people who compose them, or more precisely to the group interests that function through them, which is in type similar to the relation which a legislature or other branch of the government itself bears to interest groups; and further that they bear a relation to executive, legislature, or judiciary, similar to the relations these bear to one another.

It is no objection to this view to say that embryonic parties are everywhere observable which are clearly not such established agencies. Apart from the fact that the three generally recognized agencies themselves evolve from simple and irregular forms, there is the further fact that embryonic forms of governmental process are observable all around us in modern life, whether we look at lynching parties, at organized vigilance societies, at international law, at neighborhood improvement societies, at fraternal societies, or at associated industrial management.

Nor is it an objection to say that parties are not agencies of government because they are not legally organized and legally recognized. Apart from the fact that legal recognition and organization is rapidly being given to the parties in the American states, we must remember that some of the most important historical governing agencies have not been organized (in this terminology) in the law, but above the law. The German political scientist who would most strenuously object to treating the party as of "staatlichen Charakter" would not think of excluding the monarch on the same ground. If any legal test be applied it must be that of activity, not that of the jurist's formalism.

Parties may be found which are best to be described as the special organization for political activity of interest groups, especially of classes, direct. Others are rather the organization in a representative degree of a set of such interest groups. Certain parties in Russia at the present stage of the revolution (1906) have at times taken such forms that for some purposes they may be regarded not as agencies of the government or of interest groups in the government, but rather as partly developed substitute governments. Parties in Germany are comparatively close to the interest groups, and even the socialist party, the largest of them all, is not to be described effectively as an agency of government, though this is partly because the Reichstag itself is not a very securely seated agency. Parties in France are of different value according as one looks upon the ever-transforming "bloc" and the opposition as the parties, or gives attention to the minor constituent parties. Big party changes in the control of the French government have been usually revolutions, while small party regroupings are of almost yearly occurrence. I shall return to these in the attempt to specify more clearly the nature of these groups. In Cuba the two parties are perhaps well enough defined to be called agencies, even though, or rather because, they have worked through revolution; and in the revolutionary South American states, the parties, that is the rival hordes of politicians with their armies, are the predominating agencies of government. In England, where progress is perhaps toward a government with cabinet and parties as its main agencies, the parties are steadily advancing in their organization outside of Parliament. In the United States our massive parties with their permanent organization, seen not only at elections and between elections with a view to electoral work, but in permanent bureaus for the control of legislatures, for the disposal of favors, and the dictation of executive acts, are fully formed agencies, sometimes even making one or more of the constitutional agencies mere clerks and messengers. So Tammany Hall, in power or out of power, is in fact delegated to do much of the work of government for New York City. The city-state of Florence in the Middle Ages, especially with its Capitani di Parte Guelfa, gives us good illustrations of parties which became regular organs of government and at times even the most important organs of government.

If an executive, say, actually represented "all the people," that is the totality of the society, and a party did not, a distinction could be made. But my analysis hitherto has shown how the totality never appears, unless indeed it is totality in the special sense of one society against another, as one nation in war or diplomacy against another. The executive is buoyed up on certain groups or combinations of groups, not ruthlessly pushing toward the untrammeled realization of their ends, but allowing for resistance in other groups and bringing about in that way a balance, varying in stability from time to time. In much the same way the party machine will represent some interests more directly than others, allow for the others as far as it needs, and work out in this way a balance. Neither the lack of what is called "control by the people" in the executive nor a similar lack in the party, nor any difference in the degree of control at any time provides any fundamental distinction, however important such matters are as tests for the distinction of one agency from the other, or as issues in the practical political problems of the time.

The party agency is of course a double, or in still higher degree compound, structure, one branch rising and the other falling, and then later the positions being reversed. In this it has its peculiar characteristic, but perhaps not more peculiar than is to be found in a double consulship, one consul commanding the army one day and the other the next, or in a double legislature, one branch alternating with the other in irregular struggle according as the interests express themselves through them.

One can hardly discuss parties without introducing Burke's definition that a party is "a body of men united for promoting by their joint endeavors the national interest upon some particular principle on which they are all agreed." Here is a definition in terms of the "national interest" and of a "particular principle." But the "national interest" is rather a form of argument used by party members, than a characteristic of party tendency. It is a phrase which stands in a representative capacity to the special interest groups composing the party, and at the same time aims to reconcile other group interests to the proposed policy. And the "particular principle" is stated on the intellectual side, rather than concretely as the party tendency; it serves to indicate the presence of the party interest with its tendency, rather than to define it. Writers who accept this definition frequently mention "real political parties based on differences of opinion, not on class interests," their distinction being of course arbitrary, so far as it purports to be theoretical, since there can be no opinion which does not reflect interests or which has any value apart from interests.

It is evident that before we can understand parties we must push our analysis far deeper than words of this character will take us; not because such definitions as Burke's are incorrect, but because they are highly superficial. We must start out with that first phrase of Burke's definition, the "body of men," which seems so matter of course, and hold fast to it all the way through. We shall have to trace the representative quality of party in all its grades, from ordinary language expressions to organized political structure. We shall have to get the policies stated in terms of policy groups and show how these represent underlying interest groups, and how the mass gets knit together into great permanent organized structures, and how leadership, both of the policy type and of the machine type, appears in this mass, and how this structure as it forms develops "opportunities" for exploitation, in which appear new interest groups, which may be characterized as organization or machine interests. We must get the whole thing stated in terms of interest groups, measured by the numbers and interest intensity of their members.

Suppose we look at party formation in very simple conditions. Let us take a Spartan election by volume of applause or an Indian tribe considering a migration, a hunt, or a war expedition. We find first of all that the party phenomenon, that is, the taking of sides or the division of opinion, occurs in a bed or background of general activity. If there were no group differentiation within this general activity, there would be no division of opinion, no party formation at all. The group formation under the particular exigency is, however, so immediate that it seems the same thing as the party; that is, the party represents it immediately and directly. No doubt with fuller information we could carry our analysis back into health, food supply, and age conditions in such a matter as the plan for the hunting expedition; or in the Spartan election we might be able to discover several elements of the population which combined gave one candidate his preponderance in number and loudness of voices over another canditate. As it stands, however, we have a simple, transitory party formation, representing immediately the interest groupings of the society.

We can extend the illustration in which discussion groups are the only representative methods needed for the mediation of the interests a little way without producing any change in the party formation; as, for example, by taking cases in which a more protracted discussion is necessary, with urging and pleading on both sides. But we should soon reach a point at which we should find the party formation changing character and taking on more definite organization. This would be a result of the character of the interest groupings, of the character of the opposition between them, and of their complexity; factors which in their turn would depend mainly on the compression of the population in its environment. We should find for instance cases in which a policy in two steps would be set up, and here the realization of the policy would involve a continuing leadership, differentiated out of the party, to give it consistency and hold it together during the progress of its activity. The phenomenon which I have indicated by the phrase a "policy in two steps" is itself not to be thought of as a mere bit of head work by the leaders. Rather it itself is the outgrowth of the underlying group basis and determined in every respect by it. It is a function, partly of the larger party opposition, and partly of the group factors in relation to which the parties stand in a representative capacity. If the party leaders see that they can take step A now but not step B, and that after the readjustment brought about through step A the groups will be so arranged that step B will be possible, they set up that for their programme. They get their programme out of the groupings which they reflect, and only so far as they reflect the underlying situation correctly, by chance or by skill, will their policy work itself forward. So far as they reflect the situation wrongly, or have misjudged relative pressures, they will fail. I have used a phrasing that makes the leaders the subjects and directors of the operation, but again merely for convenience in the brief statement. It is the group process that works through them upon which we must concentrate attention in studying each case.

However, this second stage, simple as it seems, is, as I have stated it here, merely schematic. Whether or not we get this second type of party will depend on the structure of the government in which the interest groups are functioning, or in other words upon the work that is to be done. Whether the interest groups have hardened into classes or not, and what form of representation exists in the central agencies of the government, and whether all classes are independently represented in the government or approach the government by discussion groups of their own, will determine the concrete transformations.

Nevertheless, without substantial error we can analyze the elements of such an organized party a little farther without coming to concrete illustrations. As it stands, with some specialized leadership and with a programme which requires some time to carry through, it furnishes an agency through which still other policies—that is, tendencies of activity—may push themselves forward. There may be a different set of underlying groups, which nevertheless coincide as to personnel fairly well with the groups that are represented in the party, which also are working along toward the termini of their activities, and which find the existing party organization the easiest channel through which to express themselves. With a development like this the organized leadership of the party will gain a more independent, or rather a more differentiated, position; it will increase the element of discretion in its mode of representing the underlying groups, now become more complex than before. If this process continues to any great extent, we shall find developing in the party what we may call personality groups. A leader will gather a following around him which will work with him and by means of which he can adjust the emphasis which the different lines of activity receive at different times. With this we do not get to an entirely different type of party phenomena, nor to a type which can, any better than the former, be adequately described in terms of a person's "qualities." We have a different cross-section of the party and a process different in some of its details, but still one which is itself a group phenomenon, and which can only be given its value in terms of the underlying groups. Or again, if the leadership of the party becomes so organized under conditions that offer opportunities for exploitation based on circumstances that arise out of the very fact of the party's existence and of the political and other phenomena in which it exists, we may get a machine type of grouping across the party, with an interest which, although in one sense created by the party as an organization, is yet itself to be assimilated in type to the underlying groups which the party represents. It adds an important underlying group to the others, which may under peculiar circumstances come to appear the most prominent feature of the party organization; that is, it may develop abuses which arouse very vigorous groups in opposition to it, and which denounce it in unmeasured terms. Nevertheless, it will always be merely one among the many interest groupings to be considered in a full statement of the complex situation.

In this progress from the simplest to the most developed forms, the change concerns first the directness or remoteness of the representativeness of the party, and second the development of strict party, or organization, or machine interest groupings, which work through the wide party organization much as underlying interest groups do. These phenomena in their developed form are sometimes described as the "personality" of the party, but it must now be apparent on the surface that such a manner of speech tends toward obscurity, and that the method of analyzing the situation for all the forms of groupings in their various relations holds out on the contrary hope of clear and exact understanding.

The content of the party struggles is infinitely various. With that we are not concerned, but it is desirable now to note one other phase of the progress for which somewhat more concrete illustration is necessary; that is, the loosing of the parties from a class backing, and their acquisition of powers of freer functioning as the representative agents of many-sided, criss-cross groups in the developed political process.

In our simple tribe in which we find no class oppositions the party is fugitive and functions freely. When a split has come and the government rests on one class as against another or several others, held in place under a reign of custom, we shall find, so long as the government runs smoothly, that is, so long as all the class interests are fairly well reflected by the governing class, that party formations attract attention only inside the government class. There they may be numerous, or they may be somewhat consolidated and relatively permanent, appearing perhaps as personality groups, struggling within the class for immediate control of power. If it comes to pass that the classes enter into sharp opposition because of abuses in the government, each class may take on a political organization, that is form a party which represents it in the struggle The Boer governments, which have been called governments without parties, might better be called governments in which a small, compact, homogeneous class was itself the dominating party, under conditions which discouraged both party splits within the class and the formation of opposition political parties in the dominated class.

When we take the despotic monarchy, there again the party formation will be within the class upon which the monarchy is directly based, while the other classes have their interests more or less adequately reflected for them in the dominant class, without

forming parties of their own to represent them. Should the
despotism be a powerful central organization resting on an army
to hold together a number of antagonistic districts, the parties
may appear within the army in the form of cliques or factions.
Again, when a district rebels it will have its own party representation, or if a military leader contests for the central power by the
aid of his legions he may have a local support organized to some
extent in party form. If the central despotism does not need the
direct strength of the army, because perhaps of outside pressure
which holds the different districts in one system, then district parties
may appear, or perhaps class parties within each district may
strive to influence the central government. In all these cases
the form of the parties and their manner of acting will be determined by class and group considerations. The possibilities of
leadership must be worked out upon such considerations. The
possibilities of success and failure of any set of tendencies must
be based in the same way.

Let us turn now to modern England. Party phenomena are
of course as old as the nation, but the political parties as we now
know them trace their beginnings back about two hundred years,
to the time when the group process ceased to show itself as an
opposition between the king and his strength on one side and the
Parliament and its strength on the other, and began to work through
both king and Parliament acting jointly. I do not mean that there
was any particular moment when this change came about, nor
that there was no such joint procedure of king and commons long
before that time, nor that there has been no sharp opposition
between the two as aligned each with a different set of group
(perhaps class) interests since that time. The general lines of
the change are however clear enough, and are marked at various
stages of development by the selection of ministers from the
Parliament, then from one party in Parliament, and finally by their
joint responsibility to the House of Commons.

For a time with the limited range of participants in the actual
government, the parties as organized in Parliament were primarily
personal followings. The phrase, "the Whig families," which

one so often hears, stands for this fact. The changing needs of the groups of which the population was made up reflected themselves through these parliamentary party groups, and through the king, who exercised for a long time a certain representative power as the chooser between the factions. We had during this period organized permanent parties acting in the government, representing wide groups of interests, although not periodically chosen by these interest groups or parties made up out of them direct, and cohering together mainly by the use of the patronage, which was very rich, and sometimes by direct bribery, the funds for which came from the same source as the salaries of the placemen, namely the national treasury.

Now when it came about that a group interest demanding an extension of the suffrage had won the first two or three stages of its demands, a party organization outside of the Parliament at once appeared, an organization of the electorate of a primitive kind. This organization followed the lines of the two-party organization inside of Parliament, though the strong group interest of Ireland has given it a party of its own, and though the other parties have had severe shocks from sharp splits on this and other questions. At present a labor group has become strong, and an analysis of the Parliament will indicate a dozen or so fairly well-defined party groups underneath the surface, although the sharp rivalry between government and opposition is as clearly marked as ever.

As soon now as we get an organization of parties outside of the legislature we have the beginnings of a new agency of government coming up from the same source, the group struggle, from which the previously existing agencies came. In England this agency does not as yet stand nearly so independent of the Parliament as parties in the United States stand of the legislatures; the organization leaders are mainly in the Parliament personally, and those who are in the Parliament dominate completely those who are outside. Responsibility is still tested through parliamentary mechanism, but not so freely as of old. A majority does not fade away through "convictions," or through that substitute for convictions, bribe-money; it passes rather by the results of the by-elections; and the more the groups develop in the two great parties, the more perhaps we may expect to see them acting *en masse* through their extra-parliamentary organization, rather than individually within Parliament.

The whole system is nevertheless one of groups. Of the many group oppositions of the nation along different planes, we find certain ones from time to time getting out of adjustment, so to speak, or rising into vigor under new conditions of life, and forcing themselves toward political activity. Some of these group activities will be noted by the government almost before they have clearly formed themselves, and will be brought to success through the discretion of the government on its own initiative, acting of course in a representative capacity. Others again must first organize themselves, not indeed as political parties, but as discussion or propaganda groups on a level intermediate between the immediate interest groups and the parties proper. Still others will be forced to affiliate themselves with the political parties and secure expression for themselves along party lines. Finally some others, failing of success, will organize parties of their own, both within and without the Parliament, and exert themselves in that way.

Whatever be the process, however, whether through cabinet, commons, or party, the whole situation must be worked out in group terms to become intelligible. It must be worked out by the analysis of the underlying group conditions, not as they ought to be, nor as our own group tendencies may dictate them to us, nor along any lines of justice or morality dragged in from other situations, but solely on the lines of the actually given groupings, just as they stand. Policies and arguments and "class consciousness" and other such things must be taken into account as indications to help us in working out the fundamental interests on the basis of which the whole party structure must be built up. Intensities must be taken into account for just what they can be proved to be, not merely for what they claim to be at special stages of their process against obstruction. No interest group can be estimated at its right force except in terms of the amount of resistance

that others will offer to it.   And always the party process must
be reduced to the lowest terms to which our analysis can carry us.

There is a good deal to note in the English party process which
can be noted so much better in the American parties that I will
postpone discussion of it for use in connection with the American
illustrations.   But first a word or two about French parties will
be of service.   Political parties in France seem to be making
progress toward much the same status to which English parties
are tending, save that they are approaching from a different
direction.   The "bloc" is increasing in strength and cohesiveness,
the opposition which has been in the past more an opposition to
the republic's present type of government than to the cabinet is
drawing itself within the system, so that it tends to become an
opposition in the English sense, and the groups are arranging
themselves under both.   When one lists by name all the different
"parties" that appear as represented in Parliament, one sets
down more parties than can really be found.   Many on the list
would be rather personal followings within parties than independent parties.   That is, they would be groups of men whose adhesion
struck our attention more by mention of the leader's name than of
his policy, the difference, however, being strictly relative and a
matter mainly of emphasis.   The interests which are lower
lying are therefore reflected differently and through a different
technique than is the case in England.   So far as these many
French parties are direct organizations of interests, they secure
their ends by a process of barter with other similar groups which
compose the "bloc," the barter often including in its terms spoils
of a kind very familiar in the other countries we are considering.
So far as they are personal followings, they fall within larger group
territory, and furnish special tools, so to speak, through which
interests may work.   The division of the socialist parties is tested
mainly by the extent to which they recognize the strength of opposing groups, which is the same thing as saying by the extent to
which they have got their programme of action clearly and fairly
opened out before them, and also by the extent to which their
members are blocked in their lives, and by the extent to which

they are excited by their failure to secure expression—which comes to something similar to the previous point. To compare England and France on any basis that gave hope for useful knowledge, one would be compelled to get all the groups analyzed, to note the differences, to follow up the habitual forms of activity in governmental matters, and discriminate between the channels which were immediately commanded by interest oppositions, and those which are indifferently used by the interest groups because they happen to be present and can be followed without such noticeable obstruction as to stir up active effort for their alteration.

When the United States became a federal government the suffrage was limited, and the voters were organized under leaders transmitted from the earlier days. The fields in which these leaders had won their standing had been either the Revolutionary War. or the constitutional convention and its predecessor, the Congress of the Confederation. Discussion leadership and organization leadership were not well differentiated. On account of the limitation of the suffrage it is necessary to take into account in studying the parties not only their membership, but also the nonvoting interests which they represented to some considerable extent. The followings of the leaders were grouped in the main territorially, but with outlying detachments that extended well over the country.

It is well enough established that the party differentiation of the early years of the Republic cannot be more than superficially defined in terms of the theories of the leaders, such as their theories for and against a strong central government. Those theories served for little more than tags to the parties, as was well enough proved when Jefferson used the strong hand at the central place of power in defiance of all his theories. Henry Jones Ford, one of the most searching observers among writers on American politics, follows John Marshall in connecting the parties with the previous experiences of the two groups of leaders, and he emphasizes the relations between Hamilton and the commercial interests of the country on the one side and Jefferson and the agricultural interests on the other. This latter distinction offers a valuable clue in the attempt to determine what the underlying interest groups were for which the parties stood, how far the parties represented them adequately, and how through the development of the country and by compromise as the result of party struggle, adjustments were brought about and the group lines changed.

While party outlines were indicated at this time in terms of elaborate theories, and while the party process seemed to be largely a discussion process, the inadequacies of such a point of view should be noted by anyone who believes that a governmment by pure, calm discussion is the normal type by which we must test the divergences of all government as we find it. Discussion assumed most violent forms even at the start, and it is a question not for theorizing but for exact examination, with due allowance for the extension of the suffrage and for the character of the interest opposition of the time, whether the groups gained better balance through the govenment then than they do even now, when machine organization at its strongest is fresh in memory.

At the start the parties seemed to be mainly organized in Congress, but their lines could be seen on both sides stretching into the executive departments—that is, in the first part of Washington's presidency—while the state governments also furnished a field for organization. And indeed not all of the active leaders were to be found inside of the official positions. The congressional caucuses for the presidency indicate the location of the strongest organization.

We can observe first the parties as organized in the state governments contesting with Congress for the nominating power; and then later, with the rapid extension of the suffrage, the result of group struggles that went on in the state fields without rising into federal politics, and with the increase in number of elective offices, we observe the parties organizing themselves outside of both state and federal governments, and arriving finally at the convention system and the party committees.

Looking at this development along another line, we see the two-party system at the beginning; we see this system breaking down by the bad defeat of one party, and the absorption of its interests into the other party; we see groups forming within this dominant party on personality lines at a moment when no well-defined underlying group struggle was at an acute stage in federal affairs, and we see those personality groups forming the basis for a new representation of underlying interest groups as they began to press more eagerly for recognition in the government process. So we find, for example, the interest groups which were represented on the discussion plane by the tariff and internal-improvements policies operating through the government. Finally in the slavery issue, which formed very strong interest groups in the economic field, unfortunately for the country divided on terri-torial lines, and which was represented in the discussion field by intense outbursts of "moral fervor" built up complexly out of many elements, we see the party technique transforming itself into war technique. In this process the dominant party in the North came to seem a thing of pure policy, of pure morals and ideas, but that, of course, was only its superficial appearance. It is as a great mass of men with their interest groupings solidified into a huge sectional, class interest that the phenomenon of the Republican party must be examined, and not merely as an abstract economic, or as an abstract moral phenomenon.

Now when the war was over the Republican party stood power-fully organized in possession of the government. It was a mighty machine, so strongly intrenched that not for ten years did another party gain so much as a single house of Congress. It was an organization which administered the government and which stood seemingly by its own strength, when the underlying interests which had raised it up subsided. It was an engine ready for the use of interest groups which needed to push themselves toward realization through government.

Long before this De Tocqueville had commented upon the possibilities of party organization in this respect, calling it "a government within the government," and saying that "if in imme-diate contiguity to the directing power, another power be estab-lished, which exercises almost as much moral authority as the former, it is not to be believed that it will long be content to speak without acting."[1] Also he had discussed the use of spoils as party fodder, place-hunting as a trade.[2]

The history of the use of spoils in our politics both before De Tocqueville's time and after is well enough known: how the party, once organized outside the legislature as an agency of government, pressed itself into the government offices, not because Jackson was a bad man, but because of the inevitable process of groups of men and their opportunities; how the evils of the system in time stirred up a group antagonism to them, which we now know as the civil-service reform movement (I do not refer to the pious ejaculations of the excluded, but to the representation that came into being on behalf of the injured); how as a result of this antagonism we have the civil-service merit system of the present; and how, we may add, the measure of civil-service reform obtained up to the present has already produced a certain definite enough alteration in machine strength, despite the fact that large amounts of other varieties of spoils are still left for machines to thrive on.

This spoils system operated here as elsewhere to hold the party leaders from big to little together in a strong interest group, which came, on the lines of an analysis I have previously set forth, to be more like an underlying interest group than like a strict party formation on a representative level. The party stood forth rather as an agency of government than as a party in the terms of such a definition as Burke's. The Republican party I have named merely because it has been the most striking instance of this kind of organization. While the Democratic party approaches it in many respects, its chronic position as the "opposition" in national affairs makes it a less perfect illustration of the type.

Let me sum up the main features of the party as it now stands in the United States. It is an organization of voters, brought together to act as a representative of the underlying interest groups in which these voters, and to some lesser extent other citizens, present themselves. On the level of discussion groups it is repre-

[1] *Democracy in America.*, Part, I, chap. xii.

[2] *Ibid.*, Part II, Book III, chap. xx.

sented, or rather underlying groups are represented, by many theories, policies, and slogans; it has, indeed, a formally differentiated discussion phase, the platform, which offers the pretense of coherence and positive leadership on the discussion plane, but which, as every schoolboy knows, is most of the time a hollow mockery, which means merely that in the discussion plane, in the platform, the underlying groups are not accurately represented. Its leadership is a strong, though not an especially close, corporation, reaching its most compact form in New York's Tammany Hall, and indeed actually a legal corporate form in the eruptive Hearst's Independence League; a characteristic so marked that one writer a dozen years ago used the phrase "government by syndicate" to describe it.   Upon this quasi-corporate organization of the electorate the group interests of the country which are exerting themselves in the political field, must direct their efforts to secure results.   They have indeed still the legislatures upon which to bring pressure to bear, and also they can exert themselves through the presidency, but in the same way they must exert themselves on the corporative party organization if they wish results.   Of course, all group interests do not work with equal facility through these different agencies.   When the presidency is called "the people's office," that means that big widespread group interests, equipped with comparatively poor technique represented mainly on discussion lines, have been able to find expression through that office better than elsewhere.   The adjustments that are carried on through the legislature vary greatly with different legislative bodies.   In the lower house of Congress, the members adjust local demands for spoils in the form of buildings, improvements, and to some extent jobs, but the speaker, who with his two lieutenants decides most important questions, is more representative of the party organized outside the legislature than of the party as organized within it.   Through the machines go all matters which can be handled with a view to their corporate interests, whether by bribery, favoritism, political prospects, or otherwise.   Of course the machines have limits to their utilization of their corporate opportunities, limits set always by the possible stimulation of group interests directly attacking them. In short the machine is a group among groups, a group which mediates between others, and which reflects others with varying degrees of adequacy; a group whose origin, whose present standing, and whose future fate are all functions of the strength of the pressures in the given society as it stands. The analogy between the boss with his machine and a despot with his favorites is not fanciful but close, both as regards class or group support and the machine's own interests as such. The existence of the great party agencies does not, of course, do away with the lesser party phenomena. A special complex of interest groups, reacting on a special "evil," may organize a prohibition party, and many transitory party phenomena may flit across the bosom of the great party organization. All must be allowed for in the total.

It has been argued by Mr. Ford and by Professor Goodnow that the parties as we now see them were made necessary by the separation of powers in our government, by the separation of executive and legislature, and by the separation of federal from state and also in part of state from local governments. The analysis that brought this connection to light was very valuable, but even at that it remains an incomplete statement of the party phenomenon. There is no doubt that a group interest seeking expression through party activity would be compelled to operate upon executive and legislature at the same time, and in case both state and federal governments had to act, upon both of these. Moreover with divided elections and only gradual achievement of control, the party organization outside the legislature and executive would have to be maintained for considerable periods. But that our machine type of political organization would necessarily follow is a different question, only to be answered by bringing all the group interests including that excited by the spoils opportunities into accurate comparison. Where we find spoils showing a disintegrating rather than an integrating effect, that must be taken into account, and also where we find rival parties by trading dividing the fields in which they rule, that fact must be laid against the theory of unity by party. In so far also as we find party an agency for any and every interest group, or rather for selected interest groups of varying characters, to function through, instead of an agency for the representation of one great interest or set of interests, we must view it as such. When we find an interest group appearing to denounce the party machines, it is no answer to it, nor does it really bear on the situation, to argue that the machines are necessary, spoils and all, because of any work they may do or may have done in holding the organs of government together. If the machine hurts enough, the reaction on it will come just in proportion to relative strengths, argument or no argument, past services or no past services; and whether it wipes out merely the abuses or wipes out the machines along with the abuses will be largely a matter of detail, depending, however, itself on relative group strengths. And if there is a large fund of genuine work—that is work which must continue to be done, and which other agencies do not properly provide for—the very existence of the work will produce the mechanism to do it. A theoretical discussion then of the responsibility or lack of responsibility of the machine to the people will amount to much or to little, just in proportion as it reflects at their accurate weights the group forces which are now struggling to expression.

Before leaving this subject, there are a few incidental matters concerning parties which need discussion. Perhaps I have already considered at sufficient length the relation of formally expressed policies to party activity, but at the risk of repetition I will go over the point again. Like all "theory," policy has its place in the process as bringing out group factors into clearer relation, and as holding together the parties, once they are formed, by catchwords and slogans. So far as it gives good expression to the groups on its peculiar plane, all is clear. But to attempt to judge the parties by their theories or formal policies is an eternal absurdity, not because the parties are weak or corrupt and desert their theories, but because the theories are essentially imperfect expressions of the parties. The vicissitudes of states' rights as a doctrine are well enough known. Another passing illustration concerns the government regulation of commerce. If we may identify the commercial interests of a century ago with those of today for the purposes of illustration, we find that the very elements which then under Hamilton's leadership were most eager to extend the power of government over commerce are now the most bitterly opposed to any such extension. Then and now the argument made great pretenses to logic and theoretical cocksureness, and then, as now, the theories were valuable in the outcome only as rallying the group forces on one side or the other for the contest.

Public opinion, which is a phenomenon on the level of the discussion groups, is directly connected with party in many ways. It must submit to analysis and to tests for the degree of its representativeness like any other similar group expression. Sometimes it is a compound of discussion group elements, and again it is vivified by striking roots directly into the deeper-lying groups. It has enormous power, of course, but only where it expresses interest groups that mean business. The test of it is an operation of extreme delicacy in the hurly-burly of political life, and every successful politician is an expert in it, which is not the same as saying that he gives obedience to the opinion that purports to represent "all the people," but that he can estimate the opinion of the groups in which he is most strongly seated for what it is worth, and that he can use the public opinion from outside groups to test their true strength as against his own fortified position. When he fails in his reaction to the group interests as mediated through opinion, a change in leadership is quickly due. Leadership mainly on the discussion plane and leadership mainly on the organization plane are of course both found in the political process, and they may work together or work against each other at various stages of the process. The "Zeitgeist" is a spook that comes to light in the study of public opinion, when the tendency of the investigation is to individualize and personify it, not to analyze it to see what it actually represents. It may safely be asserted that any definite tendencies of action which are attributed to the "Zeitgeist" may surely and exactly be reduced to the underlying groups from which "Zeitgeist" derives his being, and that what will be left of him after analysis will be mainly trivialities and misrepresentations, in short, interesting but insignificant phenomena.

It is common to classify political parties as reactionary, conservative, and radical or progressive. Sometimes the reactionary is omitted and the classification is reduced to conservative and radical. Or again liberal and radical may be distinguished from one another. It should be apparent how extremely superficial such a basis of distinction is. Such names are indeed used by actual parties, and as names they have their reality. Also the parties so designated or classified may sometimes correspond to actual class-interest groups in a particular society; where they do it is proper to use this classification of parties, but only for the given time and place with reference to the given groups. When we come to the phenomena of the great party organizations which are agencies in government the names do not correspond at all to the facts. Indeed, under any circumstances whatever we can easily see that no party can be really "reactionary." A party must inevitably be looking to the future. Just because in the discussion plane there is much said about the "good old times," it does not mean that the party really tends backward. It is like every other bit of human activity tending forward, and we must use the talk and ideals and theories as indications from which to proceed to our analysis of the actual underlying interest groups. It may be that these groups in earlier times had much freer sway in the society and are still unreconciled to their present position, in the sense that their tendencies of activity are extreme and uncompromising. Really, however, such a party is radical, just as much as parties that call themselves radical, perhaps even more radical in some cases.

Some parties can of course be on the defensive, and all parties may be at some time. But even the distinction between the offensive and the defensive is a somewhat superficial one, when we turn our attention to the groups at the bottom of the process. Both offensive and defensive parties are pressing forward on certain lines of activity and are pressing against each other in the process. From this point of view it is rather a technical than a substantial difference whether one party is aiming to change a statute and the other to maintain it, or vice versa. The practical distinction between the party in control of the government and the party of the "outs" of course stands, but the point is that the party of the "ins" may be maintaining an established law, or it may be changing it; and both parties are exerting the strength they represent for all it is worth in whichever direction the process of adjustment is moving. Or again, in still other words, the movement of readjustment, even in the most spectacular times, is comparatively slight compared with the great mass of the pressures exerted by all the underlying groups upon each other.

Special varieties of the kind of classification I have just been criticizing are to be found when liberal, conservative, and socialist parties, for example (Kautsky), are set over against one another, each with its ideals, liberal, feudal, or socialistic, and each resting on a class of the population, capitalists, land-owners, or laborers. Such a classification may or may not be proper at any given time or place, but to erect the three so-called classes into permanent elements of the population and make them apply in all societies of the modern type, is a mere bit of metaphysics or pretentious schematism. And it can never take higher rank until direct proof is brought which rests not on the "ideals" but on independently established social groupings, which distinguish between ordinary groups and set classes with great care, and which get the whole stated as it actually is in the governing process and nowhere else. Loria, for instance, can work out a beautiful theory of the parties as based on the "revenues," and it will look attractive at long range; but wherever a disinterested student attempts to apply it to his own time and country, he will find much better methods of analyzing the phenomena than that.

Taking now a final look at the party process, we find classes sometimes opposed to each other with the government established in the hands of one class, and with a party formation on personal or policy lines among that ruling class, or among its leaders. We find that where the classes have been to great extent broken down, so that the functioning through the government is of groups of less fixed types, there parties will form to represent the groups in the political field, varying in extent and in organization according with the arrangement of the government and the supplementary work to be done. We find these parties with representation in the discussion field, and with organizations that represent them and furnish them leadership, and with various mixed forms of representation, such as special organization of propaganda. We find their intensity dependent upon the intensity of the group pressures, which include of course the amount of the obstruction as well as the amount of the demand. We find intensity in the discussion level often out of proportion to the intensity of the group pressures, and we must allow for that at all times in our judgments of the situation. We find the party organizations adding a new underlying interest which must always be taken into account and at times very acutely. We find the formal policies and theories of parties in varying degrees of representativeness, some of them maintaining themselves for protracted periods and becoming such ingrained habits on the discussion level that they survive there for considerable periods after the group interests underlying them have so shifted that they are no longer adequately represented by them. We find the theories entitled to attribution of potency in direct proportion to the adequacy with which they represent the underlying interests; with allowance only for the dregs and driblets of theory left behind, pretentious but with trifling potency, in transition periods. We find the whole process masquerading itself in the phraseology of the "public interest or welfare," which is a something non-existent except on the discussion level, save in times of a violent opposition of one nation as a whole to some other or others, in which case it represents not the whole society under consideration but only the particular nation as one group in the larger society in which the interaction—war, tariff dispute, or what not—is going on.

And above all we find that the great need at every stage in our examination of the process is for a careful analysis of all the group operations, and for a thoroughgoing statement of the most superficial and pretentious in terms of the deeper-lying and most fundamental.

CHAPTER XVIII

THE ELECTORATE AND SEMI-POLITICAL GROUPS

Passing behind the party organization we come to the electorate, out of which the parties are composed. Theoretical legal distinctions will help us here even less than elsewhere; they serve merely to define details around the edges of established activity. The Praetorian guard in its flower under the Roman Empire certainly formed an electorate. The Russian people, down even to the most oppressed of the peasants and the Jews, are attempting today according to their needs and their technique to exercise electoral functions. France at the time of the revolution developed a great electorate. On the other hand negroes in southern states with constitutional "rights" which they are kept from exercising, are not for us part of the real electorate. It is all a question of activity.

To use these illustrations is not to become involved in any confusion with regard to the suffrage as we find it permanently organized with the ballot as its instrument under complex governments of the representative type. In this latter case we have an electorate not spasmodically and irregularly working, but organized for periodical action with a definite technique. In a country like the United States it is probably entitled just as it stands, as so much "voting cattle," or "intelligent citizenship," whichever one will, to be ranked as one of the great agencies of government; and this even apart from its organization into parties. But whether it is so characterized or not is a minor matter. The important thing is to get it in proper relation to all the other processes of government.

The electorate functions through majorities or pluralities. When the majority or plurality has registered itself we say the "people" has spoken, or has "decided," but that is a bit of personification, of phrase-making. What we actually have is an adjustment or solution of oppositions, by a certain technical method which is entitled to be taken exactly for what it is, and for nothing more. It is not a direct adjustment of fundamental interests. The electorate, like every other grouping of the population in the governmental field, is itself representative in the sense in which that term has been used throughout this book. It is a differentiated activity. Its groups represent underlying groups, more or less adequately. If anyone is interested in passing judgment upon it as a "good" or a "bad" institution, the only way to reach a sane judgment is—after fixing exactly the purpose for which the judgment is desired—to reduce the electorate to terms of the underlying interests with as great a degree of exactness as available facts and methods will permit.

Sometimes the electorate passes judgment upon men and sometimes upon measures. Sometimes, that is, it elects persons to office, and sometimes it votes directly upon questions of policy. But the distinction is not a hard and fast one, good for fundamental scientific uses. A man cannot be selected or judged entirely without reference to the policy he represents or embodies. Even if "character" is set up as a test, that also is a matter of policy, since character as such in the election can cut no figure except with reference to what the man of given character will be or do in the government; honesty or dishonesty here is a matter of the use of the public funds or franchise; private moral life, where it counts, has to do in part with law-enforcement and in part with "example" in the broader field of control, while for the rest it may have bearings on personality groupings; even personal popularity is a question of the personality-leadership groups. Similarly a policy cannot be passed on save with reference to the men who are to embody it. In the discussion field, now person and now policy may get the greater emphasis, but the material we actually have to observe always includes both. However express they are, however merely implied in discussion, in fact both are together. What the distinction comes down to in its practical political use is that policy on the one side and character on the other serve in the discussion level to represent different phases of the underlying group process. They are not different things for any scientific investigation, however sharply opposed they may be in some immediate political struggle.

We have next to observe the relation of the electorate, not to the other agencies of government, but to the mass of the citizenship. The electorate never includes the whole citizenship. Always the minors are excluded, and usually all of the women. The criminal and insane elements of the population are excluded, and in most large modern states also some portion of the other adult males who cannot conform to fixed property or educational qualifications. In the United States property qualifications exist in some states, while on the other hand in many states they have been entirely abandoned, and indeed the electorate has been broadened to include males who are not, by legal definition, citizens. All of these tests and qualifications are themselves the direct result of group pressures.

Ignoring such minor peculiarities as the one last mentioned, we have to observe in general terms that the electorate is a representative institution in two different ways. In the first place, as so much political activity, it represents the other activities of its members in the way indicated a page or two back; the justification for discriminating between the electoral activity and the underlying activities of those same persons being that they group themselves differently on the two levels. The groupings of the electorate activity proper, led by party organizations differentiated out of them, are few in number compared with the complex underlying groupings.

In the next place the electorate, now most readily envisaged as a concrete body of men, represents the interests of those other elements of the population who do not directly participate in it. We have here something akin to the class as distinguished from groups in the wider sense. Take the case of the women who do not have the suffrage. As the case now stands, women-interest groups are not very markedly differentiated from men-interest groups. The family, even in its greatly weakened form, serves to keep the votes of the men in general such that they represent the women interests in a fairly adequate form. Where women's interests push themselves out in any noticeable degree as distinct from men's, or where they show themselves in specialized forms, as is sometimes the case with the conduct of the public schools— remember, I am not talking of what ought to be, but of interests as actually manifested—the women may break through to partial participation in the suffrage in that particular field. The more the family organization transforms itself and the more the women come to stand apart from the men, the more certain will be their speedy direct participation in the suffrage. This is not saying that there is any "reason" why they should not participate directly in the general suffrage now, or why they should. It is only pointing to an habitual suffrage system, grown out of earlier conditions, and lacking as yet any sufficient impetus to its transformation.

Similarly, there are the males who do not have the voting right, for lack of property or educational qualifications. They are represented by the male voters in very fact, whether they are found in large numbers with somewhat varying interests, or in smaller numbers with group interests in general identical with the various group interests of the voters. It is to be noted that the very conditions which make the women usually little forceful as a group to project themselves into the suffrage, make the male opposition likewise of little force; on the other hand, with excluded male voters the demand for direct participation may at times take violent forms, and be met with equally violent opposition, the resultant suffrage extensions or limitations being the outcome of the pressures as they actually exist within the society, the whole background and system of governmental technique being taken into account. Sometimes we find a different male electorate standing behind one branch of a government from that which stands behind another branch. It is a special result of compromise of pressures, with some indication, save so far as it is a mere survival, of the maintenance of class opposition, more fixed than the ordinary group oppositions, in the government.

Attention may also here be recalled to the fact that the suffrage is nearly everywhere now distributed on a district, or locality, basis. Russia's recent experiments have been with a suffrage grouped by classes, and Prussia has a survival of class distinctions in its three-class suffrage based on property qualifications. But usually the district is what counts. The man is an elector only where he lives, or where his property is located. Plural voting is, where it occurs, in practice a rather unimportant variation of the district system. The practical convenience of this formalism in grouping the voters is apparent, but its function in giving representation to underlying interests and its disturbing effects upon the representation of those interests have already been discussed, as well as its utility to the organizers of party machines, whereby special interests—those of the machine leaders and of their financial backers—become represented in preponderant degree.

Many phases of electoral technique might be touched on. The question of the number of offices filled by direct election could be examined from this point of view as well as from the points of view in the preceding chapters: also the extent to which the electorate chooses officers, whether it chooses all the officers of the state, or whether some, as in a monarchy like Germany, are rather co-ordinate with the electorate than resting on it, in which latter case both the electorate and the co-ordinate officers rest on the citizenship at large; also the technical methods of expression, such as secret voting by the use of the ballot, registration of voters, government inspection of elections, and so forth. I shall not go into details, but merely point out that in every case we have a phenomenon which can only be understood through an analysis of the grouped population, and that in these cases in especial the relative size of the whole society and also of its great groupings appears very plainly in its causal bearings.

Passing now behind the electorate, I wish to add a few words on the semi-political organization of the citizenship. I shall deal here with group phenomena which are neither party phenomena direct nor phenomena of the electorate in action, nor are they yet the underlying interest groupings, which, primarily to be defined as lying entirely out of the political sphere, furnish the bases upon which all the political structure is reared up. What I have to deal with is the preliminary organization of these underlying interests with a view to political operation, direct or indirect; they form a representative system intermediate between the underlying interests and the suffrage and parties.

Examining these phenomena first on the discussion level, we find many organizations engaged in propaganda of one kind or another. The varieties of such phenomena are very rich. They range from dreamland Utopias to railroad press bureaus with big budgets. Indeed, these two illustrations may be well within the outer limits, while aberrant illustrations run out to indefinite distances in every direction. When a man writes a book to advance some particular theory about society, he reflects in it a certain phase of the social process, more or less truly. If his book has any bearing, however remote, on political life, it falls within the field before us. Now the reflection of a phase of the social process is the same thing as the reflection of some group interest or set of group interests. His "theory" is such a reflection. It is such an act of "representation." As the book becomes known, there gathers round it a little group, however vaguely outlined, however uncertain in its tenets, however inclined to criticize sharply great portions of the theory. It is a group held together at the kernel. It is a differentiated representation of a certain aspect of the human groupings. The group would not form, so far as any observation of human life that we can make informs us, were not the conditions "there" at the start to be reflected in this way. Once given the differentiated discussion group, then its disappearance or its progress will be a resultant of all the rest of the given group facts of the social life, each bit of it going into the reckoning, not as so much dead surface, but weighted at an intensity which is the direct expression of the oppositions actually existing in the social groupings. We may have a very intense group of small numbers, or a very extended group of weak intensity. It is a question of fact, and the group must be valued at what it is in fact.

I have used a theoretical book for this illustration. The book is an incident to the illustration. If the group that formed itself amounted to anything the "ideas" were almost to a certainty "there" in the society before the book was published. The book was merely a little bit of activity embodying them in a good form.

Perhaps the book may have furnished the catchwords, or the particular form of the reasonings; perhaps its author may become a figurehead, full of fame and glory, in the movement. It is the grouping, nevertheless, that is important, and the grouping, at that, for just the representative value which it actually possesses.

We may find this grouping of the citizenship in many forms of greater or less detachment from the political life, running all the way from cold belief to hot temper. We may find it becoming more and more specific in its statement, till it embodies a policy or a platform. We may find it at almost any stage from the "abstract idea" up to the political party as a policy grouping.

Now a good many of these discussion groups represent vague groupings of the population, but a good many of them on the other hand represent sharply outlined and well-organized interests. We may, for instance, have a huge "consumers group" on one side and a "trust" interest on the other side. There is no essential difference between them for all of that. It is a little easier for the vague groups to talk about themselves as "the people," and a little more difficult for the well-organized groups to prove that they are "unselfish;" but that is a detail of technique. An industrial "interest" of the kind called capitalistic may put out books, revel in theory and argument, work seductively or brazenly, spread literature, organize clubs, and rally sympathizers, as well as any other kind. Either kind of group may knit its theory and its ideas up with the "established" belief groups of the time, and gain strength by so doing. It can gain strength, that is, so far as those established beliefs accurately represent underlying group interests, or so far as they are survivals which no sufficient power, that is no sufficient interest, has yet dislodged.

A particular form of this propaganda expression is to be found in the press, which is an established agency in this semi-political activity in all of the large modern states, including even Russia. The press in its news columns actively distributes all kinds of information through the society. Itself being part of the underlying interests, it provides a technique through which the others form themselves in a way they would not so easily do without it; that is evident enough. As one phase of its activity we find editorial expressions, which are differentiated opinion-group activities. It is useless to discuss "the power of the press" in general terms; for that power, considering it both as manifested in editorials and in the policy treatment of news columns, is in each particular case just the equivalent of the representative value which the paper or its particular editorial expression has, the size and character of the paper's circulation being taken into account. Not that there is any absolute value to each editorial; all fit together in systems; but the test is steadily and effectively made against the group interests which are being represented. The test does not lie in any continuity of thought or independence of thought on the part of the editor. Where a paper in general represents a very definite and coherent element of the population, it can make its pretense of being a pure reasoner with a good face; but where it functions on behalf of a mixed audience, it is mere trivial verbiage to put it to the test of reason or beliefs alone. The press shows itself in many forms, subsidized, riotous, partisan, independent, but in whatever form it appears it needs interpretation in terms of the groups it represents. Whether it sells itself to one small clique for cash, or to another by titillating its senses, or whether it is identified with some particular interest without express prostitution of either kind, is really an incident of a technical character; unless indeed now and then a group interest is moved by some peculiarly rank manifestation to take the field against one or the other form of technique, making it subject for attack and seeking its suppression or regulation.

An incidental development in connection with newspapers is the systematized writing of letters "to the editor." In England certain class interests have long gained regular expression in this way without differentiated organization. In the United States the phenomenon has been less marked, but of late it has appeared under the control of more or less strongly organized bureaus, whether representing "special interests" or broader interests of the kind that call themselves "the public."

From these various forms of discussion groupings we must turn to the organizations which are concentrated more directly on special lines of action, worked out in considerable detail. Here we find in countries like the United States a limitless number of reform organizations and special-interest organizations of unending variety. They will range all the way from those which claim to be purely motived by public spirit to those which do not even attempt to disguise rank selfishness, but each and every one of them is an interest organization of a representative character.

We may find a protectionist league, financed by certain industries and representing not merely those industries but many related interests. Now it will be agitating for new legislation, now defending achieved legislation, now working through the press, now operating on party organizations, and now on constituted legislative bodies. Its technique may be as various as the situations it is compelled to face. It may be a joke at one time and a power at another. But always and all the time it gets its value and its meaning in the process from the whole set of groupings with which it must be brought into relation. A free-trade league may be worked out similarly on its side with reference to the groupings it represents and the character of the given oppositions in the political field.

Or we may look at a civil-service-reform organization. Its roster of members may be short and its financial strength limited, but it represents an interest grouping among the population which is injured by the particular "abuses" of the government which have called the organization into being for the attack upon them. Its fight is the fight of the strength behind it as that strength can be brought to bear, and its success depends on the amount of power it can develop as against the power opposed to it, allowing for times and places of bringing its pressure to bear and proving the reality of its contention by the practical test.

Another illustration is the organization we now find in many American cities—and on the point of being imitated at Washington —for the supply of specific information about public officials, especially about members of legislative bodies, to the voters. These organizations have just the strength of the body of voters behind them, and of the recognized need they fill, which is the same thing.   Certain peculiarities of our electoral system furnish at once the opportunity and the cause for their existence.   Their future, which may range all the way from early disappearance to development into recognized structures of government, will depend exclusively on the subsidence or increase of this need, and the only way to get a solid basis for judgment is by the analysis of the group interests involved on all sides of the situation.

Again we find semi-political organizations planned to assist or supplement the administrative work of the government, where, owing to peculiarities of party rule or to other reasons, it is working poorly.   Many "citizens' associations" in the United States are in point.   Perhaps in such cases every director or contributor to such an association may think himself participating solely out of a disinterested regard for public welfare, and perhaps we may have no reason whatever to feel like entering a denial, yet nevertheless we can analyze the group need, the representative character of the organization and its leadership, and usually we can find that the men most prominent in the leadership belong to some group that has a specially marked interest.   An examination of the incidental semi-political activities of real-estate boards in big American cities would serve to bring out the point with great clearness.

Still more striking is the organization which at times can be found which produces what one may almost describe as substitute legislatures.   When there is some neglected interest to be represented, when the legislature as organized does not deal on its own initiative with such matters, when a point of support in party organization can be found—a point let us say of indifference, at which nevertheless the ear of some powerful boss can be obtained— a purely voluntary organization may be formed, may work out legislation, and may hand it over completed to the legislature for mere ratification.

These illustrations will suffice, albeit they are all taken from a single country, and that a country in which the rights of free association and free speech are guaranteed by law. The legal guarantees, important as they are from a technical standpoint, do not produce any vital difference in the human process. They simply describe and help to maintain the group process as it is actually proceeding. I have not found it necessary to emphasize them for the simple reason that I have been giving a more adequate description than they give to the very facts they indicate.

As for other countries it is only to be added that the particular forms of voluntary semi-political organization as distinct from party will depend on the group conditions and group organization of the time and place. Where the government is operated through groups, in the special political sense, as in France, instead of through parties of the American type, some of these voluntary organizations may appear as such group parties. Where the government has become an atrocity, the semi-political organizations may arise in tremendous vigor with terrorism perhaps as their weapon. Where the bulk of the representative process passes through a monarch instead of through an assembly, special forms will appear. The varieties must be studied by the analysis of the facts of the time and place.

CHAPTER XIX

THE GRADATION OF THE GROUPS

It is time now to state in a somewhat more systematic form the relationship between the various grades of groups, to which I have attempted to reduce the social process in the preceding chapters. And yet I must first make it emphatic that I am not attempting so much to get results as to indicate methods, and that I do not regard the extent of my study of the widely scattered facts of government as great enough to warrant me in being dogmatic about the exact number of varieties or even the typical relationships of groupings. So far as a scheme of group relations is put forth in this chapter it has no pretense to be more than tentative.

Tracing the thread back to the deep-lying interest groups which we find given in the population at each particular time and place, I have tried to show how the various other groups which attract attention most prominently on the surface of the governmental process can be adequately interpreted only by locating their exact representative quality with reference to the more fundamental interest groups. This representation of group by group has been traced along two general lines, that is, it has been found in two general types; one of these has been called discussion groups; the other may best be described by the term organization groups.

If I have made no attempt to define these two types of groups sharply, it is because, first of all, there is no sharp boundary line between them; and, secondly, because my purpose in this work is rather to show how both types of groups are functioning together in one system, than to set up any special line of distinction by definition. Such distinctions by definition will inevitably be made from time to time for special purposes in connection with special investigations; and they will not only be useful but absolutely

essential tools; useful, however, only so long as the special purposes
of the definitions are kept in view as they are used.

There is, of course, organization in the simplest discussion,
and discussion in the farthest stages of organization. We might
picture the process as a flowing stream in which a perpendicular
cross-section would represent the discussion phase and a horizontal
cross-section the organization phase. Sometimes passing through
a narrow channel we have a very deep narrow stream, and the
perpendicular cross-section—the discussion—seems to be the
whole nature of the happening; again the stream spreads out on a
broad level surface, and the organization phase seems so complete
that the perpendicular aspect, the discussion, seems negligible.
But such a picture is exceedingly crude, however well it may
serve to bring out this one aspect of the relationship. We have
not a single flowing stream, but a mass of myriads of currents,
plastic rather than liquid, and leaving thousand-fold shapes and
forms both of discussion and organization differentiated along its
course.

There is one point of view as to the relation between the discussion and the organization phases which tempts the investigator
at almost every step, because of its appearance of simplicity and
ease; that is, to assign to discussion an intermediate position in
the process between "conditions" and "action." To do this
does indeed mean some advance over an interpretation which
places the initiative in thinking, or in the series of thought development; but it does not allow at all for the richness of the development on the discussion side. We find there a bewildering wonder-
land of theory and dreaming, of exhortation and tirade, of fact and
fiction, every bit of it reflecting something of the living world of
men in which it arises, and nearly every bit of it presumptuously
asserting itself to be the center of the human universe, if not of a
more than human universe. We must find a way to follow the trains
of struggle and development through this mass, and to test what
part lies near the heart of the process reflecting there the strongest
pressures, and what part reflects but subsidiary currents or is
indeed but a flash and glitter far out upon the surface.

With the organization groupings we have somewhat the same observations to make. They cannot be placed offhand as stages of the process posterior to discussion. We may find organization highly developed that has not gone through differentiated discussion group process on any wide scale; we may find small groups of this kind coming, so it seems, directly out of the lower-lying groups without intermediate stages; and we may find organization groups that have been cast up on shore by the continuing process, so that they are little more than empty shells of past forces. For all of these things allowance must be made.

So far as we find organization groups and discussion groups identified with one another in great part, we must be able to get the representativeness of each worked out in terms of the underlying groups and the representativeness of each also in terms of the other. With this achieved, we can obtain a balance which will keep us from being led astray by the sweeping pretenses to dominance of any one aspect of the process.

Let us begin with the discussion groups. Some will be abstract theory, some will appear as emotional propaganda, some as definite programmes of action. Each of them will reveal to us a specialized discussion group with its leadership, the whole representing, or in other words leading, a group interest of the population or a set of such interests. A convenient illustration is socialism. The catchword socialism stands for a very large number of groupings which come to us in a confused throng when we first begin to make the analysis. We find, far out at the extreme, a theoretical discussion group, setting forth a theoretical socialism in a highly generalized form. A little farther in toward the center lie half a dozen or so theoretical socialisms much more special in the form they assume and in the particular phase of social life they reflect. Here Marxian socialism may serve as one example, with Christian socialism as another, contrasted in character. Still a little farther in, and we come to socialisms even more specific, with the center of emphasis directed on different phases of the process. Here we have marked nationality and industrial group characteristics plainly in view; also we find socialist political parties in great variety. And finally we find many special lines of activity, programmes, policies, and even laws and institutions, which, whether with the catchword socialism in evidence or not, we have to bring into relation with the other socialist phenomena. This mere attempt to list socialist phenomena shows at once how discussion and organization activities pass over into each other by endless imperceptible gradations.

In our most outlying region of pure theory we might find a certain "universal human" representation; that is, the socialism as put forth would pretend to represent human group activity detachable from limitations of time and place or at least with no further limitations than the last 500 years of Europe, with America, Australia, and a little of Asia aggregated to it. There we find a small group of men reflecting or leading in a very vague way a very wide group interest of presumably a very large proportion of the human beings. Stating itself as idea pure and simple, the discussion group is worked up in as vivid or convincing a form as any abstracted idea business could be. But we should nowhere find marked evidences of force, of pressure; there would be no adjustments under way in which we could see this group directly involved, or for which this group stood in a clearly representative relation. We should be compelled to regard it on the very proofs that we gathered, as something tossed off to one side, as poorly representative of the groupings that are counting in the governing process, as a bit of decoration rather than as an important part of the moving process.

As we move inward toward the more specialized socialistic theories, we get a chance to state them in terms of groups much more limited in character, but nearer to the groupings that are manifestly counting in the process. We can read right out of Marx's writings, for example, the specific group interests—the interests of the proletariat under certain conditions, for example— which they represent. We find the statement of these interests, however, one which does not sufficiently allow for the pressures against them—I am, of course, not talking of the validity of arguments, but of the exact place which theory of this sort holds as group representative in the actually given historical process. Broader though the leadership group may be, the represented group is still vague, ineffective, impotent.

Move next to socialist parties, considered for the moment not as participating in government, but as programmes or propaganda, and we find still greater specification, still more definite representation of interests. The pressures represented are easily discoverable and to some extent capable of exact estimate. At the same time the opposition pressures are in fact, whether in so many words or not, allowed for in the group theory.

Taking these parties close in to action, that is, passing over for the moment to the phase of organization rather than discussion, we find the programmes still more specific, we find the opposition pressures very accurately estimated, and we are able to locate the represented group interests almost entirely in powerful present-day pressures. The verbiage here may be wilder than in the most extremely "pure theory" first mentioned above, but the process itself is well in harness, and the representation of actually existing interests is vastly truer.

Finally, taking programmes and policies of the kind we commonly regard as related to these socialist programmes and policies even when the express declaration of faith in socialism is absent, we find group interests of the same kind that the socialism in the last form mentioned above had been representing, working along the same lines, without the particular kind of discussion-group representation which in other countries or other parts of the country was intermediate in their process.

When the most extremely "theoretical" groups claim to exercise any dominating influence over the more practical discussion groups or over any part of the social process, they can do it only on the basis of a theory which is merely an uncouth importation from crude individual psychology. There is absolutely nothing in the facts of social activity as given us to justify their claims to be the controlling elements in the situation. There is nothing to justify the assertion that the complex social situation can best be straightened out by working down into it from their point of view. On the other hand, when the most immediately practical policies or programmes claim dominance we need not delay more than an instant in order to recognize that they have their meaning and value, such as it is, only within the closely restricted limits of the particular situation in which they are working. It is always a question needing measurement and proof, as to just what value, what influence, any one of the phases of the discussion has for or upon any of the other phases; and such values can only be determined by reducing all phases to terms of the underlying interests.

Turning our attention now to the organization groups, the main types will at once be recalled, since in the discussion of the various agencies of government we have had specimen groups of this kind primarily in view all the way along. We find here two general varieties of representation, one in which the opposed groups reach adjustment through a single agent, the other in which they have different agents who mediate the struggle by a smaller struggle of their own. But this distinction is cut across by another distinction of even greater importance, namely, the extent in which the groups are consolidated into set classes or are found in more freely shifting forms. There is nothing inherently "good" in either variety of representation and the success with which either functions will depend on the given group and class conditions.

A despot with his army holding the balance between a number of provinces plays the part of a mediator, often in a highly useful way. So also may the president or other chief executive in governments like those of the United States. His strength at each moment is the strength of the great, shifting complexes of groups that support him. A representative assembly is typical of the second variety of representation, especially as one finds it in countries like France or Switzerland. But just as an individual as ruler may become the instrument of class dominance, so may a representative assembly. Sometimes we may have the assembly in two branches, each a class instrument. Sometimes, indeed, we have the assembly appearing in no other capacity than as class leader against a ruler who is himself a class representative; and again we may have a single individual, whether despot or constitutional ruler, given strength either as class leader or as mediator against a class-ridden assembly. The various agencies of government that have been discussed have shown these forms of representation in all varieties of intermixture.

Into the matter of types of class formation I have not thought it necessary to go for present purposes. Some writers give us a series: caste, class, trade, party; others make it caste, order, class. Hereditary membership is one of the tests that is used in making such distinctions for special investigations, and the possession of special legal privileges is another test. But even without hereditary affiliation, and without formal advantages in law, there may be a solidification of interest in fixed forms such as to justify the use of the general term class, as opposed to the freer groupings out of which class phenomena crystallize themselves. For my purpose here I have been able to set all the different kinds of class phenomena off under the one name, and use group as the more comprehensive term, embracing class, but specially applicable to the less fixed and concentrated phenomena.

In connection with both the discussion and the organization groups, one finds the personality groups, which are the outgrowths of established leadership. A leader once placed will. gather a following around him which will stick to him either on the discussion level or on the organization level within certain limits set by the adequacy of his representation of their interests in the past. That is, as a labor-saving device, the line of action in question will be tested by the indorsement of the trusted leader. The leader may carry his following into defeat in this way, but that very fact helps to define the limits of the sweep of groupings of this type.

With organization groups, just as with discussion groups, the most pretentious phases are not necessarily the ones to which the most importance must be attributed. They are not necessarily the ones which best express the underlying interests. The gleam-

ing tip of a governmental structure may or may not wield the full
weight of huge social pressures. It may be the agency for aug-
menting the strength of its subordinates, or it may do little more
than label the strengths which those subordinates employ. There
is no rule of thumb.

Neither the discussion nor the organization groups can be
interpreted except in terms of lower-lying groups. Neither can be
found in government out of relation to the other, though the
importance of the one or of the other at various stages of the
process differs greatly. Always they shade into each other without
sharp boundaries. Is there, then, any remaining reason for holding them in fundamental opposition to one another, not as merely
different varieties of activity, but as social methods or elements
which are qualitatively unlike? I think not. The citizen of a
monarchy who sees his king ride by may feel himself in the
presence of a great power, outside of him, entirely independent of
him, above him. The man busy in one of the discussion activities
of the time may look upon ideas as masterly realities self-existing.
But neither ideas nor monarch have any power or reality apart from
their representation or reflection of the social life; and social life
is always the activity of men in masses.

Both discussion groups and organization groups are forms of
the organization of social life in a wider sense of the word organization, and they show similar functional aspects. Both have leadership. Both have their set, habitual phases. Both have a certain
residual group aspect which we may call their "own interest."
Both show the phenomena of survivals. Both may be charged
with "tyranny," and in both, when a movement for "liberty" is
under way, that movement is a movement of underlying interests
which are seeking better expression for themselves.

Idea activities—to use another term in place of discussion groups
for the moment—represent underlying interests, and so do government activities. Both are differentiated structures through which
the interests work. Both are agencies for some of these underlying
interests as they strike at others. Neither ideas nor governments

in their limited immediate statement reflect fully the whole situation. They cannot be understood for what they are till they have been functioned in the social process; and to function them means to reduce them to terms of the underlying interests which give them their strength and their social meaning and value.

Not only are discussion groups and organization groups both technique for the underlying interests, but within them we find many forms of technique which shade into each other throughout both kinds of groups. In the older fighting, soldiers might sing as they went into battle, or an officer might go ahead waving the colors. The singing and the officer illustrate the technical work of the representative groups. They serve to crystallize interests, and to form them solidly for the struggle, by providing rallying points and arousing enthusiasm. For all that, it is the men as organized behind the singing, the cheering, and the colors that do the fighting and get the results.

Muscle is one form of technique for the groups, deception is another, corruption is another; tools of war fortify muscles, and tools for trickery also are to be found. Oratory and argument count as technical agencies at their proper stages in governmental development. Any such agency is employed where it answers to needs until it becomes a nuisance and is suppressed. Corruption as a technical agency is put down when it hurts groups of the population powerful enough to put it down. Again, the use of argument, of reasoning, whether in the form of clamor or of dogmatism, is technique which for itself is no more justified than is violence or corruption. The bully thinks his fist an unanswerable argument; and so the logician his logic. The logic may easily become as great a pest and nuisance in a society as the bribes or blows, in which case it will tend to the same fate. The man who tends to give final reality to his generalizations, his individualism, his anti-plutocracy, or what not, may roughen the process of group adjustment just as may the bully or bribe-giver, till at last his technique is made a content of group opposition and suppressed. There is psychic process in all social technique, but systematized theories about society do not monopolize it or even

offer the highest form of it.   The theories do not give of necessity
a better clue to the social process than would bare blows.

As between discussion and organization phases the representative relation is no more complex or mystical than is, for example,
the representative relation between written letters and vocal sounds.
We have two systems there, each of them having its value in terms
of the other; both of them activities which are socially organized
and systematized, and which may in extreme cases reach adjustment within the system through differentiated agencies of control
of their own.   All of the groups, whether underlying interests,
or discussion groups, or organization groups, have values in terms
of each other, just as have the colors in a painting, or the sounds
in music.   No color for itself alone no sound for itself alone, but
each gets its meaning from all.   There is not a bit of the process
that does not have its meaning in terms of the other parts.

We have next to ask how far we are justified in attributing
an independent influence, a pressure of their own over and beyond
the represented pressures, to the discussion groups or to the
organization groups looked on for the moment independently by
themselves.   Of course my whole attitude on such a point as
this is that the question can only be answered in each case or in
each set of cases by careful and exact analysis of the given facts.
But there are nevertheless certain observations that may be made.

Let me first call attention to certain exaggerations, or at least
to certain shades of overemphasis, in various earlier chapters of
this book.   In Part I, I was engaged in attacking the feelings and
ideas in their arrogation of independent existence and causal
power.   In so far there was no exaggeration.   But in practice
those feelings and ideas are far from being held off in any such
independence.   They are made use of to indicate a very important
part of the social activity.   And if my line of criticism should be
applied literally to this activity, there would be an exaggeration in
its statement.   The discussion activities, in other words, would
need more recognition than seemingly had been allowed them
there.   Later, in my description of the pressures of the under-

lying interests as they act through the executive and legislature, I put the emphasis continually on these underlying pressures, merely recognizing from time to time that a bureaucracy or an army or a royal family was an interest group in itself, and similarly that a legislature might have its own interest. That was done because these bodies from the ordinary point of view get immensely exaggerated emphasis as independent forces, and my object was to break down that independent position attributed to them, and to show them in their full representative aspect. On the other hand, when we came to the judiciary I went twice out of my way to show that the judiciary might be looked on from one point of view as having an interest of its own. The overemphasis in this case, so far as it was an overemphasis, was again employed for the very purpose of restoring the balance of emphasis. In the parties, and in the electorate and semi-political groupings, we got much closer to a balanced statement of the two aspects.

If we start out, now, to correct these exaggerations, we must recognize first of all that all these discussion groups and organization groups are themselves activities, themselves interests, and that therefore they are themselves pressures in the moving society, however trivial their pressures may sometimes be. At times I have spoken of these activities, the discussion and organization groups, as having their "own interest;" and at other times I have spoken of the value that must be attributed to them as "technique." The difference here is clearly one of point of view. In the first case we identify the activity with the particular set of persons in whom it is found in its differentiated form; in the second case we refer it to the represented groups, but as a "plus," a heightening of their activity, an increased effectiveness.

The term "own interest" here may again be understood in two ways. Either it may indicate a specialized underlying interest of the individuals who compose the group in question—so, for instance, the "selfish" personal interests of a despot or of a boss and his henchmen—or it may mean the tendency of the representative group to persist, i. e., its inertia, whether the case is of a belief or a governmental form. As an underlying interest, the "own inter-

est" must take its place with all the other underlying interests at
its due strength, and it does not concern us here. As a tendency
to persist we must remember that it is continuously sustained by
the complex of underlying groups. But this last statement is
vital also with reference to the "plus as technique." The underlying groups themselves create this technique, and the farther we
push the analysis, the nearer we come to stating the technique,
not as a technical instrument, a tool apart from the hand, but as
the functioning phase of tool-in-hand at work.

The problem we have here is not the same as that which arises
out of a contrast between the individual and the institution, which
is so often discussed. For us both the individual and the institution
have been absorbed into social groups, that is, restated as' social
groups. We have to deal with, not some mysterious "power"
of organization, but the actual process through representative
organization groups and representative discussion groups.

I am inclined to think that if a complete enough analysis of
the whole process could be made we could attain a point of view at
which we could see the activity of all these discussion and organization groups so completely absorbed into the represented interests,
that we should no longer feel ourselves under the necessity of
attributing any independent activity to them. But I am also
inclined to think that the point of view from which this could
practically be done is very far indeed beyond the possibilities of
our attainment. So that it all comes back to what I have repeatedly
said before, that we must push our analysis to the limit of our means,
and then allow only what remainder of pressure there is to the
"own interest" of the organization or discussion group, or to its
"plus as technique."

In different societies, societies with different types of underlying interest-group formations, we shall find the relative importance to be attributed to discussion and organization groups varying
greatly; but in no society can we find these more superficial groups
determining the fate of the underlying groups. In the societies
I know most about it is my opinion—always subject to revision
on fuller knowledge—that we already are able to push the analysis

far enough to justify us in saying that the lower-lying groups are affected by the discussion groups only in very short swings and in limited ways; and that they are affected by organization groups in slightly longer swings and more pronouncedly; but that both discussion and organization groups yield to the lower-lying groups with surprising rapidity when the actual change in the balance of pressures takes place.   And this explains why it is that no reconstruction of society in terms of the life-history of ideas, or of the life-history of governmental forms, can have more than a crude preliminary descriptive value.

CHAPTER XX

REPRESENTATIVE GOVERNMENT, DEMOCRACY, AND CONTROL BY "THE PEOPLE"

There is a theory—I do not know how far back it can be traced—that all acts of government ought to be the product of clear, cold reasoning, and that the maximum of detachment on the part of the legislator from the interests at stake will get the best results. We may say that this is "the" theory of political science, as it certainly is the professed point of view of most criticisms of government and of the theoretical statement of most schemes of reform which do not get into too close contact with immediate application. According to it every point at which government gets away from the purest and freest reasoning is an abnormal point. According to it also the standards of justice and desirability are matters which reason alone, if left undisturbed, can solve.

I will not say anything more about the psychology of this theory, for unless my previous chapters have completely miscarried it should be clear enough by this time that in government we have to .do with powerful group pressures which may perhaps at times adjust themselves through differentiated reasoning processes, but which adjust themselves likewise through many other processes, and which, through whatever processes they are working, form the very flesh and blood of all that is happening. It is these group pressures, indeed, that not only make but also maintain in value the very standards of justice, truth, or what not that reason may claim to use as its guides.

I do, however, wish to use this theory as we meet it in connection with American government to introduce what I have to say in greater detail than heretofore about representative government, democracy, and the whole topic of the control of government by "the people." Concretely, one may recall first of all the plan of the American Constitution for the election of the president, how trusted men were to be chosen in the states, how these were to get together in small meetings by states, where they would not be subject to stampeding, and were to cast their votes for the best man of the country for president; also how this thing never happened, but instead how the underlying interests of the country represented in the parties seized upon these little electoral gatherings and whirled them out of the way like feathers, playing through them according to their will.

Our early constitutional conventions were supposed to be constituted of "able men who listened to thoughtful arguments and were themselves influenced by the authority of their leaders." There it was supposed that "the councils of the wise prevailed over the prepossessions of the multitude." I am quoting from the *American Commonwealth*. Our modern legislatures are often disparaged in contrast with the good old times, and their lack of wise reasoning is made the mark of their degeneracy.

Now, we know where it is that the formal reasoning process may come to the front as the form through which government works—as technique, that is. It is where the reasoners are united in a group which is functioning in such marked opposition to some other group or groups that the various reflections of the process through the various heads become but as trifling oppositions in comparison with the greater opposition of the group to other groups: the marked opposition here referring not to verbal statements nor to the advanced stage of the pending adjustment, but to the underlying elements of the conflict.

We know also that, with the adjustment of one such opposition, new oppositions will form within the bosom of the, let us say, victorious group, and that the conditions for the whole group, as split up on new lines, will cease to be favorable to the formal reasoning process. We find, indeed, the same interest groupings, which previously in their subdued form might have adjusted themselves through the reasoning process, now forcing themselves more vehemently forward, and refusing to be content with compromise of that kind, insisting on showing their full strength by all the technical means which the prevailing habits of the time permit to them. In the United States we observe every day the forces adjusting themselves in our legislative bodies and in other officials in a way in which argument pure and simple in its own right holds a very subordinate position, confined indeed in the main to the minor groupal adjustments inside the main contending groups.

Evidently then on the very face of the facts this pure-reasoning test is not a good test for representative government or democracy; nor does its presence or absence throw any great light on the extent of popular control of government, either in the good or in the bad sense. Certainly when the presidential electoral system of the Constitution was overthrown in this country there was not a decrease but an increase in representative government and in democracy, whichever one of these vague terms one uses for the moment. Not until the party and convention system had taken the presidency under the present fairly complete control did the presidency become "the people's office." At present, while our legislatures are in the main working poorly, so that any kind of an interest with peculiar technique giving it undue proportional strength can get results from the legislatures, these bodies are catholic in their yielding to such pressures, caring not where they come from, so long as they are strong enough, or in other words, not resisting in one direction more than in another, provided the pressure is applied. They are representative bodies in their way, even though "the people" do not get their desired results with sufficient frequency.

I am not going to discuss definitions of representative government nor of democracy, inasmuch as most of those definitions belong on a discussion level very remote from the actually moving governmental process. They reflect something of the process in that "theoretical" way discussed in the preceding chapter, but they stand too far out from the heart of things to count for much in such work as this. There is one contrast, that between the representative and the delegate, however, to which further consideration should be given. These two words are not used in the same way by all writers, representative with some standing for what others mean by delegate, but that need not confuse us here. I myself in previous chapters have used the word "represent" in a most general sense, assimilating it to "reflect," and allowing it to cover cases in which all groups functioned through a common organ, as well as those in which a complex agency contained different individual members for different groups; including therefore cases of personal discretion as well as of differentiated representation. That was because it was most important for me to emphasize the similarities, not the differences. In what is immediately to follow I shall use representative in a much more conventional sense.

Now in this more conventional sense a monarch is not a representative. He is a ruler. The president is not a representative, except where we find him acting as part of the law-making body against Senate or House or Senate and House. Then he may be a representative of a certain group or set of groups which somehow have been left for the time being and on the given show of facts unrepresented in either or both houses. To catch our representative we have got to look where one group of people, formal or fundamental, has one member in some common body, and other groups have other members. And here we may find that what we really have is not a representative, but a delegate.

The representative is supposed to be a man who is intrusted with discretion to act for those who have chosen him, in such manner as he sees fit. A delegate is supposed to be a man who has received definite instructions from his electors and who is authorized to act only in accordance therewith. It is comparatively easy to find an illustration of the delegate, as in the members of the Bundesrat of the German Empire, but your representative, such as he is supposed to be, is hard indeed to find; though within his limitations the diplomat of pretelegraph days will serve. In the first place, the representative is commissioned not for any purpose whatever, but to act within the limits of a definite system. He is limited by his very function. In the next place, he has probably been chosen by his electorate or by the appointing power in competition with some other candidate, and in the competition his attitude on certain matters has been brought out before the electorate or the appointing power and to some extent passed upon by it there: whereby he is limited again. If he is a party member, he is more expressly limited by that allegiance. Also, by being in contact with his constituents from time to time, his action will probably be affected so that it will be reduced to one of a small number of possibilities. Finally we may find him swayed entirely by his constituents on some one or more issues and reducing himself to their delegate. If it were a question of formal law, the representative and the delegate could easily be distinguished. But we have to do with the practical process and so we must face the problem in all its fluidity.

Now, on the basis of the theory to which I gave attention at the opening of this chapter, one hears much criticism of the horrors which result from the reduction of wise, intelligent, and able representatives to mere delegates. A writer like Ostrogorski will grieve his heart out over it, and even one like Bryce will frequently deplore such a development. But I do not know any basis on which this tendency *per se* can be deplored save that of the particular theory which sets up the representative function in its extreme abstract form as the ideal and standard of government. And since the gradations between the representative and the delegate function are so many and so fine, and since, further, one nowhere finds a representative acting fully up to the idea of the word, I do not see how any such general line of criticism or judgment can be held valid. Of course, such expressions "represent" something themselves. They are used to indicate or label some group evil from the critic's point of view. The trouble with them is that they do not indicate the large situation with sufficient accuracy; that they are rather embroideries on the talk level than substantial reflections of the process. When even so fine a character and so admirable a statesman as Senator Hoar says, as he says in his autobiography, "I have always voted and spoken as I ought," he is not really characterizing his activity, but merely giving it a conventional and inadequate statement.

When it is said of political parties that they are no longer

instruments of public policy, but instead are this, that, or the
other non-reasoning element in the government, the same limitation in the view-point is to be noted. Morley in his essay "On
Compromise" spoke of the increasing prevalence of "the slovenly
willingness to hold two contradictory propositions at one and the
same time," and I imagine there never has been or will be a time
when critics with the superciliously intellectual point of view of
Morley will not find the same defect in the world to bewail. To
speak in terms of progress for the moment, it would surely be an
advance if parties should drop their set, formal, logically coherent
policies, providing that thereby they gave more efficient expression
to the underlying interests they represent. Along with these
illustrations might be mentioned the recent writer on the American
Constitution, who pointed proudly to "the idea of representative
government growing by its own power," thereby giving exceptionally naïve expression to a common point of view. But his super-
ficiality speaks for itself.

It is necessary then in considering representative government,
or democracy, not only past or present, but future as well, to consider it in terms of the various group pressures that form its
substance. It is useless to pause with some formal definitions,
add on a few theoretical standards, and then try to get the facts
straightened out. Instead, at every stage these forms must be
considered as they are used by the pressures. As substance,
rather than process, they can be taken into account only so far
as we gain positive knowledge that they are, in the given state of
the group oppositions, used by certain groups in such a way that
other groups, reacting against the evil in the situation, are potentially or manifestly tending toward attack upon them.

It does not seem to me necessary here to go back over the
analysis of the process as set forth in the chapters on the various
agencies of government. Merely to recall them is to point out
how the group pressures in the population form themselves on
the various discussion levels and organization levels, tending always
to express themselves in both ways or in any way, and actually
expressing themselves to such degrees as the resistance of the

other groups as represented in the government will permit at the given time. But a special reminder is desirable of the district system of representation, which in modern countries as a rule is highly formal when compared with the substance of the interests which are striving to exert themselves through it.

In governments like that of the United States we see these manifold interests gaining representation through many thousands of officials in varying degrees of success, beating some officials down now into delegate activity, intrusting representative activity (in the narrow sense) to other officials at times in high degree, subsiding now and again over great areas while "special interests" make special use of officials, rising in other spots to dominate, using one agency of the government against another, now with stealth, now with open force, and in general moving along the route of time with that organized turmoil which is life where the adjustments are much disturbed. Withal, it is a process which must surprise one more for the trifling proportion of physical violence involved considering the ardent nature of the struggles, than for any other characteristic.

We often hear of "the control of government by the people." The whole process is control. Government is control. Or, in other words, it is the organization of forces, of pressures. In a limited way I might add it is the organization of public opinion, and this indeed is a phrasing which once upon a time I would have put first in the series. But the whole process of control is too deep and vital to be stated as the organization of opinion: the opinion is but one differentiated agency to represent the process, and not at all the most accurate expression of it, at that.

What is usually meant by "control by the people" is only one of the elements in control. It is a generalized statement, poorly representative, indicating certain direct reactions by large masses of men against certain smaller masses which, as appears in the group oppositions themselves, are controlling the government process to an excessive degree. These oppositions appear, however, on what—to use the terminology of economic theory—may be called the margin of the governmental process. And the reason why the "control by the people" is a poorly representative statement is just because the great underlying masses of control are in existence, much deeper and more fundamental as facts than the contest that is being waged on the margin.

The greater portion of the detail of governmental work, as embodied especially in the law that is being daily sustained, is composed of habitual reactions which are adjustments forced by large, united weak interests upon less numerous, but relatively to the number of adherents, more intense interests. If there is anything that could probably be meant by the phrase "control by the people" just as it stands, it is this. And we may even say that without "control by the people" there would be no government, save in the cases of subjected peoples under foreign masters, with assimilation little advanced. And even here, unless the one weapon of government is the ever-drawn sword, such control is the manifested phenomenon.

There is, be it remembered, the wider field of control, that is of adjustment of group to group, outside the field of government in the narrow sense of the term, and forming the background in which the processes of government are carried on. Often a group interest, developing under some special conditions to an extreme, will give way through this outer control before the operations of government proper are appealed to. Part of this field is a sediment from the process of government itself, involving adjustments so deep set that they are dropped from the ordinary work of the organized government. All of this extra-governmental adjustment, while forming the background for the government process and capable of interpretation by very similar methods, is outside of our immediate field of study.

Now when government, as the representative of the "absent" or quiescent group interests, is distorted from this function to any noticeable extent by the concentrated pressures of smaller group interests, themselves the result of newly opened opportunities in the social mass, and fails to respond as it should, we hear the cry that there is need of "control by the people," and we see the formation of a group interest directly aroused in opposition to the interests which have gained objectionable power. And when the agencies through which the "people," or in other words such large group interests, habitually react fail to work smoothly for them—as is the case with the highly organized parties at times— we find the cry for popular control directed against those very agencies. The mysticism of "the people" is a matter of speech alone. The real facts are to be found by us in the groups as we analyze them out, and there only.

That "pure democracy" often heard of in arguments under similar circumstances and in theories which run to the far extreme from the moving process, may be mentioned in the same connection. It is supposed to be a "government by the people" directly and immediately, but the slightest analysis of the process at any point shows how very poorly representative the phrase is, save as a slogan and rallying cry for some particular groups at special stages of their activity. Freedom, liberty, independence, and other similar rallying cries in the governmental process all need the same kind of interpretation.

If now we take a different point of view and examine the set structure of control in the organized government, including the checks and balances of which American political theory has so much to say, we shall find a great variety of established methods. We have here to do with structures which were set up, and which remain, to prevent special groups, whether "the people" or the "special interests" of current speech, from getting a disproportionate power of functioning through the government. First of all we have, of course, the control of executive by legislature and vice versa, and the control of both by the judiciary. Then we have the control which is arranged by separating local from general issues, a control which in the United States is exerted in three divisions, the federal, the state, and the local governments. Then comes the control involved in the establishment of many independent offices in any one field, each of the offices subject directly to the suffrage. The majority vote on a wide suffrage basis may also be added for controlling all the agencies mentioned. Again we find parties, first as direct group representatives, and then as syndicated agencies for group representation, controlling from their own level, now one, now another, sometimes all, of the more specialized agencies of government, and at times producing a unification, as well as at times a more pronounced splitting, between them. There is also the control of party by party faction, and, of course, of one party by a rival party or by rival parties, that being essential in any party operation. Finally we have the control exerted by groups expressing themselves through public-opinion activities as these are practically analyzed by the controlled agents in the very act of their expression. And all of this controlling process takes at times the appearance of a control of persons and at times of the control of policies, according to the variations of the content that is being functioned through the process.

This structural arrangement of government is that which constitutes representative government, or democracy, whichever term is used. Definitions, or rather descriptions, which state governments in terms of the functioning of the groups through these bits of structure, to whatever extent or in whatever proportions they are present, are something that one can depend on far more than on definitions in terms of artificial men, acting in artificial ways under artificial conditions, and depending entirely on credulity for their claim to mirror rightly the tendencies of the process as it develops in time.

Besides these elements of such government we may also take into account various other methods of control which are now forming themselves as structure to some extent in a great many countries. More of them at once are perhaps to be found in the United States than anywhere else, securing their places on the basis of the actual group force they have behind them; but that is only as it happens. It is no mere accident, but a very normal fact, that the very project of a referendum on ordinary legislation, which is the monopoly of the "friend of the plain people" in the United States is put forth coincidentally by the House of Lords in England for its own official purposes.

We may enumerate here besides the referendum in its various

forms, the initiative, the recall, the direct primaries, and perhaps also proportional representation and other plans to readjust the organization of the suffrage, where its majorities and minorities seem to work too crudely.   This latter bit of structure, proportional representation, at least in the United States, has never had much actual pressure behind it; where it has been introduced it has come as a bit of the poorly representative work of the "wise men" in government; and the group pressures that accompany its use seem to be such that they inevitably break it down instead of sustaining it.   At any rate in Illinois one allied scheme has recently been abandoned, and another seems to be on the point of going, even though a very difficult process of constitutional amendment will be necessary to that end.   This, however, is only incidentally remarked.

I am perfectly well aware that these various forms of control, as we find them developing, have arguments made for them continually in the name of democracy, and against them continually in the name of representative government, with many criss-cross arguments on both sides.   But if there is anyway by which theoretically or otherwise they can be shown to be more typical of either democracy or representative government, or more filled with the "spirit" of either of these types of government, than are our present systems, I know not how it is.   That is, I know the logic of the arguments, and I know its inutility, but I do not know how the point can be made in terms of the group interests which make up the people.

Group interests there certainly are behind many of these tendencies, and strong ones at that, but they are very concrete, immediate group interests, growing directly out of oppositions which have developed in the developing process.   They can be located, most of them, with great exactness as to their strength and meaning in the whole given political system.   But they can be located as well on one theory as on another.   And the representation that they commonly get on the discussion level, whether from friends or enemies, is very poor indeed, save as so much noise, so much enthusiasm, so much quickening of the flow of blood in the members of the banded group.

These various tendencies have their usual statement as reform movements, but it hardly seems necessary to say anything more of them in that aspect. There they appear as busy discussion groupings and as voluntary organization groups, but I have already discussed this process, and I only note here how easy it is, and how essential also, to strike down through these specialized and more superficial phenomena to the underlying forces.

Out of all this mass of phenomena of representative government and democracy it is of course possible to draw off pictures mirroring, mainly with aesthetic value, the status of a whole nation as contrasted with the status in other nations, but I am inclined to think there are much better ways to do it than in terms of the democracy and representative-government theories: and to do it, while at the same time retaining the full value of "the people" in the process.

One might estimate the amount of blocking in the functioning of the government, the kinds of technique necessary, or at least tolerated for the operation of several varieties of interests, and the extent to which interests are compelled to overstate themselves on the discussion level while struggling to make themselves effective. One might work out a picture of the adjustments, "normal" for the given society, not in terms of a providence that filled every mouth, nor of a morality projected to ideality from any given point of view, but in terms of the adjustment of actual strengths in the given society, in terms of such a process that every interest forcing itself beyond the point of endurableness to the remainder of the interests would be checked before its excess had provoked violent reaction.

We should certainly not find, if we attempted such a picture, that our own modern societies were the best adjusted, the most advanced or progressive reported to us in history. And we certainly should find, that the relatively perfect adjustment of any society was a function not of some absolutely and independently stated characteristic of political structure, but instead, of underlying group conditions, of situations and disturbances of situations, due to factors far down beneath the political level, however reacted upon in special phases from the political level.

Such picturing of society lies very far outside of my sphere, farther even than the examination of the underlying conditions for this whole process; but to the latter I will devote a few paragraphs in the next chapter, more to show the field which I remain outside of, than in any way to attempt to occupy it.

CHAPTER XXI

THE UNDERLYING CONDITIONS

I have talked repeatedly about the "underlying groups" without attempting to specify them systematically. I conceive that these groups must be taken as they come, in each country and period as they are there and then found. I do not think they have as yet been worked out in sufficient detail for many countries to justify any attempt at a general classification of the types of underlying groups which enter into political life. I wish here only to show in a general way some of the conditions of the formation of these underlying groups, more by way of indicating how such matters lie outside the scope of this volume, than to make any positive contribution to their understanding.

The biologically described man is, of course, part of our given fact; but he does not as such, that is without further interpretation, enter directly into our social studies. Where the whole interpretation can be made directly in terms of vital factors, we are still within the field of biology and do not get to anything that we can call sociology, or a phase of sociology, at all. There is unquestionably a physical selection going on among men in society, as for example under the influence of war and of disease; and there are important facts of physical adaptation, as in resistance to disease, which are shown not only in the disappearance of certain plagues, but also in adaptation on the one side to the perils of tropical jungle and on the other side to the no less serious perils to the health from crowded city life. But these things must all be stated as aspects of group activity before they become significant for the interpretation of government, or, for that matter, for any other interpretation of social process. While there is systematized behavior in the animal before there is society in the sense of that word which implies structural arrangement in a mass of men, nevertheless with the very simplest differentiation of such activities in the mass, which itself is social structure, we get beyond the activity in its merely biological description; in other words, we get beyond instincts and similar factors as adequate causes of social process. Here also we must interpret in terms of the groups differentiated in the human material.

I cannot resist the temptation to point out that so far from this method of interpretation being in opposition to "natural selection," it is itself a form of truly natural selection studied under circumstances which give peculiarly good opportunities for getting intimate understanding of the process instead of merely sweeping views of results; and that, so far from the group method of interpreting society being liable to criticism from the point of view of natural selection in the restricted sense of the phrase, it is much more apt to help the students of that phase of natural selection to a better comprehension of it. There is a representative process involved in the pressures in animal and vegetable life, different enough in technique from that of the social world, which nevertheless cannot safely be overlooked.

Taking the human being from the biological point of view, we may admit a substratum of physical race for the groups, so far as such race facts can be proved to exist; whether with reference to differences as between different societies, or as to differences between different elements in one society. But they all appear in social interpretation as group facts. I have already indicated how the group factors usually attributed to race are in reality complexes of group activities, and I do not need to say anything more about them here except to point out that they rest on all the different underlying conditions mentioned in this chapter.

Passing now from the biological man to the physical environment, again we find that this does not enter as such into the interpretation of social happenings. I have here only to apply what I said about the environment in chap. vii. In the group we take up the environment as well as the men, the group itself being formed in a way that includes both. Perhaps I should best be understood if I said the physical environment is not taken into our study concretely

—as so many sticks, stones, rivers, cows, and other things. But I prefer to phrase it with greater accuracy the other way about, and insist that, while we do take it into account concretely, i. e., in the groups, we do not take it abstractly, i. e., as lying apart from men; for I conceive that as we observe it lying apart it is an abstraction from the living, moving groups.

Now, abstracting the physical environment, that is, looking at the groups from the point of view of the environment (which is permissible merely as a stage in the analysis), we may first examine the environment as a condition of the group formation. In other words, when we take up a given society for study we may, to begin with, strive to state the groups in terms of the different factors of the physical environment, as far as we can analyze them out. Most crudely put, we have groups resting on mines, farms, fisheries, cattle herds, city lots; we have groups related to steam power and to electricity. We have many forms of all of these. Deserts and rivers and space itself count with them also. But with all these we do not get so very far. Groups stated with reference to these factors which in one society appear in sharp opposition to each other may in another appear as in close co-operation.

The most important of these groups assume wealth forms. We are but developing our analysis of the groups when we get them stated as wealth groups. The capital oppositions come in all their various historic forms, down to the present-day oppositions which on the discussion level monopolize the word capital as the symbol of numerous things, actual and imagined. We are of course here considering the groups primarily with a view to their importance in the study of government; and all these various wealth groups are of special importance, because of their liability to fierce activity when thrown out of adjustment at any time, and further because of the direct and indirect technical advantages the wealthier groups secure; direct advantages being typified best by corruption, and indirect perhaps by education.

But with these we have by no means come to an end. The mass of the population, sheer number, taken of course in connection with place and wealth conditions, has an enormous amount to do both with the lines of group opposition that form themselves and with the violence of the group struggles and the whole technique of group interaction. Changes in the mass are of the greatest importance, and the difference between city and country also attract attention here.

Again there is the technique of industry, all the ways of doing things from the simplest tool-making of the savage up to the last methods of applied science. These things, themselves the products of group oppositions, become so important in the structure of the society that we are justified in setting them off abstractly as we have the preceding factors, and looking upon the group oppositions from their point of view. They too must be reckoned with in the analysis.

Also as a special branch of these latter factors there are the means of communication, both the transportation lines and the organized dissemination of information through the press and other agencies. The story of the trade routes has in recent years been told, the significance of the Roman highways has been pointed out, and that also of the great rivers of history; and in our own times we know, every one of us, right from the face of the facts, how differently we should be grouped, and hence politically organized, in the United States, without our highly developed methods of communication. We can see how some of the peculiarities in the operation of our wide-extended suffrage depend upon such factors, but we can see at the same time how these factors themselves are the outgrowth of underlying group interests and can only be given independent attention by abstraction from those interests.

Another consideration is the manner of organization of the underlying factors, considered as apart from their direct organization with reference to government. An industrial corporation is, of course, in one way the "creature" of law, but more fundamentally the tendencies to joint operation in industry are the creators of the corporation law itself. Organization as we see it in corporations and in labor unions, the structure, that is, of pressures that have gained a technical method for making themselves industrially more effective—must be taken into account as we find it. The question as to how far some groups have had historically their own organization as separate societies before they have entered into closer relations to one another in one common society is not of fundamental importance, but only one special line of variation in the general group process.

I do not mean that these are all the factors, that is to say, points of view, which must be taken into account in the analysis of the underlying groups. I give them as the great factors which stand out most clearly at this moment. They can be conceived of, and to a considerable extent actually handled, as existing apart from government. So far as this can be done they help us to the statement of the groups which can properly be described as underlying government.

But at the same time it must never be forgotten that the groups as they take their place in government tend to fix themselves in their governmental forms, and that in this way government itself, as a complex of pressures, may at times need to be regarded as one of the factors in determining the groups which, when we are studying government, we must inevitably at certain stages analyze out separately as underlying government.

CHAPTER XXII

THE DEVELOPMENT OF GROUP INTERPRETATION

For two reasons I wish now to sketch the development which the interpretation of society in terms of groups has undergone in the last generation. One is that the manner of writing in this book has not permitted sufficient reference to the previous use of the method by different investigators. The other is that this very method of interpretation is itself a group phenomenon, since each separate book that has used it is itself a phase of the leadership of a discussion group, and each such discussion group is itself representative with greater or less accuracy of wider group interests. In discussing the various theories, I shall be able to indicate in some slight measure the character of the representation which these theories give us of group interests and their places in the moving system. It is a question here, once more, not of complete description, but merely of illustration, and I make no pretense of naming all the writers who deserve to be named in this connection, nor of working out thoroughly their connection with the political process in which they are involved or which they reflect.

The starting-point for practical purposes is, of course, Karl Marx. Not that the implied use of groups in reasoning about society begins with him—it is indeed the body of all the reasoning. I shall speak of that in the next chapter. Nor can it be said that similar views were not explicitly held before him. I assert merely that the setting of activity in which he was the center threw the theory out into unusual distinctness.

With Marx it was the "class struggle," a very crude form of group interpretation, but one highly significant in its immediate use. The cause which Marx led was of course a group cause. His group was receiving through its leaders an unusually vehement verbal expression just at that time. So vehement was this expression that all other group oppositions except the one of the proletariat and the masters seemed to sink from view, to be trivial, and so negligible. The group was erected in talk into a class; the class appeared theoretically solid and firm, and the whole problem of leadership was to get its members all into action at once. Its victory, described in millennial terms, was to come forthwith.

Now Marx and his friend Engels were fresh from dalliance with Hegel and other similar` pleasures of youth, and they promptly reflected this situation in generalized terms along certain very interesting theoretical lines. The big group they were helping to lead, the class of the proletariat, they erected into a type, and history, they said, was the struggle of the classes. The directly economic character of the class they led inspired them at once to a statement of the process as historical materialism or, in more recent phrase, as the economic interpretation of history. We get from them such sentences as:

The history of all hitherto existing society is the history of class struggles.[1]

In the social production which men carry on they enter into definite relations that are indispensable and independent of their will: these relations of production correspond to a definite stage of development of their material powers of production. The sum total of these relations constitutes the economic structure of society—the real foundation on which rise legal and political superstructures and to which correspond definite forms of social consciousness· The mode of production in material life determines the general character of the social, political, and spiritual processes of life. It is not the consciousness of men that determines their existence, but on the contrary their social existence determines their consciousness.[2]

The whole history of mankind (since the dissolution of primitive tribal society holding land in common ownership) has been a history of class struggles, contests between exploiting and exploited, ruling and oppressed classes.[3]

Marx's political economy was a special method of reflecting this

[1] *Communist Manifesto*, authorized Eng. trans., p. 7.

[2] Marx, Preface to *Zur Kritik der politischen Oekonomie*, translated as *A Contribution to the Critique*, etc., p. 11.

[3] Engels, Introduction to English edition of *Communist Manifesto*, p. 5. See also preceding sentences, and Engels, *The Development of Socialism from Utopia to Science*, New York, 1892, p. 13.

group process at the particular stage he was observing, on the discussion level, but we are not interested in it here.   Our question is how far did his theory of the class struggle and his historical materialism correctly express the situation.   The proof that they reflected it but very feebly lies in the known facts of the years that followed.   The proletariat, he thought, was such a sharply defined class that it was only necessary "to point out and bring to the front the common interests of the entire proletariat, independent of all nationality."[1]   Working-men of all countries were to unite. But in fact, the International, which was to lead them, was a complete failure. A proletariat class, such as Marx and Engels conceived it, simply did not exist.   Labriola, it is true, apologizes for the International's failure on the ground that its task was "the preliminary equalization of the ideas common and indispensable to all the proletariat,"[2] and says it necessarily disappeared when its work was done, but he does not reflect here Marx's idea of what the International was to do, nor does he do justice to his own very intelligent expression of historical materialism, in allowing such a function to ideas in this connection.

An incidental proof of the weakness of Marx's theory as he himself held it was that he was unable with all his mental agility to work out a clear statement of what he meant by a class.   Even as good a socialist as Kautsky complains of this.[3]   Further, we have the fact that Marx had so little appreciation of the fundamental workings of the group process that he expected classes to disappear in the coming reign of brotherly love.   "In place of the old bourgeois society with its classes and class antagonisms we shall have an association in which the free development of each is the condition for the free development of all."[4]

Marx's theory of classes, then, was poorly representative of what was happening, because he made his classes too "hard and fast," or in other words because the particular groups which he

[1] *Communist Manifesto*, p. 16.
[2] *Essays on the Materialistic Interpretation of History*, p. 54.
[3] *Neue Zeit*, May, 1903, pp. 241, 242.
[4] *Communist Manifesto*, p. 22.

called classes were abstractions; because his theory merely indicated a connection but did not attempt to work out the position of the discussion groups among the others, and because the economic basis of groupings was overemphasized in too crude a form.

Turn now to Ludwig Gumplowicz, the writer who, so far as my acquaintance with such literature goes, has taken the most important step toward bringing out clearly the nature of the group process. With him we get away from identification with a single class in the community, and we find the group activities given a much wider and firmer foundation. He reflects the process at longer range, is as he stands much more remote from the field of acute struggle, but also offers a much more effective agency for any group interests that ultimately avail themselves of his point of view to state themselves in a way to develop their powers in accordance with the requirements of their situations.

Gumplowicz' works are so well known that I will merely indicate cursorily the points of his theory. He discards the individual as a causal factor in society, and insists that all social movements are brought about by group interactions. "When two or more distinct groups come in contact, when each enters the sphere of the other's operations, a social process always ensues."[1] He assumes the polygenetic origin of man, because he finds at the beginning of history innumerable separate small groups. When two or more of these groups clash, social structure begins to form, and not till then. Indeed it forms only when one group is absorbed by another and made a lower class in the resulting compound society. He holds that in general the classes that count most in the structure of society are classes that have thus been taken in from without and reduced from independent to dependent elements.

As a rule classes arise originally, i. e., out of different ethnical elements, or by the permanent organization of such as are at different stages of development at the time of their union.[2]

But he adds classes that appear by internal differentiation.

[1] *Outlines of Sociology*, p. 85.
[2] *Ibid.*, p. 136.

And even as to the origin of the classes of unequal power that compose the state he admits that

it might happen (?) as an exception that a period of peaceful development should result in the differentiation of the population into classes, the stronger gradually separating themselves from those who were weaker and needed protection.

For later stages of society he finds it necessary to take into account classes mainly of secondary origin, and when he gives us a table of the "group-making factors," he includes situations which as we find them are certainly far removed from the "original" group foundation. He interprets government in terms of these classes. His series of groups is, primarily, hordes, tribes, communities, peoples, states, and nations; and his classes are based on propinquity, profession, rank, property, trade, religion, language, art, and so forth.

He makes, however, a sharp distinction between social and psycho-social phenomena. The social are the group processes; the psycho-social are such phenomena as language, morals, law, religion, and systematic knowledge. These are treated by him as a sort of nondescript modification of the psychic life of individuals caused by the group process and occasionally requiring to be recognized as themselves causes in interpretation, but not as themselves really phenomena of group activity. It is hard to do justice to Gumplowicz with reference to these last-mentioned elements in his system, because his own statements are frequently inconsistent.[1] Nevertheless, despite some lapses of a kind I will mention in a moment, he is on the whole very solid in his insistence that rights are produced by the conflict of social groups, coming neither from the individual nor from any "common will," but from a struggle intermediate between these two statements;[2] and in such assertions as this concerning legislation that "the only possible solution of the social question lies in a harmonious co-operation of the social groups so far as that is possible."[3]

[1] See *Sociologie und Politik*, sec. 33; *Outlines*, Part IV.
[2] *Outlines*, p. 178; Cf. *Soziologische Essays*, p. 53.
[3] *Outlines*, p. 156.

Groups which Gumplowicz uses in his interpretations are groups that are concrete in the sense that they are composed of so many different people who can be gathered together in physical separation from other groups.   In general they are groups of such character that a man can belong only to one of them.   They are not groups as I have used the word in early chapters, but classes of an extreme type.   I do not mean to say that in the illustrations which Gumplowicz uses he never takes groups of any different nature, but that his tendency is to interpret the social process directly in terms of such groups, and not to make the further analysis into the underlying specific interest groups which they represent.[1]

This is one defect in his system as it stands.   Another is that he has left the "psycho-social" phenomena in an awkwardly nondescript position, as I have already indicated.   With groups as "concrete" as his, it will be hard indeed to assimilate these other phenomena to groups, and inasmuch as he could not make them purely individual phenomena, lest they return and take bitter vengeance on his system, he hung them in the air "betwixt and between."

In connection with these defects we find him at one time insisting that in the group struggle "the only motive is self-interest"[2] and at another telling us that "men grow accustomed year by year to submit to rights; they use legal forms constantly and learn to respect rightful limitations, until finally the conception, the very idea, of rights pervades and controls them."[3]   We find him using "material, economic, and moral (intellectual)"[4] standards alongside one another as tests in the classification, regardless of the various degrees of representativeness of the material he is handling. We find him at one time denying the existence of a "common will"[5] and at another insisting that the inoculation of all individuals

[1] For his own statement of the complexity of group formation in the class see *Sociologie und Politik*, p. 73, and *Outlines*, p. 143.   My point is not that he does not make this distinction, but that he does not develop it and use it.

[2] *Outlines*, p. 145.

[3] *Ibid.*, pp. 148, 149.

[4] *Ibid.*, p. 142.

[5] *Die sociologische Staatsidee*, 2d ed., p. 3.

whatsoever with the "higher morality" is the supreme goal of the state.[1]

A special illustration of the way in which Gumplowicz allows a very marked non-groupal factor, in the form of an idea not broken down into its representative characteristics, to intrude into his interpretations, is his assertion that the "neu aufgetauchte Idee" of the "Rechtsstaat" had a very powerful influence upon German and Austrian law-making and administration in the middle of last century.[2] The fact which he indicates in this manner is, of course, not to be denied, that there was activity in transforming legislation and administration, and that the "Rechtsstaat" was prominently mentioned as present. We may allow to Gumplowicz the implied belief that the "Rechtsstaat" idea itself can be explained as a psycho-social product of group factors. But much more than that is necessary. The "Rechtsstaat" must be functioned in its representative value in group terms at the very hour and place of its alleged working in order to find its value. When Gumplowicz gives the "idea" itself such potency as he does, he merely indicates one spot at which his theory is not adequately elaborated. In the same passage we find him also attributing to the idea, "von den socialen Aufgaben des Staates," the impulse to a series of social reformatory laws and institutions, thus again stopping his analysis half way.

It therefore appears that Gumplowicz despite all his defiance of the "ideas" still leaves them as "there," as to a great extent undigested lumps of matter in his system. He gets around them for the most part mainly by rejecting them as unimportant products of group action on the individual, and when he finds cases in which he cannot thus reject them, he has trouble in handling them, or rather he makes no pretense of handling them, but swallows them raw.

We may interpret the classes, as he makes use of them, as being a good representation of the Austrian life as he is surrounded by it

[1] *Outlines*, p. 169; Cf. also *Die sociologische Staatsidee*, p. 52, for his use of "Daseinsbedingungen der Gesammtheit."

[2] *Die sociologische Staatsidee*, p. 24.

looked at from a specially limited point of view. His theory is cold and remote from the particular groups in the Austrian struggle, but it is nevertheless focused too closely on struggles of that particular type which are so specialized and set in their forms, that they do not open the way to the fullest and freest interpretation of the group procedure.

From Gumplowicz turn to Georg Simmel. Here is a man whose work seemingly stands in the sharpest contrast to the other's, but whose acute analysis has nevertheless admirably supplemented the blunter studies of his Austrian contemporary; and the two can be made to fit together so aptly for the practical purposes of further study, that one even hesitates to assign to Simmel the lesser rank in achievement. If one were to judge these two men by current standards of mental power or delicacy, one would probably place Simmel far in the lead; but this merely serves to illustrate the relativity of such judgments. Since Simmel's work gains its main practical value in the matter of group interpretation by its supplementary aid to Gumplowicz, the latter is no doubt the more important figure from this point of view.

What Simmel has accomplished, primarily in his little book, *Ueber sociale Differenzierung*, and then in the brilliant studies that have followed it, is the analysis of the groups which cross one another in a thousand directions in the social mass, and at whose intersections "personality" and "individuality," he holds, are to be found. Taking the facts wherever he finds them most suitable for his purpose, Simmel has traced the group lines, and endeavored to make clear many of the typical forms in which group relations occur. But here is his defect. He has done this in terms of a psychology which is itself not simple process, but is too often a content which obtrudes with crude persistence into all his analysis; a defect which is all the stronger since he himself has done excellent work in banishing the most generalized forms of ideas and feelings from their pretentious appearance in social interpretation.[1]

[1] "Parerga zur Socialphilosophie," *Jahrbuch für Gesetzgebung*, etc., Vol. 18, p. 258. Also in his *Einleitung in die Moralwissenschaft*.

This defect appears in a double way. The forms which he gives us are primarily psychological, not social, or rather I may put it that his standards in classifying waver between social and individual psychological; and secondly, the detached feelings and desires and ideas continually appear to give force and power to the social process in their quality as individual content underlying and preceding the social forms and structures.

I will refer briefly to a number of passages taken almost at random from his writings to illustrate this. He tells us, for example,[1] that "spiritual structures" like language, morals, church, law, and political organization, although standing over against the individual as something objective, nevertheless "have their existence only in personal minds."   "Every attempt," he says, "to think of them outside of persons is a mysticism."   Then he appends this little confession of faith: "So far as I can see, this antinomy can be resolved in only one way. From the point of view of completed knowledge we must hold unconditionally to the fact that there are only spiritual individuals."   While permitting the treatment of such structures "as unities" because of our limited vision, his aim is continuously "to approach nearer to the individual operations which produce the social structure."

I have no objection whatever to his confession of faith, as such, nor to his epistemological principle. It is only to the use he makes of it, wherein he fails to allow his own group process full sweep, that I object. Instead of holding to the groups as groups and remembering his own demonstration that individuality occurs where the group lines cross, he uses all sorts of fragments of individuality as material of explanation. For instance, he says that the interpretation of religion can "only be approached when all the impulses, ideas, and conditions operating in its domain are inventoried."[2]   It is "our most real and personal instinct," he says, which enforces moral commands upon us.[3]   Again: "The actually dissociating elements are the causes of conflict—hatred and envy, want and desire."[4]

---

[1] *American Journal of Sociology*, Vol. III, p. 665.

[2] *Ibid.*, Vol. XI, p. 359.   [3] *Ibid.*, Vol. II, p. 184.   [4] *Ibid.*, Vol. IX, p. 490.

Along with this we find Simmel tacitly assuming that social progress is a concomitant of brain progress, as in his illustration of the monasteries and their influence on heredity,[1] and in such a reference as that of the coming to consciousness of latent mental inheritances.[2]   Also we find him over and over again attributing things to the "group will," or discussing events in terms of a group unity or a social unity.   For instance, he contrasts with majority rule which is the mere dominance of the strong, a unitary group will, and he holds the distinction to be of the highest sociological importance.[3]   Here we find him saying that "the immanent principle" of our parliamentary system is that "the majority does not speak in its own name but in that of the ideal unity and totality." In other words, he knows brute strength on one side and a cohesive power of ideas on the other side, but he does not really function them together, and he makes his own interpretations of "socialization" on the idea side.   Thus he explains the persecution of heretics as springing from "the instinct which recognizes the necessity for group unity."[4]

Now as the result of this point of view we get from Simmel such classifications as that of the elements which make for the persistence of groups; in which territory, blood relationship, loyalty, and honor are put in a series.[5]   We get so thin an explanation of the predominance of ruler over ruled as that the ruler gives all his personality to the arrangement, while the ruled only give up small bits of their personalities.[6]   We get a series of form types of groups like the trinity—"the unpartisan and the mediator, the 'tertius gaudens' and the 'divide et impera.'"[7]   Even so solid an interpretation as that of the lie and its suppression, in which the fact is brought out that each lie injures a great many more persons than it benefits,[8] we get stated more as a psychic curiosity than as a piece of powerful pushing human life.

[1] *Ueber sociale Differenzierung*, p. 130.

[2] *Die Probleme der Geschichtsphilosophie*, p. 25.

[3] *American Journal of Sociology*, Vol. II, pp. 182, 183.

[4] *Ibid.*, Vol. XI, p. 371.   Cf. also Vol. III, p. 683.

[5] *American Journal of Sociology*, Vol. III, pp. 667–83.

[6] *Ibid.*, Vol. II, p. 174.   [7] *Ibid.*, Vol. VIII, p. 166.   [8] *Ibid.*, Vol. XI, p. 447.

I would be far from saying that there was not much of the greatest value in even these interpretations that I have been criticizing. The trouble is only that one has to push down below them and straighten them out a little farther to get the statement in terms in which one can depend upon it. For the rest I imagine that almost all the typical social relations—and very many others besides—which have been discussed in this book will be found treated by Simmel, some of them in the most highly suggestive way.

But through it all, and despite the fundamental importance of his analysis of the intersecting groups, his manner of interpretation remains thin, and at times unreal.   He has not really transformed the old individual ideas and feelings into group phenomena; he treats them independently, making his interpretations all too often in terms of the idea factors alone, not in terms of the social habit in which they rest; and, often as he recurs to the topic, he does not once, to my notion, get down to square, out and out, discussion of the underlying force and stability in those situations which, as in cases of survivals and of half-developed tendencies, seem to the superficial view to be made up of ideas and of nothing else. His society is, so to speak, pasted together with ideas and feelings, and not really shown in its tremendous cohesiveness as a mass of immense human pressures.   In a way, the fault with him is much the same as is the fault with Gumplowicz, striking as are the contrasts between them in other respects; in both, the idea and feeling factors are still largely an undigested mass and so the cause of scientific indigestion.

Taken as a bit of the general social activity itself, Simmel's work then represents the social world more as it appears to the individual engaged in the process than as it appears from a point of view which gets away from that of the acting individual and looks upon the process as proceeding through him. Even his analysis of the crossing of the social groups was more a by-product of his investigation of personality than a direct interpretation of social process.   His activity therefore has less meaning, less value, as mediating the group process than that of the other writers I am here discussing. By the same token that it cannot directly be referred to national, class, or occupational activities for its origin like the others, it cannot in turn be referred back to them so readily in its functioning.

One other writer who has aided in developing the group method of interpretation requires mention. Gustav Ratzenhofer has provided us much excellent description of the practical processes of politics from a groupal point of view. How excellent this work is one can readily discover by reading Part IV of Professor Small's *General Sociology*, in which Ratzenhofer's results are set forth, not only sympathetically, but in a manner that is frequently a decided improvement on Ratzenhofer himself. His categories, while not definitive—no one looks for such as yet—must be taken into account by all students in this field.

Unfortunately, Ratzenhofer was not content to take the facts as they paraded themselves before the exceptionally well-located window which his position in life offered him through which to observe them, but instead he felt impelled to swathe them in an exceedingly wearisome and maladroit metaphysics, which he called positive monism, but which one may well describe—with apologies to a jest that was current not so many years since—as neither positive nor monistic. He was not content with the interests as they presented themselves in social group forms in the world around him, but insisted on developing behind them a world of "inherent interests."[1] Here he sets up a hierarchy of racial, physiological, individual (egoistic), social, and transcendental interests.[2] With this metaphysics he deems himself advancing beyond Gumplowicz,[3] but in reality he is retrograding.

[1] *Der positive Monismus*, p. 105. "Das inhärente Interesse—das in der Stoffconstellation des Organismus wurzelnde individuelle Streben—zwingt zur Ausführung der gebotenen Absicht durch den Willen, d. i. die im Organismus zur Befriedigung des inhärenten Interesses bereite potentielle Energie." Here we have a whole family of spooks to work the wires. Of how little use the inherent interest is except to bridge over a gap in Ratzenhofer's own analysis will be evident from such a sentence as the following (*ibid.*, p. 112): "Im Grunde genommen kann aber der weitsichtigste Gedanke auf nichts anderes gerichtet sein als auf die Erfüllung eines concreten Interesses auf Grund des inhärenten."

[2] *Die sociologische Erkenntniss*, sec. 6.   [3] *Ibid.*, pp. 288, 289.

Connected with this is the necessity he feels for giving every variety of group he discusses its own individuality or personality.[1] The group has its spiritual unity, its own will.   He thinks by naming the will he makes progress in explaining the facts, when the real problem of interpretation is always to get to a point at which it is possible to drop entirely the use of that very word.

Having set up these group personalities or group interests as independent from the individual interests, he arrives finally at the fundamental sociological law—"the reciprocal adaptation of the individual and the social interests."[2]   As an outgrowth of this he attaches ideas, and at times instincts, to these fictitious group unities, and this leads him, despite all that he says over and over again of the derivative character of the ideas, to give them an exaggerated place in his system.   Thus he allows the "Zeitgeist" to rule unchecked in many of his interpretations.[3]   Also he crystallizes instead of reducing to simpler terms his set of "political principles" and "political systems."[4]   Finally he comes out at the end, after having begun with a good working system of groups and passed through a maze of metaphysics, to a finish in which he avers that sociology as one of these group soul things in and for itself should be able to remake the world.   It should "lead to promotion of the common weal on a level above that of naïve empiricism, viz., on that of conscious and purposeful action;"[5] since human progress comes mainly "through the integration of ideas, through the intellectual control of the microcosm, through the formation of general ideas."[6]   He falls back therefore into the old error of the naïve speech forms, and his idea factors are therefore much farther from being stated at their true representative value at the end of his work than they were at the beginning.

In the very structure of his main work, his defect stands out

[1] *Ibid.*, sec. 20.

[2] *Kritik des Intellects*, p. 149.

[3] *Wesen und Zweck der Politik*, Vol. I, pp. 96 ff.

[4] *Ibid.*, secs. 14, 15.   For illustrations of a similar nature, see *Ibid.*, Vol. I, pp. 143, 237; Vol. III, p. 64; *Die sociologische Erkenntniss*, pp. 64, 256, 257.

[5] *American Journal of Sociology*, Vol. X, p. 177.

[6] *Ibid.*, p. 178.

prominently, for he holds the struggle phase of life apart from the civilization phase. Professor Small, while omitting very much of the mysticism from Ratzenhofer, has followed him in this, giving separate parts in his *General Sociology* to these two phases. As a soldier, Ratzenhofer appreciated struggle in a very realistic way; indeed he was too "realistic" about it, for he understood it under the guise of "absolute hostility" ("die absolute Feindselig-keit"). Such absolute hostility being a fiction, nowhere to be discovered in the given world, Ratzenhofer was impelled to add to it as its complement a civilization phase of social process, which he first came to appreciate through the tender heart of his wife.[1] But this civilization phase is just as fictitious as the absolute hostil-ity phase, and if one gets them functioned together in the social process one will no longer have need of any system of "inherent interests" as sticking plaster. The "concrete interests" will be material enough in themselves. I can state this in a different way by saying that what Ratzenhofer means by the civilization phase, instead of being an independent phase of the social process, is a reflection of certain group oppositions on the discussion level, with a varying value in varying situations. Or again, by saying that the individual and the social interests, instead of being different factors in opposition to each other are merely different methods of stating the same thing, so that a complete statement in terms of the individual interest would cover exactly what a complete statement in terms of the social interest will cover, no more and no less; which makes it clear enough that the two never can be added together as complementary. Not both at once but either the one or the other, is what the investigator must take.

I find that I have been criticizing these authors rather than interpreting their good work, but I will let it stand, seeing that what is most essential at the present stage of the study of society is after all to get a clear grasp of a good method of work which will reduce the number of unassimilated and misleading elements to a minimum. I can only make amends by expressly recognizing the substantial results all of them have achieved, and my own

[1] See the Introduction to *Die positive Ethik*.

personal indebtedness to the first three. I hope further that I have succeeded in making it appear how in all of these cases the works as they stand do but reflect phases of the group process,[1] how they have value and meaning only as they reflect phases of it with accuracy, and how even the most accurate reflection has value only as process through which the underlying interests work somewhat more smoothly; how, further, in all of some of the works and in some parts of all of them the reflection is primarily identified with special groups notably forceful in the social process, and how even where such identification with forceful groups is hard to make, where the reflection is at longest range and of the group process as such, it is but the manner of statement of a very small specialized group of workers in an outlying field, and can claim an ultimate value only so far as it proves useful in the actual opposition of interests in bringing about a clearer statement and smoother process—a degree of mediative value which can only be measured with the result or at most estimated roughly in immediate use, but can by no means be boasted presumptuously in advance.

This sketch of the development of group interpretation has only touched the high places. To make it at all complete it would be necessary to add mention of the class interpretations by Marxists, of whom Loria may serve as a type; and to describe the many works which are substantially interpreting society in terms of groups, despite their own failure to reach a theoretical statement in such terms. Jhering's interpretations have been most admirable, although his psychological manner of statement distorted his work so that his emphasis was not placed on the groups as such. Lorenz von Stein, when one penetrates below his "persönlicher Wille und Bewusstsein" to his study of "Kräfte und Gestaltungen," and especially of the "Vereine," certainly deserves mention. So also does Spencer in many phases of his *Sociology*. Durkheim's objective interpretation takes a good step on the road toward the

---

[1] In the case of my own variation of group interpretation, I think that any experienced reader can easily determine its representative character in terms of American life of the last decade.

use of groups, and in this country Professor Patten, Dean Bigelow, and Brooks Adams should not be overlooked. With this could properly go an examination of the extent to which various established schools of thought in the social sciences have themselves been reflections of group points of view. The various phases of political economy would be found especially illuminating in this respect. I mention all these only to pass them by at this time.

CHAPTER XXIII

CONCLUSION

If I have at any point given the impression that I think there is any special claim of "originality" to be made for the method of group interpretation set forth in this volume, it is due to faulty phrasing on my part. Originality, in affairs of this kind, is mainly sensationalism, a matter of headlines, but not of the body of the tale.

On the contrary, it is just because I am convinced that the group factors which are used in all interpretations of bits of society are the solid and substantial parts of such interpretations, that I have ventured to attempt to bring the method out into a more explicit form. Whether we have to do with a history of the older style or with a modern essay on social reform, with a Utopia or with a political pamphlet, and in whatever language the work is garbed, it seems to me that the only part that counts for our purposes is the part that reflects fairly and squarely the groups as they are. The rest has its meaning in the process, but that very meaning must be stated in group terms before we can be sure that we know it accurately.

We often hear it said that history must be rewritten with each generation; and that is manifestly a truth when we are thinking of the forms in which history embodies itself with reference to the group oppositions—otherwise, to the problems, or, more vaguely still, if you will, to the "spirit"—of the times. But from this point of view the same may be said of science, or of any field of science. Nevertheless, in a more important sense it is not true. There have been forming underneath the various dressings of history a substantial backbone and skeleton of accepted relations. And this backbone will only vary with the generations as it varies now while being more accurately worked out. We can easily conceive of a solid structure of group relationships as they have developed in historic times becoming known to us, which must inevitably define the fundamental shapes which the history-writing that varies with the generations must take, if it is to have meaning and value at all beyond the meaning and value of the most narrowly partisan outcry. Given the analysis into groups, then Tylor's suggestion of method,[1] which has so long remained unfruitful because of the lack of a unified point of view in the statement of the materials to be compared, should at once become available on a great scale.

But, of course, this work of formulating the backbone of history is not to be the work of a day or a year, but of many men through many years, perhaps through many generations. Toilsome observation and analysis, real laboratory work with society, will be necessary for it. With all the contributions that have as yet been made to it, I doubt if we can find any that are so exactly stated that they can survive as they are now stated. The gold is there, but partly in compounds, and partly mixed with much dross.

To enable this work of establishing reliable statements of the group facts to make more rapid progress, the method by which the dross can be eliminated and the compounds broken down must be clearly worked out, not necessarily in detail, but on a basis which will permit of the detail being filled in without altering the main features of the method itself. The tool must be fashioned, but it much be fashioned out of materials which in cruder forms are now available to the workers' hands.

To a certainty it is among the psychic factors, or psychic phases, or psychic what-you-will, of our social life that the labor of eliminating the dross must be carried on. To a certainty the worst confusions of our present interpretations lie here where elements enter which presistently assert their independence and persistently maintain themselves against reduction to a common denominator along with the facts which are stated in other than specifically psychic terms. To a certainty, however, any tool or method which, while eliminating the dross here, eliminates at the same time much of the gold, will be useless. Probably it will be worse than useless.

[1] *Journal of the Anthropological Institute*, Vol. XVIII.

It is our business to find out what values the discussion and theorizing forms of the social process have in terms of all the rest of the process, to find out what values the organization forms have in terms of all of the rest of the process, and specifically what values these two forms have in terms of each other.

It is our business to weigh the pressure of each bit of organization and of discussion as specialized; to weigh it in terms of the masses of men, who, not visible to the eye—I might say to the naked eye—as parts of the discussion or organization, are nevertheless its bearers and the givers of all the strength that is in it; finally to estimate as exactly as may be the plus of strength which, from any specially limited point of view, must be attributed to the organization or to the discussion groups, considered for the moment by themselves as technical agencies.

I have nowhere in this volume attempted to set forth results in particular cases of interpretation. I have, indeed, ventured the assertion that while the discussion groups are essential phases of the human social process which we nowhere know of without them, and while in their elaborated forms they correspond in many respects with the elaboration of the underlying interest groups, which often could not function except in connection with them, so far as our observation of process goes, yet nevertheless in particular cases of interpretation, when stripped of their superficial forms, such as the special turns of wording they use, and reduced to their proper meanings at given times and places, they are entitled to little emphasis as independently considered technique. And further, that any tracing of the chronological lines of such groups considered independently can throw but little light on the actual development process of the society, however interesting it may be for its decorative effects. Similarly for the organization groups, I have asserted that it is only in transition phases of society due to shifting of group balances that they appear to have notable independent power, and that here as little as in the case of discussion phases can the lines of development be traced from organization form to organization form without continuous and complete interpretation in terms of what groupal structure is underlying. But

these are merely incidental views.   They partake more of an antici-
pation of results than of a statement of method.

This in the end may not be denied, that whatever tools of method
we devise for the tasks that are to be done, they can only prove
their value in the using—in the using by many workers, not by
one, or by two, or by three.

APPENDIX

APPENDIX

The positions set forth in the preceding chapters have not been assumed without many efforts to measure the strength of the pressures which are in play underneath the superficial appearance of political struggles in the United States. Such investigations can have little meaning or value except to men who see in them short steps toward an exact analysis of social activity. Men who can simplify society to their own satisfaction by the use of convenient catchwords or who have naïve faith in the "truth" and power of arguments will inevitably regard them only as a waste of time and energy.

What may be called a qualitative analysis of the interests is nearly always possible if the investigator will seek out the proper sources of information and take the proper steps to tap them. For quantitative tests of the pressures—barring the possibilities in the use of co-operative estimates—the difficulties in the way are much more serious. Nevertheless even here there are many tempting fields thus far little utilized. For example, the machine organization of politics, where it is rankly developed, furnishes many opportunities for tests of its strength, both as exhibited at the polls in contrast with the strength of other forms of organization, and in connection with the social wastes produced by its exploitation of government agencies. With this the effect of civil service reform on machine power could well be tested by comparisons between cities and between states, with correlative use of figures from the federal government's experience. My own collection of partially worked up figures is not, however, sufficiently complete to justify any quantitative statement of conclusions at this stage.

I wish, however, to set forth in the briefest possible way the outlines of three investigations, which offer, it is true, little more than a preliminary showing of what is possible in this field, but which are nevertheless sufficiently far advanced to justify provisional conclusions. For two reasons it was not desirable to incorporate the material in the text; first, because what I have to offer should not be regarded in any sense as proof of any theoretical position taken, but merely as an illustration of the character of the results that may be reached from the given point of view; second, because any direct use of the material should include full details of methods and a carefully conditioned statement of results, for which space is not available.

I. MUNICIPAL-OWNERSHIP INTEREST GROUPS IN CHICAGO

Between 1902 and 1907 Chicago voted at referendum in every year except 1903 on one or more phases of the problem of municipalizing the ownership of street railways. Six out of a total of eleven such votes were studied to detect so far as possible the difference in the manner in which residents in different parts of the city reacted at different stages of the municipal-ownership movement and upon different phases of it. The study was made by election precincts, approximately 1,250 in number. For each vote the city was districted into from 229 to 265 districts of varying reaction, these districts casting averages of from 1,000 to 1,500 votes each. The material was sufficiently free from error to give full confidence in results for districts of this size. The assembling of the precincts into districts was made on the basis of the relative degree of interest in municipal ownership which was shown in the precincts separately. The percentages of the municipal-ownership vote, first in the vote on the proposition, and then in the total vote cast at the election, were figured for each precinct; and for each set of precinct percentages separately the sextile precincts were ascertained as a guide in constructing the districts. Large maps of the city in six colors corresponding to the sextiles were then prepared for each vote, and for each way of computing, making twelve maps in all.

General contrasts.—The maps showed that the relative strength of the municipal-ownership policy, both in the vote on the proposition and in the total vote cast, was at first much greater in what may be called the select residence regions and in the outlying residence regions than it was either in the slum or factory regions. In the latest votes this relation had been just reversed. Hyde Park, Englewood, the West Side residence district, and to a lesser extent Lake View, were relatively strong at first and weak at the end. The river factory region and the stockyards region were weak at the beginning and strong at the end. This was especially marked when comparison was made between the vote in 1904 by which the city accepted a state law empowering it to own and operate street railways, and the vote in 1907 by which carefully guarded franchises were given to the street-car companies. The interpretation of this is that at the start "municipal ownership" as a policy meant—that is, "represented"—an interest in improved street-railway service to an important proportion of the residents of the main street-car-using sections, while at the end traction settlement meant the same thing to these elements of the population. A fair inference is that while municipal ownership did not have relatively great meaning or interest at the start to sections which do not use street cars so regularly, it came at the end to represent in these sections an interest very different from what it purported to be. These meanings existed entirely apart from formal arguments on the question in any section.

Outlying territory.—A general tendency to the progressive extension of strong municipal-ownership interest toward the farther outlying parts of the city was noticed, which reached its culmination in 1905; though in 1907 the elsewhere receding wave carried farther in spots and hit one or two very small extreme outlying districts. A tabulation of the votes in a broad band of outlying territory extending entirely around the city (33,200 votes cast in 1905,

38,900 in 1907) showed, with very slight change in the proportions of partisan mayoralty votes, a municipal ownership decrease from 52 to 39 per cent. of all votes cast (city averages decrease 46 to 40), and an antimunicipal-ownership increase from 16 to 53 per cent. (city averages increase 18 to 49). With an increase of 5,700 voters, municipal ownership lost absolutely almost 2,000 votes. Nothing but the car-service needs of the population in both years can explain the high vote of the first of these two years or the low vote of the second.

Stratification of the vote.—In 1907 especially, and to a great extent in other years there was a very marked stratification of the vote in certain parts of the city. It was most marked on the West Side where numerous bands of contrasting interest running generally from northeast to southwest could be detected. Some of these bands have to do with characteristics of the population dating from early settlement, and others seem to have to do with transportation lines as affecting population; but opportunity has not yet been found to study them systematically.

Districts of persistent relative interest.—These were occasionally found, though largely obscured by the great shifts of interest in the city as a whole. A number of single precincts were found which retained an almost unbroken interest (as measured by the sextile scale) relative to the rest of the city; and a number of larger districts which retained a steady position relative to the surrounding territory.

The influence of the worst car lines.—By means of comparisons based on the sextile scales of the years 1905 and 1907 it was possible to measure the relative change of interest of residents along the worst car lines (the West and North Side cables) as compared with the change among residents of surrounding territory. The strips chosen extended to one-sixth of a mile on each side of the respective car lines, being thus one-third of a mile wide. Preliminary experiments were necessary, in lieu of weighting for heaviness of traffic, to establish the outer and inner limits of the strips. Tests were then made to determine whether the tendency away from municipal ownership and toward traction settlement was relatively strong among residents of these strips. For three lines, Blue Island, West Madison, and Clark and Lincoln (these latter two treated as one), the tests showed such a tendency. One line, Milwaukee, gave partially favorable results. For another line, Clybourn, the tests were wholly unfavorable. This gives three fully satisfactory tests out of five. The composition of the Milwaukee strip was, however, very unsatisfactory, owing to an interfering Polish community of highly specialized reaction. Both the Blue Island and Clybourn strips had some unsatisfactory features in their makeup. The two lines of heaviest traffic and best definition gave very strong favorable results. As measured by the index numbers used, the West Madison strip showed a decline in municipal ownership interest from 43 to 36, while surrounding territory declined only from 50 to 47; and Clark and Lincoln showed a decline from 38 to 35 while surrounding territory increased from 40 to 42.   The detection of one such influence does not, of course, prove that the entire voting activity was conditioned solely by a complex of such influences; but the detection of this influence, considering the poor facilities of investigation and the imperfect methods available, gives at least an added substantiality to the position assumed in this book that it is only in such group interests that the meaning and values of ideas can be found.

The mayoralty election and the municipal ownership issue in 1905.—Curves prepared to show the relation between the referendum vote and the votes for the mayoralty candidates in 1905, based on the municipal-ownership districts on the map for that year, brought out no general correlation except between the vote for municipal ownership and the vote for the democratic candidate, and very little there.   The relation between the municipal-ownership vote and the Democratic mayoralty vote was, however, further investigated with a view to detecting variations with respect to locality, if any.   Upon a study of the districts in detail it appeared that two large regions differentiated themselves clearly.   In a "slum" region, including the downtown Ward 1, the greater part of Ward 9, and the eastern parts of Wards 18 and 19, the issue ran far behind the candidate.   In an outlying region, encircling the city, the issue ran far ahead of the candidate.   Excluding these two regions, and studying the remainder of the city, it was possible by the aid of a simple, four-membered scale, showing the average percentages of municipal ownership strength for four grades of Democratic candidate's strength, to isolate six other territorially coherent areas, in which the municipal ownership reactions were either notably above or notably below the averages by the scale.   In South Chicago and Pullman the issue was far behind scale strength based on mayoralty strength, for all degrees of the latter.   In a large region including Hyde Park and Englewood the issue ran ahead of scale.   In a still larger region to the north of this, including Wards 2 to 5, together with the stockyards region and the factory region along the south branch of the Chicago River, the issue ran behind.   In the main residence part of the West Side the issue was ahead.   In the factory district, along the north branch of the river, the issue was again behind.   The North Side of the city, which remained, showed a less marked typical reaction, but was itself capable of subdivision into a number of smaller regions of contrasted reaction.   Each of these six regions contained both strong Democratic and strong Republican territory.   There were, of course, some divergencies from the type inside the limits of each of the regions, but they were not of great area, and were even less important when the degree of divergence as well as its area was considered.   The divergence of the issue from expected scale strength was thus established in a total of eight regions in the city, distinguishable from one another by special characteristics, having to do with the use made in them respectively of traction facilities.

The mayoralty election and the municipal ownership issue in 1907.—This campaign was fought with lines much more closely drawn between the candidates and the issues. The tests here were made upon the traction vote and the Republican candidate's vote. By a first test "slum" and outlying regions were found, closely corresponding to those before found. In both of them, however, the candidate ran far behind what would have been expected of him in territory of similar traction strength, considering the city as a whole. Another region also appeared, namely, the candidate's "own" wards, over which he holds a boss's sway. Here he ran heavily ahead by the same test. For the rest of the city a different test was used, namely, direct comparisons between the candidate's and the traction percentages. Regions approximately corresponding to those of 1905 could be mapped out, the candidate showing weakness under traction-settlement strength in just those sections of the city in which two years before the municipal-ownership issue had shown exceptional strength in proportion to the Democratic candidate's vote. For the whole city the only exception to this tendency was the "slum" area, where the Republican candidate was weaker than traction in 1907, while the Democratic candidate had been much stronger than normal in proportion to the given municipal-ownership strength in 1905. In other words, as between these two elections the "slum" area was the only one which showed what is commonly called logical consistency, but what anyone acquainted with metropolitan machine politics knows in this case at least to have been something very different. True "consistency" was found where the same underlying interest expressed itself in opposite ways on a "policy" at different stages in that policy's progress.

The meaning of the Socialist vote in 1905.—In 1905 the Socialist mayoralty candidate received 23,000 votes, almost double what the party candidate received either two years earlier or two years later. In this year certain scattered districts of the city showed a much weaker municipal-ownership vote relatively to the rest of the city than they showed either before or afterward. It was possible to prove by taking all districts of extreme Socialist strength in 1905 and comparing their relative municipal-ownership strength for 1905 and 1907 (allowance being made for changes in the city as a whole) that cases of heavy increase in the Socialist vote in 1905 were accompanied by a direct weakening of the municipal-ownership vote in the given localities. This conclusion was confirmed by an additional test which started with the districts of heaviest relative swing away from municipal ownership in 1905 and toward it in 1907, and examined them for their Socialist strength. In other words, in a certain limited part of the population socialism was shown to stand in 1905 in a stronger way for the same things for which municipal ownership stood at other times. There was also some evidence that in those districts in which the Socialist vote was most stimulated in 1905, an opposition to it was aroused which expressed itself in the unexpected form of an exceptionally heavy vote against municipal ownership.

A boss's influence.—In 1904 the Mueller law empowering Chicago to undertake municipal ownership was adopted by referendum vote, despite all the political machine power the traction companies could employ against it. At the same time there was another municipal-ownership vote under the "public-policy" act, which did not have binding force on anybody, and hence was relatively a matter of indifference to the traction companies. In 1905 at the mayoralty election the Republican candidate was badly "knifed" in certain parts of the city. In 1907 the Republican mayoralty candidate received most enthusiastic machine support while the Democratic candidate was "knifed" to some extent. In studying Wards 21 to 24, comprising the 1907 Republican candidate's political fief, in which the 1905 and 1907 phenomena just mentioned were most marked, a correlation could be detected between districts in which the Republican candidate of 1905 was most strongly "knifed" and those in which the Mueller-bill vote had been specially weak. This correlation did not appear on the surface for the four wards when taken as a whole, but could be seen in each of four regions into which the whole territory was capable of subdivision by tests found in the figures themselves. The showing has interest both as a measure of boss strength and because of the varying characteristics of the population in the four regions as distinguished by the varying ranges of their reaction under this influence.

In all of the investigations above outlined the referendum voting was treated simply as an activity of the massed voters, having value and meaning in terms of their underlying interests, which sometimes appeared directly and at other times in intermediate representative forms. Material for equally hopeful investigations was at hand in the reactions of massed nationality groups of the voters, and in a number of instances of stratification which would have required local study to comprehend. Material was at hand also for analysis of the possibilities of political leadership in many of its minor locality forms. In other Chicago election figures of recent years there is much material for the measurement of the extent of machine control of the voters.

II. THE PLAY OF INTERESTS IN A STATE LEGISLATURE

An attempt was made to trace the influence of definite external interests on the Illinois legislature at the session of 1905. The investigation was, however, limited to bills that became laws. This fact together with the further fact that the session was, comparatively speaking, "good" made the results much less complete on the side of oppositions than on the side of initiatives.

Two hundred and twelve measures became law. Forty-nine were appropriation bills and one fixed the amount of revenue to be raised. Appropriation bills are notoriously the result of the pull and haul of interests. To limit the study to the more doubtful field these 50 laws were removed. That left 162 laws, of which 3 were subdivided, giving 165 entries on the lists. These were examined in 11 groups according to the character of their subject-matter.

Initiative.—Of the 165 entries, 83 were assigned to administrative initiative, 34 to special interests, 20 to organized public opinion in some one or other of its definite forms, and 2 to political machines acting for their own direct interest, leaving only 26 to be assigned to members of the legislature acting in their theoretical legislative capacity.

Opposition.—Most bills that become laws do so after a fight with other bills for a place on the calendar, rather than after a fight with an opposition of a more direct kind. That fight for place is not taken into account here. Only 49 entries are made as to opposition. In 20 cases the opposition came from special interests, in 2 cases from machines acting for themselves, and in 3 cases from organized public opinion. These include a number of cases in which no negative votes were cast on roll call. In the remaining 24 cases opposition is credited to legislators in their legislative capacity. To make up this latter figure all bills were regarded as opposed in this way when over 8 per cent. of the members of either house, or when over 4 per cent. of the members of each house, voted against them on final roll call.

Other aspects of legislators' activity.—In the senate out of 401 roll calls 113 were contested; in the house out of 353 roll calls 228 were contested. A single negative vote was enough to cause a roll call to be listed here as contested. Of the 212 bills that became law 34 had one or more votes cast against them in the senate and 121 in the house. The average number of negative votes in the senate (51 members) on all bills that became law was 0.5. The average number in the house (153 members) was 5.5. Out of 162 bills (appropriations excluded) 87 were amended, most of them very slightly; this includes even trivial corrections of spelling or punctuation. Of the amended bills 22 were amended in both houses.

The figures as above given allow very liberal proportions to the participation in law-making that can be ascribed to the members of the legislature acting in their theoretical capacity as reasoners and deciders upon questions of public welfare. Had the bills been weighted for relative importance, the showing of the legislators' share in the work would have been seen to shrink materially. A partial attempt at weighting led only to the conclusion that that task should be performed by co-operative investigation and not by an individual. One group of laws, those affecting children (eight in number) were framed, discussed, and all but enacted by a volunteer substitute legislature, composed of delegates from societies interested in child-saving, which met in Chicago before the legislature itself assembled.

In this study organized public opinion in all forms was accepted as representative activity, and no attempt was made to trace its manifestations down to the underlying interests which it represented. The aim was merely to use categories which would throw a little light on the formal law-making process in an American state.

III. THE PLAY OF INTERESTS IN A CITY COUNCIL

An investigation somewhat similar to the preceding was made for eleven meetings of the city council of Chicago, in which 1,108 ordinances, orders, or resolutions were passed (*Proceedings of the City Council* for 1905–6, pp. 1–996). Only 27 roll calls were contested, affecting only 14 measures. Of the total number of acts 430 were sent up to the council by the subordinate Board of Local Improvements. Probably in almost all of them a crude and ill-governed struggle of interests preceded enactment. Fifty-one others were sent up by the Board of Education.

Ordinances.—Discarding acts mentioned in the preceding paragraph, the ordinances passed numbered 136. The results of classification and analysis showed that 85 were distinctly in private interest, while 28 involved what may be called a "locality interest." There were 8 that were designed to regulate or control the pressure of the interests, and 15 that could be classified as outside the immediate play of the interests.

Orders.—Among 491 orders of the council, analysis showed 211 directly on behalf of interests, 58 directed against definite interests at special points, 135 to be classified as affecting "locality interests," and 87 not directly to be classified on such interest lines.

Under the pressure of interests the council gave by ordinance 46 franchise grants which it had no legal right or power to give. By order it gave 55 distinctly illegitimate grants. Many of its other acts were gross abuses or marks of favoritism. Such were 88 special privileges, including gifts of city property or services and permits to violate ordinances. Four orders directing the refusal of ordinance rights to particular individuals form a climax to the system. The council's own praiseworthy, but feeble, attempts to regulate these pressures serve but to emphasize the present license.

INDEX

INDEX

Spencer, 37 ff., 310
"Spirit of the Age," 151, 419
State, 263, 300
Statehood bill, 372 ff.
State's rights, 113, 376
Statistics, 200
Steamboat regulation, 354
Stein, 121
Subjective and objective, 89, 117 foot-
note, 186, 196
Sunday-closing law, 280
Sympathies, differentiation, 6, 7, 46, 47,
52, 55
Sympathy, comparison of races, 21 ff.
"System" in law, 284
System, phase of activity, 218

T

Tariff reform, 347
Tendencies of activity, 184 ff

Theories, legal, their representative
value, 273, 294, 394
Thomas, 97
Tocqueville, de, 313, 414
Tolstoi, 117
Tradition, 219
Truth, 172, 243
Tylor, 482

V

Values, of idea factors, 172

W

Ward, 91, 155
Wealth groups, 462
Westermarck, 93–99
Willoughby, 118
Woman's suffrage, 425
Woods, 107 ff.

Z

Zeno, rest and motion, 186

Printed in the United States
204696BV00002B/58-210/P